HUMAN DEVELOPMENT
AND FAITH

HUMAN DEVELOPMENT AND FAITH

LIFE-CYCLE STAGES
OF BODY, MIND, AND SOUL

FELICITY B. KELCOURSE, editor

CHALICE
PRESS

ST. LOUIS, MISSOURI

Biblical quotations, unless otherwise noted, are from the *New Revised Standard Version Bible*, copyright 1989, Division of Christian Education of the National Council of the Churches of Christ in the United States of America. Used by permission. All rights reserved.

Excerpts from *The Jerusalem Bible*, copyright 1966 by Darton, Longman & Todd, Ltd., and Doubleday, a division of Bantam Doubleday Dell Publishing Group, Inc. Used by permission.

Grateful acknowledgment is made to the following: W.W. Norton for permission to use Diagram 3.35, Freud–critical periods and coincidences from *Genograms in Family Assessment.* Copyright © 1985 by Monica McGoldrick and Randy Gerson. W.W. Norton for permission to use Figure 1.1, Flow of stress through the family, from *Genograms: Assessment and intervention* (2nd ed.). Copyright © 1999 by Monica McGoldrick and Sylvia Schellenberger. W.W. Norton for permission to reproduce Chart 2, Psychosocial Crises, from *The life cycle completed.* Copyright © 1997 by Joan M. Erikson. Fortress Press for permission to reproduce Table 1: Erikson's life-cycle stages and deadly sins in *Deadly sins and saving virtues.* Copyright © 1987 by Donald Capps. Scribner for permission to quote from Robert Bly's poem "Sunday: What to do with objects" in *The Best American Poetry 1998.* Copyright © 1998 by David Lehman. North Point Press for permission to quote from a poem by Basho cited in D. Melzer, (Editor), *Death: An anthology of ancient texts, songs, prayers, and stories.* Copyright © by D. Melzer. Persea Books for permission to quote from a poem by Paul Celan in M. Hamburger, *Poems of Paul Celan.* Copyright © by M. Hamburger.

Cover design: Lynne Condellone; Interior design: Elizabeth Wright
Art direction: Michael Domínguez

Visit Chalice Press on the World Wide Web at
www.chalicepress.com

10 9 8 7 6 5 4 3   06 07 08 09 10 11

Library of Congress Cataloging–in–Publication Data

Human development and faith : life-cycle stages of body, mind, and soul
Felicity Brock Kelcourse, editor.
    p. cm.
  Includes bibliographical references.
  ISBN-13: 978-0-827214-42-2
  ISBN-10: 0-827214-42-1
  (pbk. : alk. paper)
1. Life cycle–Religious aspects–Christianity. 2. Faith development. I. Kelcourse, Felicity Brock.
  BV4597.555.H86 2004

    248–dc22   2004005328

To my companion teachers and learners,
especially
Paul and Rosalind

Contents

Figures and Illustrations

Preface

In my mid-thirties I faced a developmental roadblock. As a member of the baby-boom generation, raised in an extended family with ten aunts and uncles and twenty-one first cousins, I saw marriage and parenthood as predictable stages of young adulthood. I married a fellow seminarian at the age of twenty-five. Ten years and three pregnancy losses later, I was told that I would never give birth. I was angry. How was it possible that my life was not unfolding as I believed it should?

Later, during doctoral studies in psychiatry and religion at Union Theological Seminary in New York, I took my first course in human development. I learned that all people, across time and culture, have made meaning of their lives at the confluence of embodiment, with its stages of maturation, and the formative power of society, with its group norms. Our experience of embodiment is dictated in part by biology; we approach life differently depending on whether we are female or male, old or young, healthy or ill. Our lifelong acculturation begins in our family of origin and extends through the surrounding layers of acculturation that we variously attribute to economic class, ethnicity, religion, community, nationality, and generational cohort.

People who have experienced culture shock recognize the cocoons of predictable behavior our home culture takes for granted as "normal" until they are challenged. Now, at the beginning of the twenty-first century, cultures once separated by geographic distance are increasingly coming into conflict. The disasters of September 11, 2001, were fueled by disparate worldviews. The possibility of peace begins with a sincere attempt to understand the "otherness" of those who oppose us–to be genuinely curious about our differences, even though we may profoundly disagree. But there is a prior step. We are not ready for dialogue with other cultures until we have taken a good look at our own. Having a deeper appreciation of ourselves is a prerequisite for understanding the "other."

There is more than one kind of culture shock. When I was told at the age of thirty-five that I would never give birth, I felt shock, anger, and disbelief, because this pronouncement contradicted my view of the world. Marriage and children went hand in hand–that was the way life should be. I have since met women who have no desire for children. They have made a deliberate choice not to repeat the pattern of family life in which they were raised. For these women there is no shock in being childless because they have consciously chosen a different path. Our desires and expectations are influenced by all the contexts of person, place, and time that surround us, and combine with our own inner awareness of calling to shape the narrative of our lives.

The kind of disbelief I experienced at being childless can be observed in parents when a child dies, in couples when marriages end in divorce, in single people who never find the mate they hoped for, in workers "downsized" from the jobs they had hoped to keep until retirement. We grieve these losses because they don't fit our sense of the way life should be. We feel wrong, out of place, and we envy those around us who live in the "normal" world where children live, marriages endure, everyone finds a mate, and no one gets fired (Mitchell & Anderson, 1983).

The truth is that no one lives a "normal" life. Every life has unexpected losses, events that do not conform to our preconceived plan. Students struggling with the pressures of familial and cultural expectations may get angry in a human development class. They will say, "Are you telling me I'm not normal because I'm single at forty, gay, voluntarily childless, a full-time dad, or a mom with a demanding career? Sure, my life is more complicated than some people's, but I'm happy. Who are you to say that the way I live my life is wrong?"

Labeling one another "normal" or "wrong" is not the point. What *is* important is that we become conscious of the realities within us and around us. For example, women who choose to give birth have a finite biological window within which natural conception can occur. We all grow old and die—if we're lucky enough not to die young. Our limits, biological and temporal, are a fact of life. Recognizing these limits will not change them, but it does encourage us to make a conscious, deliberately chosen response to the questions life brings.

Culture also limits us. In previous generations it was not acceptable for women to gain advanced degrees and maintain professional careers, especially when married with children. In North America it was not acceptable for people of color, male or female, to attain leadership positions in a predominantly white society. Until recently it was considered unacceptable for men to be full-time parents while their wives worked outside the home to support the family. Heterosexual women, gay men, and lesbians are still barred from congregational leadership in many religious groups. Those whose lives do not conform to the dominant cultural template—whether because they are single, disabled, an ethnic minority, or homosexual—cannot take social acceptance for granted. That a few individuals in every generation have been exceptions to the rules only makes the rules more obvious to the rest of us. We defy the conventions of our generation and society at our peril. The costs may include ridicule, harassment, intimidation, even death. It takes faith—an ability to hope for things unseen—to follow a calling our culture has not condoned.

Studying human development has helped me to understand why my experience of not being "normal," not living life as I expected it to unfold, was so distressing for me at the time. Given the traditional family context in which I was raised, being barren might have called the meaning of my life into question, had it not been for faith. Through the affirmations of my faith community, I knew that my life—and the life of every person—has intrinsic worth. Because I had faith, I also had hope that out of this crisis new opportunities might appear. And they have. By faith I knew that love is stronger than blood; at the age of thirty-eight, I became the mother of an adopted baby girl who remains a source of joy as she grows into adolescence. The sorrow I experienced in my thirties drew me to my present vocation as a pastoral psychotherapist and theological educator, teaching pastoral care and counseling.

Without faith, our lives are incomplete. What is the point of being born if mere "normalcy" is the best we can hope for on the way to death? In the presence of faith, all of life takes on meaning, including the events that call our present meanings into question. With faith, we refuse to despair, wrestling the angel of death to find answers even in the midst of what could be seen as the ultimate defeat, the end of life (see chap. 14).

The present volume will prove useful to students of human development, parents, pastors, chaplains, theological educators, and psychotherapists. My own understanding of what it means to be human is necessarily limited by my social location as a middle-class, Anglo-American woman. But it has been my privilege to spend seven years living outside my own country in France; England; and Jamaica, West Indies. As a foreigner, I learned what it's like to be the "other." I am grateful for the diverse perspectives that the contributors to this collection represent based on their various ethnic and religious identities, as well as their theological and theoretical perspectives. Although this book emphasizes what we have in common as human beings, our biological, cultural, and individual differences demand to be honored. Each one of us is both fully human and fully unique. Contributors to this volume write from their distinct experiences about aspects of life that are recognizable to us all.

Felicity Kelcourse

Acknowledgments

I am grateful to Jon Berquist for his part in developing the academic offerings of Chalice Press in recent years. The concept for this book emerged from our dialogue when Jon asked what books I needed for the course I teach. Working with Jon and Jane Mcavoy, his successor, has furthered my knowledge of publishing and my appreciation for the labor of editors.

Thanks are also due to members of the Society for Pastoral Theology; the American Association of Pastoral Counselors; the Person, Culture, and Religion Group of the American Academy of Religion; the American Association for Marriage and Family Therapy; and the Association for Clinical Pastoral Education; colleagues from these professional organizations offered advice and encouragement throughout the project. The leaders, participants, and staff for the 2001–2002 Wabash Center Workshop for Teaching and Learning in Theological Education were a source of inspiration. The Butler University Irwin Library provided a refuge for writing—my thanks to Lewis Miller and Tracy Payne for making this possible. And the authors who contributed to the collection are each to be commended for their unique roles in making this book a reality.

I have benefited in many ways from the support and encouragement of my faculty and staff colleagues at Christian Theological Seminary (CTS), including our former Dean, Clark Williamson, and current Dean, Carolyn Higginbotham. The CTS Board of Trustees approved a research leave for me in the spring of 2000 during which much of the initial collection was assembled; final editing was completed during a subsequent semester leave in 2003. Members of the faculty writers' group responded to early drafts of my chapters. The pastoral theology and psychology faculty—Bernie Lyon, Brian Grant, David Marshall, and Nancy Campbell—supported my work as a team by covering for me as needed. Patricia Ikeda read through the manuscript and provided useful comments. Steven Ivy's response to the first three chapters was informative. Frank Burch Brown offered a valuable interfaith perspective for the Introduction. Joyce Krauser formatted the merged bibliography, identified reference problems, and gave editorial advice. Emilee Delbridge, Janet Hoover, Brian Anderson, and Erica Tyson contributed research and editing for the bibliography as well. Jay Harpring created Figure 6 from two print sources and Figures 3, 4, and 5 from my sketches. Jeff Siemon contributed his expertise in electronic scanning. Charlie Eldridge supplied the sand tray images for chapter 8 during a time when his wife, Vivian Thompson, the author of chapter 8, was gravely ill. Joan Vanore assisted me in recreating these images for digital photographs.

Melba Hopper, Nancy Campbell, Raima Larter, and Shermie Schafer served as midwives during the throes of delivery.

Gratitude begins at home. My parents, Mitchell and Gioia Brock, have supported my professional growth and development in many ways over the years. My students, who read and responded to early drafts, are the direct beneficiaries. As this book attests, one grows to maturity in an interpersonal context; I give thanks for teachers, family, students, clients, and friends who create the environment for lifelong learning.

Paul and Rosalind were the agents of grace. Without someone to make me laugh, to say "Mom, you're too serious," or someone to prepare gourmet meals, coordinate child care, and organize welcome breaks, the lonely work of writing would have been far less bearable. Paul's support was invaluable; and Rosalind bravely suffered through days when her parents were totally boring and wouldn't let her use the computer. The sadness we have known as a family deepens our present joy.

About the Authors

Claude Barbre, M.S., M.Div., MPh.D., is executive director of the Harlem Family Institute in New York City and training supervisor and faculty instructor at the Westchester Institute for Training in Psychoanalysis and Psychotherapy (Bedford Hills, NY). He is also editor-in-chief of *Gender and Psychoanalysis* and associate editor of the *Journal of Religion and Health* (Blanton-Peale Institute). He is also director of *Openings,* a pastoral care training program of Episcopal Social Services. His edited books include: with Esther Menaker, *The Freedom to Inquire* (Aronson, 1995), and *Separation, Will, and Creativity: The Wisdom of Otto Rank* (Aronson, 1996); with Marcella Weiner and Paul C. Cooper, *Psychotherapy and Religion: Many Paths, One Journey* (Aronson, 2004); with Alan Roland and Barry Ulanov, *Creative Dissent: Psychoanalysis in Evolution* (Praeger-Greenwood Press, 2004). He is a psychotherapist and pastoral counselor in private practice in New York City.

Pamela Cooper-White, Ph.D., is professor of pastoral theology at the Lutheran Theological Seminary at Philadelphia and the author of *The Cry of Tamar: Violence against Women and the Church's Response* (Fortress Press, 1995) and Shared Wisdom: *Use of the Self in Pastoral Care and Counseling* (Fortress Press, 2004). Use She is an Episcopal priest and a certified fellow in the American Association of Pastoral Counselors.

Bonnie Cushing, LCSW, is a family therapist in private practice in Montclair, New Jersey, and an interfaith celebrant. A graduate of the Multicultural Family Institute, she has special interest in the common ground where psychology, politics, and spirituality meet.

Russell Haden Davis, Ph.D., is the founder and current director of the School of Clinical Pastoral Education at Sentara Norfolk General Hospital in Norfolk, Virginia. He is the author of *Freud's Concept of Passivity* (International Universities Press, 1994) and has written several articles for *The Journal of Religion and Health* and the *Union Seminary Quarterly Review.* He received a B.A. degree from the University of Virginia and the M.Div., S.T.M., and Ph.D. degrees in psychiatry and religion from Union Theological Seminary in New York City. He has teaching experience at Union Theological Seminary (New York City), New York Theological Seminary, the Blanton Peale Graduate Institute, and the University of Virginia. He is the former executive director of the Association for Clinical Pastoral Education, Inc. (ACPE), and is certified as a CPE Supervisor by the ACPE. His pastoral experience includes chaplaincy (hospital, prison, and mental health), parish ministry, and pastoral counseling. He is an ordained minister and is endorsed as a chaplain by the Alliance of Baptists in the U.S.A.

Terrill Gibson, Ph.D., is a diplomate pastoral psychotherapist, American Association for Marriage and Family Therapy (AAMFT)–approved supervisor, and Jungian analyst who practices individual and family therapy with Pastoral Therapy Associates in Tacoma, Washington. He lectures and writes widely on the basic theme of the integration of psychotherapy and spirituality. He has been a frequent consultant, faculty, supervisor, and facilitator for a variety of Pacific Northwest universities, social service agencies, corporations, and religious congregations. *Psyche and Family,* a book he co-edited with Laura Dodson, Ph.D., was published by Chiron Press in 1997. He has a chapter on pastoral psychotherapy and transcendence in *The Psychology of Mature Spirituality: Integrity, Wisdom and Transcendence* (New York: Routledge, 2000), which was coedited by Melvin Miller, Ph.D., and Polly Young-Eisendrath, Ph.D. He is presently working on a collaborative project on Jungian psychology, film, and spirituality.

Alice M. Graham, Ph.D., is professor of pastoral care and counseling at Hood Theological Seminary in Salisbury, North Carolina. She is an American Baptist minister, ordained in the AME (African Methodist Episcopal) church in 1977. A fellow in the American Association of Pastoral Counselors (AAPC), her involvement in AAPC included serving as secretary of the association, chair of the African-American Task Force, and member of the association's Centers and Training Committee. Alice M. Graham is on the pastoral counseling staff of Methodist Counseling and Consultation Services and is a consultant to the Charlotte Pastoral Counseling Training Consortium. A graduate of Spelman College, she received her M.Div. degree from Garrett-Evangelical Theological Seminary and the Ph.D. degree from Northwestern University. Alice was the executive director of the Pastoral Ministries Institute for twelve years and served on the staff of Pastoral Counseling and Consultation Centers of Greater Washington for five years. She has been adjunct faculty at Garrett-Evangelical Theological Seminary, Wesley Theological Seminary, Howard University School of Divinity, Eastern Baptist Seminary, and Gordon Conwell Theological Seminary (Charlotte, N.C.).

Felicity B. Kelcourse, Ph.D., is assistant professor of pastoral care and counseling and director of training for pastoral psychotherapy at Christian Theological Seminary in Indianapolis. She has published articles in the *Journal of the American Academy of Psychoanalysis,* the *Journal of Religion and Health, Encounter, Chaplaincy Today,* and *The Living Pulpit.* She contributed chapters to *Out of the Silence: Quakers on Pastoral Care and Counseling,* edited by Bill Ratliff (Pendle Hill, 2001) and *Kitchen Talk* (Chalice Press, 2003). A graduate of the doctoral program in psychiatry and religion at Union Theological Seminary (NYC), and Blanton-Peale Graduate Institute, she is a certified fellow in the American Association of Pastoral Counselors (AAPC), a clinical member of the American Association for Marriage and Family Therapy (AAMFT), and a licensed mental health counselor (LMHC). She maintains a private practice working with individuals, couples, and groups. Recorded as a Quaker minister (Religious Society of Friends) in 1987, she has served congregations in the Midwest, England; and Jamaica, West Indies. She lives in Indianapolis with her husband, Paul, daughter, Rosalind, and sons, Jonathan and Paul.

K. Brynolf Lyon, Ph.D., is professor of practical theology and pastoral care at Christian Theological Seminary in Indianapolis. He is the author of *Toward a Practical Theology of Aging* (Fortress Press, 1985), a coauthor of *From Culture Wars to Common Ground: Religion and the Family Debate in America,* and a coeditor of *Tending the Flock: Congregations and Family Ministry* (Westminster John Knox Press, 1998). A National Certified Counselor and group relations consultant, he is completing a manuscript on congregational practical theology, *Devotion's Detail: How Congregations Think.*

Monica McGoldrick, ACSW, Ph.D., is director of the Multicultural Family Institute in Highland Park, New Jersey; visiting professor in the Fordham University Graduate School of Social Service; and associate professor of clinical psychiatry at the Robert Wood Johnson Medical School. Monica McGoldrick is widely known and respected for her training and publications in the area of multicultural family therapy, including *Ethnicity and Family Therapy* (with John Pierce and Joseph Giordano; Guilford Press, 1982 and 1996), *The Expanded Family Life* Cycle (with Betty Carter; Allyn & Bacon, 1999) and *Genograms in Family Assessment* (with Randy Gerson and Sylvia Shellenberger; Norton, 1999).

Ronald Nydam, Ph.D., is professor of pastoral care at Calvin Theological Seminary in Grand Rapids, Michigan. He is also the executive director of Michigan Adoption Dynamics He has been an ordained minister in the Christian Reformed Church since 1974. He received his B.A. degree from Calvin College (1970), his M.Div. degree from Calvin Theological Seminary (1974), his D.Min. degree from Chicago Theological Seminary, with studies at the Center for Religion and Psychotherapy of Chicago, and his Ph.D. degree from the Iliff School of Theology and the University of Denver. He co-produced a 55-minute video production on adoptive development, entitled *More than Love,* with Bethany Christian Services. He recently authored *Adoptees Come of Age: Living within Two Families* (Westminster John Knox Press, 1999).

Roy Herndon SteinhoffSmith, Ph.D., explores, in Christianity and other traditions, memories, stories, and practices of love. His most recent book is *The Mutuality of Care* (Chalice Press, 1999). He is currently completing a book to be published with Chalice Press: *Group Dynamics in a Religious Community.* He lives in Brooklyn with his partner, Carolyn, and daughters, Phoebe and Chloe.

Vivian Thompson, LCSW, ACSW, RPT-S., has studied analytical psychology at the C. G. Jung Institute, Zurich, Switzerland, and at the C. G. Jung Institute of Chicago. She has fifteen years experience teaching primary grades and eighteen years experience in counseling. Her counseling activities include crisis and suicide intervention, employee assistance counseling, and addictions counseling in both inpatient and outpatient facilities. A member of the Academy of Certified Social Workers (ACSW), a licensed clinical social worker (LCSW), and a registered play therapist supervisor (RPT-S), Vivian has worked in hospital settings with sexually abused children. Her particular areas of interest are family counseling, marital therapy, divorce mediation, custody issues, play therapy for children ages three to twelve, art and sand tray therapy, dream work, grief and loss issues, and guiding adults who were abused or molested as children into the fullness of their healing. In addition to her years in private practice, Vivian has served as a supervisor in the counseling practicum at Christian Theological Seminary.

Edward Wimberly, Ph.D., is Executive Vice President, Academic Dean, and Jarena Lee Professor of Pastoral Care and Counseling at the Interdenominational Theological Center (ITC), Atlanta, Georgia, where he also heads the Thomas J. Pugh Counseling Center. He has been an ordained minister of the United Methodist Church since 1969. He has served as a parish pastor and on the faculties of Garrett-Evangelical Theological Seminary in Evanston, Illinois, and Oral Roberts University in Tulsa, Oklahoma. He received his B.A. degree (1965) in history from the University of Arizona, Tucson, and both the bachelor of sacred theology (1968) and the master of sacred theology (1971), with a minor in the sociology of religion, from Boston University School of Theology. He completed his Ph.D. degree (1976) at Boston University Graduate School, Division of Theological Studies, in the areas of pastoral psychology and counseling. Among his many books are *Moving from Shame to Self-Worth: Preaching and Pastoral Care* (Abingdon Press, 1999), *Relational Refugee: Alienation and Reincorporation of African Americans in Churches and Communities* (Abingdon Press, 2000), and *Claiming God, Reclaiming Dignity: African American Pastoral Care* (Abingdon Press, 2004).

Karen-Marie Yust, Th.D., is assistant professor of Christian education and director of the master of arts program in Christian education at Christian

Theological Seminary. She also directs the *Faith Formation in Children's Ministries* and the *Indiana Camp Ministries Enhancement* projects, which explore the best practices for nurturing the spiritual lives of children and youth. She is an ordained clergywoman with dual standing in the Christian Church (Disciples of Christ) and the United Church of Christ and served for eleven years in parish ministry. She holds a doctorate in theology from Harvard University and is the author of *Attentive to God: Spirituality in the Church Committee* (Chalice Press, 2001) and *Real Kids, Real Faith: Practices for Nurturing Children's Spiritual Lives* (Jossey-Bass, 2004). She and her husband are the parents of three children, ages ten, thirteen, and seventeen.

Human Development and Faith

Felicity B. Kelcourse

I have nothing to offer except a way of looking at things.
ERIK ERIKSON, *Childhood and Society*

"Daughter, your faith has made you well; go in peace."
MARK 5:34

To live is to change. Individuals, communities, and societies continually adjust their "way of looking at things" in response to changing contexts. Counterbalancing the forces of change is a hunger for continuity, principles to live by–discernment that leads beyond mere survival to a faith that makes us whole.

Psychological theories attempt to bring order to the comparative chaos of lived experience. Theories of human development consider the predictable physiological and psychological changes that attend individual growth, maturation, and aging. In this book, twentieth-century theories derived from psychoanalysis provide a "way of looking at things." Equally important, however, are the lived experiences of the authors, whose diverse histories and personalities inform both their points of view and their concern for faith as a foundational dimension of life. Faith is the ground on which we stand to face life's challenges and mysteries; it is both an attitude of trust and a way of finding meaning in life as it unfolds.

This book aims to address two central questions. First, in each phase of life, from birth to death, what are the "good-enough"[1] conditions of

1

parenting, family, and community that support the growth and development of persons? Those who receive what they need to thrive from their environment are capable in turn of forming loving families and resilient neighborhoods, perpetuating the beneficent contexts that brought them into being. Human development theory's task is at once normative and idealistic—to describe, define, and advocate for the conditions of "good-enough" growth and health, both individually and interpersonally.

The second question is equally fundamental. What gives life adequate meaning as development proceeds? When we face the inevitable changes that life brings, what perspectives encourage commitment, enthusiasm, and joie de vivre? What imparts the strength of will to endure present deprivation in hope of a future good? A quality of faith informs the lives of those who meet life's inevitable sorrows with determined courage, even joy. In many religious traditions, including but not limited to Christianity, faith is the attitude of trust in God as the One who first loved us. Trust makes possible an abiding confidence in the face of fear, anxiety, and death. In the words of Job, "Yea though God slay me, yet will I trust God" (Job 13:15, KJV paraphrased).[2]

If human development describes the normative and hoped-for passages of life, then faith provides the necessary component of meaning, the foundational structures of experience and belief that allow us to weather the storms of change with fortitude and grace. Throughout the various perspectives offered in this volume we present one theme: Faith is that quality of living that makes it possible to fully live.

What Is Human Development?

Human development can be briefly defined as the study of observable physical, mental, and relational changes that occur as human beings are born, mature, age, and die. This definition includes those aspects of human experience that can be registered interpersonally, by one person observing another. But human beings also have inner lives. Intrapsychic, or inward, subjective, changes are more difficult to identify and are by definition unique to individuals, even though they may have much in common with the experiences of others. Not all developmental theories attend to the inner lives of persons.

Because questions of faith necessarily address human interiority, this volume focuses on depth psychologies that consider the inner lives of persons as interpersonally expressed and structural developmental theories that describe individuals' interpersonal expressions of meaning in the context of community.[3] Too much focus on individual experience can give the false impression that individuals exist in a vacuum, apart from the constant presence of external influence. To counter this individualistic tendency in depth psychology, family systems theory reminds us to think in ecological, whole-system terms about the interpersonal, temporal, and environmental contexts in which individual lives unfold.

Basic Assumptions of Human Development

The study of human development has evolved in relation to basic principles or formative questions that are sometimes presented as dichotomies. In this volume the emphasis will be on the dialogue between understandings of human life that may be distinct but that need not be understood as separate.

Nature versus nurture: Which came first, the chicken or the egg? Theorists who favor nature, following Darwin, would say that because it contains the DNA required to become a chicken, the egg must come first. The nature argument is similar to the essentialist perspective, which says that differences between humans, including gender and ethnicity, are biologically based. Such an approach could be used to support racism or sexism, but the mere fact of recognizing basic biological differences and their impact on our personhood need not be negative. One could argue, for example, that women do, in fact, experience the world differently from men due to their different physiology and biochemistry (S. E. Taylor et al., 2000).

On the chicken, or nurture, side are those who point out that the chicken's contribution to laying the egg and hatching it is imperative for the egg's survival. This parallels the approach of constructivists who say that groups of individuals develop as they do and express themselves differently from other groups solely because of their socialization in families and in culture. This approach can be applied to gender, class, and ethnicity to describe and define the ways in which humans may be considered different from one another. In this perspective, biology is not destiny.

When these two perspectives—nature/essentialist and nurture/constructivist—are so starkly contrasted, it becomes clear that, far from being discontinuous, they are necessarily interdependent—no chicken without an egg, no egg without a chicken. In human terms, we might say that while individuals are born with a distinct personality that constitutes their basic individual nature, the way that nature finds expression in the world is likely to be distinctively influenced by the kinds of nurture that individuals receive from the families, communities, and cultures around them.

Other dichotomies are similar: organism versus environment, ontogeny versus phylogeny, learning through biology or culture (K. Richardson, 2000). In each case, either the experience of individuals is subsumed by the emphasis on a group—the species as a whole (phylogeny)—or, alternatively, the emphasis on general human experience is largely ignored in favor of the development of individuals (ontogeny). Once again, these are clearly not categories that can or should be separated. Individuals are dependent on their environment; the development of an individual during one lifetime must build on the evolutionary and cultural accomplishments of prior generations. Learning takes place both because we are "hardwired" to develop in certain ways, as in our predisposition to acquire language as children (Singleton, 1989), and because our families and cultures encourage us to learn, hopefully in ways that are responsive to our individual gifts and abilities (Gardner, 1983).

Schemas, phases, and stages: Schemas represent the basic patterns of awareness we develop beginning in infancy and throughout life. A toddler will smile with fresh delight each time a red ball is rolled across a sunny room. An adult will look at the ball rolling once, then turn away. Schemas are essential in making sense of the world. They can also categorize experience so rigidly that there is no room left for a new way of seeing things. Clearly, a balance between the toddler's open-minded wonder and the adult's structured alienation from present sensation is desirable. Daniel Stern describes schemas as RIGs, or "Representations of Interactions that have been Generalized." He notes that language is a "double-edge sword": Although it facilitates our communication with others through the use of socially recognized thought structures, it also has the potential to alienate us from the vividly "amodal" quality of preverbal experience (Stern, 1985; see chap. 5).

Developmental "phase" sounds less rigid than "stage." Stage theory has been criticized for implying that human development is necessarily linear rather than cyclical or episodic (Knefelkamp, 1990; see chap. 3). Robert Kegan's emphasis on the developmental spiral of "evolutionary truces" between independence and inclusion serves as a necessary corrective to an overly linear understanding of stages (1982; see chap. 1). The point to remember here is that stages are simply ways of describing observable shifts in the life cycle, some of which, like menarche (the onset of menstruation), are based on human physiology. Other changes–the transition from middle to late adulthood, for example–are more subtle and dependent on factors such as individual health and social welfare.

Erikson's stage theory serves as a template for this book because it considers the life cycle from birth through old age and clearly locates individual experience within the context of culture. Erikson's stages should not be thought of as hierarchical; each stage has its own value. In many respects the earliest stages are the most important, as the foundation for later stages (Capps, 1983). Erikson's work has been criticized by feminists who hold that his stages do not reflect the normative developmental crises and opportunities of women's lives, and by others who see his work as applicable only to Western societies (Stevenson-Moessner, 2000; Sue & Sue, 1990; Cross & Madson, 1997; Gilligan, 1982; Markus & Kitayama, 1993). Despite these shortcomings, Erikson's stages have proven their usefulness as a basic overview of developmental issues that are relevant for pastoral care and counseling in many North American and United Kingdom settings (Watts, Nye, & Savage, 2002; Capps, 1983; Whitehead & Whitehead, 1982). Erikson's contribution to developmental theory will be considered further in chapter 1. The critiques just cited also apply to developmental theory in general (see below).

Developmental lines: Anna Freud is credited with the concept of developmental lines (1963). Virtually anything we consider as an aspect of human experience—sexuality, aggression, separation, individuation, and so forth—can be represented as a developmental line. Sexuality, for example, broadly defined to include all aspects of love—affiliative, compassionate, and erotic—exists in age-appropriate forms throughout life. The infant, in its tiny body, is able to passionately love his or her mother and father. The widower in a nursing home may decide to remarry at ninety because the need to express physical affection is a human urge that accompanies us from birth to death. The concept of developmental lines lends continuity to the apparent discontinuity of developmental transitions. In chapter 7, for example, the Oedipal theory of male gender identity is expanded to include the story of Electra, considering Oedipal/Electral experience as an element of every person's journey through life.

We are all the ages we have ever been: Students new to developmental theory sometimes express disinterest in the earliest stages of life. They reason that if they can't remember anything that happened to them before the age of four and they don't have immediate plans to work with preschoolers or raise children, there is really no point in attending to early human development. On the contrary, it is precisely the early experiences of which we are least conscious that play the most forceful role in structuring our view of the world. It is not until problematic early memories are made conscious that we can truly say we have a choice about the meanings we make. For this reason psychoanalytic theories including Erikson's stage theory treat the earliest, pre-Oedipal (prior to age three) dimensions of human experience as foundational. In this view, problems in later life can result from early, unresolved developmental challenges; conversely, the healing of early and later wounds can take place in adulthood. Both faith communities and psychotherapy are intended to provide opportunities for reparation and redemption. Parents, schools, and religious educators can support the future physical, emotional, and spiritual health of children by understanding and attending to their present developmental needs (see chaps. 6 and 8). At the other end of life, the adult children of elderly widowed or divorced parents who plan to remarry should not be surprised to find their parents recapitulating the behavior of giddy adolescents when they find a new love.

Critiques of Human Development

Theories of human development are not without their detractors. Feminists and womanists rightly point out that many developmental theories are based on studies of middle-class Caucasian males who are assumed to represent "normal" human development in global terms (Miller & Scholnick, 2000). Carol Gilligan (1982) and Belenky et al. (1986) have endeavored to correct this imbalance by attending to women's experiences and articulating the meanings implicit in what women say. Robert Coles has reported the life experiences of persons living in minority, poor white, and migrant worker communities whose voices would not normally be heard in scholarly discourse (Coles, 1967).

Others aver that many developmental theories presented as being universally true do not translate well cross-culturally (Ashton, 1975; Buck-Morss, 1987). This book does not purport to address the cross-cultural critique of development beyond passing allusions to the problem, but the reader is hereby reminded that cultural contexts influence all our ways of seeing and being in the world. That said, it does appear that certain structures of human experience, such as the incest taboo on which Freud based his Oedipal theory, crop up with surprising regularity in cultures worldwide.[4]

Recent studies have criticized the theoretical assumptions of developmental psychology (Morss, 1996) and the field of developmental psychology as a scholarly discipline (Broughton, 1987). In *Deconstructing Developmental Psychology,* Erica Burman notes that developmental theory can be negatively used to pathologize those who do not conform to its models (1994). The authors of chapter 11 in this volume consider the ways that mothers have carried the burden of developmental expectations in relation to their children, while the father's role in parenting has been devalued. These are crucial concerns to bear in mind when we venture to describe the "good-enough" family.

Because the present book is intended as an introduction to the subject of human development from the perspective of faith, these critiques are not considered at length. The fact that developmental theories are not without flaws attests to the difficulties inherent in self-observation. The subject of human development is ourselves, humankind. Although we share much in common, any attempt to generalize about human experience from the perspective of one group (in this case, primarily North Americans) is bound to appear inadequate to others. Social power remains a factor as well. Privileged groups are more likely to speak and be heard, and in so doing claim the power to name reality. The impact of racism and all forms of discrimination on individuals and families is considered throughout our presentation of development (see especially chaps. 3, 4, 10, and 11).

While this book covers three broad spectra of developmental theory—depth psychologies, structural developmental, and family systems—the full theoretical spectrum is far more diverse. The theories presented here have been chosen both for their breadth and for their relevance to questions of faith. Suggestions for further readings can be found at the end of this chapter.

What Is Faith?

Theories of human development and faith development seek to address essential aspects of our lives. After a review of basic theoretical assumptions in human development, it makes sense to consider definitions of faith before asking the question, "Does faith develop?" It is beyond the scope of this book to consider in their full range the philosophical and theological dimensions of faith. In this context it is sufficient to approach faith from the standpoint of theological anthropology. How does the presence or absence of faith affect human relationships, whether with oneself, others, or God?

Basic Assumptions about Faith[5]

Faith as trust versus faith as cognition: When we consider the etymology of the word *faith,* two separate Latin meanings appear. *Fiducia* refers to a trusting and confident attitude toward God and others. *Fides* is defined as a cognitive state in which people are said to know God or have knowledge of God (Hick, 1966). *Fides* could refer to non-ordinary religious experiences such as those reported in biblical narratives and by mystics of all times and places. It may also refer to a more rational apprehension of God for those who, like Einstein, believe in God because they see creation as too sublimely ordered to be random. James Fowler and other structural developmental theorists tend to speak of faith primarily in intellectual terms. But the fonts of faith are deeper and broader than our conscious thoughts. The trusting confidence of *fiducia* can be understood as an aspect of faith that is our human birthright, one that can be nurtured, damaged, or destroyed by our families, through our own actions, and by the communities in which we live.

In anthropological terms, trusting faith is foundational. Without a prior orientation of trust toward God, knowledge of God would be unlikely, if not impossible. In chapter 2, faith as basic trust is seen as a red thread that links all our experiences of receptivity to self, others, and God. Yet without reflection on experience, basic trust remains static and mute, unable to mature in response to changing circumstances (see Fowler's stages in chap. 1).

Propositional faith versus religious experience: In twenty-first-century North America, people who base their personal knowledge of God on non-ordinary religious experiences may be hesitant to talk about them for fear of sounding crazy. It is not necessary to have *fides* in the sense of religious experience to live a life of faithful commitment to a good that is greater than ourselves. Faith is not only a product of religious experience; in theological terms, faith is relational. Like the hemorrhaging woman, we intuitively reach out to God as the source of health and healing (Mk. 5:25–34). But God also reaches toward us. Those whose religious experiences, often arising in times of crisis, have proven fruitful in their lives will agree with Jung's answer when asked if he believed in God: "I don't believe, I know" (Meany, 1990).

Without the eternal light of religious experience there would be no sacred texts, no saints, and no history of faith. Yet propositional faith, as expounded in the foundational statements and creeds of faith communities, provides the language through which religious experience can be shared and expressed. Propositional faith also establishes norms for fruitful faith. If faith is entirely individual, subjective, and egocentric, it will generally fail to communicate well as a source of inspiration for others and may even devolve into madness. Fruitful faith proves its value not only to individuals but also to the faith communities that surround them.

Nature versus grace: Faith is recognized in community by its fruits, yet it is ours by grace, not by works. Questions about the relationship between faith and grace are comparable in some ways to the "chicken and egg" question of nurture versus nature. Is there something inherently divine in us, as humanists might say? Or are human beings incapable of seeing beyond our own immediate experiences of alienation and brokenness unless an Other–God, the Holy One–initiates contact and offers comprehension of faith through the gift of grace? Karl Barth (1928), Hunsinger (1995), and Loder (1998) would agree that communication and communion between God and humanity can only occur as a result of God's divine initiative, the gift of God's grace freely given. This approach emphasizes God's transcendence. Other theologies emphasize God's immanence; there is "that of God" in us, even though we are not God, that allows us to find faith from within, not as something externally given (G. Fox, 1694/1976; see chap. 2). Simone Weil writes that our desire "draws down God" (1951). Even theologians who favor divine transcendence also emphasize our freedom before God. In this respect, faith is ours to receive or reject; it is never coerced.

Belief versus disbelief: If faith is our ability to trust in the reality and goodness of things not seen, it is also important that we practice discernment in relation to what we refuse to believe. Many faith traditions are based on hierarchical dualisms that elevate one aspect of human experience or humanity by debasing another. Such dualisms–soul versus body, male versus female, Christian versus Jew or Moslem, humanity versus the rest of creation–have often contributed to atrocities committed in the name of religion. In *Not Every Spirit: A Dogmatics of Christian Disbelief,* Christopher Morse makes the case that what we refuse to believe, and why, can be as important as what we choose to affirm (1994). Statements of disbelief can help us recognize our own shadow (see Carl Jung, chap. 1), those disavowed parts of ourselves that we so easily project and persecute in the person of the rejected "other."

Because faith can take toxic as well as beneficial forms, the nature and tenets of our faith need to be constantly reexamined. Without openness to new experience, any faith can become at best limiting and at worst deadly rather than life affirming. When faith is beneficent, it draws us into closer, trusting, more loving, and just relationships with ourselves, others, and God.

Faith and God

Faith is still faith whether it deliberately calls on God or not. When one professor of religion hears students say that they don't believe in God, he replies, "Tell me about the God you don't believe in—I probably don't believe in that God either" (James Jones, personal communication, spring 1996). God images can be problematic if they are based on negative experiences with one's parents, who represent the love (or neglect) of God to a small child, or on theologies that instill fear, hatred, or rejection of self and others (Armistead, 1995; Gerkin, 1994; Rizzuto, 1979; see chap. 2).

The religious imagination of many Christians is thoroughly steeped in biblical and theological traditions that seek God through the way of abundant life (Jn. 10:10; C. Williamson, 1999). What constitutes abundant life may not be immediately apparent to individuals, families, or cultures; abundant life makes itself known by its fruits. In the presence of abundant life, we feel more possible, more courageous, more loving and connected, able to usefully share the talents we have been given in ways that are respectful of other persons and the living systems that sustain us.[6] These are useful criteria by which the meaning adequacy of any faith or representation of God may be judged (Buber, 1937/1970; Niebuhr, 1962; Morse, 1994; Brock, 1988; McFague, 1987).

There are no atheists in foxholes, it is said. Even people who do not normally address God except when swearing are likely to utter heartfelt prayers when their lives are threatened. All traditional cultures point to some form of "higher power." While the elephant-headed God Ganesh of Hinduism might superficially bear little resemblance to the crucified God of Christianity or the no-God of Theravada Buddhism, the world's major religions are like wells that draw from a common underground river of faith (M. Fox, 2000). In an age when Pierre Teilhard de Chardin's "noosphere" has found concrete expression through the Internet, it behooves us to be respectful of those whose statements of faith may take different forms from our own (1969).

Yet the differences we find in religious traditions are also significant. If the freedom of all persons to express their God-given sense of vocation for the benefit of their communities is a criterion for fullness of life in faith, we may be inclined to pre-judge some traditions as more faithful than others. It is important to hear the voices of those who live within a given religious tradition before we judge it from an external cultural perspective. Specific traditions form cultural templates—structures of perception within which the potential raw material of faith can either thrive or be thwarted.

In the considerations of faith that follow in this introduction and in chapter 2, the living, available presence of God will be assumed based on the observable tendencies of human beings to imagine, desire, and seek the God of their understanding and the way of abundant life for themselves and others (Ulanov and Ulanov, 1991). This is not meant to imply that God is only a projected wish, an illusion, as Sigmund Freud maintained (1927c/1953). Nor do I mean to suggest that God is a passive, distant entity that winds the universe up like some immense clock and then withdraws. By grounding this presentation of faith in human experience, I do recognize that the fullness of God in Godself is essentially unknowable to humankind. This is hardly surprising when one considers the fact that even human beings in intimate relationships remain in many ways unknown to themselves and to each other. Yet we recognize ourselves and those around us through memory and predictable patterns of behavior. In like manner, religious traditions seek to remember and represent patterns of experience in the lives of individuals and communities that reflect their knowledge of the divine. In the religious traditions of Judaism and Christianity, for example, two salient attributes of God include God's *hesed,* or steadfast, abiding love, and God's concern for justice, a preference for harmony in creation based on the value of all life. As one might search for a familiar face in a crowd, so faith communities seek God's presence in history by expecting to find evidence of God's love and justice.

Why Human Development and Faith?

Human development seeks to describe and understand the intrapsychic (inward), familial, and social conditions under which health will prevail over illness, relationship over isolation, love over hate. This is precisely where human development, as the study of "good-enough" living, and faith traditions, as the guardians of religious wisdom, can make common cause. The Ten Commandments can be seen as a moral structure that safeguards fullness of life and gives it meaning. The first and second great commandments–to "love the Lord your God, with all your heart, and with all your soul, and with all your might/mind" (Deut. 6:5; Mt. 22:37) and... "your neighbor as yourself" (Mt. 22:39)–enjoin us to explore the interdependence of self-acceptance, empathy for others, and gratitude for the essential goodness of Being (Eigen, 1981).

Human development teaches us that our individual lives–our expectations and perceptions of what is good, right, and desirable–are embedded in the meanings we make in our original family constellations and in the ways in which each family mediates the expectations of its immediate community and national culture. To come to terms with these influences and gain a measure of independence from them while allowing them to support our own growth and development is the work of a lifetime. The free expression of a sense of calling or vocation frequently requires the ability to differentiate from one's social context. Our time and place in history will necessarily influence our sense of what is meaningful (see chaps. 3 and 4).

Theological and Philosophical Antecedents of Developmental Theory

In *The Religious and Romantic Origins of Psychoanalysis: Individuation and Integration in Post-Freudian Theory* (1996), Suzanne Kirschner traces three stages of developmental psychology's earlier cultural forms. She identifies goals generally found in Western developmental theory as well-established cultural themes: self-reliance, authenticity, and intimacy. She finds in these themes parallels to earlier Judeo-Christian images of salvation where "images of the idealized self are secularized versions of Protestant ascetic and mystical visions of the soul's election" or reunion with God (1996, p. 5). In her reading, developmental psychology's older cultural forms include:

- Christian doctrines of humankind's fall and ultimate redemption; The Neo-Platonic vision of radical Protestant mystics such as Jacob Boehme;[7]
- Secularized narratives of fall and redemption articulated by English and German Romantic philosophers during the nineteenth century.

Kirschner sees all three of these earlier cultural developments contributing to the story of development as told by contemporary Anglo-American psychoanalytic theorists, including the schools of ego psychology, object relations, and self psychology. Much of the psychoanalytic language of the idealized self, or ego ideal, can be meaningfully correlated to earlier theological understandings of soul. One thinks of Kohut's "nuclear self" (1984, p. 152), Winnicott's "true self" (1960a/1965), and Jung's understanding of individuation (1934/1951), recently popularized by Hillman as "the soul's code" (1996), to name a few.

Other developmental theorists have identified moral and existential concerns implicit in secular literature that can be correlated with earlier religious themes. Crain (2000, p. 327) finds an implicit ethical emphasis in developmental theory and cites Maslow's understanding of the "biological brotherhood" (1998, p. 185) that developmental theory implies. The emphasis here is on our necessary interdependence as persons and the ethics of care such interdependence requires (SteinhoffSmith, 1999). Jesus' saying "...as you did it to one of the least of these [my brethren] you did it to me" (Mt. 25:40) links religious devotion with loving action, as does the biblical emphasis on caring for vulnerable widows and orphans in covenant community so that all may experience shalom (Psalm 146; Acts 6).

Gibbs (1977) finds in developmental theory both a "naturalistic" argument, in which developmental phases link us to cycles of birth, maturation, aging, and death; and an "existential" argument, in which the awareness and vocation of self are seen as key. In theological terms, one might say that attention to embodiment is intrinsically incarnational–it draws our attention both to the immanence of our ephemeral humanity and to the transcendence implied in religious understandings of the *imago dei*. One thinks of Jung's emphasis on wholeness and balance as essential for individuation. This concern for wholeness can be understood as the psychological counterpart to Jesus' injunction "Be perfect [complete, on the right path]... as your heavenly Father is perfect" (Mt. 5:48).

Kohlberg and Mayer (1972) identify in developmental theories the educational ideologies of romanticism, with its emphasis on personal transformation or conversion, and cultural transmission. The latter emphasizes the importance of tradition and progressivism, which echoes Christian eschatological hope for the realm of God that is both coming and already present, through the redemptive action of Christ as Savior, in the Eternal Now.

If developmental theories are adequate to lived experience, they must recognize and reconcile a variety of aspects of self and community life. The development of self has been studied by object relations theorists such as Donald Woods Winnicott (1971) and self psychologists such as Heinz Kohut (1978). Jung's depiction of individuation stages as adult maturation represents an understanding of persons that is both culturally and intrapsychically informed (Jacobi, 1962; see chap. 1).

Each of these approaches can be assigned lesser or greater degrees of adequacy in theological terms. Psychoanalytic theorists, most notably Freud, may be seen as overly pessimistic; they present humanity as being subject to the repeated blows of unconscious forces. But this state of being at odds with oneself echoes Paul the evangelist, "For I do not do the good I want, but the evil I do not want is what I do" (Rom. 7:19), and can be readily correlated to Christian understandings of original sin. It may be Freud's very pessimism about the human condition that endears him to pastoral counselors despite his avowed atheism. Jung is not at his best when he ventures into theological territory (cf. "A Psychological Approach to the Dogma of the Trinity" and "Transformation Symbolism in the Mass," in *Collected Works,* vol. 11 [1948/1969]), but he writes with understanding and respect about religious experience, the *imago dei,* and vocation as God's claim on our lives (Jung, 1932/1954). Jung's Self, not to be confused with our conscious sense of self, stands for a center of knowing that transcends the ego's perspective—in essence, the soul's eye view (chap. 2).

In an essay entitled "Can psychology escape religion? Should it?" Don Browning contends that psychology, as a discipline, would do well to give attention to its inextricable ties with religion (1997). He notes that the psychological theories of Freud, Rogers, Maslow, Erikson, Kohut, and Skinner are rife with religious themes, narratives, and metaphors. Browning argues for a religiously informed philosophical anthropology that can more adequately account for the human condition when religious metaphors are brought into conversation with psychology (1987).

By the same token, religion and contemporary understandings of faith do believers and seekers alike a disservice when insights into the human condition that have been identified using developmental theories are discounted or ignored. Science need never be the enemy of faith if we take seriously the idea that both are part of the seamless whole that we refer to in religious terms as God's creation. There are predictable, recurring structures of being that can be identified in the human body, mind, and soul, just as there are patterns that repeat across time and space from the smallest observable wave or particle to the farthest known star. It is the intent of this volume to identify patterns of human experience and behavior that can help us better understand ourselves and others. Understanding, in turn, encourages acceptance, respect, love, and justice among people of all sizes, types, and conditions.

Overview of Chapters

This introductory chapter identifies an understanding of the human life cycle that is informed both by developmental theory and by an appreciation for the dimension of faith as essential to our humanity. Part One considers the context of development. Even though we are each born with patterns of behavior that tend to remain constant over time–our in-born personality–it is clear that the familial, cultural, and temporal settings into which we are born are more than a mere backdrop for our individual lives. The forces of family, community, and time forge us in powerful ways of which we are often only dimly aware. Part One begins with a chapter outlining the basic assumptions of the three main schools of developmental psychology that inform the authors of this volume: depth psychology, structural developmental theory, and family systems theory (chap. 1). Each theoretical school is considered in relation to its assumptions about faith or its primary system of meaning.

Chapter 2, "Finding Faith: Life-Cycle Stages in Body, Mind, and Soul," offers a basic overview of the stages covered in this book, including reflections on the soul's-eye view as a developmental line and life before birth that do not appear elsewhere. The emphasis here is on challenges to faith throughout life–the successive ways we make, find, and recover meaning based on our embodied experience. Chapter 2 reflects the editor's commitments and experience as a Quaker minister, pastoral psychotherapist, parent, and theological educator.

Chapter 3, "Human Development in Relational and Cultural Context," presents the idea that development is best described as "complex, organic, and intrinsically relational." The author, Pamela Cooper-White, addresses this subject out of her experience as a seminary professor, Episcopal priest, and pastoral psychotherapist. She begins with a psychoanalytic approach to the familial context in which our sense of self first forms, then turns to the wider cultures and subcultures that continue to mold our identities as we move beyond the family circle. As a feminist, she acknowledges that culture can deform as well as inform, especially for those with less power (Cooper-White, 1995). As a person of faith, she recognizes that change is possible both in clock time, or *chronos,* and in God's time, through the *kairos* of in-breaking grace and the hope for healing.

Chapter 4, "The Family Context of Development: African American Families," offers an overview of family life-cycle issues, including predictable rites of passage. While the chapter gives particular attention to the needs of African American families–based on the author's experience as a seminary professor, pastoral counselor, and ordained United Methodist minister– the family systems perspective Edward Wimberly presents is instructive for all families. Wimberly makes the case for a cross-generational and community-based spirituality that serves to reconnect couples and families to these broader contexts as a source of strength in changing times. He gives specific examples of approaches to pastoral care and pastoral counseling that meet the needs of individuals and families in transition.

After the context is established for life-cycle transitions in relation to developmental theory, faith issues, culture, and family, part 2 describes life-cycle change in ten stages, from infancy through death. This represents an expansion of Erik Erikson's eight-stage template as found in *Childhood and Society* (1950/1963). Because change occurs so rapidly during adolescence, there are separate chapters on early adolescence (puberty through junior-high age, chap. 9) and middle-to-late adolescence (senior high to college age, chap. 10). Given this book's emphasis on the relevance of human development to pastoral care and counseling concerns, the inclusion of a final chapter that looks beyond late adulthood (retirement age) to the experience of death and dying and the hope of resurrection was essential (chap. 14). From a faith perspective, the reality of death need not be denied (Becker, 1973; Bregman, 1999), but can be squarely faced as the ultimate context for our ephemeral and meaningful journeys through life.

The authors for chapters 5 through 14 have brought their life experiences and various theoretical perspectives to bear in addressing the following topics as they relate to the developmental tasks for each stage of development:

- *Physiological and cognitive change:* Physical changes that affect the sense of self, such as changing body size and capacities for children or diminishing physical capacities for the elderly; cognitive changes including changing awareness of self, others, environment. and community.
- *Intrapsychic and interpersonal change:* Psychological changes that affect the sense of self and other, such as degrees of emotional dependence or independence from family and community; shifting awareness of self and others based on developmental transitions.

- *Moral and faith development:* The development of conscience, super-ego, the capacity for integrity, and moral discernment; faith, trust, and hope as "developmental lines" that exist in a variety of forms and expressions throughout the life cycle.
- *Social location:* The influence of family, community (including religious beliefs), setting in time (*Zeitgeist*), and setting in culture (*Sitz im Leben*); their positive and negative influences on the sense of self, others, and soul.

In the first of the life-cycle chapters, chapter 5, "Infancy: Faith before Language," Roy SteinhoffSmith offers a distinctive presentation of Daniel Stern's *The Interpersonal World of the Infant* (1985). Stern attempts to match what we know about infants through direct observation with the subjective reports on which psychoanalytic theory is based. SteinhoffSmith, who has served as a theological educator, psychotherapist, pastoral counselor, and minister, considers the registers of body, soul, and spirit at this early stage of faith formation in relation to Stern's categories of self experience in infancy. (The attentive reader will note that "soul" is defined differently in this chapter than in chapter 2.) Chapter 5 presents early self experience in relational context, emphasizing interpersonal communion as the basis for love.

From the ages of twelve months to three years, preschool-age children begin to experience a wider world beyond the family. In chapter 6, "The Toddler and the Community," Karen-Marie Yust, a Christian educator, seminary professor, theologian, and minister in both the Christian Church (Disciples of Christ) and the United Church of Christ (UCC), identifies the significant ways in which faith formation begins for small children when communities give attention to their developmental needs. Toddlers absorb life-long impressions of their faith traditions through stories, particularly when these are presented in ways that engage the toddlers' senses and address their aptitude for kinesthetic (physically expressive) learning. Responding to these smallest members of our faith communities with the loving, informed attention they deserve creates a positive foundation for their sense of meaning in relation to self, others, and God.

The Oedipal age, identified by Freud as three to six years, is usually described from a psychoanalytic perspective. This is the age at which a core sense of gender identity solidifies as our life-long orientation to femininity or masculinity. In Chapter 7, "The Oedipal Child and the Family Crucible: A Jungian Account," Terrill Gibson, writing as a pastoral psychotherapist, marriage and family therapist, and Jungian analyst, offers a unique perspective of this stage by presenting the Oedipal/Electral cusp as a developmental line, tracing its implications throughout the life cycle. The incestuous longings we experience at this age have significant implications both for our gendered sense of self and for subsequent interpersonal and familial developmental challenges.

Vivian Thompson brings to her understanding of latency-age children an extensive background as a play therapy supervisor, clinical social worker, and teacher of primary grades. The concerns of this age, which covers the grade school years up to puberty, are addressed in chapter 8, "Acculturation and Latency." As children absorb the lessons of their culture, they continue to require the loving attention of their families. The challenges to normal development that children this age may experience are presented with illustrations from play therapy cases that demonstrate the mythic-literal character of school-age children's faith.

Early adolescence, typically occurring between eleven to fifteen years of age, is the period in which we first experience the transition out of childhood toward adult sexual maturity. It is a confusing time for many youth; there are pressures of change from within, a rapidly changing body, and pressures from without in the form of social demands for which young people may be ill prepared. Ronald Nydam, in chapter 9, "Early Adolescence: Venturing toward a Different World," addresses the question so often posed in the news: Why do young adolescents turn violent? What are the challenges to their faith that must be addressed if they are to move toward the different world of adulthood with a sense of hope rather than despair? This author's understanding of early adolescence is informed by his experience as a theological educator, Christian Reformed Church minister, and psychotherapist specializing in the developmental challenges faced by relinquished and adopted children (Nydam, 1999).

Alice Graham, the author of chapter 10, is an active member of the American Association of Pastoral Counselors, a theological educator, and minister in the American Baptist Church, first ordained in the African Methodist Episcopal tradition. She brings her experience in counseling and ministry to bear on the subject of "Identity in Middle and Late Adolescence," addressing the concerns of senior-high and college-age youth preparing to meet the challenges of adulthood. Despite the temptations to despair that can beset this age group, it is also a time of great potential for intellectual and creative flowering as young people develop a sense of the identity that is uniquely theirs. The author suggests ways that parents, teachers, and faith communities can help youth find and affirm their sense of vocation at this critical stage of life.

An understanding of young adult development from a family systems perspective is presented in chapter 11, "The Differentiation of Self and Faith in Young Adulthood: Launching, Coupling, and Becoming Parents." Co-authors Bonnie Cushing and Monica McGoldrick are marriage and family therapists with a strong commitment to multiculturalism. Monica McGoldrick, well known for her contributions to the literature of family therapy (McGoldrick, 1980; Carter & McGoldrick, 1999; McGoldrick, Gerson, & Shellenberger 1999), serves as the director of the Multicultural Family Institute in New Jersey. Bonnie Cushing, a family therapist in private practice, brings insights from her Jewish faith of origin to her understanding of spirituality and psychotherapy. Together they explore "the pivotal decades of the twenties and thirties," identifying this as a time when our self-understanding develops in relation to others who may enter our lives through marriage and parenting. The young adult's relationship to spirituality, faith of origin, work, money, and sexuality is addressed with attention to the importance of social context.

The middle years, ages forty to sixty, are for many the most generative period of life as this age group claims its place in relation to work and takes responsibility for both older and younger family members. Russell Haden Davis, the author of chapter 12, is former executive director of the Association for Clinical Pastoral Education, Inc. (ACPE), a CPE supervisor whose experience includes seminary teaching, chaplaincy (hospital, prison, and mental health), parish ministry, and pastoral counseling. Chapter 12 covers the predictable physical, psychological, social, and faith concerns of this cohort, including existential angst as they face the prospect of death with more immediacy than at earlier life stages.

Chapter 13, "Faith and Development in Late Adulthood," addresses a period of life that is in many ways a product of the modern era. In past times few people lived to be sixty or beyond. Most of us now expect to live past seventy and hope to enjoy relatively good health until just before death. Informing the developmental challenges of integrity versus despair (Erikson, 1950/1963) is the hope "that we may gain a wise heart" (Ps. 90:12) in late adulthood and finish our life span in a manner that is a testimony to our faith. K. Brynolf Lyon is known for his work on aging (1985, 1988, 1994) and brings to this subject his experience as a theological educator, consultant to congregations, and psychoanalytically trained psychotherapist working with individuals and groups.

In chapter 14, "The Wages of Dying: Catastrophe Transformed," Claude Barbre considers the threat that death presents to the living–the ultimate loss of self–but also the hope that something of value in us will live on. If we are remembered in love and through love, if we find ways to take our joys with us into death, then we may experience the dreaded angel of death as partner to the angel of life when we complete life's journey. There is certainly struggle on the way to death, but through faith that struggle can be a catastrophe transformed. The author, a psychotherapist writing from a depth psychology perspective informed by analytical (Jungian) psychology, brings to the subject of death his experience as a chaplain and as executive director of the Harlem Family Institute in New York City, a place where children and families can renew their creative strengths despite the death-dealing adversities of urban poverty. In the context of pastoral care and counseling, death is more than an ominous future, casting its cold shadow over life. Death becomes a reminder of the fragility, beauty, and sanctity of all life, even as it forces us to hallow our diminishments and mourn.

Conclusion

Faith and human development designate essential elements of human experience. They are presented here as distinct perspectives that belong in dialogue. Through the dual lenses of developmental psychology and faith informed by religion and theology, our human condition becomes more fully visible.

The preceding brief presentation of chapter topics serves to orient the reader to the wide variety of viewpoints the authors represent. In this collection, each author's theoretical, experiential, and faith perspective can be expected to lift up certain aspects of development and faith while de-emphasizing others. Readers new to the subject of human development are encouraged to consult texts such as Colarusso's *Child and Adult Development* (1992) and Erikson's classic *Childhood and Society* (1950/1963), both written from a psychoanalytic perspective, as well as Fowler's *Stages of Faith* (1981), informed by the work of structural developmental theorists such as Piaget and Kohlberg. For an introduction to family systems theory, works by Betty Carter and Monica McGoldrick, including *The Expanded Family Life Cycle: Individual, Family and Social Perspectives* (Carter and McGoldrick, 1999) and *Genograms: Assessment and Intervention* (McGoldrick, Gerson, & Shellenberger, 1999), are recommended.

To gain a broader view of developmental theory, readers may wish to consult Patricia Miller's *Theories of Developmental Psychology* (1993), William Crain's *Theories of Development: Concepts and Applications* (2000), or Keith Richardson's *Developmental Psychology: How Nature and Nurture Interact* (2000). Critiques of developmental theory are offered by John Broughton, *Critical Theories of Psychological Development* (1987); John Morss, *Growing Critical: Alternatives to Developmental Psychology* (1996); and Patricia Miller and Ellen Scholnick, *Toward a Feminist Developmental Psychology* (2000).

Books on development that consider a faith perspective include Don Capps' *Deadly Sins and Saving Virtues* (1987), which pairs traditional sins with Erikson's life-cycle virtues; James Loder's *The Logic of the Spirit: Human Development in Theological Perspective* (1998); James Hightower's *Caring for People from Birth to Death* (1999), aimed at orienting pastors to the specific spiritual needs of each developmental stage; and Elizabeth Liebert's *Changing Life Patterns: Adult Development in Spiritual Direction* (2000). Froma Walsh's *Spiritual Resources in Family Therapy* (1999) is the most useful book in the family therapy field with respect to the interface between faith and family systems theory since Edwin Friedman's *Generation to Generation: Family Process in Church and Synagogue* (1985).

Thanks to the editorial efforts of Jeanne Stevenson-Moessner and Maxine Glaz, a multi-authored trio of books addresses women's pastoral care needs and developmental issues: *Women in Travail and Transition: A New Pastoral Care* (Glaz & Moessner, 1991), *Through the Eyes of Women: Insights for Pastoral Care* (Moessner, 1996) and *In Her Own Time: Women and Developmental Issues in Pastoral Care* (Stevenson-Moessner, 2000). While not specifically focused on developmental issues, *Feminist and Womanist Pastoral Theology* (1999), edited by Bonnie Miller-McLemore and Brita Gill-Austern, brings a critical theological perspective to bear on women's concerns. *In a Different Voice: Psychological Theory and Women's Development* (Gilligan, 1982) and *Women's Ways of Knowing: The Development of Self, Voice, and Mind* (Belenky, Clinchy, Goldberger, & Tarule, 1986) are recommended for their distinctive presentations of women's experience.

This book addresses developmental issues that arise for both women and men. The implications of difference in gender, ethnicity, faith, social location, culture, and sexual orientation are noted but not exhaustively explored. With so broad a task, it is inevitable that some important concerns related to development and faith may be overlooked. My hope as editor is that you, the reader, will think of this collection as an on-going conversation. If these essays raise useful questions or enlighten your understanding of yourself, others, and God in some small measure, they will have served their purpose.

Notes

[1]Winnicott's phrase, the "good-enough" mother or caregiver, makes clear that the child's caregiver need not be perfectly attuned to her or him, as long as the care the child receives is not overly frustrating, intrusive, or neglectful. This "good-enough" care is essential—we are all dependent from birth on the beneficent presence of others (Winnicott, 1960/1965).

[2]Job 13:15 reads quite differently in other English translations (Kelcourse, 2001). The Jerusalem Bible translation—Job addressing God—reads "Let him kill me if he will; I have no other hope than to justify my conduct in his eyes." According to Gerald Janzen (personal communication), this passage is problematic in that *lo eyachel* can be translated either "I will hope in him" or "I will have no hope." The Hebrew word for "hope" ("trust" in the *King James Version*) has the connotation of "trembling with anticipation." In this sense the *King James Version* (KJV) captures the spirit of Job's struggle with God.

[3]"Structural developmental theory," also referred to as theories of cognitive development, is used here to include the work of Piaget, Kohlberg, Gilligan, Fowler, and Kegan. The work of Fowler and Kegan has been further identified as "constructive developmental" theory. I am indebted to Steven Ivy for noting these distinctions (personal communication, 2003).

[4]To give one example, Angela Kakerissa, a student from Indonesia, recounts a Javanese fable in which Sangkuriang falls in love with his mother, Dayang Sumbi, who has become immortal. Both are killed by Brahma to prevent the disgrace of a marriage between a mother and her son (personal communication, 4/8/2003).

[5]This consideration of faith is expressed in theistic terms and is therefore not intended to represent the perspective of non-theistic religious traditions.

[6]As a Quaker minister, I interpret Jesus' saying "I am the way, and the truth, and the life. No one comes to the Father except through me" (Jn. 14:6) in universalist terms. Anyone who gives evidence of living the abundant life to which Jesus invites us is on the way to the Father, striving for right relationship with self, others, and God.

[7]Although Kirschner does not cite Augustine's *Confessions* (400/2001) as a study in human faith development, the *Confessions* have influenced Christian understandings of the subject (personal communication, Frank Burch Brown).

PART ONE

The Context of Development

CHAPTER 1

Theories of Human Development

Felicity B. Kelcourse

The specific theories of human development that inform the authors of this book each presume a particular orientation to faith as the ability to receive, find, and make meaning in our lives. Theories of depth psychology originating with Freud and Jung, cognitive-structural-constructive developmental theories based on the work of Jean Piaget, and family systems theories have been chosen among many for their relevance in the work of pastoral care and counseling. Because these theoretical perspectives give attention to individual self-awareness as well as intersubjective, relational patterns in families and society, they serve to describe "good-enough" development–the desired conditions for meaning-making–in relation to self, others, and God.

Depth psychologies consider both conscious and unconscious components of human awareness. Unconscious awareness can have developmental significance as it appears in recurring dreams and fantasies and in complexes, or feeling-toned thought patterns, that may impede desired functioning. For example, a person who has consistent difficulty relating to men in authority might have a father complex based on negative interactions with his or her father as a child. Projection, the largely unconscious process by which we see disavowed characteristics or experiences of our own in others, can cloud our perception of relationships. The insight-oriented process of psychotherapy favored by depth psychology aims to make us more conscious of, and therefore more responsible for, our patterns of attention and inattention to the world around us.

23

Unconscious beliefs can be transmitted intergenerationally, as family patterns that repeat from one generation to the next, and cross-culturally, through folk tales, mythology, and religion. Depth psychologies explore the intrapsychic (inward) and interpersonal (relational) dimensions of meaning and motivation in human experience.

Sub-groupings of depth psychology include psychoanalytic theory and analytical or Jungian psychology, ego psychology, object relations, self psychology, and theories of intersubjectivity. Psychoanalytic theory gives attention to human development and faith through the work of Sigmund Freud (1953–1974), Melanie Klein (1932, 1957), Anna Freud (1966), Erik Erikson (1950), Donald Woods Winnicott (1965), Daniel Stern (1985), William Meissner (1984), Anna Maria Rizzuto (1979), and Calvin Colarusso (1992), among others. Chapter 3 offers an overview of object relations, and chapter 5 presents the work of Daniel Stern with regard to the earliest stages of self/other awareness in infancy. Chapters 12 and 13 are also psychoanalytically informed.

Analytical or Jungian psychological theories begin with psychoanalytic understandings of persons, but also depart from them in significant ways. Analytical psychology gives attention to vocation, the individuation of adulthood, as an expression of faith, and is represented in this volume by the work of Carl Gustav Jung (1953–1961), Marie-Louise von Franz (1999), James Hillman (1992), John Sanford (1979), Donald Kalsched (1996), and Ann Ulanov (2001), among others. The authors of chapters 7, 8, and 14 draw on principles of Jungian psychology.

Psychoanalysis sees faith and meaning-making as capable of change through the dialogue between conscious knowing and unconscious, body-based awareness, or what psychoanalyst Christopher Bollas calls the "unthought known" (1985). As a developmental theory, it begins with the concern of Darwin and other students of animal behavior and habitat (ethologists) to discover the basic biological underpinnings of human behavior, especially sexuality and aggression (Freud, 1905d/1953). It shares with ethology the conviction that early experiences are at the root of later behaviors (Ainsworth et al., 1978; Bowlby, 1988, 1999). Words originating in psychoanalytic theory that have now passed into common parlance include id, ego, superego, projection, and libido, among others (Reber, 1983/1995, p. 300; see definitions of these terms below).

Theories of cognitive development, including structural and constructive developmental theories, document observable responses to changing levels of intellectual maturity as well as changing circumstances. They consider schemas, or the mental constructs we use to interpret sense perception.[1] Structural theories of development study the actions and reactions of children and adults, attempting to infer from observed behavior the mental processes and inner logic that informs them. Theorists building on the work of Jean Piaget (1937/1954, 1967), including Kohlberg (1981),

Fowler (1981), Gilligan (1982), and Kegan (1982), identify the stages and processes of reasoning through which decisions are made.

Cognitive development is the general rubric used to group these theories due to their focus on the development of logic in childhood (Piaget), moral reasoning (Kohlberg), conscious articulations of faith (Fowler), moral decision-making in women's experience (Gilligan), and the conceptual demands of modern life (Kegan). But theorists within this school use the term *structural* to identify their approach to development. Following Piaget, developmental change is understood to unfold in stages that are sequential; unfolding in a logical progression; invariant, in that the order of stages does not change; and universal–the same for all people regardless of their cultural context. Though each of these Piagetian categories has been nuanced or questioned by subsequent theorists, they continue to provide the template by which this group of theorists is recognized.

Robert Kegan prefers the term *constructive-developmental* to emphasize "the development of the activity of meaning-making" (1982, p. 4). Given this definition, Fowler, Gilligan, and Kegan could each be considered constructive developmentalists; compared to Piaget and Kohlberg they are relatively more willing to take into account the contexts in which meaning is made and place more emphasis on meaning-making as a process involving both affect and cognition that evolves over time. Chapters 5 and 6 best present a structural approach to development, but the influence of cognitive, structural, and constructive developmental theories can be found throughout this volume. While Erikson's epigenetic chart is grouped with the psychoanalytic theorists based on his attention to unconscious, intrapsychic dynamics, his work forms a bridge between psychoanalytic and structural understandings of development given his attention to developmental stages. Faith, in the understanding of structural development, has to do with our ability to find and make meaning as the sequential phases of our lives unfold.

Family systems theories consider individuals within the context of their relationships, both familial and societal. These theories lift up the developmental contribution of community and culture, the multiple forms of influence family members have on one another, and the observable patterns of intergenerational behavior couples bring from their families of origin. Family systems theories serve to counterbalance the relative individualism and essentialism of depth psychologies and structural developmental theories, although Erikson, Winnicott, Fowler, Gilligan, and Kegan also give attention to contextual dynamics and cultural concerns. Compared to the other schools considered here, family systems theories are thoroughly postmodern: It is generally assumed that there is no established "right" way to be a family or develop as an individual. Judgments about the adequacy of development in families, individuals, and cultures are based on mutuality and consensus–whatever serves to balance intimacy and independence, justice and responsibility must be good.

Systems models of human interaction assume that we are each so influenced by those around us that it is virtually impossible to say where interpersonal and societal influences begin or end. Monica McGoldrick's books (1980, 1999) offer an excellent introduction to family systems theory, as does the work of Murray Bowen (1978) and Edwin Friedman (1985). Chapters 4 and 11 consider ethnicity, intergenerational support systems, and couple relationships from a family systems perspective. But attention to familial and cultural dynamics informs other chapters as well. And the field of human development itself is giving increasing attention to the profound influence of culture and context on the unfolding of individual lives (Liebert, 2000; K. Richardson, 2000; Miller & Scholnick, 2000; Morss, 1996). Faith, from the standpoint of family systems theories, must be understood in ecological rather than individual terms; life, health, and meaning are found through the confluence and balance of interacting systems. While individuals are responsible for their choices, families, communities, and cultures are ultimately charged with providing the contexts within which faith can be found and meaning made.

Taken together, these three conceptual frameworks—depth psychologies, cognitive-structural-constructive developmental theories, and family systems theories—provide a comprehensive understanding of human behavior and motivation within the context of developmental change. My own primary theoretical grounding is in depth psychology. Yet I find it useful to juxtapose these theoretical groups in teaching human development because each group of theories appeals to different personality types and viewpoints. Depth psychologies often fail to give adequate attention to the influence of familial and societal factors such as racism, sexism, ageism, and the like as they inevitably influence individual development. Family systems theory does this well. Structural developmental and family systems theories, with their greater emphasis on observed behavior, are much better suited to quantitative and qualitative research than depth psychologies, which rely on highly subjective reports and interpretations. On the other hand, the subjective emphasis of depth psychologies makes them better suited to map the landscape of human interiority; theories that rely primarily on observed behavior have relatively less access to the inner lives of persons (Bittner, 1991). Many cognitive-structural-constructive developmental and family systems theories are based on the self-report of individuals. But interviews tend to emphasize what is consciously known and are therefore less able to account for the presence of irrational, unconscious factors in human experience.

Because a basic familiarity with the three theoretical perspectives in question is assumed in the chapters that follow, it is useful to review their origins and principles here in light of the following questions: "What does this theory teach about faith as our ability to trust, and our ability to receive, find, and make meaning? What does this theory recognize as expressions of vital concern?" Note that this chapter will not attempt to give equal time to each theoretical group, in part because cognitive-structural-constructive developmental and family systems theories are relatively new, with many of the founding theorists still living. It is also the case that depth psychologies are the primary ground from which subsequent structural and family systems theories have grown. Readers who find themselves drawn to a particular theorist or group are encouraged to use this overview as a large-scale map from which to choose a more detailed orientation.

Depth Psychologies

Freud and Psychoanalysis

Sigmund Freud (1856–1939) was raised in a Jewish home and trained in neurology. For all but the earliest and last years of his life, he lived and worked in Vienna, Austria, beneath the shadow of rising anti-Semitism. He became a psychoanalyst because university positions were closed to Jews. Barred from the more empirical sciences, he applied his appetite for research to the distressed women and men in his care, extrapolating from their difficulties developmental theories to explain the underlying causes of psychopathology. Psychoanalysis, as founded by Freud, begins with the cognitive and affective self-report of adults in psychotherapy and looks back in time to discern the psychosexual origins of their complaints. Sexuality, in this context, should be broadly understood as including the entire spectrum of our affiliative and erotic longings. To gain access to the unconscious workings of the mind, Freud favored dreams, as the "royal road to the unconscious," and free association, understood as the practice of saying whatever comes to mind without the usual social censorship (Bollas, 2002).

Freud compared the interaction of the ego, or primarily conscious sense of "I," and the id, or reservoir of embodied but generally inarticulate impulses, images, and ideas, to the relationship between a rider and horse. Only the skillful rider, in cooperation with the horse, is able to access the powerful precision that horse and rider together can express. Psychoanalysis aims to make us more self-aware and therefore more responsible for our actions, more accepting of self and others; from this standpoint it can be considered a form of spiritual discipline. To the extent that psychoanalysis enhances our ability to love our neighbor and ourselves (Lev. 19:18; Mt. 22:39), encouraging ethical behavior, good deeds, and *mitzvah,* it can be said to promote the love of God (Grant, 2001; LaMothe, 2001). Freud's avowed atheism not withstanding, psychoanalysis supports faith as it assists persons in their search for meaning and abundant life.

While Freud's neurological studies and early clinical work launched his initial theorizing, his own self-analysis, as found in *The Interpretation of Dreams* (1900), was a major breakthrough, both personally and professionally. Through analyzing his dreams, Freud was able to overcome complexes that limited his productivity. At forty he began the work and writing that would make him one of the leading intellectual influences on twentieth-century thought.

In addition to Freud's theory of libido as the basic life energy we express or sublimate through various forms of sexuality and aggression, his psychotherapeutic research explored the interplay of primary process–the irrational, illogical structures of unconscious thought–and secondary process–the more rational, logical thought processes that dominate our conscious ideas and interactions. In his later writing, he used the terms *Eros* and *Thanatos* to describe our developmental strivings on the one hand, and our desire for a cessation of effort on the other. While these terms are difficult to operationalize for the purposes of qualitative research, they effectively name the struggle psychotherapists frequently observe between the need to know, grow, and change, and the fear of knowing (Maslow, 1963). Truth has the power to set us free, but freedom, and the effort required to attain it, is usually hard work.

Freud's psychosexual theory of development identifies the oral phase, from birth to about eighteen months, as a time when orality characterizes the child's preferred mode of discovery. Developmental disturbances from this period may lead to addictions, eating disorders, or overly dependent behavior in adulthood. Next is the anal phase, from about twelve months to three years. During this time the child learns to control his or her bowels and is focused on developing physical mobility. Difficulties at this age, whether in the form of physical limitations, overly vigilant adult authorities, or absent, abandoning caregivers, may result in passive-aggressive behavior, covert aggression, or obsessive-compulsive, anal-retentive behavior in later life.

Freud was most interested in the Oedipal period, from three to six years, considering the resolution of incestuous Oedipal longings the cornerstone for healthy superego development. At this stage the child, formerly focused on the mother or primary caregiver, enters the relational triangle of "Mommy, Daddy, me." The child, if heterosexual, will be attracted to the opposite-sex parent and tempted to compete with the same-sex parent (see chapters 2 and 7 for additional perspectives on Oedipal development). The boy concludes that competing with Dad is too risky. Fearing castration as the ultimate punishment for such hubris, the boy elects to identify with Dad and move away from Mom, thereby establishing his future independence and (in Freud's view) laying the groundwork for superego development as the basis for conscience and morality in later life.

The girl's developmental task is less clear in that she has to find positive ways to identify with Mom, who is usually her primary caregiver all along, while claiming appropriate attention from Dad, whose positive regard affirms her self-worth. Freud believed that superego development in women was compromised as a result (Freud & Breuer, 1905d/1955). Although Freud's understanding of male and female development has been criticized (Gilligan, 1982; Fliegal, 1986), it is clear that gender identity formation is an important developmental task at this stage (see chap. 7). Psychotherapists observe that when children receive enough of the positive, appropriate attention they need from each parent at this age, they are more likely to grow up confident in their gendered sense of self.

Having successfully met the Oedipal challenge, the child moves on to latency, the period of school age (six to twelve) in which overt interest in sexuality goes underground while the child absorbs the knowledge of her or his culture. At the beginning of adolescence (twelve to twenty), sexuality once again comes to the fore. These five stages and others added by Erikson to cover adulthood will be considered in greater detail in chapter 2 and in Part Two: Life-Cycle Stages of Development.

Perhaps Freud's most impressive accomplishment was to demonstrate, through self-experimentation and careful attention to the suffering of others, that psychoanalytic methods can and do produce healing through insight regarding our earliest stages of development. The work of analysis can be slow and time consuming, but it can also achieve lasting results without the side effects of medication. Psychoanalysis has been called a "cure through love" (Freud & Jung, 1974, p. 10).

There is a substantial body of literature regarding Freud's theories, life, and times. The following list offers a representative sample: *The Life and Work of Sigmund Freud* (Jones, 1953–57); *The Development of Freud's Thought* (Fine, 1987); *Freud: Conflict and Culture* (Roth, 1998); *Freud: A Life for Our Time* (Gay, 1998); *Freud: Darkness in the Midst of Vision* (Breger, 2000); and *Freud and His Followers* (Roazen, 1992).

Jung and Analytical Psychology

Carl Gustav Jung (1875–1961) was born in Switzerland nineteen years after Freud's birth. Jung's father studied ancient languages as a doctoral student but failed to obtain a teaching position and became a country pastor by default. Jung's mother suffered from an unidentified mental illness; she was hospitalized for several months when Jung was three. D. W. Winnicott, in a review of Jung's autobiography *Memories, Dreams and Reflections* (1963), said he thought that Jung suffered from a childhood psychosis (1964). This would be consonant with the effect on a child of being raised by a mentally ill parent (Kelcourse, 1998).

Due in part to these parental influences, Jung maintained a life-long interest in ancient languages and cultures, religion, and the nonrational thought processes found in dreams, fantasies, psychosis, and religious experience. Having earned his medical degree, Jung worked and lived for nine years at the Burghölzli, the psychiatric clinic of Zurich University, where he served as a staff psychiatrist. There he developed his understanding of complexes (feeling-toned thought patterns) through his use of the word-association experiments that form the basis for our modern lie detector tests.

Early in his career, Jung read Freud's *Interpretation of Dreams* (1900). Correspondence between the two men developed into a mentor relationship, as chronicled in their published letters (Freud & Jung, 1974). They eventually parted on bad terms, ostensibly due to theoretical differences. Freud linked his concept of libido, or basic life energy, to embodied expressions of sexuality and aggression. Jung was not willing to limit libido, also known as instinct, to these categories, maintaining that we have many instincts, including a religious instinct. Freud was also leery of delving too deeply into what he called "the black tide of the occult," which he associated with pre-verbal, pre-Oedipal experience (Freud & Jung, 1974, p. 103n). Jung was more interested in allowing the pre-Oedipal "language" of image, fantasy, myth, and symbol to have its own voice. Like Freud, he believed that the unconscious could be dangerous if allowed to overwhelm the capacity of consciousness for dialogue, discernment, and reflection. Unlike Freud, he emphasized not only the personal unconscious, which is based on our embodied early and repressed experience, but also the cultural or collective unconscious. Jung conducted research into the collective unconscious by comparing themes that reoccur in religions, myths, and folk tales across time and culture.

Freud and Jung enjoyed, for a time, an intense father-son bond (1906–1913). Both were disappointed with their own fathers. Ambivalent toward their mothers, both longed for and feared intimate relationships. When their friendship effectively ended in 1913, Jung experienced a six-year "creative illness" (Goldwert, 1992). Though he was able to continue seeing patients at his home, he stopped participating in international psychoanalytic gatherings and published very little during this time.

This was Jung's period of healing through self-analysis. During these years (1913–1919), he chronicled his dreams, creating illuminated manuscripts to represent his dream images (Woollen & Wagner, 1990). In addition to techniques that would later be developed as art therapy, Jung discovered the rudiments of play therapy; each day during his lunch break from seeing patients, he would go down to the shores of the lake near his home and create miniature villages (Jung, 1963). Eventually, Jung was able to reemerge from this period of intense introspection, and, as with Freud, prolific publication followed his years of self-analysis.

Jung's legacy includes distinctive approaches to clinical work such as dream amplification, active imagination, play therapy, art therapy, and theories of personality on which the Myers-Briggs Type Indicator is based. In Jung's view, individual dreams and fantasies are not limited by the personal unconscious but can also express larger cultural themes as evidence of what he called the archetypes or the "inherited instincts and preformed patterns" found in the collective unconscious (Jung, 1936/1969, p. 66).

Jung was clearly influenced by Freud's understanding of the unconscious; there are many points of comparison between psychoanalysis and analytical psychology. But there are also important differences in theory and vocabulary. Most significant within the context of human development is Jung's theory of individuation.[2] While Freud and his followers stressed the importance of early development through adolescence, Jung is known for his theories of adult development, which emphasize the changes that are possible and desirable in the second half of life.

According to Jung, the first half of life, roughly up to age forty, was spent developing one's ego, or sense of "I." But the second half of life should be devoted to living out one's true calling or vocation (1932/1954). Like other developmental theorists, Jung identified stages by which individuation proceeds. In the first half of life one establishes a persona, like the mask an actor might wear. One learns to play the roles of (in Jung's case) doctor, husband, father, and analyst, knowing that one is always more than these roles. Over-identification with our roles can lead to severe depression when a role is lost, as when parents "lose" a child who grows up and moves away, or when a worker loses her or his employment.

Once the ability to function comfortably in a given persona role has been established, the next task is to face one's shadow. The shadow is a collection of "not-me" attributes that do in fact belong to an individual but are incompatible with one's conscious sense of self. It is possible for positive as well as negative traits to be hidden in the shadow, waiting to be rediscovered. As persons come into their own in the second half of life, with greater ego-strength and the capacity for greater wisdom and self-knowledge, their shadow traits, both good and bad, can be reclaimed into conscious awareness. The benefit of this effort to become self-aware is better discernment, but also more responsibility for the characteristics that one can no longer deny.

A simple exercise acquaints us with our shadows. First, think of a person who makes you uncomfortable. Then name one trait about this person you particularly dislike. When you have clearly identified the person and the trait, ask yourself this question: "Is there any aspect of what I dislike about this person that is also a part of me?" The point of this exercise is to recognize that what we most dislike about others is often related to disavowed traits in ourselves (an example of projection). In reclaiming one's shadow, one becomes more accepting of oneself and others.

The next stage on the journey of individuation is to face the syzygy, or anima and animus. Jung believed that we are all capable of expressing traits that society divides into male or female categories (Ulanov & Ulanov, 1987). Growing up male or female, we are taught by our families and cultures to identify traits associated with the opposite gender as "inappropriate."[3]

In the second half of life, men and women who have repressed aspects of their humanity that they were taught to view as unacceptable for their gender can reclaim these contrasexual human qualities (Jung, 1925/1954; 1932/1954).

Jung saw this internal reconciliation of the woman's disavowed animus, or culturally identified "masculine" traits, and the man's anima, or culturally identified "feminine" traits, as being an essential bridge to the Self. I have capitalized the word *Self* here deliberately to distinguish Jung's use of this word from the self of self psychology. In many psychology lexicons, self is synonymous with ego or our conscious sense of "I." This is not true for Jung. Jung's understanding of the Self has much more in common with religious understandings of the soul or *imago dei,* that of God in us. The dialogue between ego and Self is important precisely because the Self has a broader view than the ego. Whereas the ego tends to be limited by the dictates of time and culture, the Self will not hesitate to call persons to forms of self-expression that the society of their time and place would never condone. While an imbalance between ego and Self can lead to forms of psychic inflation in which we suffer from delusions of grandeur, too little dialogue between ego and Self results in chronic dissatisfaction, depression, and despair in the second half of life.

One quality that clearly distinguishes shadow contents from anima-animus contents is the way each cluster of complexes rises into conscious awareness. Shadow contents generally repel us, while contrasexual contents (qualities typically associated with the opposite sex) are often experienced as enlivening and alluring. In the second half of life, heterosexuals may find themselves strongly attracted to a person of the opposite sex who holds a particular fascination for them. People sometimes divorce and remarry or enter into affairs on the basis of such attractions. In a Jungian view, recognizing this attraction as an anima or animus projection allows us to consciously choose not to act out (take action) based on this attraction, but to recognize it as calling our attention to aspects of our own being that we have ignored. In so doing, we gain the increased self-awareness and ego strength that facilitates the dialogue of ego and Self (Ulanov & Ulanov, 1987).

Analytical psychology's approach to faith differs from a psychoanalytic view by virtue of its understanding of the relationship between consciousness and the unconscious. Faith, from a Jungian standpoint, is based on (re)discovering truths that may address us from beyond our individual experience. By entering into intentional dialogues between conscious and unconscious knowing, we draw closer to the guidance of the Self. The search for meaning includes the freedom to imagine and create as we learn to hear and trust the deeper knowing we each carry within us. Religious traditions speak of this as a mystical awareness of the holy in daily life. Catholics, Episcopalians, and Quakers are often drawn to Jung because their understandings of faith emphasize the nonverbal power of images, symbols, and silence as they inspire our receptivity to the divine.

Suggestions for further reading include Jung's autobiography *Memories, Dreams and Reflections* (1963); *The Psychology of C. G. Jung* (Jacobi, 1962); *The Freud-Jung Letters* (Freud & Jung, 1974); *C. G. Jung: His Myth in Our Time* (von Franz, 1975); *A Life of Jung* (Hayman, 1999); *A Most Dangerous Method: The Story of Jung, Freud and Sabina Spielrein* (Kerr, 1993); and *Boundaries of the Soul: The Practice of Jung's Psychology* (Singer, 1972).

Object Relations Theory and Ego Psychology

Melanie Klein (1882–1960) and Anna Freud (1895–1982) are progenitors of object relations theory and ego psychology, respectively. Each wished to be considered the true intellectual daughter of Freud. In an era when most analysts were psychiatrists, both were "lay" analysts without medical training; as women of that generation their opportunities for higher education were limited. Through their own study and experience they were qualified to conduct training analyses and taught in London as European expatriates during and after World War II. Melanie Klein's work influenced Donald Woods Winnicott, and Anna Freud's work influenced Erik Erikson.

Klein and Anna Freud were known for their theoretical disagreements. Melanie Klein's work explored in depth, through play therapy, the pre-Oedipal fantasy life of children three years old and younger as a way of extending Freud's work into the realm of early preverbal experience that both fascinated and repelled him (Freud & Jung, 1974). Klein analyzed Winnicott and group psychology theorist Wilfred Bion. Unlike Freud, she believed that the seeds of superego development and conscience can be identified during the first three years of life (Klein, 1932, 1957; Grosskurth, 1995). Klein's contributions to object relations theory are summarized in chapter 3.

Anna Freud's work took a different direction. In *The Ego and the Mechanisms of Defense* (1936/1966), she focused not on pre-Oedipal experience but on the defenses employed by the ego to negotiate between unconscious influences from within and environmental pressures from without. Having trained Erik Erikson in Vienna before fleeing the Nazis with her father in 1938, Anna Freud provided a foundation for the ego psychology writings of Heinz Hartmann (1964) and the documentary biographies of Robert Coles (1967). Her work has contributed to developmental psychology in the United States through the research of Margaret Mahler and Fred Pine (Mahler, Pine, & Bergman, 1975). The faith of ego psychologists is based in the developing ego's ability to mediate between instinctual and environmental demands. The hoped-for outcome of this balance is a sense of self that is strong, creative, flexible, and capable of intimacy.

Donald Woods Winnicott's (1896–1971) theory of transitional objects and transitional space has been useful in describing the function of religion, art, and culture as spheres of imagination and creative play in the development of the self (Winnicott, 1953/1971; Ulanov, 2001). Just as the teddy bear takes on a life of its own, becoming the first "not-me" possession that receives the child's love and aggression, so culture, art, and religion become expressions of the human spirit that allow us both to imagine life as it should be and to safely rage at the destructive aspects of existence. Winnicott trained first as a pediatrician and treated children in London during the bombing raids of World War II. His insights regarding the mental and emotional life of children became the basis for his work with adults as a psychoanalyst. Winnicott understood that the capacity to be alone begins in the presence of a loving but nonintrusive other (1958/1965); at the beginnings of life, we find ourselves only as others are able to love us into being. He described the necessary interplay of affiliative and aggressive impulses in the full expression of intimate connection with the other (1969/1971). Faith, from an object relations perspective, resides in the creative balance of self-other relating that allows freedom of expression for both self and other. The "true self" protects meaning that can only find expression when it is safely held; the "false self" becomes a necessary shield with which to face a threatening world (1960a/1965). The true self knows its experience is true because the guidance of the true self bears good fruit.

Margaret Mahler (1897–1986) was born in a small Hungarian town near Vienna. Despite being both Jewish and female at a time when women where not expected to pursue higher education, she was able to train first in pediatrics and then in psychiatry. She had a training analysis with Helene Deutsch, who was among the first generation of female psychoanalysts. Working with children was Mahler's passion. She became chair of the child analysis training program at the Albert Einstein School of Medicine in 1950. Her theories have since been challenged by later researchers such as Daniel Stern (1985), but this does not obviate their pioneering value to the field of early childhood development. She proposed three stages during the first three years of life. In Stage 1, the autistic phase (1–2 months) the infant appears to be turned inward, oblivious to everything outside its body. In Stage 2, the symbiotic phase (3–5 months) the child begins to recognize others, not yet as separate persons, but as extensions of his or her sense of self. Stage 3, the separation-individuation phase (5–36 months), consists of four overlapping sub-phases: differentiating, practicing, rapprochement, and object constancy (see Colarusso, 1992). During Phase 3, the psychic life of the individual is formed, and this serves as the foundation for children's early structures of meaning and response to their environment. The first three years of life are therefore primary determinants in the unfolding of personality and the establishment of mental health. See Mahler's classic works, *On Human Symbiosis and the Vicissitudes of Individuation*

(1968) and *The Psychological Birth of the Human Infant: Symbiosis and Individuation,* co-authored with Fred Pine and Anni Bergman (1975).

Erikson's Stage Theory

I have chosen Erik Erikson's epigenetic chart as a unifying template for this book because I find it the most comprehensive and least constricting of the various stage theories. The term *epigenesis* has been used to describe the intracellular unfolding of fetal development in response to a given prenatal environment. The concept of epigenesis as used by Erikson refers to the fact that each stage carries within it the seeds of its future unfolding, the basis for subsequent development, and the capacity to respond to the environmental conditions found within the family and in society.

Erikson (1902–1994), né Erik Homburger, was sired out of wedlock by a Danish father he never knew, born to a Jewish mother, and later adopted by his pediatrician. He studied art and worked with children before training to become a psychoanalyst. In adulthood he chose his own surname as a statement of his life-long quest for identity. His envisioned trajectory of a life includes both crises to be resolved and virtues to be claimed through their resolution (Erikson's eight-stage epigenetic chart can be found in chapter 2).

While his first five stages were borrowed from Freud, Erikson gave greater weight to the adolescent identity crisis and the influence of social context on all stages of development. Both Freud and Erikson were well aware of the essential relational family trinity of "mommy, daddy, me" and considered to some degree the influence of siblings and other relatives. Their work laid the foundation for the subsequent development of family systems theory with its emphasis on the broader intergenerational and interpersonal contexts of development.

Erikson, like his analyst, Anna Freud, was primarily interested in ego psychology, which focuses on the conscious sense of self while maintaining a depth psychological perspective that includes the influence of the unconscious. Erikson's stages are chronological, but they are not hierarchical in that each stage is an important component of the whole. If there is any sense of hierarchy in Erikson's template, it favors the earliest stages, as these are the sine qua non of "good-enough" development. This attention to preverbal stages has important implications for a psychoanalytic understanding of the value of religious ritual as embodied faith (see chap. 6). It also means that the preferred verbal and rational modes of adulthood cannot be privileged with respect to image and intuition, but that all stages must be regarded as valuable dimensions of personhood. As James Loder notes (1998), a non-hierarchical understanding of the relationship of developmental stages allows for a correspondence between developmental time, which is linear, and God's time, the Eternal Now (Tillich, 1963). Then the threads of meaning connecting all the moments of our lives can be seen, in retrospect, to interweave, like the patterns of a finished tapestry. The warp and woof of the tapestry are to the complete pattern as the developmental lines and stages of our lives are to the meaning of the whole. A complete overview of Erikson's eight stages, with two additional stages added for this volume, appears in chapter 2.

In Erikson's view, we live faithfully by negotiating life's predictable crises and finding in them opportunities for greater trust, a stronger will and sense of purpose, with confidence in our competence and fidelity as we mature. Living faithfully in adulthood allows us to love and care, and gains us a heart of wisdom. Through faith we express our capacity for mutuality in relation to others and, ultimately, in relation to God.

Suggestions for further reading in object relations, self psychology, Winnicott, and Erikson's stage theory include: *Schizoid Phenomena, Object-Relations and the Self* (Guntrip, 1961); *Melanie Klein: Her World and Her Work* (Grosskurth, 1995); *Love, Guilt, and Reparation* (Klein, 1975); *Anna Freud: The Dream of Psychoanalysis* (Coles, 1992); *The Ego and the Mechanisms of Defense* (A. Freud, 1936/1966); *In Search of the Real: The Origins and Originality of D. W. Winnicott* (Goldman, 1993); *Playing and Reality* (Winnicott, 1971); *Erik Erikson: His Life, Work and Significance* (Welchman, 2000); and *Childhood and Society* (Erikson, 1950/1963). *Ego Psychology: Theory and Practice* (Blanck & Blanck, 1974) offers a useful overview of ego psychology, while *A Primer of Object Relations Therapy* (Scharf & Scharf, 2003) serves as a clinical introduction to the subject.

Self Psychology and Intersubjectivity

Heinz Kohut (1913–1981), the founder of self psychology, furthered our understanding of pre-Oedipal developmental needs by modifying Freud's focus on sexuality and aggression, emphasizing instead the role of empathy in early and later self experience. Kohut advocated a healthy narcissism, which results in a cohesive self expressing ambitions and goals that actualize one's talents and abilities (1978). To form such a strong self, we each need self objects, usually other people, whose beneficent presence brings out the best in us. This does not mean that optimal development is based on an exclusive diet of coddling and praise. There is a disruption-restoration process that leads to transmuting internalizations, both in early experience and in the reparative work of psychotherapy. This can be understood as "tough love"–the parent or mentor knows when to say "no," thereby frustrating the learner's tendency to dependent regression and encouraging the appropriate growth of resourcefulness and self-reliance (Kohut, 1977, 1984). The goals of ego psychology and self psychology are comparable in that the strength and health of the ego remains the focus of development. But faith in self psychological terms must clearly be based in a beneficial reciprocity between self and other. Self psychology acknowledges our profound dependence on others for developing the self we become.

Atwood, Stolorow, Brandschaft, and Orange have extended the concept of empathy to encompass a two-person systemic understanding of intersubjectivity. In their phenomenological approach to human interaction, meaning is constructed in the intersubjective field that forms between two persons. The open dialogue and emotional attunement between self and other establishes intersubjective truth. Intersubjective faith adheres in the willingness to set aside defensive disbelief and enter into the phenomenological reality of another. In religious terms, we remain ever hopeful that we can find and respond to "that of God" in another. In intersubjective terms, it is our receptivity to one another's experience that provides the basis for healing.

Suggestions for further readings in self psychology and intersubjective theory include the following: *The Essential Other: A Developmental Psychology of the Self* (Galatzer-Levy & Cohler, 1993); *The Freedom to Inquire: Self Psychological Perspectives on Women's Issues, Masochism, and the Therapeutic Relationship* (Menaker, 1995); *The Search for the Self: Selected Writings of Heinz Kohut: 1950–1978* (Ornstein, 1978); *Structures of Subjectivity: Explorations in Psychoanalytic Phenomenology* (Atwood & Stolorow, 1984); *The Intersubjective Perspective* (Stolorow, Atwood, & Brandschaft, 1994); and *Emotional Understanding: Studies in Psychoanalytic Epistemology* (Orange, 1995).

Cognitive, Structural, and Constructive Theories of Development

Piaget and Cognitive Development

Jean Piaget (1896–1980) was a Swiss theorist known for his interest in biology and philosophy, two fields of inquiry he combined to explore genetic epistemology, or the study of how we come to know what we know. He published his first scholarly article at the age of ten and earned his doctorate in natural science from the University of Neuchâtel at age twenty-one; by the time of his death he had authored more than forty books and one hundred articles on child psychology alone (P. Miller, 1993). Piaget was exposed to the psychoanalytic theories of Freud and Jung before working for a time at the Binet Laboratory in Paris administering intelligence tests to school children. There he observed consistent patterns of "mistakes" made by children of different ages. This sparked his lifelong interest in the development of reasoning during childhood (Singer & Revenson, 1996).

Piaget took refuge in intellectual pursuits at an early age; this allowed him to withdraw from the conflicts he witnessed as a child between his studious, rational father, a medieval historian, and his emotionally labile Christian mother (Crain, 2000). It may be that these earlier experiences in his family of origin predisposed him to de-emphasize the role of affect in cognition, a subject since taken up by Sylvan Tomkins (1962) and others. From a faith perspective, Loder notes a "potentially spiritual quality" in the "reliance on transformation" that appears in Piaget's later work (1998, p. 26). Loder goes on to say that "for Piaget, intelligence derived its significance from a comprehensive sense of the order of all that is, including the sensory motor behavior of the knower, the moral order of human existence, and the ultimate comprehensibility of the universe" (1998, p. 26). In this way, Piaget's work combines the rational scholarship of his father and the spiritual concerns of his mother. Because Piaget's theories emphasize the development of rational, logical thought processes, he is known as a theorist of cognitive development. His work on children's moral reasoning (1932/1965) provides a foundation for the subsequent work of Lawrence Kohlberg and James Fowler.

Piaget did not see the mind as a *tabula rasa,* or blank slate. Like Jean Jacques Rousseau (1712–1778) and Maria Montessori (1870–1952), he believed that development begins with the unfolding of the child's innate potential as a learner predisposed to actively engage her or his environment. Based on detailed observations of his own children beginning in infancy and interviews with children as young as three through adolescence, Piaget also adduced that the development of cognition proceeds by stages. These stages may be described as "an integrated set of operational structures that constitute the thought processes of a person at a given time" (Fowler, 1981, p. 49). Cognitive development takes place as the knower assimilates what is known to achieve an accommodation between what is experienced and one's structures of perception. Piaget's work lays the foundation for subsequent structural theories of development because it posits that cognitive, functional change occurs within the developing neurological structure of the child. The structuralist perspective supports stage theories of development in which each stage is qualitatively different from the one that precedes it, while building on the developmental achievements of the previous stage. Each individual psyche contains the seeds of change as a genetic inheritance, but adequate stimulation from the environment may be required to unlock the full potential of each stage.

Piaget sees development as a largely predetermined sequence of biological maturation that causes individuals to respond differently to their environment as each new stage of maturation is achieved. Specifically, Piaget's theory of cognitive development posits four genetically determined stages that unfold in an invariant sequence:

1. *Period I–Sensori-Motor Intelligence (birth to two years):* Movement is essential for learning at this age as babies organize physical schemes for interacting with their environment. Actions such as sucking, grasping, kicking, and hitting aid in the discovery of one's body and surrounding objects.

2. *Period II–Preoperational Thought (two to seven years):* The thought processes of young children are quite different from those of adults. While preschoolers are able to think in terms of symbols and internal images (the *semiotic function*), their thinking is still illogical and

unsystematic. *Egocentrism, animism,* seeing dreams and fantasies as external events, and a lack of ability to classify dissimilar objects characterize this stage. Also characteristic are *moral heteronomy,* a sense of morality entirely dependent on what one is taught by others and a lack of *conservation,* or the ability to recognize that the volume of water in a glass remains the same when it is poured from a short wide glass into a tall narrow glass.

3. *Period III–Concrete Operations (seven to eleven years):* Children can think systematically at this age if they are able to refer to concrete objects and activities such as using blocks to add and subtract. At this stage the logic of conservation has been achieved.

4. *Period IV–Formal Operations (eleven to adulthood):* As children enter adolescence, they gain the capacity to think in abstract, hypothetical, and systematic terms. Only at this age can children follow adult logic and reasoning as they begin to develop their own ideals and moral loyalties (Piaget, 1926, 1953).

Critics of Piaget's work observe that his stages are more culture-specific than he believed. Cross-cultural research using Piaget's stages indicates that while the stages he described do seem to name basic human potentials for cognition, the time frame for the emergence of particular stages is likely to depend on the skills that are valued by a particular culture (Ashton, 1975). Recognizing that children younger than adolescence tend to use play rather than words as a primary language, one might question the usefulness of verbal interviews designed to ascertain children's thought processes (see chap. 8). Piaget's research methods were descriptive and naturalistic; he observed children as one might observe animals in their native environments. Subsequent researchers have certainly criticized these methods, but as Patricia Miller observes, "For developmentalists, problems resulting from Piaget's lack of uniform testing procedures and statistical analysis and his small number of subjects were more than offset by his remarkable naturalistic observations" (P. Miller, 1993, p. 82).

Piaget may have underestimated children's intelligence in certain respects (Crain, 2000). Although it is true that Piaget's research tended to emphasize children's logical deficits from the standpoint of adult cognition, we are indebted to him for recognizing that children's thought processes are qualitatively different from those of adults. To understand how best to teach children, we must first understand how children of different ages view and interact with the world. Piaget's theories have important implications for parents and educators. Is it right, for example, to require that children in the preoperational thought stage of two to seven years "tell the truth" when their understanding of reality is so different from that of adults? Should children ages seven to eleven be expected to take a stand on moral issues when they have not yet acquired the capacity for abstract thought? When dealing with children in the early teen years and younger, it is important that adults take into account the child's understanding of the world around them, lest parents and teachers unwittingly subject children to emotional abuse through the imposition of inappropriate expectations.

Despite their shortcomings, Piaget's stages remain the standard by which other theories of cognitive, structural development are measured. The theoretical descendents of Jean Piaget in this country include Lawrence Kohlberg, Carol Gilligan, James Fowler, and Robert Kegan; each of these scholars has made significant contributions to our understanding of structural development. All four present some theory of stages to account for the maturation of cognition in relation to moral, ethical, and faith-related issues. Kohlberg, Gilligan, and Fowler have followed Piaget's empirical model in using verbal interviews as their primary method of research. Kegan's stages are based on his own experience as a psychotherapist, parent, and educator.

Following Piaget, the faith of cognitive, structural theories of development begins with creation; we carry within us the ability to learn, as well as a hunger to draw adequate stimulation from our environment. If the environment doesn't thwart our quest for understanding and if we are sufficiently motivated to continue extending our cognitive abilities in adulthood, each individual is equipped to realize his or her God-given potential. But it is surprisingly rare in the case of Piaget's stages, as well as the stages of Kohlberg, Fowler, Gilligan, and Kegan, to find adults who consistently function at, or even reach, the highest stages that each theorist identifies. Piaget notes that adults will use their highest intellectual capacities in pursuing the tasks they most value, whether scientific research, car mechanics, or international peacekeeping (Crain, 2000). This suggests that from the faith standpoint of cognitive development, the grace inherent in our innate human potential is counterbalanced by the need for works; we will tend to fall short of our full intellectual and moral potential if we are not prepared to focus our best abilities on the tasks at hand.

Suggestions for further reading on Piaget include: *Piaget's Theory of Intellectual Development* (Ginsburg & Opper, 1988); *The Language and Thought of the Child* (Piaget, 1926); *The Origins of Intelligence in the Child* (Piaget, 1953); and *A Piaget Primer: How a Child Thinks* (Singer & Revenson, 1996).

Kohlberg and the Development of Moral Reasoning

Lawrence Kohlberg (1927–1987) was born in Bronxville, New York, to a wealthy family. He rebelled against family expectations by joining the Merchant Marines after high school. In support of the Israeli cause, he participated in smuggling Jewish refugees from Europe into Palestine to elude the British blockade during World War II. The moral dilemmas inherent in this situation influenced his choice of moral judgment as the topic for his doctoral dissertation at the University of Chicago: *The*

Development of Modes of Thinking and Choice in the Years 10–16 (1958a). The boys he initially interviewed were posed a series of moral dilemmas including the scenario entitled "Heinz Steals the Drug": Should Heinz steal the drug that might save his wife's life if he can't afford to buy it? Kohlberg was more interested in the reasoning process used to arrive at an answer to these scenarios than in the answer itself. As a result of this research, Kohlberg posited three moral levels in six stages, as follows:

LEVEL 1 — PRECONVENTIONAL MORALITY

There is no internal sense of right or wrong at this stage—moral judgments are based on the rules imposed by external authorities.

Stage 1: Punishment and obedience orientation: An event is judged to be right or wrong depending on its consequences.

Stage 2: Individualism and exchange: A person conforms to rules to gain rewards—"If you scratch my back, I'll scratch yours."

LEVEL 2 — CONVENTIONAL MORALITY

At this stage, the hope of praise and avoidance of blame replace tangible rewards and punishments.

Stage 3: Good interpersonal relationships: Behavior is good when it pleases and helps others.

Stage 4: Maintaining social order: What is right conforms to the law and reflects the will of the community.

LEVEL 3 — POST-CONVENTIONAL MORALITY

At this stage right and wrong are defined in terms of broad principles of justice that may conflict with the dictates of local authorities or one's immediate community.

Stage 5: Social contract and individual rights: The purpose of just laws is to express the will of the majority, but unjust laws can and should be challenged.

Stage 6: Universal principles: Principles of universal justice, the dictates of one's own conscience, and respect for individual rights transcend any law or social contract that conflicts with them (Crain, 2000).

Kohlberg's understanding of universal justice reflects the moral philosophies of Kant (1788/1956) and Rawls (1971). It is also in keeping with the worldviews of great twentieth-century leaders such as Gandhi and Martin Luther King Jr. Both Gandhi and King deliberately broke civil laws in the name of higher principles of justice. Only persons whose moral reasoning reflects post-conventional principles of morality are cognitively prepared to engage in civil disobedience. This is a point that ministers and educators do well to bear in mind when issues of social justice are being considered.

Kohlberg, following Piaget, believed that his stages always unfolded sequentially. But some longitudinal research suggests that persons may remain in a given stage, and that they may sometimes skip a stage as well (Kohlberg & Kramer, 1969). Unlike Piaget's stages of cognition, Kohlberg did not believe that his stages of moral development naturally appeared in the course of maturation. Nor did he believe that moral development was the direct result of ordinary socialization in the absence of deliberate moral education. He attributed the emergence of new stages to critical reflection on moral dilemmas, though he recognized that social experiences can stimulate our thinking in a way that encourage us to reevaluate our positions on ethical issues.

Despite the value he placed on cognition and reflection, Kohlberg recognized that moral reasoning was no guarantee of moral action; people whose reasoning indicates a high level of moral development may not always act in accordance with their espoused beliefs. Ultimately, Kohlberg's understanding of moral development has to do with our ability to step outside our own experience and dispassionately weigh the needs and claims of others in a way that respects the worth and value of all persons. It would be logical to suppose that moral reasoning might be a necessary precondition for moral action, especially when action for the good of others is costly to oneself. But this point has been questioned by Carol Gilligan and others.

Criticisms of Kohlberg's theory include the fact that, as with Piaget, the assumption that Western social values are normative blinds him to important cultural differences. His initial interview studies were also primarily limited to middle-class boys and men. When women were included in subsequent studies, their answers as a group placed them on average at a lower stage of moral development than men as a group. Can one conclude from this result that women are less likely to extend themselves for the benefit of others? On the contrary, they may be more likely to do so in actual fact, even though their responses to Kohlberg's interviews suggest otherwise. Can we conclude from this that moral education is not a fundamental necessity for democratic societies? There will probably always be people who are more adept at moral reasoning than they are at moral action, whereas others may behave in a heroic, self-sacrificial manner when the need arises yet not be able to articulate the philosophical principles that motivated their action. Yet there is no doubt that encouraging moral reflection, whether in the context of faith communities or schools, does make a difference in how people understand their ethical responsibilities in relation to others. The great value of Kohlberg's legacy lies in his insistence that moral reflection can and should be taught. At a time when some schools still promote a "values free" approach to education, Christian educators, teachers, parents, pastors, and all concerned for social justice need to be providing the kind of opportunities for moral development that Kohlberg's classic moral dilemmas are designed to inspire.

Kohlberg's approach to faith might be summarized in the words of the great commandment "'Hear, O Israel: the Lord our God, the Lord is one; you shall love the Lord your God with all your heart, and with all your soul, and with all your mind, and with all your strength';...'You shall love your neighbor as yourself'"(Mk. 12:28–31; see also Mt. 22:34–40; Lk. 10:25–28; Deut. 6.4). Kohlberg's scenarios for moral discernment all pose the same implicit question: What do we hold most dear, most sacred, and why? These are questions any person of faith will be required to answer.

To learn more about Kohlberg's approach to moral development, the following readings are suggested: *Kohlberg's Stages of Moral Judgment: A Constructive Critique* (Gibbs, 1977); *Vision and Character: A Christian Educator's Alternative to Kohlberg* (Dykstra, 1981); *The Philosophy of Moral Development* (Kohlberg, 1981); *Lawrence Kohlberg: Consensus & Controversy* (Modgil & Modgil, 1985); *Moral Development, Moral Education and Kohlberg* (Munsey, 1980).

Gilligan and Women's Judgments

Carol Gilligan (b. 1936) earned a master's degree in clinical psychology at Radcliffe (1960) and a doctorate in social psychology at Harvard (1964). She taught with Erik Erikson at Harvard beginning in 1967, and beginning in 1970 she worked as a research assistant with Lawrence Kohlberg. In 1986 Gilligan was tenured as a full professor at the Harvard Graduate School of Education. She has since coordinated Harvard's Center for Gender and Education. A feminist scholar, she has interests in conflict resolution, adolescence, moral development, and women's development.

Gilligan became critical of Kohlberg's emphasis on individual rights, which she contrasts with women's perspective on relationships based on caring for others with the expectation of being cared for in return. She is known for her "difference feminism": While some contextualist feminists insist that women and men are basically identical apart from differences in socialization, Gilligan is more essentialist in that she does recognize women's physical difference from men as a factor in their moral development. Gilligan's alternative to Kohlberg, *In a Different Voice: Psychological Theory and Women's Development* (1982), urges us to attend to individual difference and circumstance. She asks us to consider the speaker; his or her embodied, lived experience; the story he or she tells; as well as the cultural framework in which the story is presented. Gilligan faults Kohlberg for not paying sufficient attention to class differences and other issues of social location.[4]

Carol Gilligan and others have claimed that Kohlberg's theory is biased against women because it tends to elevate the abstract principles of justice apparently favored by men over women's tendency to focus on the needs of individuals and groups in real-life circumstances (Gilligan, 1982). Gilligan argues that because both Piaget and Kohlberg derived their stage theories from studying boys and men, their models fail to accurately reflect important differences in women's moral development (Burman, 1994). Both Gilligan's ethics of care and an ethical system based on philosophical and religious principles are essential for human growth and development, in that the morality of justice can inspire oppressed groups to challenge their oppression (Broughton, 1983). Yet the ethics of care is often more germane for day-to-day interpersonal dilemmas faced by families and faith communities. In the ethics of care, context and individual difference cannot be subsumed under abstract ethical principles and must be taken into account (SteinhoffSmith, 1999).

For example, Gilligan asks women to consider an ethical dilemma with which many women are faced: Is it wrong to have an abortion? Some believe that there is only one right answer to this question, based on their fundamental principles of faith, morality, and justice. But is it right to impose an abstract principle on women without considering the context in which their decision must be made? Is conception following rape or incest to be equated with conception that occurs between consenting adults? Does it matter whether a woman living in poverty is pregnant with her seventh child, when her resources are already insufficient to support the children she has? In the case of women who are willing to risk their own health and well-being to give birth to a child they relinquish for adoption, does society adequately recognize the altruistic nature of their choice, or are these women somehow stigmatized for giving up their babies? Do societies make every effort to protect women's right to wanted pregnancies while providing legal and physical protection from unwanted pregnancies? Gilligan would argue that one must listen to women tell their stories, seeing the world through their eyes, before one is entitled to pass judgment on their decisions. She notes that women are generally less inclined to be judgmental of others because they recognize the complexities of life (1982).

Faith for Gilligan is found dialogically, in conversation with others. There can be no adequate discernment that does not take the voice and context of the other into account. Faith is found relationally, not in isolation. Gilligan would say that we listen each other into being. To fail to listen and honor another's experiences diminishes both the other and ourselves. Failure to listen to women's stories leaves them speechless, unable or unwilling to speak for fear they will not be heard.

For an alternative to Gilligan's view of development, see "Women's Rationality and Men's Virtues: A Critique of Gender Dualism in Gilligan's Theory of Moral Development" (Broughton, 1983). Carol Gilligan's 1982 book, *In a Different Voice: Psychological Theory and Women's Development,* extends and rethinks Kohlberg's stages in the context of women's experience: Her three stages include a progression from selfishness to conventional morality, with the highest stage being a post-conventional, principled morality. Because women are heavily socialized to put the interests of others before their own, considering their own needs as well as those of others is a developmental achievement for many.

Gilligan's subsequent books include *Meeting at the Crossroads: Women's and Girls' Development* (Brown & Gilligan, 1992) and *Between Voice and Silence: Women and Girls, Race and Relationship* (Taylor, Gilligan, & Sullivan, 1996). For a summary of her contribution in the context of feminist theory, see *Moral Voices, Moral Selves: Carol Gilligan and Feminist Moral Theory* (Hekman, 1995).

Fowler's Structures of Faith Development

James W. Fowler (b. 1940) is an ordained Methodist minister who graduated from Drew Theological Seminary in 1965 and earned a Ph.D. in Religion and Society at Harvard University in 1971. A member of the Candler School of Theology faculty since 1977, he served as the first director of the Center for Faith Development at Emory University. His *Stages of Faith: The Psychology of Human Development and the Quest for Meaning* (1981) has remained continuously in print since it was first published and has been widely translated.

Fowler identifies seven stages of faith development (Stages 0–6) based on his synthesis of Piaget's, Kohlberg's, and Erikson's stage theories and more than four hundred interviews with adults and children. Theological sources for his work include H. Richard Neibuhr and Paul Tillich. The word *faith* in the title of this book reflects Fowler's broad understanding of faith as that which gives meaning and purpose to our lives.

The initial, or "0" stage is the *undifferentiated faith* of infancy (from birth to age two). Here, "the seeds of trust, courage, hope and love are fused in an undifferentiated way and contend with sensed threats of abandonment, inconsistencies and deprivations in an infant's environment" (1981, p. 121). Fowler follows Erikson in seeing the central crisis and opportunity of this stage as the balance of trust and mistrust. In this stage, the beginnings of mutuality, as the capacity for interpersonal empathy and connection, are either firmly established or threatened.

Intuitive projective faith (ages two to six) is Fowler's stage 1. The thinking of children at this age is characterized by cognitive egocentrism, a predominance of fantasy and a lack of logic. The need for concrete symbols and stories of one's faith community that can be learned by preschool children in embodied ways is addressed in chapter 6.

Stage 2 is the *mythic-literal faith* of grade-school children (ages seven to twelve). Stories remain prominent due to their ability to either liberate or "trap" meaning (Fowler, 1981, p. 149). This stage is characterized by the emergence of mutual interpersonal perspective taking: "I see you seeing me; I see me as you see me; I see you seeing me seeing you" (1981, p. 150). Each cognitive change that Fowler identifies affects one's ability to relate to self, others, and God. There is a risk of alienation for children at this age through becoming stuck in a rigid perfectionism or mired in a pervasive sense of one's own "badness" (see chap. 8).

The *synthetic-conventional faith* of stage 3 first emerges in adolescence and is found in many adults. Identifying a "personal myth" can provide a coherent means of navigating the complex world that extends beyond home, friends, and school or work. Persons at this stage are largely dependent on the views of significant others; beliefs are typically inhabited rather than being subject to critical reflection. Unless an ability to step outside the prevailing worldview develops, "autonomy of judgment and action can be compromised; or interpersonal betrayals can give rise... to nihilistic despair" (1981, p. 173). The suicidal urges experienced by many adolescents can frequently be linked to a crisis of faith at this stage (see chaps. 9 and 10).

Fowler's stage 4, *individuative-reflective faith,* may or may not emerge in young adulthood and is often first encountered by persons in their thirties and forties. A person in this stage begins "to take seriously the burden of responsibility for his or her own commitments, lifestyle, beliefs and attitudes" (1981, p. 182). The dichotomies that must be faced include individuality versus group loyalty, individual subjectivity versus objectivity and critical reflection, self-fulfillment versus relational demands. While persons at this stage are able to differentiate from others with a clear sense of their own identity and worldview, they also have a tendency to place too much confidence in their own rationality and capacity for critical thought. An in-breaking sense of mystery may move individuals out of this stage and into the next.

Conjunctive faith, which Fowler identifies as stage 5, typically does not appear until midlife. Persons in this stage develop what Ricoeur called a second naïveté, "in which symbolic power is reunited with conceptual meanings" (Ricoeur, 1967, p. 351; Fowler 1981, p. 197). They return to the religious practices of their childhood that were left behind during the "de-mythologizing" stage of individuative-reflective faith because they are now more open to the paradox and mystery that religious symbols and rituals seek to mediate.

The conjunctive faith stage requires persons to become receptive to the "voices of one's 'deeper self'," including "a critical recognition of one's social unconscious," composed of the ideals and prejudices that we absorb from our own families and culture (1981, p. 198). One becomes receptive both to paradox and to the "otherness" of those whose views may threaten our own. Persons in this stage may become committed to justice as a way of honoring the truths of others, but they can also become mired in cynical complacency because they recognize the relative nature of all worldviews. A conjunctive faith person might agree with Trudy, Lily Tomlin's bag lady, who says, "I refuse to be intimidated by reality anymore. After all, what is reality anyway? Nothin' but a collective hunch" (Wagner, 1986, p. 18). Yet the ability to transcend the limitations of one's own tribal loyalties, at least conceptually, lures persons in this stage toward the radical commitments that appear in stage 6.

The last stage that Fowler identifies, *universalizing faith,* is one that appears to be quite rare, based on the hundreds of interviews that he and his fellow researchers have conducted. Fowler writes that persons in stage 6 "have become incarnators and actualizers of the spirit of an inclusive and fulfilled human community. They are 'contagious' in the sense that they create zones of liberation from the social, political, economic and ideological shackles that we place and endure on human futurity" (1981, p. 201). For this reason they are seen as subversive of the very social and religious structures to which persons in stage 5 still cling out of a concern for their own identity and personal security. Stage 6 describes persons whose saintliness is generally most appreciated after their death: Fowler points to Gandhi, Martin Luther King Jr., Mother Teresa of Calcutta, Dag Hammarskjöld, Dietrich Bonhoeffer, Abraham Heschel, and Thomas Merton as representatives of this group (1981, p. 201). Persons in stage 6 are citizens of the realm of God, unencumbered by lesser allegiances and unfettered by concern for their own well-being. Fowler asks, "What is it about these persons that both condemns our obsessions with our own security and awakens our taste and sense for the promise of human futurity?...These persons embody costly openness to the power of the future.... [They are ready to] spend and be spent in making the Kingdom actual" (1981, p. 211).

Regarding Fowler's contributions to our understanding of faith development, Sharon Daloz Parks notes the following questions that have been raised about Fowler's work: (1) Is his definition of faith so broad that it fails to consider important distinctions between faith, religion, and belief? (2) Is it theologically adequate in light of particular religious traditions? (3) Does it adequately account for the role of affect, the unconscious, and imagination? (4) Does it make sense to identify the highest stage of faith development as one that can be attained only by martyred leaders, messiahs, and saints? (5) Is the very term *development* too heavily laden with the cultural baggage of North America to be useful in other cultural contexts (1991)?

Despite the above critiques, it is clear that Fowler's work gives us a way to think of faith that potentially transcends the narrow confines of particular religions traditions and can therefore contribute in useful ways to ecumenical, international, and intercultural dialogue. In addition to Fowler's highly readable *Stages of Faith,* those interested in learning more about his work may wish to consult the following resources: *Faith Development and Fowler* (Dykstra & Parks, 1986); *Faith Development and Pastoral Care* (Fowler, 1987); *Faithful Change: The Personal and Public Challenges of Postmodern Life* (Fowler, 1996); *Stages of Faith and Religious Development: Implications for Church, Education, and Society* (Fowler, Nipkow, & Schweitzer,

1991); "The North American Critique of James Fowler's Theory of Faith Development," in *Stages of Faith and Religious Development* (Parks, 1991). For specific applications of Fowler's work, see *Developing a Public Faith: New Directions in Practical Theology* (Osmer & Schweitzer, 2002).

Kegan's Constructive-Developmental Theory

A licensed clinical psychologist and practicing psychotherapist, Robert Kegan focuses on adult development and learning; he is also known as a consultant on professional development. Kegan has served as chair of the Harvard Graduate School of Education (HGSE) Institute for Management and Leadership in Education, as co-director of a joint program between HGSE and Harvard Medical School using principles of adult learning to inform medical education, and as co-director of a project funded by the Gates Foundation to train leaders as coaches for change in schools. He counts Hasidism as an important religious influence.

In *The Evolving Self* (1982), Robert Kegan presents a nonhierarchical understanding of developmental spirals that is relatively free of gender bias as it identifies both men's and women's need to negotiate developmental truces between the poles of inclusion or dependence and independence. Kegan's stages are as follows (the ages given identify the usual predominance of the stage):

Stage 0: Incorporative (in utero and at birth, balanced between inclusion and independence)
Stage 1: Impulsive (ages 0–2) More inclusive (dependent) than independent
Stage 2: Imperial (ages 2–5) More focused on independence than inclusion
Stage 3: Interpersonal (ages 5–7) More inclusive than independent
Stage 4: Institutional (ages 7–11) More independent than inclusive
Stage 5: Interindividual (ages 12–adulthood) Tending toward inclusion– but the spiraling oscillation between the independence-inclusion poles can continue to oscillate based on life events (Kegan, 1982)

In a subsequent book, *In Over Our Heads: The Mental Demands of Modern Life* (1994), Kegan considers the impact of cultural demands and the development of cognitive capabilities from adolescence through adulthood. With this contribution Kegan joins Jung, Vaillant (1993), Levinson (1978), and Colarusso (1992) as a theorist of adult development. With Lisa Lahey he has written *How the Way We Talk Can Change the Way We Work: Seven Languages for Transformation* (Kegan & Lahey, 2000). Robert Berchmans has compared the thought of theologian Bernard Lonergan with Kegan's evolving self to suggest a framework for Christian anthropology (2001).

In sum, a major benefit of the theories derived from Piaget, especially those of Kohlberg and Fowler, is that the clarity and specificity of each stage allows these theories to be empirically verified. While Piaget's stages are accurate for children in Western cultures, his stages do not translate cross-culturally as well as Piaget believed (Ashton, 1975). We have seen that structural developmental theories sometimes appear to be gender-biased as well (Gilligan, 1982). Because of the emphasis on reason, the role of affect in cognition, or the impact of emotion on what we learn and know, is discounted, and despite Piaget's psychoanalytic background, his theories of cognition are not designed to take the influence of the unconscious into account. Kohlberg's stages have been criticized for implying a hierarchical relationship between stages. Nevertheless, these theories address the important epistemological question of how we know what we know about our ability to reason, engage moral dilemmas, and reflect on our faith. As a template for considering these questions, they are invaluable. This approach to faith trusts that human understanding unfolds in accordance with established principles. The faith of structural developmental theories lies in reason, reflection, and the apprehension of creation through the senses.

Family Systems Theory

Family systems theories offer an approach to human development that emphasizes the influence of families and society on individuals, as presented in chapters 4 and 11 of this book. In this view, the life cycle begins when a couple comes together to form a new family. Each family member is influenced not only by the presence of others in their immediate family but also by intergenerational patterns that are transmitted, largely unconsciously, as family norms. The goal of development is to differentiate sufficiently to be true to one's sense of identity and vocation while maintaining a connection with other family members. Family therapists believe that the family "cut-offs" that occur when family members avoid each other have an adverse affect on the emotional life of individuals and decrease the stability of the family as a whole (McGoldrick, 1995).

Psychoanalytic models of development usually focus on individuals. Family therapists have found that issues related to marital discord, divorce, remarriage, "problem" children, adolescent rebellion, intergenerational conflicts, and other difficulties that may initially be presented as individual problems are frequently best addressed by counseling with both members of a couple or all members of a family in the room. Marriage and family therapy began to gain adherents in the 1950s, but it draws from a variety of earlier sources. Key influences include systems theories from the science of cybernetics, or the study of complex, interactive systems; psychoanalytic theories emphasizing ego psychology and object relations; and group theories that study the influence of group norms on individual behavior.

Some histories of family therapy present it as a novel approach that first flowered in the 1950s. Christian Beels goes further back, tracing the influences that culminated in the development of systems thinking to sources as diverse as social work, social psychiatry, the pragmatism of William

James and John Dewey, and the communications theories of Edward Sapir. Beels also includes the eighteenth-century proponent of hypnotism, Anton Messmer, whose work laid the foundation for the later hypnotherapy techniques of Milton Erikson, which in turn influenced the structural and strategic work of Jay Haley (see Jay Haley below; Beels, 2001; Newmark & Beels, 1994). The following brief history of family therapy is confined to more recent influences.

Norbert Wiener (1894–1964), an American mathematician, used the word *cybernetics* (from the Greek, meaning "steersman") to describe the control mechanisms observable in communications systems, especially *feedback mechanisms*. Systems tend to move from *disequilibrium to homeostasis*. Feedback loops help to restore balance and tend to mitigate against change. *Gregory Bateson* (1904–1980) attempted to apply principles of cybernetics to therapeutic work with schizophrenics and alcoholics, and their families. Therapists no longer believe that dysfunctional families are the primary cause of schizophrenia or alcoholism, since both appear to have a biological component in many instances. But the research Bateson conducted with Jay Haley, John Weakland, Don Jackson, and others has been helpful in understanding the communication difficulties that "normal" families and groups encounter. A classic example is the "double-bind" or lose-lose scenario, where family members find themselves tied in knots by conflicting injunctions such as "always be nice" and "always tell the truth" (Bateson & Bateson, 1987).

The work of *John Bowlby* (1907–1990) represents a link between the Child Guidance movement and earlier psychiatric standards of individual treatment. Bowlby is best known for his work on attachment, separation, and loss (1999), focusing on the importance of the infant's early attachment to the mother. Psychoanalytically trained, his experience as a child and family psychiatrist lead him to be interested in the prevention of mental illness through attention to the pre-Oedipal *attachment* needs of infants and older babies. He recognized in human infants the same stages of *protest, despair,* and *detachment* during prolonged separation from their mothers that can be observed in primates. *Ethology,* the study of animal behavior, influenced Bowlby's understanding of human development. For all higher primates, the first year of life is important in developing healthy patterns of attachment that encourage appropriate trust, dependence, and cooperation that begin in infancy and continue throughout life.

Nathan Ackerman (1908–1971), a psychiatrist and educator, founded the Family Mental Health Clinic in 1954 in New York City, which was renamed the Ackerman Institute after his death. After he was born in Russia, his parents immigrated to the United States in 1912 and were naturalized in 1920. In his early clinical work Ackerman followed the then prevailing model of care by having a psychiatrist treat the "identified patient" problem child while a social worker saw the mother. But Ackerman soon became a strong advocate of the approach that would become a hallmark of family systems thinking–including the entire family in treatment to address the difficulties of one family member. In a family system's view, the problems of one family member are a symptom affecting the family as a whole, which cannot be adequately resolved without reference to the entire family context. In 1960 Ackerman founded the Institute for Family Studies and Treatment, a nonprofit organization dedicated to the proposition that if the family is healthy, individuals will be healthy and will in turn promote the health of society as a whole (cf. *The Psychodynamics of Family Life: Diagnosis and Treatment of Family Relationships* [Ackerman, 1958]).

Mary Ainsworth (1913–1999) is not often grouped with family therapists, but her work on attachment, in concert with John Bowlby, has had a significant impact on our understanding of the developmental needs of children in the first year of life. Born in Ohio, she earned her Ph.D. in developmental psychology from the University of Toronto in 1939. Ainsworth worked with Bowlby at the Tavistock Clinic in London before moving with her husband to Uganda, where she continued the work she and Bowlby had begun in studying the dynamics of mother-infant attachment. Her research on this subject was published after she later joined the faculty of Johns Hopkins University. She is best known for developing the "Strange Situation," a procedure used to evaluate the nature of a child's attachment to her mother through a series of separations and reunions. Ainsworth characterized toddlers as (1) *anxious/avoidant* (the child may show no distress when the mother leaves the room and will usually avoid her when she returns), (2) *securely attached* (the child shows distress when the mother leaves and seeks to be comforted by her when she returns), and (3) *anxious/resistant* (the child becomes distressed when the mother leaves but rejects comfort from her when she returns) (cf. *Patterns of Attachment: A Psychological Study of the Strange Situation* [Ainsworth, Blehar, Waters, & Wall, 1978]). Subsequent family systems applications of this research would not blame the mother for the child's response but would instead consider the circumstances of family context and history that may have contributed to difficulties in early bonding between mother and child. Often, reparative work can be done in supporting mothers that will in turn allow them to be more emotionally available to their children.

Murray Bowen (1913–1990) grew up as the oldest child in a large, close-knit, alcoholic family. Bowen, in his comprehensive theory of human behavior, emphasized theory and insight in contrast to some of his more behaviorally focused colleagues, who emphasized action and technique (Bowen, 1978; Nichols & Schwartz, 2001). He trained in psychiatry and in 1954 became the first director of the Family Division at the National Institutes of Mental Health (NIMH). He is known for his emphasis on *differentiation* of self in relation to one's family and group, which is best accomplished by avoiding *triangulation,* or the tendency for dysfunctional (ineffective) communication to proceed through a third party rather than face-to-face (1978). The work of *Edwin Friedman* (1932–1996), a rabbi who applied Bowenian systems theory to congregational life in *Generation to Generation,* is useful in pointing out the pitfalls religious leaders can avoid by practicing differentiation and eschewing triangulation (1985).

Virginia Satir (1916–1988) has been described as "The Mother of Family Systems Therapy." She began treating families in 1951 and established a training program for psychiatric residents in 1955. She emphasized the roles family members can assume, such as "rescuer" or "placator," that serve to limit family interactions (Nichols and Schwartz, 2001). A master therapist, she highlighted nurturance and compassion as the most healing aspects of therapy (Satir, 1972). In developmental terms, one might say that individual lives unfold at their best when the family environment can be influenced to move in the direction of greater affection and mutuality. Satir also pioneered a focus on personal growth and health that has come to characterize the emphasis of marriage and family therapy as a discipline. She is the author of *Conjoint Family Therapy* (1964) and *Peoplemaking* (1972).

Ivan Boszmormenyi-Nagy (b. 1920), a student of Virginia Satir's, is known for his emphasis on relational ethics, loyalty, and trust as expressed between the family and society and within the family (Nichols & Schwartz, 2001). His contextual and ethical approach to family therapy reflects his psychoanalytic training. In Nagy's view, the therapist can help troubled families reestablish a climate of trust and loyalty by encouraging them to face conflicted emotions they have avoided, thereby reestablishing a sense of fairness between all members of the family (cf. *Invisible Loyalties: Reciprocity in Intergenerational Family Therapy* [Boszormenyi-Nagy & Spark, 1973]). Nagy founded the Eastern Pennsylvania Psychiatric Institute (EPPI) and has taught at Hahnemann University.

Carl Whitaker, who died in 1995, was known for his spontaneity, disarming wit, and creativity. Trained as a psychiatrist, he treated the family as a unit, liked to work with large groups, and encouraged all family members to attend counseling sessions. His intuitive method, based on his personality and clinical wisdom, was designed to unsettle the family through therapist interventions with the goal of promoting flexibility and honesty among family members. His approach was irreverent, confrontational, and iconoclastic, but despite his provocative methods, families trusted him because they sensed his caring concern. Whitaker was an early proponent of working with a co-therapist in family sessions to promote therapist self-awareness and objectivity. During his years as chairman of the department of psychiatry at Emory University, he treated schizophrenics and their families. Whitaker's spontaneity is best appreciated through audiotapes and videotapes of his work. *Dancing With the Family: A Symbolic-Experiential Approach,* co-authored with William Bumberry (1988), offers an overview of Whitaker's inspired approach to family therapy.

Salvador Minuchin (b. 1921) is known for his structural theory of families in which relationship patterns are seen on a continuum from *enmeshed,* or chaotic and closely interconnected, to *disengaged,* in which family members are seemingly disconnected and unrelated (1974). His attention to *subsystems* in families, such as the parental subsystem and the sibling subsystem, helps therapists understand the importance of intergenerational *boundaries.* Minuchin's cross-cultural experience as a person born and raised in Argentina who spent most of his working life in the United States helped him to recognize structures that apply to all families regardless of cultural background. Rather than judging families of various cultures for having family structures different from the North American norm, Minuchin focused on the family's strategies to cope with their environment and encouraged them to adopt family patterns that worked best for them. Minuchin became the director of a leading therapy training center, the Philadelphia Child Guidance Clinic, in 1965 and used his position to develop a training program for paraprofessional family therapists who could effectively meet the needs of urban African Americans and Latinos in the inner city (cf. *Families and Family Therapy* [Minuchin, 1974]).

Jay Haley was born in Wyoming in 1923. His development of *structural and strategic* approaches to family therapy includes an emphasis on changing clients' actions rather than focusing on insight in the context of brief therapy. Having studied with Gregory Bateson, Milton Erikson, and Salvador Minuchin during his training as a psychologist, he co-founded the Family Therapy Institute in Chevy Chase, Maryland. Based on his work with hypnotherapist Milton Erikson, Haley developed a model of brief therapy that considers the possible function or "secondary gain" of the family's dysfunctional behaviors and instructs them to act in ways that force them to behave differently. Haley believed that taking responsibility for one's actions was the most important outcome of therapy (cf. *Problem Solving Therapy* [Haley, 1991] and *The Art of Strategic Therapy* [Haley & Richeport-Haley, 2003]).

Betty Carter trained at the Ackerman Institute in New York while earning her M.S.W. degree at Hunter College. She has popularized the concept of the family life cycle and has developed it as a tool for family assessment (cf. *The Expanded Family Life Cycle: Individual, Family and Social Perspectives* [Carter & McGoldrick, 1999]). An outspoken feminist, she served as co-director of the Women's project in family therapy with Peggy Papp and others. Her clinical specializations include work with divorced and remarried families. Carter encourages therapists to consider the historical origins of family difficulties and the intergenerational dimensions of the family life cycle that may impinge on nuclear families in the present. She founded the Family Institute of Westchester in 1997, where attention is given to the family costs of gender and ethnic inequalities.

Michael White, trained as a social worker, resides in Adelaide, South Australia. He became interested in the ways that stories people tell about their lives reflect their construction of meaning. As the founder of *narrative family therapy,* he encourages therapists to consider the broad historical, cultural, and political context of the family. Narrative therapists consider the ways in which a family's beliefs about itself shape the self-concept of family members. White's method is relentlessly optimistic. By consistently challenging negative self-beliefs, he encourages families to develop more positive ways of telling their story and seeing themselves in the world. In this volume, Ed Wimberly illustrates this approach through his combination of narrative therapy and biblical narratives as these serve to empower African American families (chap. 4). To learn more about Michael White's approach, read *Narrative Means to Therapeutic Ends,* coauthored with David Epston (1990).

From this brief overview of founding family systems theorists, it is clear that the origins of this theoretical school are remarkably diverse, ranging from the so-called "hard" sciences, such as physics and cybernetics, to studies of animal behavior, to social work, social psychology, and psychoanalytic theories of ego psychology and object relations. The evolution of family systems theory includes the practical clinical wisdom of psychiatrists, psychologists, pastoral counselors, social workers, and other therapists who give attention to context, the influence of culture, society, and relationships while emphasizing strengths and coping skills as opposed to pathology and emotional deficits. Today, many members of the American Association for Marriage and Family Therapy serve as pastors, are ordained ministers, or are committed lay leaders in their faith communities. Giving attention to context and emphasizing sources of hope is an approach fully compatible with pastoral care and counseling.

Figures 1 and 2 serve to illustrate basic principles of family systems theory. **Figure 1** depicts the flow of stress through the family. The horizontal line stands for the progress of time. The individual is seen at the center of concentric circles including immediate family (usually those living in the same household); extended family; the larger community–including one's neighborhood, workplace, friends, faith community, and community organizations–and society as a whole, which comprises all sociocultural, political, and economic aspects of a person's milieu. Horizontal sources of stress tied to particular events that impinge on the individual include life-cycle transitions, migration, untimely death, chronic illness, accidents, and unemployment. Sources of stress that affect communities and societies include war, economic depression, political climate, and natural disasters. Chronic sources of stress identified as vertical stressors include racism, sexism, classism, ageism, homophobia, consumerism, poverty, loss of community, too much work, too little leisure, inflexibility in the workplace, and lack of time for friends. Family sources of stress include dysfunctional emotional patterns: detrimental family myths ("boys are better than girls," for example), triangulation between family members, secrets, legacies, and

Figure 1: Flow of Stress through the Family

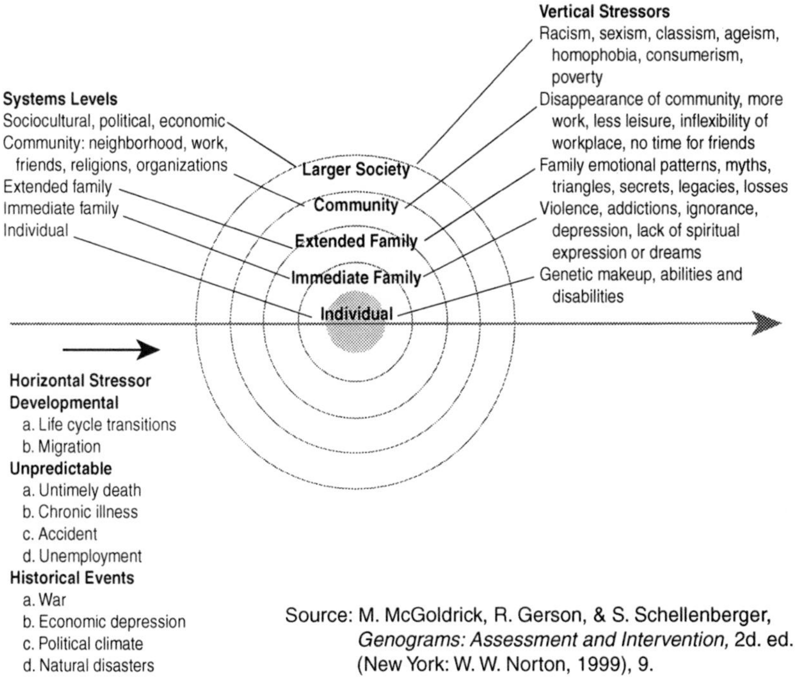

Vertical Stressors
Racism, sexism, classism, ageism, homophobia, consumerism, poverty
Disappearance of community, more work, less leisure, inflexibility of workplace, no time for friends
Family emotional patterns, myths, triangles, secrets, legacies, losses
Violence, addictions, ignorance, depression, lack of spiritual expression or dreams
Genetic makeup, abilities and disabilities

Systems Levels
Sociocultural, political, economic
Community: neighborhood, work, friends, religions, organizations
Extended family
Immediate family
Individual

Larger Society
Community
Extended Family
Immediate Family
Individual

Horizontal Stressor
Developmental
　a. Life cycle transitions
　b. Migration
Unpredictable
　a. Untimely death
　b. Chronic illness
　c. Accident
　d. Unemployment
Historical Events
　a. War
　b. Economic depression
　c. Political climate
　d. Natural disasters

Source: M. McGoldrick, R. Gerson, & S. Schellenberger, *Genograms: Assessment and Intervention,* 2d. ed. (New York: W. W. Norton, 1999), 9.

losses. Violence, addictions, ignorance, depression, and lack of spiritual expression or dreams all take their toll on the individual members of the family and the family as a whole.

No other theoretical school we have considered is as consistent in giving attention to the contextual dimensions of individual lives and family life. Before labeling an individual or family as difficult, crazy, anti-social, dysfunctional, or the like, family systems therapists argue that it is important to consider the sources of stress impinging on them from these larger contexts. This way of thinking is gradually gaining credence in North America as the consequences of familial stress, such as "battered wife syndrome," are now recognized as a legal defense, as in the case of abused women who kill their husbands (Hansen & Harway, 1993). The goal of family therapy is to help families move away from levels of chaos that can lead to harm or death and toward patterns of communication that are life enhancing.

Figure 2 shows the *genogram* as an analytical tool for plotting the movement of family constellations, and the individuals within them, over time. In this genogram, Sigmund Freud (1856–1939) is the focus. All male family members, including Sigmund, are represented by squares, with

Figure 2: Freud's Genogram

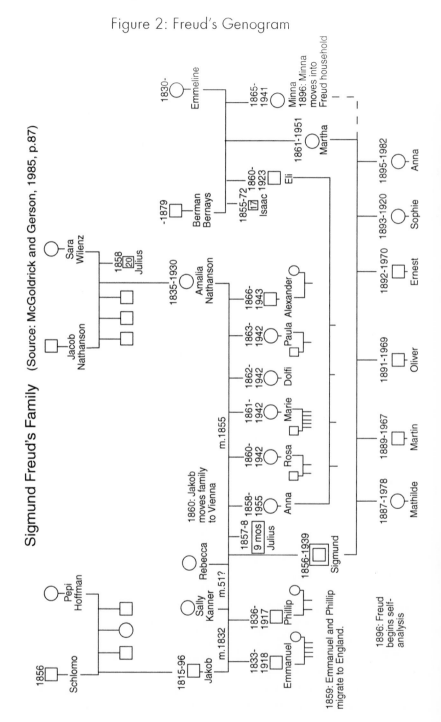

Sigmund Freud's Family   (Source: McGoldrick and Gerson, 1985, p.87)

female members represented by circles. Marriage bonds are depicted as horizontal links between men and women, with the lines descending from a given union representing their offspring. What is fascinating about genograms, as one learns to interpret them, is that intergenerational family patterns can be seen to have a lifelong influence on the lives of individuals. For example, Freud's emphasis on the Oedipal complex was noted earlier. One can see from examining his own family constellation why the relationship between mother, father, and child would be a source of confusion and fascination in his experience. Freud's father, Jakob, was twenty years older than his mother, Amelia, while his half-brothers from Jakob's first marriage, Emmanuel and Philip, were virtually the same age as Amelia. With Jakob often away on extended business trips and Phillip living across the street until Freud was three years old, it must have been hard for a small child to tell the father from the brothers. Add to this the fact that the next child, Julius, was born within a year of Sigmund and died at the age of nine months, and you have a family context that might well produce anxious attachment, due to maternal stress and grief, in Amelia's first-born child.

Freud was ambivalent toward both his parents and only partially resolved the detrimental effects of that ambivalence through his own self-analysis (Freud, 1900/1953; 1912x/1953; Margolis, 1996; Krüll, 1979). There has been speculation about a possible affair between Freud's mother and his half-brother Phillip (Kerr, 1993). All that is known for certain is that Freud's nanny was fired, ostensibly for stealing; the two older brothers migrated to England; and the rest of the family moved from their small town to Vienna, Austria, all in Freud's third year of life. If an incestuous affair did occur, it would help to explain Freud's later close emotional and possibly sexual ties to his sister-in-law Minna, who moved into the Freud household in 1896. Such an affair would represent a transgenerational pattern of familial incest. At the level of societal context, the fact that the Freud family and the Bernays family are doubly intermarried attests to the relative social isolation of the Jewish community within the dominant Catholic context of late nineteenth-century Vienna (McGoldrick, Gerson, & Shellenberger, 1999).

Much more could be gleaned from this genogram; this brief introduction is intended to illustrate the genogram's use as a tool for self-awareness in the context of one's family constellation. Genograms can be used by pastors seeking to understand the familial relationships in congregations. Genograms are also useful for therapists who wish to work with individuals, couples, and families, with attention to the impact of relational dynamics and the intergenerational transmission of family patterns.

Faith, from a family systems standpoint, can be seen to reside in the power of healthy families and communities to support their individual members through trust and honesty, expressed by means of loving and direct communication. These theories emphasize our radical dependence on the families that give us life and the communities that sustain us. The Christian doctrine of the Trinity can be understood as symbolizing the importance of relationships in our understanding of God.

It is impossible to adequately represent the full range and diversity of family systems theory in this brief introduction. Suggestions for further readings, in addition to the sources cited above, include *Transformations of Gender and Race: Family and Developmental Perspectives* (Almeida, 1998); *Basic Family Therapy* (Barker, 1992); *Family Therapy in Clinical Practice* (Bowen, 1978); *Black Families in Therapy: A Multisystems Approach* (Boyd-Franklin, 1989); *Generation to Generation: Family Process in Church and Synagogue* (E. H. Friedman, 1985); *Genograms: Assessment and Intervention* (McGoldrick, Gerson, & Shellenberger, 1999); *Family Therapy: Concepts and Methods* (Nichols & Schwartz, 2001); *Families Across Time: A Life Course Perspective* (Price, McHenry, & Murphy, 2000); and *Peoplemaking* (Satir, 1972).

Conclusion

Underlying all these theories, like the red thread of meaning in a psychoanalytic hour, runs the belief that a life without faith is like a body without breath. Without the ability to place trust in something greater than our individual experience, the sequence of birth, life, and death becomes, in Shakespeare's words "a tale told by an idiot, full of sound and fury, signifying nothing" (*Macbeth,* Act 5, scene 5). With faith, we live not only for ourselves, but to celebrate the original Life through whom we come to be. Whether a theory is focused on the inner lives of persons or on the broader context of society, each one of us and all of us together, need reasons to live and ways to find meaning in existence. When meanings elude us, when life appears grim and pointless, these theories of development may offer a way to uncover the psychological origins of our distress. Despite our suffering, God is never far from us, as we discover by considering a broad overview of the life cycle in chapter 2, seen through the soul's-eye view.

Notes

[1]Stern's work, as presented in chapter 5, is informed by both psychoanalytic and cognitive approaches to human development (Stern, 1985).

[2]Jung's use of the term *individuation,* which typically refers to adult development, should not to be confused with separation-individuation as understood by Margaret Mahler (1968) and other theorists of child development.

[3]Clearly this is most true for heterosexuals, less true for gay, lesbian, bisexual, and transgendered persons for whom the traditional categories of what it means to be male and female are often experienced as being more flexible.

[4]For a discussion of essentialism and constructivism as it relates to feminism and theology, see *Feminist Theory and Christian Theology: Cartographies of Grace* (S. Jones, 2000) and *Feminist and Womanist Pastoral Theology* (Miller-McLemore & Gill-Austern, 1999).

CHAPTER 2

Finding Faith

Life-Cycle Stages in Body, Mind, and Soul

Felicity B. Kelcourse

We are all more human than not.

HARRY STACK SULLIVAN

...[T]hose who lose their life for my sake will find it.

MATTHEW 10:39B

What are the faith issues that face individuals, families, and communities on the journey from birth to death? In Chapter 1 we considered these questions from the standpoint of developmental theory. Here, we take a closer look at faith–our ability to trust, receive, and make meaning–in relation to successive life tasks.

Why a Life-Cycle Approach?

Viewing human experience within the context of the life-cycle arc from birth to death offers a useful framework for individuals, parents and families, teachers, pastors, faith communities, pastoral counselors, and other healers. Individuals can better understand life's challenges when they are seen as the developmental tasks that many, if not all, persons must learn to negotiate.

Faith communities can be a powerful influence for good when they surround *kairotic,* transformative, life events such as birth, coming of age, marriage, illness, and death with traditions and rituals that speak to our human need for meaning. These corporate observances of faith invite us to trust in something or Someone greater than ourselves. Pastoral counselors are more effective when they can accurately correlate adult difficulties, including loss of faith or problematic God images, to earlier instances of developmental arrest (Rizzuto, 1979; Armistead, 1995).

Despite our obvious differences as individuals, we were each conceived from two sets of DNA, born from a woman's body, protected from death in infancy, and provided sufficient nurture to reach maturity. We each face the challenge of adapting the personalities with which we were born to the expectations of our family and culture. We each must come to terms with what it means to be embodied as a man or a woman, to grow up, mature, grow old (perchance), and die. Although differences of gender, sexual orientation, social class, and culture are far from insignificant, as recent pastoral care and counseling literature attests (Stevenson Moessner, 2000; Miller-McLemore & Gill-Austern, 1999; Glaz & Stevenson Moessner, 1991; Couture, 1991; Couture & Hunter, 1995; Marshall, 1997), this chapter seeks to lift up the common themes of faith that all human beings must face to some degree in the course of life.

Faith was previously defined as the fruit of our search for meaning, the ground that we find to stand on as we face the ordinary challenges and unexpected storms of life (Tillich, 1957; Frankl, 1969/1988; Fowler, 1981; Ashbrook, 1996). Short of severe physical and emotional abuse, no one can ultimately deprive us of our ability to make meaning, but we are fortunate if our community is able to confirm and support the meanings we find.[1] We have seen that knowledge of developmental psychology is useful as individuals and communities discover the importance of "good-enough" developmental parameters in support of optimal meaning-making (Winnicott, 1965). When basic developmental needs are not met, community life suffers, individuals miss their vocation, and the ability to find faith is compromised. This chapter considers the dialogue between human development and faith in lived experience.

There is more to human existence than meets the eye. How do we account for grace that seems to find us out of the blue or explain the religious experiences of those who are ill, suffering, or nearing death? What explains a sudden conversion, a profound intuition, or a change of heart?

Psychological theorists use words like *Self* (Jung) or *true self* (Winnicott) for that part of us that seems to know more than the ego or conscious sense of "I." Christian traditions speak of the *imago dei,* or that of God in us, that may be heard more clearly when we attend to it through prayer and spiritual disciplines. I call this inner Self the *soul* and distinguish it from the psyche as one might make a distinction between body and mind: Soul is embodied spirit; psyche is embodied mind. All persons have spirit, soul, body, psyche, and mind existing as different lenses through which to view the unity that we are. We can understand the soul's perspective as a developmental line, a thread that, like the need for faith and meaning, runs through all the moments of our lives.

The Soul's-Eye View as a Developmental Line[2]

The soul lives at the divine center; it is the part of us that sees and knows God. There can be no integrity without the voice of the soul, no true sense of vocation without the soul's direction, no fruitful discernment without the soul's-eye view.

If the soul sees and knows God, what does it see? Christians say that God is good, that God is love. If these affirmations are fundamentally true, then the soul continually sees God's goodness and love for us. Just as the sun continues to shine on a cloudy day when the earth is dark, so the soul receives the Light of Christ, even when the ego or conscious self is shrouded in desolation. This helps to account for persons suffering from life-long depressions, preoccupations with suicide, or self-destructive behavior who, against all odds, find themselves at a therapist's door. The soul holds *hope,* and *receptivity* to the Light beyond the clouds and mediates *intuitions* of an unseen but dimly remembered time when we were as one with God.

If we could keep to the soul's-eye view, as some saints have done, we could float in trust, free from fear. But for most of us, the genetic and environmental inheritance of the psyche is a maze through which we must find our way to arrive at the soul's perception of God. Too often what blocks the way to God are the god representations we have derived from parental introjects (Rizzuto, 1979). So God the Father, Mother, Creator, Redeemer, Friend, Lover becomes god the drunk; god the unholy terror; god the absent, unavailable, or demeaning father; god the poisonous mother.

People of faith affirm curious things. Against all evidence to the contrary, we affirm that God is good, that the universe can be trusted. George Fox wrote: "I saw also that there was an infinite ocean of darkness and death, but an infinite ocean of light and love, which flowed over the ocean of darkness" (1694/1976).[3] Fox's statement is comparable to Julian of Norwich's affirmation that, "All shall be well, all manner of things shall be well" (1670/1978). Mystics in all ages have searched the inner world of the soul to bring us the soul's-eye view. The soul knows and rests in the goodness of God. Such a view is quite different from Jung's understanding of the collective unconscious, in which all symbols are bivalent, both good and evil. It also contrasts with religious understandings that pit God against the devil, and heaven against hell, or that emphasize original sin. Fox sees the conflict of light and dark, but his vision also points to a place of resolution that, while outside linear time, is real and present in the *kairos* of the Eternal Now (see chap. 3).

Here we have the basic tension between the sight of the psyche and the sight of the soul. The psyche knows torture as well as delight, fear as well as joy. The soul knows, as its core reality, only bliss. Yet in this life the two are inseparable and completely essential. In this life there can be no mind without body, no soul without psyche.[1] Soul is embodied spirit, the living *nephesh* that expresses our unique idiom and connects us to all of life.

What most of us experience in the first two to four years of life is a fall from grace in the psyche that is comparable to the expulsion of Eve and Adam from paradise (chap. 7). Paradise is the country of the soul at one with God. Sin is the state of separation from God in which the Light of Christ is hidden from view and the self feels alone, cast out, and bereft. One of Fox's more arresting images of sanctification is that we can move back through the sentinel angel's flaming sword into paradise (1694/1976) toward what Ricoeur calls a second naïveté (1967). This may also be understood as the place of freedom we may rediscover through psychotherapy when, as adults, we dare to face the childhood fears we were loathe to remember and consciously acknowledge (Grant, 2001).

I find that the students, church members, and psychotherapists I meet in classrooms and workshops are generally quite receptive to this understanding of the soul as a metaphor for the distinctive form of energy that comes into being when human life is created and leaves the body in death. Scholars, on the other hand, are often wary of this concept because it has historically been used in hierarchical and dualistic ways to privilege mind over body and, by extension, male over female and human over non-human life. By identifying the sight and voice of the soul, I do not intend any such dualism, much less an assumption of hierarchical privilege. There can be no mind without body, no male without female, no human life without the living envelope of creation that sustains our lives on earth. Our lives are in reality a seamless whole, with no way to truly separate self from other, much less our own internal biological and psychological "parts." But, for the purposes of discernment, it is useful at times to distinguish between different aspects of reality, not to separate them in any rigid or final way, but as a means of bringing different aspects of our experience into dialogue, making the unconscious conscious.

Figure 3 presents a schematic view of a person as a sphere afloat in the Sea of Being. The inner oval represents an individual fully surrounded by a cocoon of others, including family, community, and culture. The horizontal line represents a boundary (actually far more permeable than this solid line) between conscious and unconscious awareness. Above the line is the individual consciousness of "I" surrounded by the collective consciousness of others. Beyond the human sphere is the outer world or objective cosmos including all of life on earth and, beyond earth, our physical place in space and time. Below the horizontal line is the individual or personal unconscious based on embodied experiences "I" have that are

Figure 3: A Schematic View of Persons

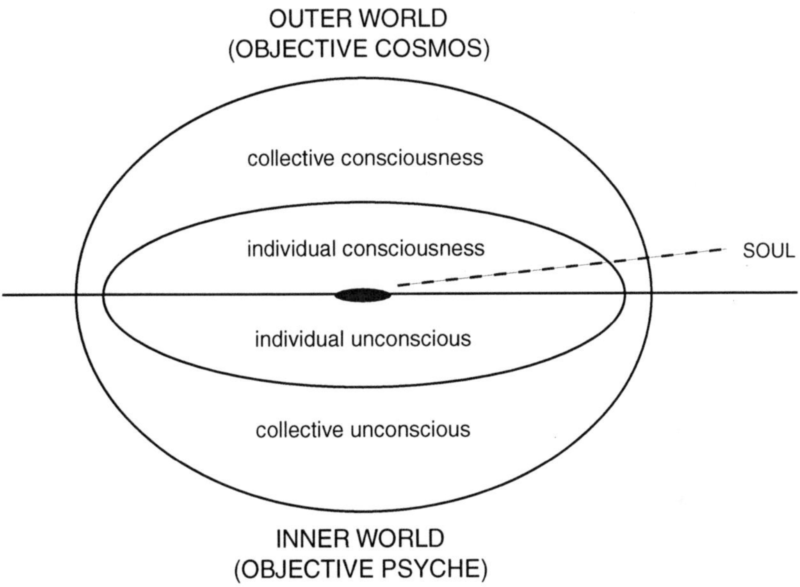

OUTER WORLD
(OBJECTIVE COSMOS)

collective consciousness

individual consciousness — — — SOUL

individual unconscious

collective unconscious

INNER WORLD
(OBJECTIVE PSYCHE)

not consciously known. The collective or cultural unconscious below stands for the "unthought known" of those around us, including the inheritance of family patterns and culture (Bollas, 1985). Beneath this is the inner world of the objective psyche that is manifest to us through archetypal patterns in individual experience and culture. The archetypes of the objective psyche are to conscious awareness as starlight is to our senses—we know the stars are there because we see their light, yet the reality of a star in outer space is beyond anything we can directly experience.

At the center of each person is the soul, accessible to us both consciously and unconsciously. The "eye" formed by the person and the *imago dei* constitutes the "soul's-eye view." In the following stages I suggest that the soul's perspective can be fully present even when it is not consciously known. Jung spoke of the journey of individuation as taking place along the axis between ego (or conscious "I") and Self, or, as depicted here, soul. From midlife through death, our task is to become more fully conscious of the soul's-eye view.

Developmental Stages of Psyche and Soul

In this chapter a brief overview of developmental stages begins with life before birth, then turns to the template of stages identified by Erik Erikson in *Childhood and Society* (1950/1963). I will consider the virtues Erikson identifies for each stage from the perspective of psyche and soul, as well as the vices identified by Donald Capps in *Deadly Sins and Saving Virtues* (1987). My focus will be on the dialogue between psyche, including what we experience and consciously know, and soul, or what is known in and through us of God. This chapter is intended to provide an overview of faith concerns across the life span with reference to the role of faith communities. It does not replace the more detailed and specific perspectives offered by the chapters in Part Two: Life-Cycle Stages of Development.

What follows is a description of the soul's embodied life from the time before conception until death. This view is combined with what we know about physiological, cognitive, intrapsychic, and interpersonal changes through experience and observation. Attention is also given to moral and faith development, and the impact of social location on every aspect of our experience.

Prior to conception, the soul exists as a drop of water in the Sea of Being. Although it has its own integrity, it is not separate from the enfolding love of God.[5] Like a worshiping community bound together by communion, each individual soul is surrounded by a community of others, joined to them as one. This understanding of the soul's life before life parallels Karl Rahner's view that we join the primary energy of the universe after death (Rahner, 1961). **Figures 4** and **5** depict the hypothetical flow of energy in worship that would be the nearest equivalent in adult experience to what I describe as the Sea of Being. Figure 4 represents the individual's experience when surrounded by others in worship, connected to them through the

Figures 4 and 5: Hypothetical Flow of Spiritual Energy in Worship

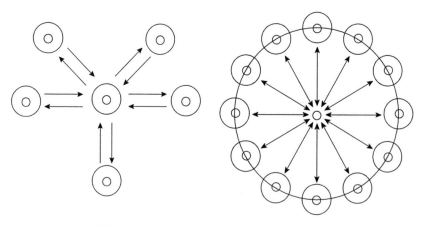

Individual
connects to center circle = soul or
"that of God" in themselves
& in others

Group connects
to the "Presence in the midst"

flowing energy, embodied spirit, of each soul. Figure 5 stands for the group's experience as all focus on what is most holy in worship, symbolized for many Christians by communion with bread and wine and recognized by "the unity of the Spirit in the bond of peace" (Eph. 4:3).

At conception, intrauterine life begins. The soul has moved from the Sea of Being to the dark waters of a mother's womb. As an embryo with a developing body, it swims, overhears the voices of its parents, and dreams. Perhaps the beginnings of distinction and dialogue are there ("this is mother's voice, that is father's voice"), but for the most part the unitive consciousness that bathes it in love continues. If the mother is addicted to drugs or alcohol or finds herself in frightening, dangerous circumstances, the soul may struggle even before birth to retain its vision of the love of God. Both the body and the soul of the developing child can be damaged by such experiences. Pregnant women need loving, supportive communities to surround them, just as the fetus needs the mother's healthy body to nurture it as it develops.

In utero, it was thought that a fetus had little or no capacity for awareness. Yet the fetus clearly responds to stimulation in ways that indicate comfort or discomfort (Richardson, 2000). Although the developing fetus is not initially neurologically equipped to have thoughts in the ways that adults recognize them, what he or she experiences in utero, including parental attitudes towards the developing child, can have implications for her or his responsiveness to parental caregivers after birth. For this reason, neonatologists encourage expectant parents to actively begin the process of bonding with their child before birth (Wirth, 2001; Newman & Newman, 2003).

At birth, the child is separated from the body of its mother and begins to have even more definite, potentially traumatic experiences of physical, emotional, and spiritual separation from its origins in the Sea of Being. If the mother has had a positive experience of pregnancy in an emotionally supportive environment, the dreaming child *in utero* may have few anticipatory fears about "outside" and "other" voices. I put these words in quotes because some developmental psychologists believe the newborn is "symbiotic," having no ability to clearly distinguish between self and other (Mahler, 1968). Others believe the child has a rudimentary sense of self from birth, if not before (Stern, 1985). In any event, the child at birth experiences a rupture from the protected precincts of the mother's body and discovers the terrors of physical helplessness for the first time. Freud recognized this birth trauma implicitly when he observed, in *The Future of an Illusion* (1927c/1953), that our emotional need for God stems from a deep-seated fear of our own fundamental helplessness, especially evident during times of suffering and loss. Freud thought that our need for God and religion, "the universal neurosis," stemmed from nothing more than our childhood longings for a loving mother and father to hold and protect us. I believe that Freud was accurate in his observations but wrong in his conclusions. Any "neurosis" that is "universal" must be normal. Our fears of helplessness are well founded, our need for God's loving protection very real.

We do long, at the deepest levels of our being, for the "everlasting arms" that can keep us from falling. Some of us were blessed with loving parents whose tender physical and emotional attention to us as infants came as close as any love in this world can to the enfolding, inexhaustible love of God. Others were not so fortunate. But even those of us who suffered various degrees of physical and emotional deprivation from birth somehow knew that we were missing something and found ways to actively look for it.

If the sight of the psyche, our physical and mental experience of life, were all we had to go on, how would we know on some deep level that loving care is our human birthright, that we were wronged when that birthright was damaged or withheld? We know because our souls tell us that there is more to life than neglect and abuse. If we hold fast to this knowing, we can hold on to life and hope for healing. If we lose hope, we slide toward the lure of a quick death by suicide or a slow death through addiction and other self-destructive behaviors. How we are "held" by our parents, extended family, and community–physically, emotionally, and spiritually–can either help us or hinder us in retaining our memories of the soul's-eye view.

Stage 1 — The Oral Phase: 0 to 12 Months

Physiological and cognitive changes: In the early oral phase of development, the infant still has limited mobility and physical coordination as its nervous system continues to develop after birth. Freud designated infancy as the oral phase in part because of the infant's early preference for exploring the world by putting things in its mouth. At this stage parents bond with their infants through eye contact and cuddling, instinctively engaging their baby with high-pitched sounds and repetitive games that give the baby pleasure and form the rudiments of interpersonal relatedness in later life (Stern, 1985). If all goes well, the familial environment formed by those around us loves us into being (see chap. 5).

It is humbling to realize how utterly dependent each of us has been on the loving care of others. Infants who are neglected exhibit a failure to thrive and may never live up to their intellectual potential as a result of inadequate care in these critical early months. In studies of children orphaned during war, developmental psychologist Rene Spitz (1945) observed that children who received adequate physical care but were deprived of physical and emotional affection lost their will to live, and died, in essence, from a broken heart.

Intrapsychic and interpersonal changes: During the first twelve months through age three, the child is gradually developing a sense of *object constancy*.

Babies are visibly turned inward during the first three months of life, which Margaret Mahler identified in her theory of *separation-individuation* as the *autistic phase.* The transition out of this phase is marked by what Spitz named as the *smile response,* the first of three early *psychic organizers;* this response demonstrates that children know and recognize familiar others (1965). From three to twelve months, in the *symbiotic phase,* babies are clearly more curious about their immediate environment, but they still require the constant presence of familiar caregivers. According to Piaget, this is so because the schema of object permanence is just beginning to form between seven and eight months. At this age infants love to play the "peek-a-boo" game. Their endless fascination with the game attests to the fact that an unseen object may literally be understood as ceasing to exist.

Spitz's second psychic organizer is *stranger anxiety,* which usually appears at eight months. The child is now aware of who is familiar and who is not (Colarusso, 1992). When a loved one is away for more than a brief period, the baby will begin to mourn; the absence of the caregiver is also experienced as a loss of self. The first year of life is critical for secure emotional attachment. It is only in the toddler stage (twelve months to three years) that the child begins to exhibit a clear sense of distinction between self and caregivers. Erik Erikson (see chart on p. 68) described the basic developmental challenge of the oral stage in terms of *trust versus mistrust* (1950/1963). Clearly, if we are "disappointed in love" at this early stage in our development, it will be difficult to open our hearts in love to others, trusting that the light of God's love is always available to help us grow. The virtue Erikson identifies for this stage of life is *hope.* If we are lovingly welcomed into the world and safely held in infancy, we have a reservoir of hope to sustain us through the inevitable storms of life. From the soul's-eye view, there persists a memory of enveloping love, the original template we seek to reclaim in our families of origin. For all but the most severely abused and neglected children, this remembered love is enough to sustain embers of hope. When neglect and abuse are too severe, the child suffers an empathic disconnection between the little self that suffers and the big others who hurt. Such children may grow up to identify with the aggressor by becoming either perennially victimized or abusers seeking to inflict on others the pain that was inflicted on them (A. Freud, 1936/1966).

Moral and faith development: Donald Capps, relating the traditional "seven deadly sins" to Erikson's stages, identifies *gluttony* as the sin of infancy (1987). He notes that gluttony can be the result of indiscriminate trust. Infants (and later adults) can be so starved for love that they ingest food and other substances to soothe the insatiable hunger of their longing, failing to recognize that even good things are toxic in excess. When a person not genetically disposed to be heavy suddenly starts to put on weight, pastors and other caregivers need to be curious about the sense of loss that is being silenced with excessive food or alcohol. Twelve-step recovery programs are often successful precisely because they link the hunger for emotional connection back to the original source from which it can be satisfied, the soul's memory of the love that shines for us all above the clouds of sorrow and loss (Clinebell, 1990). The addict's hunger for love is tangibly met by

Source: Erik Erikson, *The Life Cycle Completed* (New York: Norton Press, 1997).
Source for vices only: Donald Capps, *Deadly Sins and Saving Virtues* (Philadelphia: Fortress Press, 1987).

Figure 6: Erikson's Epigenetic Chart with Virtues and Vices

Psychosocial Crises

	1	2	3	1	5	6	7	8
Old Age VIII								Integrity vs. Despair WISDOM vs. MELANCHOLY
Adulthood VII							Generativity vs. Stagnation CARE vs. INDIFFERENCE	
Young Adulthood VI						Intimacy vs. Isolation LOVE vs. LUST		
Adolescence V					Identity vs. Role Confusion FIDELITY vs. PRIDE			
School Age IV				Industry vs. Inferiority COMPETENCE vs. ENVY				
Play Age III			Initiative vs. Guilt PURPOSE vs. GREED					
Early Childhood II		Autonomy vs. Shame, Doubt WILL vs. ANGER						
Infancy I	Basic Trust vs. Basic Mistrust HOPE vs. GLUTTONY							

the human community of voluntary recovery programs, where members are both more accepting and more confrontational than most church communities.

The stage of infancy is foundational because at this stage we are forming our basic structures of experience. Our embodied impressions of mother and father are all the more powerful for being preverbal, affect-laden, and inarticulate. Beginning in infancy and throughout early childhood, our god-images form and are based not only on what we are told about God but also, and more centrally, on the love we receive or fail to receive from those who care for us (Armistead, 1995). The soul's-eye view can remain strong or fade from consciousness depending on whether it is met with confirmation or disappointment in its hope for a loving environment.

Yet it would be too simplistic to equate the love of parents with an individual's awareness of the love of God. Some abused persons, whose parents were definitely *not* loving to them in many ways, can nevertheless retain a sense of love and hope available to them from a source they later came to identify as God. Many of these persons grow up with an interest in theology, spirituality, and ministry that is not readily traceable to their upbringing. This suggests the ability of "that of God" in us to look beyond the object relations of our early life, toward the original source of love from which we came.

Fowler, in his understanding of the *undifferentiated faith* of infancy, writes that the danger or deficiency in this stage is a failure of mutuality in one of two directions, either an excessive narcissism in which the experience of being "central" continues to dominate and distort mutuality, or experiences of neglect that may lock the baby into patterns of isolation (1981, p. 121). The excessive narcissism or tendency to isolation Fowler refers to develops as a defensive response to fears of abandonment. It is a sin in the sense that it creates disconnection between self, others, and God, not in the sense that the narcissistic or isolated person is being willfully destructive of community. Such behavior in adulthood is an indicator of early damage to the loving connections between self and others. As difficult as such persons may be within the context of community life, pastors, teachers, and counselors will relate to them with greater empathy if they have compassion for the neglected infant within them, rather than simply seeing them as adults who seem incapable of relating well to others. The antidote to narcissistic wounding is loving presence patiently offered, within reasonable limits.

Social location: An understanding of the importance of *attachment* and object constancy during the first twelve months of life has clear implications for public policy. Infants who are removed from their parents during this first year, often the children of the poor, may suffer lifelong difficulties with love and intimacy based on separations of a few months that seem insignificant in adult terms. Babies who are clearly suffering abuse and neglect at the hands of their parents can physically recover quite quickly when removed to a safe, caring environment. If they cannot be returned safely to their homes, they will be far better served if, before the age of twelve months, they are permanently placed with a family where they can form stable emotional bonds rather than being placed in temporary foster care and then returned to the neglectful homes from which they came. But permanent placement is also a last resort. Providing social and economic support for struggling parents who want to keep their babies is the best solution for all concerned. Pamela Couture, in *Blessed Are the Poor? Women's Poverty, Family Policy, and Practical Theology* (1991), notes that the American belief in self-sufficiency helps to perpetuate societal neglect of single mothers and their children. Faith communities perform a significant service when they actively support families and advocate for a society that values all children as the children of God. (For a comprehensive view of the healing and nurturing roles faith communities can support throughout the life cycle, see Margaret Kornfeld's *Cultivating Wholeness: A Guide to Care and Counseling in Faith Communities* [1998].)

Stage 2—The Anal Stage: 12 Months to 3 Years

Physiological and cognitive changes: Now the child is mobile, exploring the world on her or his own two feet and beginning to take charge of basic bodily functions such as eating and elimination. If all goes well at this stage, the toddler is able to experience a developing independent sense of self by retaining a positive connection to a family that loves and accepts him or her while setting limits in a consistent manner.

During this time, the toddler begins to speak. Language serves to connect the child to family and culture, but it also disconnects him or her from the amodal quality of preverbal perception (Stern, 1985). Amodal perception engages the whole person more vividly than mere reason or ordinary rational thought. Art, poetry, music, being in love, and religious experience afford opportunities for adults to experience what the preverbal child may feel much of the time, a vivid interconnectedness of sense and feeling. In amodal perception, red tulips "shout" with color; a symphony sends chills down the spine; poetry allows us to feel the textures of another's being through words. In religious experience, mystics of all ages have known the paradox of being one in loving union with God yet still an individual self who can speak of that noetic encounter in ordinary life (chap. 14). Acquiring language, fitting oneself into the verbal categories of one's culture, is part of the toddler's expulsion from Eden, even as it brings a measure of control over one's environment (see Fig. 7, chap. 7).

Intrapsychic and interpersonal changes: Erikson identified the task of the toddler (or anal stage) as *autonomy versus shame and doubt.* If all goes well at this stage, the child develops a healthy sense of autonomy. When parents are too physically or emotionally intrusive, too quick to say "no," or fail to limit, protect, and instruct the child in appropriate ways, the child feels shame and begins to doubt her or his own abilities. An important part of toilet training includes coming to terms with the fact that we have a "backside" that we cannot see. Because others can see this part of us, this backside becomes a metaphor for everything we wish to declare "not-me," to split off as dirty, bad, or wrong. But if we become divided from parts of our being, we cease to know the truth about ourselves. Knowing and accepting ourselves as we are, an acceptance we internalize from the adults who care for us, allows us to feel confident. Healthy autonomy helps us strike a balance between "masculine" independence and interpersonal harmony as a "feminine" ideal identified by Gilligan (1982).

The toddler's defiant "no!" and "me do it!," so annoying to the parents who must be ever vigilant for their child's safety, constitute Spitz's third psychic organizer, which first appears at about eighteen months. It can be understood as an *identification with the aggressor* (A. Freud, 1936/1966), because the parents are always saying "no" to the child. It can also be understood as an expression of *object constancy,* which is fully developed by age three. The child can now risk asserting a separate sense of self because she or he trusts that the essential other will not disappear.

Moral and faith development: As children, especially before language, we experience the vivid intensity of loving union with others and all creation. The eye of the soul can still be one with all it sees. Gradually, if we are disappointed in our experiences of love, we shut down most of our aliveness into the depression that often passes for a normal middle-aged existence. But unless the soul's sight has been thoroughly blinded, there is always something within us that hungers for more. Toddlers give evidence of the vivid delight we depict in stories of Eden, when the world was a garden and there was an innocent, naked openness to all of life. But even in Eden some fruits were forbidden and not all animals benign. The toddler needs to learn from the limits that loving parents set, because we live in a world in which not everything or everyone is safe.

If all goes well enough at this stage, we have the full use of our own *will.* Toddlers, when they are not tired, overwhelmed, or frustrated, have boundless energy and enthusiasm for life. With this enthusiastic life energy intact in adulthood, we are able to connect with "that of God" in us and believe that we have what it takes to accomplish our goals. Capps identifies *anger* as the vice of this developmental stage. If we fail to find and accept useful limits, we can become consumed with anger at the idea of not having our way. This anger can be expressed in direct or passive-aggressive acts. Pastors may recognize this "stuck place" in parishioners who seem perennially disgruntled and frequently at odds with those in authority. Because one does not feel positively connected to the "powers that be," one finds oneself behaving in passive-aggressive ways, chafing against necessary rules and regulations. In adulthood, the antidote for this angry sense of disempowerment is to work toward claiming our own authority.

In terms of moral development, this is the stage at which we internalize the concepts of "clean" and "dirty" and begin to distinguish right from wrong, initially through identification with the watchful other who says "no" (see chap. 6). From the soul's perspective, we can experience appropriate autonomy and expression of our will only when we are lovingly related to and guided by the One who first loved us. In the eyes of the toddler, the parents are surrogates for God (Rizzuto, 1979). But if parents fail to be "god bearers" in the life of the child, both supporting and protectively limiting the child's independence, the result may be a timid, shame-based, self-doubting child or a child who angrily resists and opposes any limits.

Social location: If we were giving significant attention to cross-cultural child-rearing practices beyond the scope of this volume, we might note the ways in which toilet-training practices at this age are correlated with cultural understandings of individual, interpersonal, and group shame, as well as the sense of balance different cultures favor between autonomy and doubt, will and anger. In Japan, for example, there is a saying, "The nail that stands out will be hammered down." Such a culture clearly does not value autonomy in the same way that Western cultures do (Soo-Young Kwan, 2001). Erikson's stages were developed in a Western context and may not match the developmental goals of other cultures.

Stage 3—The Oedipal Age: 3 to 6 Years

Physiological and cognitive changes: Preschoolers face significant developmental milestones. At this age children become more thoroughly verbal, able to adequately express their needs to caregivers. Most people have few conscious memories from before the age of three or four, possibly because the sense of self is more fluid before that age. Antonio Damasio, a neurologist, writes, "Extended consciousness occurs when working memory holds in place, simultaneously, *both* a particular object *and* the autobiographical self"(1999, p. 222). In other words, *I* need to be consciously present with the objects of my awareness for lasting memories to form. At this age, building on the "me" consciousness of the toddler, children become a fully distinct "I" for the first time.

Intrapsychic and interpersonal changes: This is also the age at which a definite sense of gender is formed. Gender conditioning begins at birth (Leaper, 2000); hospitals put pink caps on baby girls and blue caps on boys. Oedipal-age children have internalized these earlier messages. Little girls often, though not always, want to be pretty and emulate the nurturing activities of their mothers by playing with dolls or caring for toy animals. Little boys are encouraged to relate more instrumentally to objects with less emphasis placed on harmonious interpersonal interaction, as expressed in the phrase "boys will be boys." But both genders will, if unhindered, often show "cross-gender" behavior—boys by dressing like girls, girls by being aggressive in "unfeminine" ways. This simply confirms the fact that there is much about gender identity that is not inborn but must be culturally instilled (Gelman & Taylor, 2000).

This is an age at which nightmares are developmentally normal (Colarusso, 1992). Oedipal-age children may be more fearful because they have become painfully aware of how small they are in relation to adults. It is also normal at this age for children to be sexually curious. According to one preschool owner, it is common to find Oedipal-age children hiding in the coat closet to play "doctor." Masturbation is also developmentally normal. Colarusso, writing as a psychiatrist, notes that "parents should neither encourage nor criticize masturbatory activity," but goes on to say that "compulsive masturbation at this age is usually a sign that the child has been over stimulated sexually" (1992, p. 75).

Moral and faith development: Freud placed great emphasis on what he called the "positive resolution" of the Oedipus complex as the cornerstone of moral development (see chap. 7). As outlined in chapter 1, the little boy becomes attracted to his mother: He proposes marriage to her. The mother's appropriate reply to this would be "You're so handsome, thank you, but I'm already married to your father." This response affirms the boy in his gendered sense of self but makes the generational boundaries clear. An inappropriate response would be to ridicule the boy's emotionally serious proposal or collapse the generational boundaries in a manner that causes anxiety by saying, "Your Dad's a louse, I'd much rather marry you," making the small boy feel responsible for his mother's happiness. Such a response will tend to produce an adult male who is reluctant to be emotionally vulnerable with women for fear of feeling emotionally engulfed by them. This "Oedipal triumph" (actually a defeat of the boy's interpersonal freedom) may complicate his efforts to relate to both genders and skew the developmental balance between initiative and guilt.

Freud maintains that the boy's appropriate renunciation of his mother as an object of desire lays the basis for the *superego* as an agency of the mind that affirms the child in doing what is right in the eyes of his parents and society. Superego formation contributes to a *conscience* that is useful to the adult if parental standards and prohibitions are not experienced as overly strict or punitive.

The "negative" *resolution* of the Oedipus complex in Freud's theory describes the experience of gay or lesbian children who can often recall from this early stage of development a definite attraction to their same-gender parent. Freud did not intend the term to imply a negative judgment on homosexual orientation; he maintained that we are all essentially "polymorphous perverse" in childhood, meaning that we are all potentially bi-sexual during this period of Oedipal sexuality in which our sense of object choice is still fluid.

Because this watershed for moral development is described in masculine terms, it has been criticized by feminist theorists as representing a prejudicial view of the girl's moral development. To summarize Freud, the girl feels attracted to her father and may seek his attention, but if he responds appropriately to affirm her femininity while maintaining generational boundaries, her recourse is to identify with her mother. Unlike the boy, she does not have a clear path for separation from the mother in the interest of her own autonomy. She needs to establish a positive sense of identification with her mother as a basis for having a positive sense of herself as a girl. If her relationship to her mother is conflicted or ambivalent, this may be difficult. Little girls who fail to establish a positive identification with their mothers may be disinclined to embrace the project of becoming mothers themselves in later life. Girls whose longing for a positive tie to the mother is thwarted may turn their emotional longing toward father figures, with the risk that men in authority may take advantage of their vulnerability through sexual exploitation.

Carol Gilligan, in her studies of the decisions and meaning-making of girls, maintains that the girl's sense of morality is not "worse," only different (1982). According to Gilligan, girls value harmony over rule-keeping. Freud might see "bending the rules" to make everyone in the group happy as an example of fuzzy ethics. Gilligan sees it as a female tendency–whether biologically informed, as psychiatrist and Jungian analyst Jean Shinoda Bolen maintains (Bolen, 2001), or socially constructed–to elevate interpersonal harmony above abstract standards of right and wrong. Girls develop, in effect, different standards of value and different criteria for meaning in interpersonal settings than boys.

Erikson's balance of *initiative versus guilt* may be more problematic for girls because girls are socialized to consider the needs of others before their own. From this standpoint, any initiative that could displease others may provoke a sense of guilt. The balance of virtue and vice for this stage, as identified by Erikson and Capps, is *purpose versus greed.* Any purpose that can be seen to benefit others will not be problematic for a girl, whereas the purpose of "getting what I want" may be associated with greed.

Fowler associates the Oedipal-age with *intuitive-projective* faith (1981). He notes that children at this age are generally uninhibited by the need for logical thought. The child's experience of the world is dominated by imagination (which the child cannot clearly separate from fact at this age) and powerful images. Positive images may include the example of adults practicing their faith through corporate worship (chap. 6). Fowler notes that "The dangers in this stage arise from the possible 'possession' of the child's imagination by unrestrained images of terror and destructiveness…" (1981, p. 134). Children in this stage of life should not be threatened with images of hell or stories that would confuse their efforts to sort fantasy from fact. Statements at a funeral such as "Jesus took your mother to be a flower in his garden" can be damaging to children of this age as they literally imagine a Jesus who goes after people with garden shears.

Many first-born children are presented with a younger sister or brother while in preschool. If parents do a good job of balancing their attention between children of different ages, older children should handle the arrival of a new baby relatively well. The greed Capps identifies as the vice of this stage will be exacerbated if the older child feels that there is suddenly not enough parental love and attention to go around.

For the preschool child, God is likely to take on the features of the opposite sex parent. Parents continue to be idealized by children up to and sometimes through adolescence. If the parent is abandoning, abusive, or sexually inappropriate, the child's sense of purpose as a meaning-maker in the world may suffer. But even under these negative circumstances, it is possible for children to retain their soul's eye view and hope for a powerful Other who will love them and not mistreat them as their parents do.

Social location: The intuitive-projective faith of this age can be re-experienced in adulthood through dreams. A female minister dreamed that she was shown a room in which men were conducting a ritual. As part of the ritual the men said, "God prefers men." The dreamer responded, "That's not true." On considering this dream when she awoke, she realized that some part of her must still be struggling with the idea that "God prefers men," even though she consciously affirmed, "That's not true." This woman grew up in a time when, as an Oedipal-age child first becoming aware of her own gender, she would have seen only men as ritual leaders in the church. Her dream is evidence of the powerful meanings that can be internalized by children at an early age and carried into adulthood in the unconscious. According to psychoanalytic theory, we don't have the full power of choice over these early beliefs until we make the unconscious conscious.

Pastors, pastoral counselors, and faith communities need to be mindful of the understandings of gender that we each have formed at this early, very impressionable period in our lives. These gendered understandings of self can either liberate or hinder us in significant ways. A faith perspective that takes the idea of vocation seriously must be prepared to call social constructions of gender identity into question, as expressed in the saying, "There is no longer Jew or Greek, there is no longer slave or free, there is no longer male and female; for all of you are one in Christ Jesus" (Gal. 3:28). When we try to squeeze into socially prescribed roles that don't fit us, we fail to fulfill vocations to which we are called by God. What matters is that our roles fit the gifts and graces that we have each been given.

Stage 4—Latency: 6 to 12 Years

Physiological and cognitive changes: Latency is considered the golden age of childhood. In virtually all cultures, fairy tales, with their combination of reality and fantasy, assist children in the task of distinguishing fact from imagination and also serve to impart morals and cultural injunctions, for good or ill. Popular culture reinforces standard gender roles with stories of princesses who wait passively to be rescued by princes. But traditional fairy tale collections include stories of brave, active heroines as well.

Latency-age children worldwide are focused on absorbing the knowledge of their culture. While part of the child's consciousness remains in the mythopoetic mode of the preschooler, another part is outwardly focused on absorbing information and learning facts. Children of this age are better able to "tell the truth" than younger children, although they are still likely to tell adults what they think the adults want to hear.

Intrapsychic and interpersonal changes: Girls at this age are generally taller and do better in school than boys. In the "tomboy" stage that many girls go through before adolescence, girls experience what Erikson identified as a *psychosocial moratorium:* They are not yet called on to take up the cultural roles assigned their gender and may enjoy a sense of freedom and self-confidence that is lost at the onset of puberty.

Latency-age boys and girls tend to avoid each other, although, as Vivian Thompson points out in chapter 8, fraternizing with the opposite sex is usually more of a taboo for boys than for girls. This may have to do with an awareness that girls hold an "inferior status" in patriarchal societies. Befriending them might compromise the task of becoming a man.

Moral and faith development: Fowler describes the *mythic-literal faith* (stage 2) that characterizes the beliefs of school-age children in these terms:

> Mythic-Literal faith is the stage in which the person begins to take on for him or herself the stories, beliefs and observances that sym-bolize belonging to his or her community Story becomes a major way of giving unity and value to experience Marked by increased accuracy in taking the perspective of other persons, those in Stage 2 compose a world based on reciprocal fairness and an immanent justice based on reciprocity They do not, however, step back from the flow of stories to formulate reflective, conceptual meanings. For this stage the meaning is both carried and "trapped" in the narrative (1981, p. 149).

This is the ideal age for children to learn the stories of their faith tradition, their nation, and their family of origin or ethnic group. Erikson identifies the psychosocial crisis of this age as the balance between *industry and inferiority.* Children must realistically learn that it is important to work diligently even though they are not going to be the best at everything. On the other hand, it is important that all children find opportunities to establish competence in something, lest they internalize a sense of inferiority that will sap their confidence and motivation to face adult challenges. *Competence* is the virtue that school-age children internalize through hard work as they attempt to succeed in the tasks their culture values. *Envy* is the painful emotion that causes school-age children to wish they were popular or good in sports or had curly hair.

Even though envy is painful, it can be salutary if one takes a positive approach. In *Cinderella and Her Sisters: The Envied and the Envying,* Ann and Barry Ulanov explore the lessons implicit in the Cinderella story (1983). They observe that a negative approach to envy causes us to wish for the destruction of the good we see in another and find lacking in ourselves. A positive approach allows us to recognize that feelings of envy are evidence of our hunger for the good we behold in another. If we are willing to do the work to get it, some semblance of that good can be ours too.

Social location: Children who fail to develop a positive sense of competence during their school years may experience life-long difficulties. The majority of inmates in the nation's prisons did not excel at the standard measures of competence in reading, writing, and arithmetic. These same people may have other talents that are not as rewarded in our society, such as musical and creative abilities. Taking the arts out of school curricula not only removes a positive means of self-expression for latency-age children, it may also doom children with different gifts to a sense of failure (Caffrey & Mundy, 1995).

The faith of latency resides in the ability of confident children to imagine themselves as fully grown and capable, living out their dreams in an adult world. Children in this "golden" age may lose hope and despair in the face of trauma or loss (chap. 8). Faith communities can be the place where latency-age children come to see themselves as children of God, loved and valued even when they are not "the best" at everything.

Stage 5, Part 1 — Early Adolescence: 12 to 15 Years

Physiological and cognitive changes: In early adolescence, children are faced with the need to revise their sense of self in relation to a body that is undergoing a gradual transition toward sexual maturity. Girls may experience *menarche,* or the beginning of menstruation, as early as nine. The physical development of boys usually lags behind that of girls at this stage, which may cause boys to worry about whether they will grow as tall and strong as their family and culture expect them to be. Physical changes can be experienced as embarrassing or even frightening if the child does not receive good information about puberty. In Freud's day many women were kept deliberately ignorant of any information having to do with sexuality, while men were raised to be "worldly" in sexual matters. As a man of science, Freud felt it essential to combat the neurotic distress caused by the prudery and double standards of the Victorian era with sound medical information. Some parents still fear that accurate sexual information will cause their children to be promiscuous, whereas the opposite tends to be true. Young teens who lack accurate information about sexuality are more likely to endanger their health and emotional well-being through uninformed experimentation (Adams, 2000).

It is at this age that young people begin to make the intellectual leap into what Piaget calls *formal operations.* These are the cognitive abilities that adults are expected to exhibit: the ability to consider abstractions and reflect critically. Junior high-school youth can be observed to move in and out of this new cognitive ability, virtually from one moment to the next. This is not the age at which to ask a youth group to write a "credo" or statement of belief. Youth at this age are generally not sure who they are or what they believe because their bodies, and therefore their sense of self, are changing from day to day. Freud wrote that "the ego is first and foremost a bodily ego" (S. Freud 1923b/1961, p. 26). This is nowhere more evident than in the lives of young adolescents (see chap. 9).

Intrapsychic and interpersonal changes: At this age youth are beginning to question their parents and look for their own place in society while preparing to take an adult role. Even though they appear to be critical and rejecting of parents, they need the loving support, reassurance, and realistic limits that parents can provide. Scott Sells and others who specialize in working with troubled youth emphasize that the assurance of loving and consistent parental support is what the angry and rebellious teen really needs. Coaching parents to express their love effectively resolves many of the problems young adolescents may encounter (Sells, 2001).

Peers become important in adolescence. Young teens may change friends frequently as a way of "trying on" different identities (Colarusso, 1992). *Identity versus role confusion* is the task Erikson designates for adolescence. The corollary virtue is *fidelity;* the corollary sin is *pride.* Donald Capps pairs pride with fidelity, reasoning that "Fidelity…provides a genuine alternative to pride in the constructing of our lives. By encouraging loyalty to others, it stands for a risk-taking engagement with life…" whereas pride leads to isolation (1987, p. 99). Pride is a sin not only because of its results but also in its origins. If sin is defined as separation from self, others, and God, pride begins as a sense of separation from others that is so painful it must be countered with an overweening and defensive pride. In extreme forms this can result in *narcissistic rage,* in which a teen who feels rejected by peers and society will take revenge on the rejecting other in violent ways, as in the Columbine High School shootings (see chap. 9).

Moral and faith development: Teens begin to give evidence of a *synthetic-conventional faith* (Fowler's stage 3). They confront their parents with moral inconsistencies and have a nose for adult hypocrisy. It is important for young teens to find role models outside the home whose values they can emulate and respect as they seek to differentiate from their parents in preparation for adult independence. Peers that exert a positive influence help to support the young teen's often shaky sense of self.

The faith of young teens lies in their hope that their developing bodies will sustain a positive sense of identity, allowing them to find their place in the world. God can become a needed confidant and friend for junior high youth who have been introduced to the practice of prayer. Faith communities can be a positive source of moral support. If their hope in the future is not crushed, young teens retain the joy and wonder of their earlier years as they prepare for adulthood.

Social location: With their fluctuating, vulnerable sense of self and their need for adult mentors outside the family, faith communities perform a great service by welcoming youth into adult membership through confirmation classes and bar or bat mitzvahs. In traditional societies, youth approaching puberty frequently undergo specific rituals of transition into adulthood. The pattern of inner-city youth joining gangs results in part from a lack of positive community rituals for transition into adulthood. Gangs can be counteracted by providing not only membership in youth groups but also rituals and positive traditions of inclusion that help the adolescent find a stable sense of acceptance in the face of tempestuous physical change and demeaning oppression (Barna, 1995).

Stage 5, Part 2—Middle and Late Adolescence: 15 to 20 years

Physiological and cognitive changes: In middle and late adolescence, the capacity for abstract reasoning, independent thought, and reflection comes into its own. Wise educators of senior high- and college-age youth will draw out this propensity for creative and critical thinking. Faith communities can harness the idealism that flowers in late adolescence by encouraging participation in community service projects, providing the adult guidance needed to support and structure adolescent energy and enthusiasm.

With the physiological aspects of sexual maturity firmly established, youth gain a sense of confidence in their physical ability and newfound "powers," as portrayed in the transitions of comic book superheroes from wimp to wonder. Young men literally grow muscle, while many young women assume the willowy form that popular North American culture considers the apex of feminine beauty.

Intrapsychic and interpersonal changes: Erikson notes that adolescents need to be seen, heard, and affirmed by their communities. Faith communities provide the context in which minority youth who may be constant targets of prejudice in the dominant society can be recognized and appreciated for their good qualities and emerging potential (see chap. 4 and 10). Feeling securely "held" in the loving regard of parents and community is essential for the adolescent to successfully launch herself or himself into young adulthood. The faith of late adolescence tends to be somewhat narcissistically focused on the self; faith in oneself is best discovered in a community of faithful others.

Moral and faith development: Fowler calls the faith orientation that he sees emerging in adolescence *synthetic-conventional faith* (stage 3). He writes that in this stage:

> ...a person's experience of the world now extends beyond the family. A number of spheres demand attention: family, school or work, peers, street society and media, and perhaps religion. Faith must provide a coherent orientation in the midst of that more complex and diverse range of involvements...The emergent capacity of this stage is the forming of a personal myth–the myth of one's own becoming in identity and faith, incorporating one's past and anticipated future in an image of the ultimate environment unified by characteristics of personality (1981, pp. 172–73).

In essence, the late adolescent moving toward adulthood must become the hero of his or her own story. She or he must discover what "bliss" is, to use Joseph Campell's expression, and be prepared to follow it (Campbell, 1996; see chap. 10).

Social location: The older adolescent's sense of potential and openness to life can be severely curtailed at this age by teen pregnancies or the need to go to work to support the family rather than pursue further studies. Some poor and working-class youth have little opportunity to encounter the wider world beyond their immediate neighborhoods, so that their vision of what is possible for them in life becomes unduly restricted. Because youth represent our future as a society, it is important for faith communities to support the practice of providing scholarships for youth to travel or go on to college. Expanding the horizons of youth at this impressionable age can make a world of difference for them and, ultimately, their communities.

The faith of late adolescence includes the sense of intellectual and physical mastery and potential gained at this stage. The idealism of youth also leads them to look beyond themselves toward their vision for a better world, the Realm of God. Adolescent interests and enthusiasm may hold the seeds of future vocation, a true expression of the soul's eye view for the adolescent's life purpose.

Stage 6—Young Adulthood: 20 to 40 years

Physiological and cognitive changes: In physical terms this is often the period of life in which people feel most alive and most "themselves." For women, these are the prime years for reproduction, especially between the ages of twenty and thirty, when the body is fully mature but reproductive abilities have not started to wane as they do beginning in the early thirties. This biological reality poses problems for women who wish to establish themselves in careers and must therefore postpone childbirth, problems North American culture does little to help them resolve. Men at this age begin to experience a gradual sexual decline from the peak capacities of adolescence but are less limited in their ability to successfully father a child before the age of fifty. Men also face the challenge of establishing themselves in a career. If a person is still uncertain about his or her life's work at age forty, we say that they haven't "found" themselves. Yet seminaries and other graduate schools are full of second-career students in their forties who may have launched themselves on one career path in their twenties only to find themselves dissatisfied as they move from early to middle adulthood and begin to face their own mortality. Some persons "find themselves" at forty for the first time and do not fully claim their vocation until the end of young adulthood or later.

Piaget does not extend his understanding of cognitive development beyond the critical conceptual abilities that first begin to flower in adolescence. But Jung sees this period as important for the consolidation of ego identity, living into a variety of familial and societal personas, and finding one's place in the world.

Intrapsychic and interpersonal change: Erikson defines the task of young adulthood in interpersonal terms—the quest for *intimacy.* Those who are not able to establish life partnerships during this stage are likely to face *isolation,* both because societies are often biased in favor of couples and families and because it becomes more difficult to form a couple as persons mature. Men who marry late are apt to marry younger women, which makes it harder for older women, generally more numerous in the population, to find a mate. This doesn't mean that pairing after age forty is impossible or necessarily less successful, only that it may be more difficult. Erikson identifies the virtue of this stage as *love;* Capps identifies the correlated sin as *lust.* Lust results from a failure of mutuality if one continually objectifies sexual partners without seeking to understand them as persons. Love is only possible as one learns to extend oneself for the good of another, realizing that happiness is compounded when it can be shared.

Persons who are single during these years usually devote themselves to their work, to the service of others, or to both. Single people can be a tremendous resource to communities as they are often less burdened with sustaining a family and more available to be present as friends, neighbors, and mentors. It is entirely possible to express love and have intimate relationships as a single person, but it may mean swimming upstream against the familial and societal expectations that view pairing at this age as "normal." Couples without children, either by choice or due to infertility, may also experience familial and societal pressure to conform to the "married with children" norm.

There is a great need for gay and lesbian couples who are committed members of faith communities to feel welcomed and supported in their faithful unions. Discomfort about same-gender couples may be fueled by the sexual anxieties of heterosexual members with regard to traditional gender roles and is sometimes a result of heterosexual members' disowned experiences of sexual wounding. Committed same-gender relationships need to be carefully distinguished from sexual relationships that are in any way unjust or predatory. The same congregations that fail to welcome homosexual members frequently turn a blind eye to the sexual harassment, adultery, pedophilia, and incest committed by heterosexual members in their midst. Sex can certainly be the occasion for sin, but discernment is required to be clear about which behaviors are actually damaging to victims, to sexual predators, and ultimately to their communities.

The quest of many young adults for love and intimacy is sadly complicated by the prevalence of sexual harassment and violence. In *When Violence Is No Stranger: Pastoral Counseling With Survivors of Acquaintance Rape,* Kristen Leslie refutes the common myth that rape is most often committed by strangers; in fact, the reverse is true. Despite growing public awareness of sexual violence, only 16 percent of acquaintance rape cases are reported (Leslie, 2002). Pastors and faith communities, being ill-informed and avoidant around sexual issues, have often been less than effective in recognizing or supporting victims and confronting perpetrators. Congregations and seminaries can offer a prophetic witness against interpersonal violence by presenting alternatives to the stereotypes of aggressive masculinity and submissive femininity popular culture promotes (Chopp, 1995). Sue Cardwell's research using the Minnesota Multiphasic Personality Inventory (MMPI) to test incoming seminary students does suggest a higher-than-usual incidence of cross-sex-linked traits: male seminary students tend to be more caring and cooperative than the norm, female students more assertive than the norm (Cardwell, 1965).

Moral and faith development: Kohlberg saw young adults as generally expressing the values of his stage 4 within the context of *conventional* morality. Persons at Kohlberg's stage 4 seek to maintain the *social order,* believing that whatever conforms to the law and reflects the will of the community must be good. While this characterization may be true of many young adults, it would not be true of social activists, avant-guard artists, or communitarian religious groups that carry the socially critical attitudes of adolescence into adulthood and appeal to moral standards based on a *post-conventional* morality that grants the individual or counter-cultural group the right to set their own moral standards.

In terms of faith development, Fowler posits young adults as inhabiting an *individuative-reflective faith* that allows them to reassess the values of their families of origin. Travel and other experiences that take one outside the cocoon of one's familiar social milieu are likely to galvanize this transition. Fowler notes that many adults remain suspended between the stage of synthetic-conventional faith, which relies on external authority, and individuative-reflective faith, where an internal locus of authority predominates. In the latter stage, individuals may begin a quest for meaning intended to make sense of the particular narrative of their own experience, even if this puts them in opposition to the symbols and rituals of their original communities. Christian educators, congregational leaders, chaplains, and pastoral counselors need to consider the predominance of synthetic-conventional faith among the adults they encounter. The question of why so few adults move beyond this faith stage is one these groups may wish to address (cf. Fowler, Nipkow, & Schweitzer, 1991).

Social location: Because coupling is, for many, an important task of young adulthood, faith communities can support the needs of this cohort by providing singles ministries, premarital counseling, marriage enrichment, and divorce recovery programs. Those who do not find partners, lose their partners, or do not choose to partner will benefit from community support of their gifts and personhood. Pastors need to be mindful of the fact that not all members will be happily married with children. Celebrations of "Mother's Day" and "Father's Day" need to recognize the nurturing and mentoring contributions of those who are not biological parents. Infertility is a painful fact of life for up to one in four couples today (Diamond et al., 1999; Shapiro, 1988). Pregnancy loss deserves attentive pastoral care because there are no funeral rites for bodies too small to be buried (Moe, 1997). The loss of a child at any age is more painful than most deaths because we expect children to outlive their parents (Johnson, 1987; Mehren, 1997). Pastoral counselors may also be called to minister to those who have fallen into sexual addictions–Capps' sin of lust–due to a damaged capacity to love self and others (see chap. 4).

The faith of young adulthood is informed by the ability to critically reflect on our beliefs and discover the vocations for which we were created, even when these fall outside the norms prescribed by our families and culture. Loving commitment to a partner and children can be a human expression of divine love. Persons bound by lust or unwanted isolation may require community support and therapeutic healing to recover a sense of loving connection to self, others, and God. Low self-esteem can cloud the soul's eye view, making it difficult to discern one's vocation or enjoy intimate relationships with others.

Stage 7—Middle Adulthood: 40 to 60 years

Addressing this stage gives me pause, as I am about to write beyond the life stage I presently occupy, the first decade of middle adulthood. As each of us looks beyond our current life stage to what lies ahead, we face an unknown land that we can only map through the experience of older persons we know. Our parents are guides into this uncharted future. If parents suffer death, illness, or loneliness at or before retirement age, the future may seem ominous for those in their middle years who must increasingly care for elderly parents. And as elderly parents require more care, there may still be children who have not yet left the nest or who, having left, repeatedly return. For these reasons this generation is aptly called the "sandwich" generation (Abrams, et. al., 2000; Zal, 1992). The intergenerational demands on this age group may be light or onerous depending on the family systems within which they have become key players.

Physiological and cognitive change: Physical changes related to aging are a fact of life after forty. Keeping weight off and retaining muscle strength requires a conscious effort. Parents may feel threatened by the youthful, vigorous, sexual presence of their adolescent or young adult children. Fathers who did not benefit from good parenting may themselves become negatively competitive with their sons. Mothers may attempt to compete with their beautiful young daughters. Whether or not these feelings are conscious or acted on, they all have to do with a sense of physical insecurity that faces the middle-aged person whose body is no longer as strong, attractive, and healthy as it once was.

As noted in chapter 12, women go through menopause at this age, which may cause sex to become less enjoyable due to a decrease in hormone levels. Men, too, experience a diminution of their sexual drive and ability to maintain an erection. Even in this age of Viagra and hormone replacement, such unwelcome developments may cause the middle-aged person to ask, "What meaning does my life have now as changes in my body force me to reevaluate my understanding of sexuality, potency, and fertility?" On the positive side, many women report "post-menopausal zest"; released from the possibility of pregnancy, their lives are now their own in a new way. Men may also become more receptive to the "feminine" values of nurture and care for others as they age.

Intrapsychic and interpersonal change: Erikson identifies the crisis of this age as *generativity versus stagnation.* A positive resolution results in the virtue of *care,* the ability to remain meaningfully connected to our own sense of vocation and the lives of those around us. The sin Capps identifies is *indifference,* meaning that we have stopped caring and become cynical or depressed. Persons in middle age may become indifferent through sheer overwork. A retreat or sabbatical leave may be required to reconnect them to their sense of meaning and purpose in life.

This is also a life stage when many feel overwhelmed by relational demands or burdened by loss. Middle-aged adults must choose their boundaries carefully to set realistic limits on how many family members they can support and how many tasks they can successfully undertake. This is particularly true for middle-aged African American women, who are often expected to care for their extended families while they are still responsible for their own children and work outside the home to learn a living. Congregations must be careful not to pile responsibilities on those who are already burdened by multiple intergenerational demands, but seek instead to offer support whenever possible. Elder care day programs can provide welcome respite for middle-aged caregivers. Family leave policies that do not penalize workers for attending to the needs of their children and aging parents are a public policy priority for this age group.

Because marital roles and expectations tend to shift in midlife, pastors and therapists need to be prepared to address the needs of couples locked in what Harville Hendrix calls the "power struggle" phase of the marriage (1988; see chap. 12). This often takes the form of wives wishing to assert greater independence and autonomy and husbands trying to resist this shift into a new way of being a couple. Counselors who understand what is at stake in this transition will be better equipped to help the couple weather their fears of change and avoid a painful divorce.

Moral and faith development: Time for rest and reflection may be the greatest need of this age group. Fowler notes that the *conjunctive faith* (stage 5) some persons arrive at in middle adulthood and beyond supports a renewed appreciation of the symbolic power that resides in the religious rituals and traditions of one's faith of origin. Conjunctive faith is characterized by openness to dialogue between self and other, conscious and unconscious meaning. But for the fruits of this stage to become manifest, midlife persons must claim what they need to refresh and renew their spirits, lest their desire to care and be generative harden into indifference.

Midlife is the age at which Jung says persons come into the fullness of their own unique personality and gifts through the journey of individuation. The personality traits and interests that have sustained persons until midlife may now be complemented by a counterbalancing focus. Men who have been career-driven may become better related, more nurturing. Women who have been focused on meeting the needs of others for most of their adult lives will now begin to ask, "Who am I, and what do I want from life?" They may leave the domestic sphere to run for public office or embark on a new career. New outlets for generativity are required as parents experience the empty nest and workers lose jobs or redefine their vocation.

The faith of midlife resides in a growing ability to look beyond the pressures of the present moment toward an appreciation of the deeper meanings symbolized in religious tradition. Time for refreshment and reflection supports the active expression of generativity and care. Persons at this stage of life are, ideally, prepared to answer the following questions posed by Fowler:

- What are you spending and being spent for?
- What commands and receives your best time, your best energy?
- What causes, dreams, goals, or institutions are you pouring out your life for?
- To what or whom are you committed in life? In death?
- What *are* [your] most sacred hopes, those most compelling goals and purposes in your life? (1981, p. 3).

Those who fail to find answers to these questions, who suffer from a sense of *stagnation* in midlife, will benefit from setting time aside for prayer, spiritual direction, and spiritual renewal. Time spent in dialogue with a pastoral psychotherapist can be claimed for reflection on life's purposes, an opportunity to listen for the voice of the soul. Answers can be found, but they are difficult to hear amid the pressures of daily living.

Social location: The satisfaction persons feel at this stage of life may depend on how well they match the notions of success with which they were raised. Persons single, divorced, or widowed at midlife may struggle with a sense that their lives are not as they hoped they would be. Being unsettled in work is also a cause for concern. Unrealized dreams may haunt those who see diminishing prospects for their fulfillment. In all these difficulties, faith communities can be a place of refuge where persons disappointed with aspects of their own lives can reaffirm a deeper sense of meaning that transcends their immediate concerns. In the soul's eye view, it is never too late to find redemption, meaning, and purpose in life.

Stage 8—Late Adulthood: 60 and over

Physiological and cognitive change: By this stage, if not earlier, many parents have become grandparents and have faced the loss of their own parents. Having no generation between ourselves and mortality is like a cold wind at our backs, reminding us that time is limited and fleeting. Health at this stage becomes more important than chronological age. Some are already facing serious ailments in their sixties, while others enjoy good health well into their eighties. Regular exercise will benefit even those whose mobility is limited. The ravages of diminished mental capacity can be forestalled in many cases by exercise for the brain—taking courses, learning new skills, and so on. "Use it or lose it" becomes the watchword for physical and mental health.

Intrapsychic and interpersonal change: Grandparents may enjoy their grandchildren more thoroughly than they did their children because they now have more time and the wisdom to appreciate the discoveries of the young. But this is only possible when family connections have been maintained—family feuds and "cut-offs" that sever ties between family members diminish the opportunities for grandparents and grandchildren to bond (McGoldrick, Gerson, & Shellenberger, 1999; McGoldrick, 1995). This is a great loss, because for many children the love of a grandparent is the closest thing to unconditional love that they will know, short of the love of God.

Persons who lose a life partner during these years may need to learn new skills of self-sufficiency. Some widows and widowers end up in the hospital, questioning their will to live without their mate. Others find new love, perhaps the love of their lives, during these later years. Many older women who are widowed or divorced enjoy the autonomy of life on their own, with the support of friends and extended family. Widowers are more likely to remarry and tend to live longer when they do (Tengbom, 2002; Tagliaferre & Harbaugh, 2001).

Loss and grief can be experienced in all stages of life, for all persons, but nowhere more so than as one nears one's own end. A woman who lived to be 102 in reasonably good health spent the last twelve years of her life lamenting, "Everyone I know is gone." One loses friends, family members, familiar places, and familiar ways of life. All these losses must be mourned. Pastors, congregations, chaplains, and counselors perform a valuable service by giving people a place to own their grief and encouragement to truly mourn. The work of mourning involves a gradual letting go of the loved one. Without this grief work, the dust and cobwebs of melancholy inevitably descend to cast their pall over the present (S. Freud, 1917e/1957; Mitchell & Anderson, 1983).

Moral and faith development: The challenge Erikson identifies for this age is *integrity versus despair.* Those who continue to find life coherent and meaningful in the face of diminished physical capacities and multiple losses have discovered the virtue of *wisdom.* Those who despair are likely to be mired in the *melancholy* of many elderly persons whose life stories are always told in terms of failures and disappointments.

According to Fowler, persons who arrive at the stage of *universalizing faith* are those who have transcended concern for their own well-being and experience their connection with all of life in a way that few of us have felt or imagined. Fowler gives the example of modern-day saints such as Mother Theresa, spending her life for the dying in the streets of Calcutta. A universalizing faith sees beyond the ego's limited perspective to embrace the soul's-eye view—the interconnectedness of all beings.

Social location: For those who have not arrived at a universalizing vision of life, financial security normally has much to do with whether one's "retirement" years can be enjoyed in comfort or whether they will be a trial. Not all persons over sixty have the means or desire to retire. Some find life without work uninteresting. The plight of the elderly poor, who may also be physically ill and emotionally isolated, is an indictment of the capitalist emphasis on self-reliance. Communities of faith, with their programs of visitation and activities for the elderly, not only support caregivers but also may be just the antidote to despair and melancholy that the elderly require. The ministries of persons who are active and healthy in retirement are essential in sustaining the outreach of today's faith communities. Young people can be encouraged to record the history lessons the elderly have to share. This allows the younger generation to learn about the past and the older generation to engage in the age-appropriate task of *life review* (Butler, 1982).

Faith at this stage of life may be relatively easy to find for those who have their health, who are surrounded by a loving extended family, enjoy a measure of financial ease, and have invested their talents to earn the blessing, "Well done, thou good and faithful servant" (Mt. 25:21, KJV). Finding faith in the face of failing health, the death of loved ones, regrets, and financial insecurity is more of a challenge, but if one has gained a wise heart (Ps. 90:12), it can be done. The loving support of family and community can ease the process of relinquishment that facing the end of life requires. Those who have truly learned to see beyond the ego's limited perspective become radiant in the light of the soul's-eye view.

Stage 9—Death, Dying, and Resurrection

Physiological and cognitive change: We live in a culture that denies death (Becker, 1973; Bregman, 1999; chap. 14). Medical personnel tend to see death as a defeat, even though death is the natural conclusion of advancing years. Hospitals frequently call on chaplains to sit with the dying, those for whom "nothing more can be done." Chaplains and hospice workers have come to recognize this as a precious time; it is a privilege to be called to share the last few months, weeks, days, or hours of another's life. Those who minister to the dying need to be well informed about the natural physiological processes of death so that the loved ones surrounding the dying person will know what to expect (Callanan, & Kelley, 1992). It is wise to prepare a living will so that family members can be spared difficult end-of-life decisions. With good palliative medicine and hospice care, much can be done to relieve the physical suffering of the dying person and the emotional suffering of their loved ones.

Intrapsychic and interpersonal change: The dying process involves letting go (Mairs, 2001). As a chaplain I have been present in intensive care settings where a dying person held on to life until the last family member had flown in to be at the bedside. Only then was the one nearing death ready to say goodbye. Some families will surround the dying person's bed for days. Eventually they decide to take a break and are distressed to learn that their loved one died without them while they were gone. This may be the dying person's choice—it's as though the presence of family members holds them in life. Being alone gives them permission to let go.

Moral and faith development: In the book *Final Gifts: Understanding the Special Awareness, Needs and Communications of the Dying,* two hospice nurses, Maggie Callanan and Patricia Kelly, write about the ordinary and extraordinary experiences of persons nearing death (1992). This subject is considered in chapter 14, where Claude Barbre reflects on the meaning of the angel of death archetype for the dying person. Both families and those who are dying can benefit from experienced hospice guides who understand the predictable stages of death and appreciate its numinous qualities. To be present for a birth or a death is to experience a sacred liminal, transitional, space in which the visible world we know touches life energies we feel but cannot see.

Social location: No one deserves to die in pain, alone, without adequate physical care and emotional contact. The cultural value of self-sufficiency is worse than irrelevant for the elderly poor as they face death. A preponderance of the elderly poor are women; this compounds their distress, as the ones who cared for others all their lives fail to find care. Is it any wonder that some dying women seek euthanasia rather than face an extended, solitary dying process?

In ministering to the dying, especially those who are poor, isolated, and lonely, faith communities witness to their respect for life and serve as the hands and feet of God on earth. Faith at the end of life resides in the hope that we will once again be reunited with the love of God that first enfolded our being, waiting to receive us again in the Eternal Now. Moments of insight from the soul's-eye view remind us that nothing can ever separate us from the love of God (Rom. 8).

Conclusion

The dimension of faith requires us to consider the possibility that there is more to life than the ego's limited perspective. When Jesus says, "[T]hose who lose their life... will find it" (Mt. 10:39), he is referring to a vision attested to by the world's major religions: the paradoxical awareness that our greatest experience of joy and purpose in life, our best understanding of faith and hope, may come precisely in those moments when we are least concerned about our own individual well-being. Then we are attuned to the flow of life itself, able to affirm that it is good to be alive. In these moments, gifts of grace, it is as though we are rediscovering a truth once known but long hidden. As William Wordsworth (1770–1850) puts it in his "Ode to Immortality from Recollections of Early Childhood" (1964):

Our birth is but a sleep and a forgetting:
The soul that rises with us, our life's star,
Hath had elsewhere its setting,
And cometh from afar:
Not in entire forgetfulness,
And not in utter nakedness,
But trailing clouds of glory do we come
From God, who is our home:
Heaven lies about us in our infancy!

Life holds meaning if we remain mindful of our origins, held in faith by a loving Spirit known through the soul's eye view. The language of faith describes enduring patterns of human experience that transcend culture and history. As the following chapter reminds us, no matter what befalls us in time, we remain citizens of Eternity. We have only to remember–through prayer, ritual, reflection, acts of faith, or gifts of grace–the loving Other from whom we come, ever present to us in the Eternal Now.

Notes

[1] In making this statement, I am assuming sufficient physical and mental health to make meaning effectively and that the meanings we find are not destructive to ourselves or others.

[2] An earlier version of this section appeared as "Discernment: The Soul's Eye View," in *Out of the Silence* (see Ratliff, 2001).

[3] Note that Fox's revelation is quite similar to the prologue of John's gospel: "The light shines in the darkness, and the darkness did not overcome it" (Jn. 1:5).

[4] A neurologist, Antonio Damasio, in *Descarte's Error* (1994), gives detailed physiological evidence for the mind's complete dependence on the body. Whether a similar analogy can be made between soul and psyche is unclear to me. The fact that we make distinctions, for the purposes of awareness, need not result in a hierarchical dualism that places mind over body, male over female, soul over psyche. None of these pairs can exist without both parts.

[5] We need not think of the soul as "disembodied" at this point. Traditional Christian doctrine holds that there is a bodily resurrection after death, despite the corpse that the departing life energy visibly leaves behind. What the soul's form might be before birth or after death is a mystery. Like love and God, it is both real and unseen.

CHAPTER 3

Human Development in Relational and Cultural Context

Pamela Cooper-White

"In the beginning is the relation."

Buber, 1936/1970, p.69

Human development does not occur in a vacuum. To be human is to be in relation from the moment of conception. The development of human consciousness is a process of meeting, an increasingly rich and complex knowing and experiencing of oneself in context. There is never a moment of human existence without a surrounding environment of sensations and relations, beginning with the experience of the mother herself as total environment and living, breathing home. While researchers and theory-makers differ somewhat on the perception of differentiation between self and others that is possible at birth, life begins in the matrix of "I and Thou" (Buber, 1936/1970). Martin Buber wrote, "It is not as if a child first saw an object and then entered into some relationship with that. Rather, the longing for relation is primary, the cupped hand into which the being that confronts us nestles" (1936/1970, p. 78).

Toward a New Metaphor for Human Development

This basic relationality of human existence may seem obvious, but traditional models of human development have tended to paint a different

91

picture. Human development is still frequently taught as an extension of Descartes' famous dictum, "I think, therefore I am (1641/1992)." Traditional models of development, while recognizing the challenges of interpersonal relating, particularly from early childhood onward, have tended to focus on the course of growth of individual persons. With the individual as foreground, the environment and the people in it form the background against which the individual's development proceeds. Frequently, the environment is depicted as posing obstacles or impediments to forward movement of the individual. An overarching pattern or archetype presented in these traditional models of development is the hero's journey (Jung, 1952/1967). The individual yearns, or is "hardwired" from birth, to move forward toward ever increasing capacities, particularly in the realm of cognitive, rational, and principled moral thought. Obstacles are seen as problems to be overcome, and each developmental stage or level is an achievement over the previous one. The use of the term *mastery* in many developmental theories is not accidental. The hero's journey has a goal, that of increasing mastery of the environment through ever more efficient thought and skilled action.

The hero's journey is also depicted as linear. Traditional models have tended to present human psychological growth as progressing forward along a developmental path. Furthermore, the path has milestones. Development is understood in virtually all traditional models as occurring in *stages,* that is, a predictable sequence of psychological achievements that could be charted as a series of rises and plateaus. The most famous of these perhaps is Erik Erikson's (1950/1963) "Eight Stages of Man," but the basic idea of stage theories originate as early as 1905 with Freud's (1905d/1953) psychosexual stages (oral, anal, and phallic/genital). Jean Piaget (1937/1954; Ginsburg & Opper, 1988) also presented his highly detailed theories of cognitive development in terms of minute changes, which he observed over time in infants' and children's perceptual and cognitive capacities. The stages are understood as normative—when all goes well, the psychological stages should occur more or less in synchrony with advances in physiological maturation. From Anna Freud's point of view, pathology could also be understood as occurring along a series of parallel developmental lines, which need to proceed more or less synchronously toward healthy maturity (A. Freud, 1963). Pathology is thereby understood as a failure to achieve stages more or less on time, whether this is caused by constitutional deficits or disruptions from the environment. Another way of thinking about what goes wrong would be a "boxcar" model, in which each stage is a boxcar being added to a train; if something goes wrong at a particular stage, the individual's growth is "derailed."

Stage theories obviously have a place in understanding how the individual human person acquires capacities for increasingly complex cognitive and physical tasks. The stages described in traditional developmental theories do have descriptive power. They represent physiological and cognitive "milestones" that serve a heuristic and diagnostic purpose, allowing for the measurement of a child's growth against a norm of average, expectable development. All stage theories are based on close observation, either of infants and children directly, or, in psychoanalytic theories, also on reconstructions from adult patients' memories and experiences. Beginning with Erikson (1950/1963), the study of developmental stages was expanded beyond early childhood to encompass the lifespan. Longitudinal studies, such as Vaillant's *Adaptation to Life* (1995), have contributed important observations about normative phases of human life. Stage theories have also served as the framework for more specific research into the development of morality (Kohlberg, 1973; Gilligan, 1982), of lifelong meaning-making (Kegan, 1982, 1994), and of faith (Fowler, 1981; Meissner, 1987; Loder, 1998).

The whole notion of stage theories has, however, increasingly been challenged in the last two decades, with regard to most if not all of its fundamental presuppositions: linearity, progress, the prescriptive quality of stages, individualism, and the privileging of rational thought. Advances in both philosophical and scientific realms have brought a collective critique of the notion that truth itself is singular, universal, or even wholly knowable. The broad philosophical movement called "postmodernism" and the scientific field of quantum physics both, from very different perspectives, have questioned the Enlightenment-age assumptions that the world is always orderly, that all knowledge is rational, and that objective knowledge of a phenomenon (whether a person, other living being, thing, or event) can be possible apart from entering into a relationship with that phenomenon, which in turn influences it. Some of the limitations of research in the 1960s and 1970s have also been challenged, particularly the establishment of norms based on white, middle-class boys and college-educated men (Gilligan, 1982; Belenky, Clinchy, Goldberger, & Tarule, 1986; Brown & Gilligan, 1992; Taylor, Gilligan, & Sullivan, 1996).

A sense of directionality may be unavoidable in the way we perceive development phenomenologically, as growth occurring in a forward movement over time. But development is not only linear. It is an organic unfolding, similar to the process shown in slow-motion films of the growth of flowers. Growth occurs not in a single direction, but outward, like the concentric rings of a tree trunk. Plants and trees do not only grow up, but toward all their sources of energy. They reach up toward the light, outward into the air, and downward into their source of nourishment. Trees also build structure as they grow—over the years, layers are added to the trunk, building a structure of support, storage of nutrients, and an outer layer of bark that protects the tree against the buffeting realities of wind, fire, and the axe. This is a much more adequate and organic metaphor for human psychological development than a linear model.

In theological terms, this conception of time is closer to *kairos*, time-in-eternity, than to *chronos*, the category of hourly time marked progressively by the ticking of a clock. Time not only is linear, but participates in eternal cycles of birth, change, death, and renewal. Such a concept of time might be represented not by a straight line, but by a Möbius strip, a symbol of eternity. This is an image that can represent the diversity and complexity of human developmental phenomena such as love, dependency, grief, fear, pleasure, power and attainment (as well as their opposites), and the narratives about them, which appear, change, multiply, and loop back to reappear in new configurations with many different meanings over the lifespan.

In the model presented in this chapter, development is also not conceived with the individual in sharply focused foreground. Rather, it is a multidimensional interrelation. The individual self participates in and co-constructs the realities of intimate relationships, culture, class, and society and shares mutually in endowing these with meaning and the power to impact ongoing being. As Erikson (1950/1963, 1980) himself recognized, social context has an important influence on the formation of identity, including social, historical, sexual, racial, ethnic, and religious influences.

It is therefore the thesis of this chapter that development is not only a linear, heroic, individualistic process, but also a complex, organic, and intrinsically relational human phenomenon that operates simultaneously and dynamically in at least four dimensions: the internal or intrapsychic world of fantasy and experience (conditioned by the earliest relationships with primary caretakers); the interpersonal, gendered world of intimate relationships and families; the wider context of the cultures and subcultures into which the person is born and the other cultures with which she or he comes to interact; and the overarching dimension of time, both linear and eternal.

The Internal World of Experience and Fantasy

"There is no such thing as a baby…If you set out to describe a baby, you will find you are describing a baby and someone. A baby cannot exist alone, but is essentially part of a relationship" (Winnicott, 1964/1987, p. 88). Although no one can say for certain what goes on in the interior life of an infant, it is quite clear that environment and context play an ongoing role in development. A baby is not born as a psychological tabula rasa, or "blank slate." The human person comes into the world already equipped with the capacity to receive and process information on a number of levels, including bodily sensations, cognitive abilities, affects, feelings, and emotions, all of which have a relational dimension:

Bodily sensations: These may include internal and external perceptions of pressure and touch, smells, taste, sounds, and sight. On the inside, the baby experiences his or her own vital functions and digestive system as central, organizing events. Breath, heartbeat, the bubbling of stomach juices and gas, the sensations of hunger and satiety, sleepiness, and urges to perform vigorous movement constitute the core inner rhythms of daily life. But even in this most interior realm, the inside is in constant relation with the outside world, the "cupped hand" to which Buber refers. The baby is utterly dependent on the environment for the alleviation of all internal discomfort–especially hunger.

External sensations also bring comfort or discomfort. Sounds can be intriguing and pleasurable, or painfully loud or startling. Light can bring objects into better focus, or hurt the eyes. There are wonderful smells and horrible smells. The milk from breast or bottle can taste sweet, rich, sour, or watery thin. The surfaces of things–clothes, diapers, beds, blankets, and stuffed toys can be cozy and comfortable, or they can be scratchy, cold, squishy, or wet. The baby's own skin can betray him or her with rashes that itch and burn. At the most primal level of the skin, the baby first experiences the boundary between self and other (Bick, 1968; Ogden, 1989). Although the primary caretaker(s) cannot soothe every sensory pain and irritation (no cure for colic has yet been discovered!), a "good enough" response (Winnicott, 1960/1965, pp. 49, 145) by a caretaker who is reliably present establishes from the earliest days of life a sense of trust in the potential goodness of the outside world, the core of faith.

Cognitive abilities: Infants come "hardwired" neurologically to receive and process a huge variety of stimuli. Recent neurological research (Greenspan, 1997; Siegel, 1999) suggests that particularly in the years between birth and age three, there is an explosion of growth in neurological pathways that become the basis for learning even in adulthood. When a child's brain is given optimal stimulation, neurological pathways develop, and patterns of recognition are laid down. In the absence of stimulation, certain pathways do not develop, and there is a process of "pruning" that takes place. Over time, every baby's brain becomes more specialized, as certain pathways are developed and others diminish with lack of stimulation.

While there is still a great deal that is not known about the neurobiological basis of development, researchers have identified a close relationship between infant brain development and such developmental areas as emotions, behavior, learning, the acquisition of language, and social development. Evidence supports the idea that the environment strongly impacts development. Positive or negative stimulation from primary caretakers and others early in life can nurture or interfere with healthy brain growth and can have ramifications for all areas of a child's psychological and social development (Schore, 1999; Perry, Pollard, Blakly, Baker, & Vigilante, 1995; Siegel, 1999).

Affects, feelings, and emotions: Researchers have now recognized that not only are infants "hardwired" for cognitive learning, they also come equipped with a set of eight basic affects, which can be observed by facial expressions: surprise-startle, interest-excitement, enjoyment-joy, distress-anguish, contempt-disgust, anger-rage, fear-terror, and shame-humiliation (Tomkins, 1962, 1962). These early affects are not quite the same as emotions (Basch, 1988). They are biological reflexes originating in the autonomic nervous system, not yet attached to voluntary action or symbolic or verbal meaning. But they do represent primal reactive states that are excited by environmental stimuli in a range from mild to intense. Environmental stimuli may be personal, such as a parent's smell or touch, or impersonal, such as a bright light or loud sound. Basch (1988, p. 78) defines "feeling," which arrives developmentally around eighteen to twenty-four months, as an affective reaction connected to a sense of self, with a basic verbal capacity not only to experience, for example, the state of anger, but to articulate it: "I am angry." Emotion is a yet more mature affective phenomenon, in which feelings, experiences, and the meanings given to them are joined to produce complex concepts such as love, hate, and happiness (Basch, 1988). Basch proposes that "the final maturational step in affective development is the capacity for empathic understanding," (1988, p. 78), similar to the concept of "emotional intelligence" (Salovey & Sluyter, 1997; Goleman, 1997), in which the individual is capable of entering into the affective, feeling-toned experience of another outside the self.

These powerful relational tools of affect, feeling, emotion, and empathy further confirm the intrinsic relationality of human nature and of the close relationship between affective communication and the development of identity (Beebe & Lachmann, 1988). Researchers have, for example, studied the importance of the effect of shame on development of the self, concluding that an overwhelming amount of shame-laden experiences in early childhood can create serious deficits in all areas of development (Lewis, 1981). The quality of early attachment between infants and their primary caretakers also may have a profound effect on later learning, social relationships, and even mental and emotional health (Bowlby, 1988). Warm, sensitive nurturing by primary caregivers tends to result in healthy, secure attachment, while inconsistent, unresponsive, or rejecting parental interactions tend to result in patterns of attachment that are anxious in the form of either ambivalent clinging or avoidant distancing behaviors (Ainsworth, Blehar, Waters, & Wall, 1978). Significant negative effects on development have been observed in cases where the infant's experience of attachment is traumatically interrupted (Spitz, 1945). Trauma, although seldom discussed in the literature of developmental psychology, has a profound impact on multiple aspects of development (Cooper-White, 2000).

The emotional surround of early childhood, in fact, has physiological consequences for brain development. One of the leading researchers on the developmental aspects of neurobiology, Allan Schore, asserts that the child's future social and emotional development, including the actual structure of the brain, is determined by his or her social environment, with the primary caregiver having significant responsibility as mediator for that environment (1999). Thus, cognitive and emotional development and neurological maturation are not separate processes, but are intertwined. Growth in all areas is intrinsically dependent on relationships. It is not too much to say that the brain itself is shaped by social and emotional relations from birth.

Recent studies based on infant observation (Stern, 1985, chap. 4) confirm the inherently relational nature of human development at the earliest phase of life. In particular, the level of attunement of a primary caretaker with the infant's and small child's shifting affect states will have an impact on the child's own capacity for affective maturation. As the child acquires verbal ability, the parent's ability to observe and accurately name feelings for the child lay the foundation for the child's own ability to recognize and name his or her own feelings and, in time, complex emotions. Empathy, the foundation of all capacity for "I-Thou" relationship, is thus a learned capacity. It is first acquired at a rudimentary level through the experience of empathic attunement of primary caretakers, and later (sometimes remedially) through both experiencing and practicing the affective recognition, respect, and mirroring from and with others. This process is never finished, but continues to increase in depth and complexity over the lifespan.

Such infant observation studies have added credence to many of the more relationally centered concepts of psychoanalytic theory, particularly from the school of psychoanalysis known as "object relations." Melanie Klein (1882–1960), an analyst from Freud's own circle who emigrated to London, was one of the first theorists to investigate the earliest relationship between mother and infant.

Object Relations Theory

Klein (1932, 1957) proposed a theory of the infant's inner experience that did not entirely replace Freud's view of the centrality of sex and aggression, but placed far more emphasis on the formative nature of the infant's earliest inner experience of his or her caretakers. Based on reconstructions from her adult patients' memories, fantasies, and projective processes at work in the analytic relationship, Klein proposed that the infant's experiences of hunger, thirst, pain, satisfaction, soothing, or fright are stored by the infant in a rudimentary system of classification into "good" and "bad." Relational experiences of the primary caretaker (for Klein, this was always the mother) can be good if perceived as adequately responsive, or can be bad in either of two ways: overwhelming and intrusive, or depriving and inadequately responsive. These good and bad experiences coalesce in the realm of fantasy into symbolic mental representations, or "objects." Initially, good and bad are split domains, with an all-or-nothing quality. A primary caretaker, or even in the earliest months a part of a caretaker, particularly a breast, can exist in the interior fantasy world as both a good object and a bad object or objects. Klein called this early period of development the "paranoid-schizoid position," in which the infant's early mental life is organized around an absolute split between good and bad and efforts to avoid experiencing the bad.

After the first six months of life, Klein proposed, the infant begins to gain a rudimentary experience of the destructive potential of his or her own hunger and need. There can be a dawning sense that the wish to devour the breast could destroy it. With this sense can come a feeling akin to sadness, and a desire for reparation. She called this the "depressive position" and considered it the lifelong foundation for emotional and psychological health. It is significant that Klein did not use the term *stage,* but rather *position* (Ogden, 1989). Because her theorizing was based on adult clinical cases, she saw the relevance of both positions throughout life, and saw the paranoid-schizoid position as one in which adults might still be predominantly functioning or to which they might regress during times of great stress or trauma.

Other object relations theorists extended Klein's theories further, in particular, British psychoanalysts W. R. D. Fairbairn (1952), D. W. Winnicott (1953/1971, 1964/1987, 1965), and Harry Guntrip (1961), and more recently, two American groups of psychoanalytic theorists who have posited a two-person, relational, or "intersubjective" dimension to every individual's construction of meaning and even reality (e.g., Mitchell, 1988; Davies, 1988; Stolorow & Atwood, 1992; Stolorow, Atwood, & Brandchaft, 1994; Orange, Atwood, & Stolorow, 1994; Bromberg, 1998). For these theorists, the inner world, from infancy throughout the lifespan, is made up of varying numbers of internalized others, or "objects," as well as multiple representations of the self or aspects of oneself at different times and under different circumstances. These inner mental representations function somewhat like templates, against which new experiences, particularly relational experiences, are tested. As a child grows up, he or she comes to expect certain kinds of behaviors from other people, based on the internalization of earlier experiences. The earliest internalized objects or representations, because they occur in infancy and toddlerhood, are preverbal and therefore not necessarily attached to any sort of narrative memory.

Narrative meaning, when attached to these early representations, is always necessarily retrospective, from the vantage point of an older, verbalizing self. Not all early representations are ever explored or processed verbally, but nevertheless exist as powerful forces governing behavior and experience. Some of a person's earliest childhood experiences may not even reach the cognitive level of symbolization, but rather may be retained at the level of behavior patterns or bodily sensations (Segal, 1957/1981). Particularly in the case of trauma, researchers have observed that overwhelmingly terrifying or painful events are not processed cognitively as are other narrative memories, but are stored in fragments that separate cognition; affective or emotion-toned experience; behavioral patterns; and/ or visual, auditory, olfactory, taste, and tactile sensation. Some traumatic memories may only exist as unsymbolized body memories (Van der Kolk, 1994; Davies & Frawley, 1994).

Inner objects or representations are also not merely inert pictures or sensations in the mind. As object relations theorists have proposed, inner objects also have their own dynamic life. They function as internal motivating forces or parts of the self, with varying degrees of autonomy, acting and reacting in relationship with external and internal others. A person may feel "fragmented" or "divided" internally as different forces come into play based on differing childhood experiences and internalized significant others. He or she may have little or no conscious awareness of these inner forces or parts of the self. The less aware she or he is, in fact, of these inner forces, the more likely they are to be projected, similar to the way a movie is projected, onto the "screen" of other people. This process has the power to distort the person's perception of others and to cause him or her to misperceive a new reality as an old (usually painful or self-destructive) one. When early experiences have been consistently painful or depriving enough, projections tend to be negative and bring even more pain. Expectations that in childhood might have been helpful or even life-saving often outlive their usefulness and in adult life may serve to create more problems than they solve.

Projective Identification

Especially in cases where childhood experience has been consistently depriving or traumatic, a more intensely projective process called "projective identification" may occur. In projective identification, projections may be experienced by the other as entering within them and actually changing their behavior in relation to the person doing the projecting. Considered mysterious or quasi-telepathic by some, the process of *projective identification* is really conveyed by a series of subtle or not-so-subtle behavioral cues, which invoke reciprocal behaviors in the other person. A form of self-fulfilling prophecy results, in which the inner expectations of the person doing the projecting become incarnated in the other. A vicious cycle may ensue, in which the expectation based on a negative experience of a primary caretaker in early childhood becomes confirmed again and again in ongoing living.

The cycle is hard to break, because projective processes are not only powerful, but frequently are mutual, as individuals become locked into mutually reinforcing negative patterns of projection. The cycle can be broken, however, by the in-breaking of an unexpected new relational experience that is powerful enough and feels real enough to overcome the veil of projections and allow for the internalization of a more positive reality, a new object that neither abandons nor retaliates (Winnicott, 1969/1971). Sometimes this can happen in everyday living, but more often, if the inner representations are too painful or persecutory, a therapeutic relationship is needed to allow for and contain the projective processes at the level of intensity necessary for healing. Much clinical work in object relations–oriented psychotherapy is founded on this principle, and the projective processes that begin to develop in the therapeutic relationship become the focus for mutual exploration between therapist and patient.

This object-relations model also has implications for faith, particularly as individuals conceive of God and the quality of their relationship to God or the sacred. Internalized representations of primary caretakers early in life are not only projected onto other people. These representations, particularly internal parental figures, also constitute the core of a person's internal representation of God, or God-*imago*. Ana-Maria Rizzuto (1979) demonstrated in her studies of children's and adults' drawings of their concepts of God that God images are powerfully influenced by the positive or negative internalized experiences of primary caretakers in early childhood. In her pastoral psychotherapy work with adults, Valerie DeMarinis (1998–99) also found that the therapeutic process allowed for an emergence of more complex, life-sustaining images of God.

Thus, the inner life is the place of primary experience, mediated through ever-increasingly complex symbols and verbal narratives, which are continually co-created in the intersubjective matrices of intimate relationships. Inchoate experiences, symbolizations, and narratives (both positive and negative) combine to form the deep structures underlying each individual's motivation, moral choices, and construction of ultimate and/or spiritual meanings–the unconscious foundation of an individual's faith (religious or secular–see Fowler, 1981 and Armistead, 1995).

The Interpersonal World of Intimate Relationships and Families

Individuals most often are raised in the context of families, whether the white middle-class nuclear family of *Leave It to Beaver* or more varied, culturally normed configurations of single-parent and extended families. The relational life of every family includes both conscious and unconscious dimensions, with an interlocking network of mutual projective processes at work among the individual "I's" and "Thou's" within it. These processes result over time in the formation of certain characteristic patterns, boundaries, and styles of relating within the family (whether harmonious or conflictual). Conflicts may harden into predictable polarities between certain dyads, or rigid triangular configurations (Bowen, 1978; Friedman, 1985). The functioning of families as whole organic entities, or systems, has been elaborated by family system theorists (e.g., Bowen, 1978), who emphasize the transmission of these family patterns across generations.

These multigenerational patterns can be observed using a family tree–like diagram called a genogram (McGoldrick, Gerson, & Shellenberger, 1999).

Families, like individuals, also have a developmental "life cycle," with certain somewhat predictable "stages" that occur as the family moves through time (Carter & McGoldrick, 1999, p. 2). Intergenerationally, this cycle has no definite beginning or end. Carter and McGoldrick choose leaving home as the entry point to describe the family life cycle, a time at which single young adults "leave the nest" and accept responsibility for themselves. A new generation of adults is thus launched. The cycle continues with a number of steps, not all of which apply to all families or generations: the joining of families through marriage; families with young children (whose task is to incorporate and nurture new dependent members); families with adolescents (whose task shifts toward greater tolerance for children's growing independence, as well as caring for elder family members); launching children and moving on (making the transition to the "empty nest)"; and finally, families in later life (whose task is to accept a shifting in their generational roles from parents to grandparents/nurturing elders). Individual development is closely entwined with larger family realities. Individuals' identities are profoundly shaped by the roles, conflicts, and particular phases of the life cycle that characterize the experience of collective family life. Certain other groups, particularly close work groups (Bion, 1959; Obholzer & Roberts, 1994) and religious groups such as churches and synagogues (Friedman, 1985), also function unconsciously and systemically and may have a reciprocal formative impact on the development of the individuals within them.

Contemporary American media frequently depict family life, at its best, as representing a place of safety and nurture for children and a haven for adults from the pressures of the outside world. This ideal of domestic life as separate and fortressed from reality is limited, however, and at worst may become insular and self-absorbed. Sociologists such as Robert Bellah (1985) have increasingly begun to challenge the privatization of family life as a symptom of unhealthy individualism in American society. Just as individual development usually proceeds within the interpersonal context of family life, so do families grow and develop within the wider context of culture and society, and contribute to it.

The Wider Context of Cultures and Subcultures

Psychoanalytic theorists have become increasingly sensitive to the formative impact of the interpersonal context of relationships. Group relations and family systems theories have extended this sensitivity to the context of groups and families. However, most theorists stop short of considering the significance of the wider circles of cultures and subcultures in which individuals and families are embedded. This is in part due to the once unquestioned practice, particularly in developmental psychology, of establishing norms based on the study of white, middle-class male subjects. But it is also due to the tendency inherent in psychoanalysis to focus on the interior life of individuals and to pay less attention to the real impact of the environment (cf. Altman, 1995).

Just as individuals do not exist and grow in a vacuum, neither do couples, families, or groups. All children are born and develop within a culture—or, more typically, within multiple cultural systems that may overlap (Carter & McGoldrick, 1999). Culture is often thought of as the particular imprint of an individual's national or ethnic heritage, a world into which a child is born and develops that includes distinctive languages or dialects and patterns of speech; styles of dress; particular aesthetic forms of music, art, drama, and literature; particular foods; and particular forms of religious expression and identity. Culture may also include social mores, proper manners for social and business interactions, and moral taboos. Accepted norms for forming intimate social friendships and sexual partnerships and for child rearing also fall within the umbrella of "culture." They are the cultural maps through which "I-Thou" relationships are expressed. These are most often the rich qualities that come to mind when considering the value of cultural identity. They are the cultural treasures that individuals and groups love, identify with, and seek to protect.

Culture is not only a national or ethnic phenomenon. Cultures and subcultures may form around particular occupations, lifestyles, or sexual practices. Movements for social change frequently begin as "countercultural" groups that question the authority of prevailing cultural paradigms. Religious groups may become cultures or subcultures organized around religious identity and practice as a primary definer of self and group. Religious, artistic, social, and political subcultures frequently exist as havens of protection for individuals who do not conform to the mainstream of social norms and privilege. While an individual child may not grow physically, intellectually, or socially according to traditional developmental criteria, which were normed to middle-class, able-bodied, male Anglo-American subjects, there may be a subculture in which that child can flourish. Schools for the deaf, schools for the arts, religious schools, and all-girls' schools are all quite different examples of places in which the growth of children who do not necessarily do well according to established competitive norms may be positively encouraged so that they may reach their own unique potential. Such subcultures also allow for individual growth without sacrificing each child's unique constitutional or cultural endowment to a goal of assimilation.

Particular ideologies can also serve as organizing cores of cultures or subcultures, some more positive and growth-fostering than others. Ideological cultures, which do not necessarily identify with a national or ethnic heritage, may attract or even recruit new members. The more strongly ideological the subculture, whether a political group or a religious group or cult, the more likely it is to interact at an unconscious, projective level with the psychodynamics of the individual member to create a strong bond of mutual need, loyalty, or loss of autonomy in favor of a group identity.

Although ideological groups and cults are not rare, they do not constitute the center of most individuals' lives. No one escapes the force of culture, however. Ultimately, culture is the medium for all development, and for reality itself.

The Social Construction of Reality

Reality does not exist apart from the meaning that humans make of it. Therefore, the perception of reality is the chief "product" of all cognitive and emotional development. Because development does not occur in a vacuum, but in the context of culture and society, *reality is socially constructed* (Berger & Luckmann, 1966). This social construction, further, is a construction not only of what is, but of how things happen. At the scientific level, this is the construction of "paradigms," in which theories about the way the world works generate certain questions for investigation and preclude others (Kuhn, 1970). At the social level, it is the construction of familial, group, social, and institutional arrangements and structures of political power. It is the usually unconscious and unnamed "way things are" that keeps decision-making in the hands of some groups and individuals, and not others. How does this work?

All development takes place in a social matrix in which reality is defined in and through relationships. People, places, and things, and particular aspects of them, are given existence through the social act of naming. This act of naming is inescapably an exercise of power, which can take the form of either stewardship or domination. As in the biblical creation story in Genesis 2:19–20a, God entrusts Adam with the stewardship of all the animals by giving Adam the power to name them. But not all practices of naming are so benign. Power and privilege are distributed according to the meanings given to certain realities and according to the naming or lack of naming of certain individuals' experiences. Groups hold social dominance by naming and conferring meaning on certain realities, but also by refusing to see and to name realities that are experienced by other social groups. Many realities are not named, especially realities experienced by groups who do not share social dominance and privilege. These are most often realities that, if named, would reveal the pernicious aspects of the prevailing social power structure, such as gender and race discrimination or assumptions about able-bodied-ness (Eiesland, 1994). They are therefore left unnamed and are not given the status of reality. Individuals and groups who do attempt to give voice to their experience often find themselves in the position of having to choose between their own reality and the authorized, named reality of the dominant group. The act of choosing their own reality is an act of courage, because it carries the risk of being labeled delusional.

Language and Power

Language is central to the maintenance of structures of power in another way as well. As the philosopher Michel Foucault (1988, 1994) showed in his monumental studies of early twentieth-century mental institutions and medical clinics, professional training often is not only an education about the subject matter of concern to the profession but is also an initiation into an exclusive world of coded language, to which only professionals are given the key. Foucault showed how much of the role of the professional or expert revolved around the maintenance of social power (Foucault, 1980), again, conferred by the power of naming.

All human persons are thus born into a world of language in which the acquisition of language itself serves as a primary initiation into a social and systemic construction of reality. In the theory of the French psychoanalyst Jacques Lacan (1966/1977), this primary acquisition of language is both a vehicle for and itself a constitutive element of the child's inevitable acquiescence during the Oedipal phase to what he terms the "symbolic order," and the "law of the father." Feminist theorists, particularly Julia Kristeva (1986), Hélène Cixous (1994; Cixous & Clement, 1975/1986), and Luce Irigaray (1974/1985), have further clarified that language itself is both the medium and the message of patriarchy (see Moi, 1985; Kim, St. Ville, & Simonaitis, 1993).

Development, particularly cognitive development, is inextricably related to the capacity first for symbolization and then for verbalization of experience. But all verbalization is learned in a social context, and the acquisition of language is a culturally mediated process that also is inextricably related to social structures of power and privilege. At the most obvious social level, children who grow up in environments of relative lack of power and privilege are not only frequently deprived of the material resources that would support their growth, such as adequate housing, nutrition, clothing, and education, but they also grow up within a different "language game" (Wittgenstein, 1953; Lyotard, 1979/1984). Children of privilege tend to learn only the dominant language of the culture and are initiated into increasingly complex usages of that one language. Children who, because of racial or economic oppression, grow up excluded from circles of privilege often learn to become "bilingual" or, in the words of W. E. B. DuBois (1903/1961), develop a "bicultural consciousness." Like all children, they are acculturated into the language and meaning-making patterns of their own immediate cultural environment, but also, as a matter of survival, may become increasingly adept at decoding the language of privileged groups as well. This brings the benefit of survival, but with it also comes the absorption of meanings from the dominant culture's language that devalue and denigrate oppressed groups and name them as inferior. As this "language game" is internalized, so hatred can be internalized as self-hatred. The saying "Black is beautiful," coined by the Black Power movement in the 1960s, is a good example of a conscious attempt to counter this process of internalization of oppression. It was a reclaiming of sacred creative power of naming, to restore pride in African American identity, and to declare it good. It takes many such acts of power to overcome the dominant social structures of power and to reclaim the power of naming for oneself and one's own group.

Gender and sexual orientation are social constructions that exist in complex relationship to other realities of power, privilege, and oppression. Although the biological realities of male and female bodies may be understood as givens, the meanings given them are again socially constructed. What it means to grow up in a male or female body may be taught as an unquestioned reality, but is, in fact, an interpretation. Similarly, to grow up gay, lesbian, or bisexual may have very different meanings in different cultures and subcultures. In most contexts, feminine gender and gay, lesbian, or bisexual sexual orientation are categories of oppression. For women and for lesbians and gay men of color, these socially constructed realities add a "double whammy" to the experience of racial and economic oppression. For white women and for white lesbians and gay men, there is a fragmentation experience in which social and institutional power is conferred due to race privilege, but at the same time, gender and/or sexual orientation oppression is a constant, though often unnamed, reality. Children who grow up female or homosexual may be initiated into the language game of privilege, only to find that, for them, it does not open the doors that it opens for white, heterosexual males. Economic class oppression further heightens this disparity of power, so that working-class and poor women and girls, gay men, and lesbians are excluded even more from decision-making positions in institutions of power, including education, industry, and government.

All forms of ongoing, structural, institutional oppression are maintained by economic, physical, and sexual violence, which are the largest but often least clearly named signs of injustice. In the United States, certain forms of oppression–especially racial violence, economic oppression, and violence against women and homosexuals–establish the particular map of reality into which each person is born. Every human person without exception around the world is also born, and must develop, embedded in his or her own culture. And every culture is formed by a combination of language and, to varying degrees, violence, which may be racial, economic, or gender-based, or a combination of these and other forms of oppression. Language and violence combine to create a "reality" that defines each individual's identity and names his or her place within the hierarchical structures of power.

Developing a Critical Stance

Persons are born into cultures and receive their imprint. Individuals are also constitutive members of their cultures, and from birth they help to shape and construct the cultures in which they are embedded. Culture itself, then, is a "Thou" with whom a person, an "I," may enter into a mutually formative relatedness. What gives an individual the resilience to take one step back psychologically from the culture(s) in which one is embedded, to see and name realities that commonly have been left unseen or unnamed and to develop a critique of one's own cultural inheritance, including its most oppressive aspects?

At least two factors seem to be essential in allowing an individual to develop a critical stance toward his or her own cultural surround: exposure to other cultures and worldviews, and a capacity for empathy and mutual perspective-taking. First is the exposure to alternative cultures, which present alternative "language games" and ways of understanding one's own embedded worldview. One cannot take the perspective of another person, another worldview, without coming into meaningful contact with the other. The more insulated an individual is from other national, ethnic, and linguistic communities, the less opportunity there is to place one's own assumptions into a critical or even self-reflective light.

But the capacity for taking the perspective of another is also, as traditionally understood by most developmental theories, a cognitive and emotional achievement. It requires, at minimum, the cognitive capacity for reciprocal operations (Piaget, 1937/1954). Making the imaginative leap of seeing from another's point of view also means taking the risk of being exposed to criticism or harm, as well as the risk of being changed by what one learns from the new perspective. This requires a capacity for empathy, the ability to stand in another's shoes. This capacity, as discussed above, requires a sufficient foundation of having been treated empathetically and responded to in such a way that the world seems safe enough to risk setting aside one's own aims, at least temporarily, in the service of greater understanding (Kohut, 1977). Empathy can be seriously impaired by childhood trauma, which has the power to wound one's primal sense of security, basic goodness, and trust in the reliability of the world, and also one's confidence in the basic sufficiency and goodness of one's own self.

One of the benefits of greater knowledge and insight about one's own individual developmental process and the contours of one's own inner landscape, is that the tendency to project one's own fantasies, experiences, and inner objects onto (or into) other persons and institutions tends to recede. Sometimes, especially where there has been significant trauma or deprivation, psychotherapy can foster a healing process of self-reflection that can in turn nurture one's capacity for empathy. Sometimes, constructive new relationships and learning experiences can serve a similar function in strengthening one's ability to enter into meaningful encounters with other points of view.

Cultures are not monolithic (Geertz, 1973). Whenever the issue of cultural context is invoked, individual cultures tend to be described in terms of general characteristics, which frequently do not adequately depict the richness of variations within their communities. Individuals within cultures are not only embedded in them, but act upon them and create new variations within them. As an individual grows and develops, he or she makes meaning of the cultural surround. Some of these meanings will subtly or even radically shape the culture itself.

Further, cultures themselves do not simply exist, they also grow and develop, like the individual self. And like the individual self, they do not grow in a vacuum. Multiple national, ethnic, and linguistic groups coexist and comingle, and international migration brings increasing numbers of groups into contact with one another. Each contact has the potential for genuine encounters in which new meanings, and thus new realities, may be made. Idealized or "pure" cultures that are invoked to represent the identity of individuals, families, and groups actually function as "imagined communities" (Anderson, 1983; also cited in Benhabib, 1995). As Seyla Benhabib has pointed out, recent debates about culture have tended to operate on four faulty assumptions: regarding cultures and value systems as "self-consistent, pre-reflexive wholes; as sealed off from one another; as internally unified"; and as "systems of meaning, value, and interpretation which must also be reproduced over time by individuals under the constraints of a material way of life" (1995, p. 244).

Just as interpersonal relationships are increasingly being recognized as co-constructing the reality that is shared between two individual I's and Thou's, and thereby in some sense continually recreating and reconstituting the sense of self, meaning, and purpose of each partner, so, too, do cultures interact in a "potential space" (Winnicott, 1971, p. 41) in which new meanings are given and new realities can be created. This interaction of cultures does not usually happen *en masse,* however. It is carried out most often in intimate dyads and in genuine interactions among small groups of people. Individuals who are committed to change can do so most effectively not through maneuvers to replace one dominant force with another, but rather through engagement with others and participation in a process of mutual creation.

Lives of Commitment

Within most developmental schemata, there is usually a "stage" assigned to the years beyond midlife, in which individuals are said to achieve a more altruistic, generative, or universal perspective (e.g., Erikson, 1950/ 1963; Fowler, 1981; Maslow, 1998). Beyond the capacity for one-to-one perspective taking comes a capacity for commitment to constructive change in the world. In order to inquire about what constitutes such commitment, social researchers Daloz, Keen, Keen, and Parks interviewed 145 individuals whom they identified as having a commitment to the common good, evidenced in their ability to articulate how their life work served the well-being of society as a whole, as well as qualities of perseverance, resilience, and ethical congruence between life and work. Through these interviews, the authors identified several key factors that appeared to be significant in the development of sustained "lives of commitment" (1996, p. 17). These factors include a loving home environment in childhood, the example of at least one parent who worked actively for the public good, opportunities and challenges to be of service to others during adolescence, exposure to cross-cultural experiences, and a good mentoring experience in young adulthood. The more such experiences were present, the authors found, the more likely the individual would be to grow into a mature adult life of commitment to the common good.

Families collectively may also participate in this ongoing process of mutual influence and social change. It is not only true that "it takes a village to raise a child," but it might equally be said that it takes individual children and adults, families, and groups to "raise a village." Anderson and Johnson (1994), based on a Christian theological framework, have proposed a model of family as a "just community" (p. 81), and a "crucible" of social responsibility, in which "the needs of the individual and the needs of the community are negotiated and balanced" (p. 107).

Time and Eternity

All such social and cultural developments finally occur not as single events, but as ongoing processes within the overarching framework of time. In the context of faith, this may also be understood as occurring not only within the generally linear human perception of time, but within the eschatological future-present of God's time.

Theologians are familiar with the notion that there are at least two kinds of time, represented by two words in biblical Greek: *chronos* and *kairos*. As mentioned at the beginning of this chapter, development is usually discussed only in terms of the first, a concept of time as linear, forward moving, and measurable. But development occurs in the context of both linear time and eternity.

In linear time, individuals are born, grow, and die within identifiable historical epochs. Every individual is born into a "cohort group" of persons born roughly during the same political and historical era (Ryder, 1965; Elder, 1998; Elder, Modell, & Parke, 1994). Significant events, particularly traumatic ones such as natural disasters, wars, or assassinations, can serve as symbolic markers for the experience of entire generations of people. Generations are sometimes even identified by the dramatic events, social trends, or political movements that occurred during their formative years. A child born at the turn of the twentieth century and a child born at the turn of the new millennium might go through nearly identical physiological stages of maturation and somewhat similar psychological changes, but theories of individual development would not adequately explain the differences in the lives of those two individuals and their respective beliefs and behaviors.

Technological changes alone would account for a very different experience of the world, and a different set of expectations about how to live and even about longevity itself. Large-scale historical events can also shape the worldview of entire groups of individuals. For example, the generation who served in World War II tends to have a very different view of the morality of war and the trustworthiness of political institutions than those who were drafted during the Vietnam War. Children of individuals who experienced historical periods of enduring hardship or crisis also tend to be formed in their worldview by the experiences of their parents–for example, the children of parents who lived through the Depression. Children whose parents survived extreme trauma, as in the Holocaust, also may be heir to the previous generation's worldview, as shaped by those traumatic historical events. Meanings, philosophies, and commitment or lack of commitment may be shared by large groups of people who have endured shared losses, victories, or disillusionments.

Time is not only linear. The human life journey is not only a forward moving line, but a circle or spiral, in which meanings are made, changed, remade, and regathered in dynamic relation with persons, groups, and cultures, past, present, and in potential. The meaning of a life cannot adequately be charted only as a story of progress. Life is also a process of continual formation and re-formation as other lives enter the story. Finally, our stories are given residence within the hearts and experiences of other people and their stories. Religiously committed individuals further understand their personal stories, and the stories of others with whom their own lives are intertwined, as resonating with God's eternal story, as revealed in their holy scriptures. The stories of individuals, families, and groups also participate in ancient sacred patterns, such as biblical narratives of liberation from bondage, of exile and return, of brokenness and healing, and of death and resurrection.

All human life from before birth is created within and for relationship. Genuine encounter with the other, however, past the inner realm of fantasy and projection, past reified boundaries and mores of family and group, and past cultural barriers often is fragile and fleeting. Moments of joining nevertheless do take place at both conscious and unconscious levels and in the space between individuals, in the words of Winnicott (1965), in the "potential space" where imagination, fantasy, and mutual experience come together to create new understandings. Furthermore, true meetings, however fleeting, are not simply isolated moments. When individuals become intentional about seeking genuine I-Thou encounters with the other, this has the potential for building greater ongoing possibilities for connection and cooperation. In the words of Buber, "the moments of supreme encounter are no mere flashes of lightning in the dark but like a rising moon in a clear starry night" (1936/1970, p. 163). When this openness to encounter becomes a *habitus*, a committed practice, it promotes dialogue not only between individuals but also among groups, communities, and cultures. We study development in relational and cultural context, finally, so that our awareness may expand and enable us to participate more fully in the sacred, storied conversation that embraces all people across all time.

> The anchoring of time in a relation-oriented life of salvation and the anchoring of space in a community unified by a common center: only when both of these come to be and only as long as both continue to be, a human cosmos comes to be and continues to be around the invisible altar, grasped in the spirit out of the world stuff of the eon.
>
> BUBER, 1936/1970, P. 163

CHAPTER 4

The Family Context of Development

African American Families

Edward Wimberly

The society in which we live is characterized by the realities of a high-tech economy: de-industrialization and the relocation of industrial jobs to the Third World, the predominance of consumer values, the loosening of cross-generational ties, and the weakening of support systems and mediating structures that once assisted persons through the life cycle (Billingsley, 2000; West, 1993; Wimberly, 1982). The resulting impact of these many social and cultural factors on the life cycle of all ethnic groups, particularly African Americans, is profound. Racial discrimination further exacerbates the impact on the life cycle.

For example, racial discrimination and economic marginality influence how life-cycle tasks are negotiated, how identity formation is developed, and how the stresses of life-cycle transition are handled (Wimberly, 1997). Andrew Billingsley has pointed out that the strengths of black families that have existed since slavery are now being eroded as a result of the modern era. Strong family-oriented values, strong emphasis on blood ties and bonds, reverence for elders, caring for children, individual rights being subservient to relational ties, a deep sense of spirituality, and the conviction that life is sacred are in severe decline (Billingsley, 2000). Cornel West has pointed out that there is a prevailing nihilism that seems to be related to the changes in values. For him, nihilism is evident in the loss of meaning and purpose in life that accompanies the social forces undermining the African American family (West, 1993). All these factors lessen the cross-generational ties that are needed for African Americans and other ethnic groups to successfully negotiate life-cycle tasks and transitions.

I see the impact of these many factors in my counseling practice with African American young adults who have made it into the job market but lack the necessary emotional and social skills to sustain close and intimate relationships. Such relational skills are an outgrowth of the successful negotiation of earlier developmental stages, particularly identity versus role confusion in the Eriksonian epigenetic scheme of individual development (Erikson, 1950/1963). The point that subsequent development in the life cycle is built on previous stages of the life cycle has proven to be clinically accurate for African Americans.

An illustration from my counseling practice will be instructive. A thirty-year-old African American male counselee described himself as sexually addicted. He spent hard-earned money on phone sex and strip shows. He had no close relationships and felt alienated from his family. He felt emotionally abandoned by his parents in his early childhood and lost his closest childhood friend at four years of age when his parents moved to another part of the country. He said he had never regained the closeness to friends that he had when he was four. In fact, he thought that his social skills were arrested at that point, and he had used sexual outlets as a substitute for true intimacy ever since. He found it hard to maintain close relationships and feared such contact.

The family within which this young man grew up taught him that manhood meant being disconnected from others, developing strenuous willpower to overcome personal failures. He therefore learned very early not to depend on relationships in handling life-cycle transitions. This young man's father was a high-tech enthusiast who sacrificed his family relationships in order to pursue the American dream. He mentored his son to be a relational refugee (Wimberly, 2000) who relied on himself alone to transit through the life cycle. He felt as if he could not rely on his mother emotionally, because she was too angry at his father for emotionally abandoning her.

In my mind, this young man aptly illustrates the fallout of the societal factors mentioned earlier. Both high-tech, market-driven values and nihilism can be seen in the young man's life. The impact of race is not as evident. Yet the way his father was driven to succeed and move his family from the South was motivated by the racial discrimination of the 1970s.

In order for African Americans and other ethnic groups to negotiate the life-cycle tasks that are common to all human beings, the support structures that once sustained African American families prior to 1960 must be restored. Basic to this restoration is an understanding of the relational and spiritual needs of human beings that are being trivialized by our high-tech and market-driven society. This chapter focuses on restoring the cross-generational support systems needed to successfully negotiate individual, marital, and family life-cycles transitions.

Human Beings as Social Creatures

One of the major assumptions of this chapter is that participation in cross-generational relationships serves to mentor children, youth, and young adults throughout the life cycle in the wisdom of past generations and the communal traditions conveyed through ritual. For example, African American sociologist Benjamin Bowser says that there was a time when the elders in the community were the primary socializing agents orienting young people and young adults to the practices, customs, patterns, and beliefs of that particular community and the world. Membership in a church and participation in family life were seen as central and important (Bowser, 1989). He goes on to indicate that this is no longer the case. Urbanization, radio, and television have eroded the once coherent world of the past to the extent that today's youth and young adults are the first generation to be completely reared by electronic media and its images, according to Bowser. The strengths of the past, including church membership and participation in family life and rituals, are being replaced by substitutes for direct experience and participation in these communal dimensions. Youth and young adults sense a loss of participation and experience isolation and abandonment of a kind not experienced by previous generations.

Participation, not isolation, fuels successful negotiation of the life cycle. Full participation in communal life has a positive impact on life-cycle transitions such as birth, death, marriage, employment, midlife transitions, retirement, and others. Black developmental psychologists point to the significance of cross-generational mentoring relationships not only for children, youth, and young adults but also for those adults moving toward midlife and retirement. One study, for example, focuses on the role of cross-generational support systems in the lives of African Americans throughout the life span. Support systems are patterns of consistent communal ties that help people maintain emotional, physical, and spiritual well-being as they transit through the various stages of the life cycle (Wimberly, 1976). The functions of the support systems are to provide stability, connectedness, and reciprocity in relationships along the life span. They also help to establish obligations and normative expectations about such things as care and assistance (Taylor & Chatters, 1989). These support expectations help to foster long-term bonds and associations. Bonds foster closeness in formal and informal support systems and are surely needed during life crises and transitions.

The church is one of the major support systems for African Americans. Taylor and Chatters conclude:

Blacks are often affiliated with a church at an early age and develop long term associations with them. Churches are integrally involved with a variety of life events and transitions such as marriage, the birth of children, personal illness, and death of significant others. Several studies suggest that church involvement variables (i.e., frequency of attendance, perceived importance of church attendance and religion, and church membership) are important as determinants of the receipt of support from church members. (1989, p. 250)

There is also additional data indicating that cross-generational support systems are significant to African Americans across the life span. For instance, African Americans are more likely than whites to live in extended family households (Taylor & Chatters, 1989). Such arrangements in living not only benefit the individual, marital, and family life cycles, they also assist family members with other important survival needs, including economic needs and racial discrimination.

The purpose of this brief review of support systems is to emphasize that the quality of survival for African Americans in the United States has depended on their participation in support systems such as the local congregation and the extended family. Economic hardships and racial discrimination necessitated this, as did the fact that human beings are social and participatory creatures who need human interaction and involvement. African Americans, however, are increasingly participating in our high-tech and de-industrialized economy with all of its worldview influences and accompanying negative impact on support systems. Part of the fallout of our high-tech culture is the separation of human beings from their relational roots, resulting in a sense of nihilism or meaninglessness. Children, youth, and young adults today are more vulnerable to this reality than their parents or grandparents.

Over the years, I have encountered many African American families who have had enough of the so-called good life of climbing the corporate ladder of success. Many have become tired of uprooting their families every three or four years in pursuit of the American dream of economic prosperity and financial independence. Some have decided to stop the endless climb and lay down more permanent roots by establishing networks of relationships, particularly through the church.

One particular family had moved on average of once every three years. Finally, they decided not to move anymore. Their children were tired of leaving friends behind and having to make new ones all the time. The wife wanted to pursue some career options that she had not been able to fulfill. The husband was feeling the need to get more connected to church activities as a family and to deepen his relational and spiritual self. Slowly, this family realized that the corporate vision was preventing them from meeting many of their needs.

Once the family decided to stay put and to give up the economic rewards of continued upward mobility, the impact on the life-cycle transitions of each person was significant. Geographical stability gave them time to attend to each family member's life-cycle tasks. It also gave them time to deepen relational and spiritual roots. In other words, rooting geographically facilitated individual, marital, and family life-cycle transitions.

Support systems are not luxuries like jewelry or sports equipment. They are necessities of human existence. Part of our job as pastoral counselors is to make sure that this message is communicated loudly and clearly. Neither overt nor covert high-tech consumer values need to drown out relational voices, though the positive message of relationships may be hard to hear in our contemporary climate.

The Life Cycle as a Universal Reality

Another assumption of this chapter is that a life-cycle orientation is basic to all cultures whether the perspective employed relies on the behavioral sciences or analogies from the rhythms of nature. Not only are support systems universally needed for human beings throughout the life cycle, the reality of cycles of development for human beings and human institutions is universal as well; however, the content of the individual stages may vary from culture to culture and within cultures.

Several critical issues have emerged from a cross-cultural perspective regarding the human life span. One issue is whether the descriptive characteristics and contents of life-cycle transition vary across cultures and across gender. More specifically, the question is whether developmental theorists such as Freud, Erikson, and Levinson are describing a biased sample of white males from the middle class whose experiences are culturally bound or limited.

Carter and McGoldrick (1989) do not assume the universal application of white, middle-class, male categories to all cultures and to gender. African American scholars point to the fact that economic, gender, racial, and environmental factors influence life cycle-development as well (Ruffin, 1989; Gooden, 1989; Harrison, 1989; P. Bowman, 1989). For example, Winston Gooden and Janice Ruffin conclude that African Americans need a much broader model of human development than that provided by Freud and Erikson. Gooden and Ruffin note that the focus of stage theory is on pattern sequences of stages with particular physical, emotional, and cognitive spheres. They find Levinson's concept of life structure more suited for African American adults because the focus transcends individual personality factors alone and brings into focus the social and cultural worlds that impact the life cycle (Levinson, 1978). Thus, they emphasize the significance of both intrapersonal and extrapersonal dimensions in life-span theory.

Though Gooden and Ruffin found Levinson's life structure helpful to them, they demonstrated that the specific characteristics of the life structure were culturally different because of race and ethnicity. For example, Ruffin (1989) studied black women, who revealed that they could not rely on whites to mentor them in their careers and had to rely on support systems and families within the African American community and other types of professional assistance. The process of mentoring was completely different from that of white women, who could often expect "on the job" mentoring by white colleagues. It can be concluded from Ruffin and others that the development of life structure through the life span is impacted greatly by the socialization process. Values, beliefs, and convictions that make up the worldview of many support systems in the black community also sustain persons as they develop their life structures.

Life structure refers to that bridge between the inner life of the individual and the social world that is made up of choices one makes with regard to marriage, occupation, key friendships, and relationship to parents (Gooden, 1989). At each stage of the life cycle, the life structure that is developed and modified during periods of transition is solidified during stable periods of the life cycle. It is the fact that African Americans must develop their individual life structures in a hostile racial environment that makes the concept of life structure important. Participation in the life of the community contributes significantly to the development and enhancement of life structure. According to Gooden (1989), without engagement in roles that are valued by the community and in relationships of personal significance, development of the life structure and life's meaning are held together by fantasy.

Gender and African American Women's Life Cycle

Not only do race and ethnicity impact the life structure within life-cycle development of African Americans, gender is also an important variable as well. This is particularly the case with regard to African American women. For example, Janice Ruffin (1989) empirically explored the applicability of Levinson's concept of life structure to the lives of African American women. Although several of Levinson's premises were not supported by her research, Ruffin's data did suggest that the concept of life structure was valuable in organizing the life histories of the women studied and in describing the changes that took place in their lives, particularly when race and ethnicity were factors. She also found that the concept of choice proved very helpful in describing the restricted choices African American women faced given the racial climate that influenced their lives.

Specific gender findings of the research revealed greater variation in the timing and sequences of the periods of stability and transition in their adult lives when compared with white women. Another finding is that childbirth was a significant factor for them when compared with African American men at the same point in the life cycle. Yet their concern for autonomy and separation was comparable to that of African American men given their long heritage of work outside the home while raising children and caring for the home. Additionally, they were more embedded in social relationships than men were at the same period of the life cycle.

Spirituality across the Life Cycle

So far two assumptions have been explored. One assumption is that participation in community life is essential to human beings throughout the life cycle. The second is that life structure, the overarching pattern of choices that guide people's behavior and participation in community, is the key concept needed to connect the inner lives of people with their social and cultural context. However, it is not possible to talk about cultural and ethnic dimensions of the life structure of African Americans and many other ethnic groups without talking about spirituality.

In this section, a third assumption will guide our discussion. This assumption is that participation in community life means that African Americans are also impacted by spiritual values and convictions that influence life-cycle transitions and the development of life structures. Related to this assumption is a fourth, which assumes that spirituality is the fuel that powers the restoration of meaningful cross-generational support systems and mediating structures. *Mediating structures* are those institutions such as the family, extended family, local congregations, neighborhoods, supportive networks, and voluntary associations that stand between the individual and larger institutions of the public sphere (Wimberly, 1982). Spirituality is an important dimension in strengthening cross-generational support systems and mediating structures, because it facilitates successful development of life structures during life-span transitions.

Spirituality refers to the overarching meaning system–the dynamic force of cross-generational support systems and mediating structures–that holds together communal life. Systems of meaning and cross-generational support facilitate the development of life structures and successful movement through life-cycle stages. Spirituality can be understood in two basic ways: namely, as non-sectarian and sectarian. Non-sectarian refers to spirituality that is not tied to any particular religious community and is normally secular. On the one hand, non-sectarian spirituality generally refers to the dynamic that links human life to meaningful and purposeful ends, including values, beliefs, convictions, metaphors, and narratives that orient people to life (Fowler, 1981). Sectarian spirituality, on the other hand, performs essentially the same function of linking people to meaningful and purposeful ends and orienting people to life, but specific religious traditions are drawn on for this purpose (Wimberly, Wimberly, & Chingonzo, 1999). The understanding of spirituality put forward below is sectarian in the sense that it reflects a particular narrative orientation to a biblical worldview that has been appropriated by many African American Christians.

A narrative spirituality informed by stories from the Hebrew Bible and the New Testament is an overarching system of orientation that grows out of many African American Christians' reflection on their experience of racism in this culture. This orienting system performs many different functions that help to build relational bonds in community and assist individuals, couples, and families in successfully negotiating life-cycle transitions. These functions are symbolic, ritualistic, supportive, reparative, and meditative (Wimberly, Wimberly, & Chingonzo, 1999).

Symbolic functions refer to the ways that communal narratives, metaphors, and images bring meaning and purpose to the lives of their members and prevent nihilism. The dominant narratives that have assisted African American Christians have been biblical stories of the exodus, experiences in the wilderness, and Jesus' life, death, and resurrection. African American Christians have found analogous experiences with which to identify, and they have been able to fashion for themselves a spirituality that gives meaning to their lives.

Closely related to the symbolic function is the *ritualizing function,* which refers to the repetitive patterns of communal life that reinforce the narratives and their related orienting values. It is not enough to have narratives and images that orient life. Such narratives and images need to become the center around which the total community life is organized. Thus, it is through ritualistic memorials and practices that certain stories, images, and metaphors are celebrated and made part of the daily life of the community.

From narratives and metaphors that are ritually celebrated come support system values and expectations to maintain the very relational bonds that foster physical, emotional, relational, and spiritual wholeness. This is the *supportive function.* These values and expectations are what assist people in developing their life structures. Not only do narratives, metaphors, values, and expectations help maintain the ties that facilitate the development of life structures, they also bring healing during painful periods of life transition and crisis. Specific narratives, scriptures, religious poetry, and sayings are invoked by community members to address the needs of those who are in crisis and transition.

An example of how rituals support life structures comes from the experiences that my wife and I had in Zimbabwe. These experiences involved the reformulation of ritual ceremonies performed at one time in the village. Because of the breakup of the village, these rituals are being re-created in city churches in Zimbabwe. My wife and I have been teaching these rituals in our classes as a way to recover the value and functions of ritual activity.

The first examples are ceremonies for both future brides and grooms in which they are taught their specific roles in marriage. These ceremonies involve several phases. In village life, the aunts and uncles of the future bride and groom set aside time to teach the future bride and groom about the values and expectations of married life in the village. Today, women and men from church groups now take over the teaching as the aunts and uncles once did. At the appointed time, the group gathers by gender. The first hour there is preaching, singing, and story-telling using the Bible. In the second hour there is story-telling about the participants' relationship with the future bride and groom, similar to what we call "roasting." In the third hour, there is very frank and open talk about the sexual act and the expectations related to marital intimacy.

The purpose of such ritualistic activity is to order experiences in ways that preserve cherished marital values. This activity also privileges selected community and faith tradition stories that help to support the communal life of all. These acts reinforce certain values and contribute to the meaning-making surrounding this critical life-cycle transition. These activities also set the stage for the couples' meaning-making after the marriage.

A growing percentage of churches don't take these rituals for granted. Many pastors have gotten intentional about making sure these ancient traditions are preserved in the churches. There is an awareness of the collapsing ritual traditions in Africa, and faith communities are actually reinforcing them whenever they get a chance. My wife and I are sharing these traditions in this country as well.

Another example is a cake ceremony that is performed at the wedding. It symbolizes the joining of two extended families and not just two individuals. In many of our marital ceremonies in the United States, the unity candle is lit, symbolizing the uniting of the couple. African culture takes seriously the joining of two extended families where traditional obligations are performed throughout the couple's married life.

The ceremony is very simple. The pastor provides a brief sermon on the purpose of the ceremony, reflecting traditional village values as well as the values of the Christian community regarding marital and family life. Then, each spouse takes a piece of the wedding cake to each of the in-laws, symbolizing the act of becoming one family. The wedding attendants then take a piece of cake to each church member present, symbolizing the unity of the eschatological family of God in the person of Jesus Christ. The ritual is concluded with the appropriate prayers.

The cake ceremony was performed at my niece's wedding reception. I presented a brief homily focused on the family systems theory observation that two families were coming together. Each spouse was raised in a particular family of origin, and the family patterns from each spouse's family of origin could be a source of support as well as conflict as they sought to become a couple with a unique story. The cake ceremony was not to be a magical act in which the family differences are lessened; rather, the cake ceremony was an effort to make sure that all family members work hard to support marital life in the most mature and helpful ways possible. Firm boundaries needed to be established for each spouse's individual identity as well as clear boundaries separating the new couple from family members and in-laws. Balancing individuality and marital exclusiveness while maintaining extended family relationships was lifted up as very important.

Undergirding the thinking related to the cake ceremony was Murray Bowen's understanding of remaining self-differentiated while at the same time being connected with the family of origin. African Americans often get into trouble because there are African traditions regarding family of origin obligations. Sometimes family of origin expectations are stronger than marital obligations. Bowen's emphasis on balancing family ties with the need for individual autonomy helps us understand how it is possible for each spouse to maintain his or her self-differentiation and the boundaries of the marital subsystem while at the same time keeping contact with the extended family members (Bowen, 1978). Periodic contact with the extended family helps lessen the tension caused by the couple, firmly maintaining their spousal boundaries.

Finally, sectarian spirituality requires the transmission of its contents to the next generation. This is called the *mediating function.* Through this function, the stories, images, and values that build and sustain life throughout the life cycle are handed down from one generation to the next. This mediation is at the heart of the cross-generational family context of development. The elder generations are responsible for ensuring that the next generation has what it needs to negotiate its life-cycle tasks and build meaningful life structures.

The point to emphasize here is that spirituality is part and parcel of community life and encourages successful transition throughout the life cycle. The enumerated symbolic, ritualizing, and supportive functions are essential for maintaining adequate communal support systems and must be fostered intentionally in this high-tech, postindustrial age.

Spirituality impacts individual, marital, and family life cycles. An illustration of spirituality's impact is instructive. An African American family in which the husband and wife were in their early thirties with two very young children was in the expansion phase of the family life cycle. In the expansion phase of family life, young children are coming into the family, extending its boundaries (Wimberly, 1997). In the marital dimension of the couple's life cycle, they were still learning to accommodate each other's deep emotional needs while the husband pursued his career goals. The husband put in twelve-hour days while his wife performed the traditional homemaker roles. She was, however, getting increasingly frustrated with not getting any relief and help from him in the home, nor was she developing her own career identity.

Both realized that they were heading in a dangerous marital direction that could have negative consequences for their marriage and family. As one measure to try to break the lifestyle impasse, they decided to start attending church as a family. The wife found prayer partners and Bible study, and the husband joined a men's group. As a result, they became more sensitive to the other's emotional and vocational needs and found ways to accommodate each other's goals and aspirations. They attributed their growth as a couple to the spiritual and relational support they received from Bible study and church involvement. Thus, spirituality and relational support enabled them to deal better with individual, marital, and family transitions.

The relationship between spirituality and life-cycle development is emerging as an important area of research in the public health movement (Borysenko, 1993). Spirituality's link to the working of the immune system is being demonstrated scientifically, and church involvement is being linked to having healthy immune function as well. A healthy spirituality contributes to a positive outlook in life, and a positive outlook in life contributes to hope in our family relationships. Hope in a benevolent dynamic at work in our marital and family relationships in turn facilitates life-cycle transitions for families and their individual members (Butler, 2000).

Spiritual Mentoring

Living in a high-tech, postindustrial age requires more than an understanding of the meaning of spirituality and how it functions within community. There is also the need for those who are guides in support systems and mediating structures to provide a mentoring form of spirituality. Mentoring spirituality is crucial today because many of our children, youth, and young adults are similar to the young man introduced at the beginning of this chapter. Many people are what I have termed "relational refugees." Relational refugees have physical parents, but they feel left alone to negotiate the difficulties of life because they feel abandoned by their parental mentors (Wimberly, 2000). They desperately need mentoring from someone who guides them into a meaningful life. Mentoring has been understood solely in terms of role modeling, but it actually is much more comprehensive. Mentoring is a style of being present, a way of making persons who feel homeless and abandoned in the world feel at home. Such mentoring involves several levels of mimetic activity.

Those who need mentoring copy personality-building traits from their mentors through the psychological process of internalization (Wimberly, 2000). Following the principles of depth psychology, mentoring involves taking in personality traits of the mentor that can help those in need of mentoring to value themselves as whole human beings. By internalizing the mentor's positive attitude and approachability, the person being mentored discovers important dimensions of himself or herself and his or her life structures that he or she had not previously discerned.

The person being mentored also internalizes positive interactions between herself or himself and the mentor and utilizes them in ways that nurture the self through the life-structure–building tasks. Positive and nurturing interactions become focal scenes that are drawn on by the person developing a life structure, and these scenes help facilitate and clarify the choices that the person needs to make.

Persons being mentored also internalize the plots of stories mentors use in the mentoring process. Plots generally refer to the direction or movement of stories in positive or negative directions. Identification with positive plots moves people in positive and growth-facilitating directions, whereas identification with negative plots generally does the exact opposite. The presence of a mentor helps the seeker to identify with self-enhancing plots that she or he can use in developing adequate life structures.

Finally, mentoring includes role identification. Role modeling in building life structures involves exploring those roles that the mentor discerns as possibilities for the seeker. The mentor discerns gifts that the person being mentored has and calls those gifts to her or his attention. They explore together the implications these gifts have for that individual's life structure and for full participation in life as a whole.

While the mentoring described here may seem elementary and basic, it is not advisable to take anything for granted in this high-tech and postindustrial age. Many people come into adulthood without adequate mentoring and are in need of persons with whom they can temporarily identify in order to further their life-structuring tasks at different stages of the life cycle. For African Americans and other ethnic groups who have been reared in supportive religious networks, the life-structuring tasks will take on a spiritual direction. Therefore, spirituality and its intimate connection with the cultural life of the community cannot be ignored. Mentoring as described above is a form of spiritual direction when narratives and plots are used to help persons develop adequate life structures. Moreover, mentoring helps the person being mentored to dip into the resources of the spiritual legacies that lie behind faith communities. In short, the mentor in this model is an extension of the faith community that helps those needing mentoring to keep their connections with cross-generational support systems.

Emerging Moral Issues

The content of the values that get passed on from one generation to the next through ritual traditions and mentoring is very important. From the previous discussion of spirituality, there are certain values and moral themes that need to be highlighted. First, religious faith is very important, because it provides the language and symbols that integrate the life of the people. Second, human beings are viewed as spiritual and religious beings who interact and participate in community where central values are to be celebrated. Third, the role of communal stories and biblical stories is critical in the growth and development of persons. And finally, ritual is significant because it is fundamental to the communal life of the people. These values undergird the moral structure of society and are passed on through the mediating structures of the culture.

One moral issue in transmitting values from one generation to the next has to do with how mediating structures support the growth and development of its members when those members act differently from the cherished values held sacred in the mediating structures. Divergent values often come to the surface in life-cycle transitions and as a result introduce conflict into the resolution of the transitions.

One positive thing about many African and African American mediating structures is the narrative process and grace orientation undergirding them. The narrative orientation in mediating structures and support systems has historically emphasized the connection between its relational structures and the extension of grace to those who are different. Exclusion of people for difference is not the primary goal. Rather, the primary goal is to keep all members connected with the community regardless of their difference. Traditionally, it was believed that connecting to the mediating structures and support systems was crucial in facing racial oppression, and being disconnected left one unmercifully vulnerable. This value and emphasis on connecting has allowed a great deal of behavioral and attitudinal latitude within mediating structures and support systems.

As the mediating structures and support systems break down in the African American community, the propositional and legalistic approach seems to be replacing the narrative orientation to nurturing persons. The level of impact on the lives of persons in these mediating structures is not as significant as it once was. Unfortunately, one of the ethical and moral strengths of African American churches, the former emphasis on inclusion and grace, is breaking down. As a result, some people are being alienated from the church.

Historically, African American mediating structures and support systems have emphasized development of human character as the result of participation in community and being shaped by its story. This is a narrative view of human character formation and not a propositional view. The propositional view sees human character formation primarily as the result of the making and enforcement of laws; the narrative orientation places the emphasis on full involvement. This means that legalism in morality was not central. Love, grace, and nurture are (or were) the central values governing character formation.

Systemic Narrative Pastoral Counseling

Several different perspectives have come together to help give shape to this chapter. These perspectives include cross-generational thinking, life-cycle understandings, spirituality, and family systems thinking. The critical concern of this section is how these different perspectives are held together in a systemic and integrated whole, providing a conceptual framework for intervention in African American families. The integrative dimension proposed here is systemic narrative pastoral counseling.

Systemic narrative pastoral counseling is grounded in the faith story of African American Christians and draws resources from faith narratives, the historical and cultural past of African Americans, and family systems theory to respond to African Americans in need of care. Systemic narrative pastoral counseling begins with the belief that African Americans are part of God's eschatological family (Wimberly, 1997). The universal eschatological family of God is made up of all who allow God's salvation drama to become the center of their lives. Members of this family see themselves as loved and cared for by God and invited to this family by God. God is the welcoming host, and no human being can deny anyone entrance into this family. The invitation is initiated and confirmed eternally by God. African Americans have adopted this view of themselves as members of God's household, and as a result, we have also affirmed our right to be full participants in God's creation here on earth. Thus, our marital, family, and extended family stories are linked forever with God's story, because our stories are now part of God's legacy as well as God's unfolding future.

This affirmation of being God's children in God's family has undergirded the worldview of African American Christians and has been the central norm used to support certain strengths of African American families. For example, the extended and communal nature of family life is a cherished value of African Americans. Being cross-generationally connected is another important value for African Americans. The emphasis on being cross-generationally connected racially and culturally as well as being members of God's eschatological family has been a central resource for our meaningful participation and survival in the United States.

These understandings are crucial when pastoral counselors work with African American marriages and families. Nancy Boyd-Franklin (1989) emphasizes the need for family therapists to include the legacy of religious values in working with African American families. Using religious values deeply lodged in African American marriages and families, along with a multisystems approach based on a variety of family systems practitioners and thinkers, serves to undergird the narrative approach to marriage and family counseling recommended here.

Systemic narrative pastoral counseling is also grounded in life-cycle and systemic understandings (Wimberly, 1997). Life-cycle theory emphasizes the movement of the extended family through a series of stages and phases throughout the life span. There are certain predictable periods of transition through which the extended family goes as it grows and develops. Moreover, as the extended family grows and develops, boundaries or lines of flexible demarcation between individuals, family subsystems, and generations must be formed. The family systems theories of Murray

Bowen have been very helpful in understanding these boundaries. Interventions with families and extended families emphasize self-differentiation as well as relating cross-generationally while maintaining clear generational boundaries. In summary, systemic narrative pastoral care of African American families is the result of a rich correlation of several different theological, cultural, historical, and behavioral science disciplines and practices. It is a major resource for assisting African American families strained by economic, transitional, or relational challenges in becoming whole and functional.

Conclusion

The focus of this chapter has been on the restoration of those support systems and mediating structures that African Americans and other ethnic groups need to negotiate life-span transitions (see also Lyon & Smith, 1998). To this end, emphasis has been placed on the fact that human beings need cross-generational supportive relationships throughout the life span. This chapter also explored the relevance of life-cycle perspectives for cross-cultural application, whether they were based on behavioral science models or on analogies from the world of nature. We concluded that people in all cultures go through life-cycle transitions, although the specific content of the phases or stages is different and unique reflecting the particular cultural experiences of those within that group. This chapter supports the consensus among African American life-span theorists that Daniel Levinson's (1978) concept of life structure is theoretically useful because it helps them describe the interaction between inner dimensions of personality growth and cultural factors.

Because cultural factors are intricately involved with the development of life structures, spirituality was explored for its impact on life-cycle development. Spirituality permeates support system and mediating structure processes. Spirituality supports life-cycle transitions and life structure development. Spiritual mentors or guides help those needing mentoring to draw on specific spiritual resources. Systemic narrative pastoral counseling also is a major resource on which spiritual mentors can draw to assist African American families. In conclusion, spirituality is a necessary component in restoring the viability of cross-generational support systems and mediating structures in African American and other ethnic communities.

PART TWO

Life-Cycle Stages of Development

CHAPTER 5

Infancy

Faith before Language

Roy Herndon SteinhoffSmith

Numerous students of the relation between the individual human life cycle and faith have paid special attention to infancy. For example, Erik Erikson (Wulff, 1997) describes the basic task of infancy as the establishment of enough trust in the self, others, and the world that the becoming person can hope in the future. Infants learn this trust with an empathic primary caretaker who forms an especially close bond with the baby. The caretaker and infant experience moments of positive emotional attunement to each other as numinous–filled with light, security, and joy. Religious institutions, especially through their rituals, provide opportunities for adults to renew their trust and hope through a return to this numinous world. These institutions also help the caretaker to enter into the numinous meetings with her or his infant.

Body, Soul, and Spirit

Students of infancy and faith agree that what they study cuts across the three registers that define human existence. The *body* comprises the physical givens of human reality, the register that biologists, physiologists, and geneticists study. *Soul,* the register that some psychologists, philosophers, religious scholars, and theologians study, includes all that a human being consciously and unconsciously senses, experiences, knows, and remembers.

Some psychologists, sociologists, philosophers, religious scholars, and theologians study the third register, that of the *spirit*. Martin Buber (1936/1970) defined the *spirit* as that which lies between a person and another. In this *between, I* and *Thou* co-create each other. I prefer to use *spirit*, defined in this way–rather than its possible synonyms, *social, cultural, interpersonal,* or *intersubjective*–to name this relational register, for three reasons. First, each of the synonyms wrongly suggests that this *between* exists as an epiphenomenon of society, culture, persons, or subjects. *Spirit* correctly connotes the *between* as a necessary and primary reality. Second, none of the synonyms connotes as well as does *spirit* the co-creativity of beings in relation. Third, *spirit* correctly suggests that these mutually creative relations take place not just between persons, but also between persons and other natural and socially constructed beings.

A reading of the research on infant development in infancy leads to a reformulation of Erikson's understanding of the relation between infancy and faith. *Faith* denotes an orientation, a particular set of characteristic behaviors, beliefs, attitudes, and feelings with which one faces, relates to, and moves into reality. A child emerges from infancy with the first such orientation. Infancy thus establishes a primary faith. Later events, in childhood and adulthood, may modify this initial orientation or even replace it with another. Still, this infant faith remains as the direction one faced at the beginning of life.

I have deliberately avoided using exclusively theological or religious definitions of terms such as *faith, soul,* and *spirit.* Theological definitions tend to capture these terms for a particular, usually Christian, religious tradition, whereas I seek to use them in such a way that people with very different religious or secular perspectives can grasp them. I do not seek to add a *faith* dimension to psychological and social scientific studies of infancy, but to discover what *faith* might mean in the light of these studies.

In the following discussion, I use Daniel Stern's *The Interpersonal World of the Infant* (1985) as the primary resource. I have not found a more comprehensive and elegant exploration of the psychology of the first two years of life. We can break infancy into three phases, each characterized by:

A period of time: the first, between birth and two to four months; the second, between two to four months and seven to nine months; the third, between seven to nine months and fifteen to eighteen months

A primary register or focus of research: the body, the soul, or the spirit

An emergent dimension of faith: in the first phase, hope; in the second phase, trust; in the third phase, love.

Three Phases of Infancy

Phase One: Hope

In the first phase, beginning at birth and lasting until the second through fourth month of life, researchers primarily observe what is happening *to* the infant's *body*–changes in the infant's biology, behavior, and perception.

During this phase, the infant's nervous system matures (as it will continue to do until late adolescence). In the cerebral cortex, new neurons develop, nerve cells get larger, and the interconnections among neurons increase greatly. Myelin sheaths, which allow for quicker interaction among neurons, begin to cover these connecting extensions. These changes both make possible and are the result of the newborn's behavioral and perceptual interactions with others and the world (Sroufe, Cooper, & DeHart, 1996).

Newborns move quickly among a number of different states of sleep, distress, and wakefulness. In the first months of life, the onset of, time spent in, and transitions between these states become more predictable, largely as a result of interactions with caregivers (Sroufe et al., 1996; Stern, 1985).

Infants have certain reflexes that help them to survive. Some of these–such as "blinking, sneezing, and gagging" (Sroufe et al., 1996, p. 129)–remain throughout life. Others–such as rooting, sucking, grasping, and stepping–disappear in the first months as babies replace them with learned behaviors (Sroufe et al., 1996).

As babies' bodies rapidly grow, their motor skills become more differentiated. Increasingly fine control develops from the head downward and from the trunk outward. Interaction with others and the environment, in addition to neurological and physical maturation, shapes what skills develop, how they develop, and the speed of their development. Most importantly for researchers on the first months of life, infants can visually track objects and lift and turn their heads toward a sight, sound, or smell (Sroufe et al., 1996).

Newborns can discriminate as well as adults among different sounds, smells, and tastes. Their visual acuity develops rapidly, probably largely as a result of experience. Within the first months of life, they are able to see that an object has the same shape, even when viewed from different angles, and that it is the same size, even when viewed from different distances (Sroufe et al., 1996, pp. 138–48).

"Infants seek sensory stimulation" (Stern, 1985, p. 41). Their preferences for certain kinds of stimuli are innate. For instance, from birth on, a baby prefers to look at human faces, to listen to his or her mother's voice, and to smell his or her mother's milk. Newborns discriminate between what is the same about a familiar percept and what is new or different. They quickly learn to sense patterns and categories (Stern, 1985).

Amodal Perception

Infants have *amodal perception,* the ability to sense similarities in the *shapes, intensities,* and *temporal patterns* of percepts coming from different senses. For example, newborns can recognize that the pacifier they just touched is the same pacifier they are now seeing, the similarity between a bright light and a loud noise, the similarity between a visually presented rhythm and an auditory presentation of the same rhythm, and the similarity between the shape of a sound and the shape of the mouth as it makes that sound. Perhaps most significantly, infants can perceive the similarity between the sense of their own bodily movements (which psychologists call the *proprioceptive* sense) and something they see or perceive in another way. For instance, if an adult sticks out his or her tongue or even protrudes a pencil eraser from between his or her fingers, a watching infant will likely stick out his or her tongue (Stern, 1985).

Newborn infants can "reliably imitate an adult model who either smiled, frowned, or showed a surprise face" (Stern 1985, pp. 50–51). Researchers do not yet know whether this response is more like a reflex or is due to another "kind of amodal perception" (Stern 1985, pp. 51–53). Heinz Werner (1948) thinks that newborns directly perceive and sense these different "category affects," that they translate certain sounds and visual percepts directly into sad, happy, and angry feelings (Stern, 1985, p. 53). Researchers think that people sense each of the discrete category affects–"happiness, sadness, fear, anger, disgust, surprise, interest, and perhaps shame, and their combinations"–"along at least two…dimensions: *activation* and *hedonic tone. Activation* refers to the amount of intensity or urgency of the feeling quality, while *hedonic tone* refers to the degree to which the feeling quality is pleasurable or unpleasurable" (Stern, 1985, pp. 54–55).

Stern also thinks that

> There is a third quality of experience that can arise directly from encounters with people, a quality that involves vitality affects…These elusive qualities are…captured by dynamic, kinetic terms, such as "surging," "fading away," "fleeting," "explosive," "crescendo," "decrescendo," "bursting," "drawn out," and so on. These qualities of experience are most certainly sensible to infants and…will be elicited by changes in motivational states, appetites, and tensions. (1985, p. 54)

In discussions of amodal perception, category affects, and vitality affects, researchers do not just observe what is happening to the infant; they begin to infer how infants *experience* themselves and the world. (I use *sense* to refer to perception or perception-like responses and *experience* to refer to more highly organized responses in which something like a perceiving *subject,* though not necessarily a fully organized *self,* may be present.) The most important inference researchers make is that infants directly experience the organization into unified wholes of separate stimuli from separate modes (sight, sound, smell, taste, touch, and proprioception) and domains (actions, perceptions and cognitions, category and vitality affects, and states of consciousness) (Stern, 1985). "Infants are not lost at sea in a wash of abstractable qualities of experience. They are gradually and systematically ordering these elements of experience to identify self-invariant and other-invariant constellations" (Stern, 1985, p. 67).

SCHEMAS AND AFFECTS

Most cognitive psychologists have followed Jean Piaget in focusing on how people use cognitive *schemas* or structures to integrate actions and perceptions. In this model, people learn by *adapting* to changing circumstances. Adaptation occurs in two ways. People use existing schemas to *assimilate* new and different situations. And they *accommodate* or change these schemas in order to respond in a more fitting way to new situations. Effective adaptation results in a movement from *disequilibrium,* in which a person's responses only roughly match environmental demands, to *equilibrium,* in which demands and responses fit smoothly and gracefully together (Sroufe et al., 1996).

According to Piaget, during the first month of life, newborns learn by refining reflexes. Infants in what I call the first phase of life conceive that a perceived object remains the same if it is moved. They are able to perceive a moving object as a whole, even if part of it is hidden. They can remember an object that a researcher first shows and then hides from them. At first, they only remember an object when they perceive it again (*recognition memory*). During the first phase of life, they begin to be able to recall information about an object even in its absence (*recall memory*). Some researchers think that increases in the amount of information a baby is able to hold in his or her *working memory* explain these changes (Sroufe et al., 1996).

Psychoanalysts, psychoanalytically oriented developmental psychologists, and psychologists with training in biology, ethology, and anthropology have tended to focus on the affective life of infants. They follow Sigmund Freud in inferring that desire for pleasure and aversion to unpleasure are the fundamental motivators of human behavior. They observe that newborns first organize stimuli according to whether they are pleasurable or unpleasurable (*hedonic* tone). As infants grow, they become able to differentiate levels of affective activation and, finally, discrete category affects (Stern, 1985).

SELF, SOUL, AND SPIRIT

From observations, most psychologists infer that, during the first phase of life, the infant does not yet organize the self-invariant constellations of percepts into one "self." And yet, like all adults who relate to infants, these researchers tend to assume that the newborn is a unified actor and subject.

They talk and write about the *infant's* experiences and activities as if there already exists a boundary between this unified infant's inner life and the outer world. When they recognize the prospective character of their responses, they quickly note that the "self" they are discussing is "virtual" (Kohut, 1978) or "emergent" (Stern, 1985).

This terminology obscures two realities. First, this way of experiencing, in which the differentiation between inner life and external world is not primary, does not just exist as a way station or prelude to the achievement of selfhood. Throughout life,

> this global subjective world of emerging organization is and re-mains the fundamental domain of human subjectivity. It operates out of awareness as the experiential matrix from which thoughts and perceived forms and identifiable acts and verbalized feelings will later arise. It also acts as the source for ongoing affective ap-praisals of events. Finally, it is the ultimate reservoir that can be dipped into for all creative experience. (Stern, 1985, p. 67)

Second, not all perceptions, experiences, emergent organizations, or even achieved organizations make it into the world divided by the boundary between self and not self. Inborn constitutional predispositions, physical or psychological trauma, parental non-responsiveness or rejection, and social conditioning split off some perceptions, senses, experiences, and organizations from this world.

Because of these realities, I have chosen not to use the terms *emergent self* or *virtual self* to name how the newborn and, indeed, all humans exist as sentient beings. Instead, I use the word *soul* to refer to this register of human subjectivity that includes all that is organized, that is becoming organized, and that remains separate and unorganized. The emergent, virtual, or realized *self* thus appears on the register of, but is not equivalent to, the *soul.*

A discussion of the *spirit* shifts the focus from what happens *to* or *in* the infant to what happens *between* the infant and other beings (see chap. 2). Outside of the spirit, the infant does not come into being. The fetus comes to be in the mother's womb. Birth results in a separation from the womb, but not from the newborn's physical, psychological, and social dependence on a caregiver and others. The interactions *between* the baby, his or her caregiver, and the environment decisively form the baby's body and soul. Although later relations will continue this shaping work, these meetings, precisely because they are primary, have an inordinate effect on the child and then the adult this infant becomes.

Co-creativity and Imagination

These relations also shape the parents, the caregivers, and, finally, the whole social fabric. Pregnancy, birth, and the time immediately after birth change mothers' and, in most cases, fathers' lives. The particularities of the newborn decisively shape her or his caregiver's experiences and behaviors. A relatively calm, happy baby seems to include her or his primary caregiver in a joyous aura. A primary caregiver of a relatively fussy and unresponsive baby sometimes responds to the child with depression (just as a caregiver who is depressed for other reasons will affect the baby's mood).

Imagination mediates this co-creativity. As caregivers provide for newborns' physical needs, they talk to, look at, and touch their babies as if these infants were already unified selves with motives and intentions (Stern, 1985). In other words, they imagine that their babies are already full social partners.

Newborns are "preadapted" for such "social" interactions (Sroufe et al., 1996, p. 201). Prior to being intentional selves, they reflexively cry when they are in need and smile at various other times. When adult caretakers are not experiencing undue stress, these behaviors almost automatically elicit appropriate responses. In other words, babies specifically shape their caretakers' behavior.

They also shape their own behaviors in response to what their specific caretakers do. They notice when caretakers respond to their behaviors and repeat the behaviors to get the responses (Sroufe et al., 1996). They choose to look at human faces rather than other visual stimuli, and to listen to human voices rather than other auditory stimuli. They respond in a more organized fashion to human faces than they do to other visual stimuli. They respond differently to and imitate adult models' smiles, frowns, and expressions of surprise. They can differentiate between different human voices (Stern, 1985, p. 63). A newborn adapts his or her movements between states of sleep, distress, and wakefulness to fit the particular rhythms of his or her primary caretaker. A study shows that infants who experience a change from one primary caretaker to another show "marked disruptions in sleeping and eating" (Sroufe et al., 1996, p. 203). In other words, the baby differentiates between different caretakers. These observations show that newborns finely attune their behaviors to the cues that signal caretakers' changing thoughts and feelings (Sroufe et al., 1996; Stern, 1985).

These observations point to a paradox. When caretakers imagine newborns to be what they have not yet become, they are responding more sensitively to what newborns already are than if they allowed more "realistic" or "objective" appraisals of the newborn's abilities and limits to wholly shape their responses. Imagination opens the caretakers to the fact that the newborn does not exist primarily as an object with qualities, capacities, and abilities. Rather, an infant (like human beings of all ages) exists as a movement in continual co-creative relation with other beings, other movements. Through their imaginations, adults accurately perceive the infant as this responsive relational movement.

PERCEPTION AND HOPE

Recognition of the imagination as *perceptual* points to the constructive character of perception. Like infants, adults organize unities out of collections of percepts. These unities do not merely reflect sensory givens. Perception is not merely a passive reception of reality. Perception shapes reality. Infants' and adults' particular perceptions of each other form, out of innate and other potentialities, the people these infants and adults become. Caretakers' imaginings of infants are accurate perceptions partly because, through these imaginings, the caretakers help form what the infants become.

Together, newborns and their caretakers find and create *hope.* Stern (1985) infers that infants' experiences of emerging organizations of percepts are like adult déjà vu experiences. In both, one experiences a new and present event as familiar, as if one had experienced the event in the past. In addition, the infant also experiences a "premonition of a hidden future," a sense of an organization that has not yet emerged. Similarly, in relation to a newborn, an adult senses the movement toward a familiar, yet new and possibly better, future. Both newborn and adult hope for what is becoming.

Any particular infant and caregiver construct a limited set of hopes. In general, four interacting factors shape these hopes: the baby's innate constitution, environmental conditions, social expectations, and the caretaker's particular attitude toward the newborn. In each of the following examples, one or two of these factors are primary, while the others play a secondary role.

Stern describes a newborn named "Eric," who constitutionally prefers a lower level of stimulation; he "is a somewhat bland baby" (1985, pp. 193–94). Eric's mother is "more affectively intense [and] likes to see him more excited, more expressive and demonstrative about feelings, and more avidly curious about the world." With sensitivity, she encourages his excitement. With her, he learns to tolerate and enjoy—even to hope for— more stimulating situations, which he associates with his mother's support. While his constitution determines the limits of this hope, his mother's attitude shapes it.

Robert A. LeVine summarizes "a general picture of infant care" that emerges in poorer tropical countries:

1. The infant is on or near a caretaker's body at all time [*sic*], day and night.
2. Crying is quickly attended to and becomes rare relative to Western infants.
3. Feeding is a very frequent response to crying.
4. There is, by Western standards, little organized concern about the infant's behavioral development and relatively little treatment of him as an emotionally responsive individual (as in eye contact, smile elicitation, or chatting). (LeVine, 1977, p. 23)

According to LeVine, in these countries, environmental threats–such as exposure to heat and cold, disease, malnutrition, and accidents–result in "high infant mortality rates" (1977, p. 21). Parents care primarily about the infant's survival and only secondarily about behavioral, cognitive, and emotional development. In a study of the Gusii people, who live in Kenya, LeVine discusses the effects of such parenting. Gusii infants and adults can hope for ongoing support from others as long as they conform to strict social norms designed to secure individual and social survival. They cannot hope for support for "self-assertion and pride in personal accomplishment" (1990, p. 466).

Jane Flax summarizes feminist psychoanalytic thought about the way social expectations shape gender differences, beginning in infancy, through the assumption that mothers, not fathers or other men, are the primary caretakers. Feminists theorize that mothers treat male and female newborns differently:

> Women as mothers produce daughters with mothering capacities and the desire to mother...by contrast women as mothers (and men as not-mothers) produce sons whose nurturant capacities and needs have been systematically curtailed and repressed. This prepares men for their less affective later family role and for primary participation in the interpersonal extrafamilial world of work and public life. (1990, p. 162)

Observations of mother-infant interactions support this speculation. In general, mothers talk more to, engage in face-to-face interactions more with, and remain physically closer to female infants, while they encourage male infants to interact more with objects and the environment (Stratton, 1988). In other words, social expectations shape differences in the *hopes* mothers construct with male as opposed to female newborns.

Peter Stratton discusses studies that show how mothers' *perceptions* of their newborns (apart from more objective descriptions of the infants) directly affect how they treat their babies, which in turn predicts how their children will behave in the future. For instance, a mother's belief that a newborn is "difficult" (even if others do not view the baby in that way) tends to result in the child's becoming "difficult" (according to others, as well as the mother) in later years (1988, p. 16). Caretakers' attitudes about their newborns thus shape the hopes they construct together.

Phase Two: Trust

At the age of two to three months, infants begin to give the impression of being quite different persons. When engaged in social interaction, they appear to be more wholly integrated. It is as if their actions, plans, affects, perceptions, and cognitions can now all be brought into play and focused, for a while, on an interpersonal situation. They are not simply more social, or more regulated, or more attentive, or smarter. They seem to approach interpersonal relatedness with an organizing perspective that makes it feel as if there is now an integrated sense of themselves as distinct and coherent bodies, with control over their own actions, ownership of their own affectivity, a sense of continuity, and a sense of other people as distinct and separate interactants. And the world now begins to treat them as if they are complete persons and do possess an integrated sense of themselves. (Stern, 1985, p. 69)

From observations of changes in the relations between babies and caretakers, Stern infers how infants come to integrate a "sense of a core self" and a sense of a "core other" in the register of what I have called the *soul* (1985, p. 70). Before about two months, the interactions focus on regulating the babies' changes of states of consciousness (from wakefulness to sleep and from fussiness to calmness) and meeting the babies' needs (for food, warmth, and comfort). After about six months, the interactions focus on supporting the infant's manipulation of objects. Between two and six months, the focus is on the interactions themselves. Stern concludes that this phase is "the most exclusively social period of life" (1985, p. 72).

Babies in this phase seek out face-to-face interactions. They look at their caretakers and seek to keep their caretakers looking at them. They vocalize to their caretakers and clearly enjoy their caretakers' verbal responses. Caretakers adjust their voices and activities to keep their babies engaged. For example, responding to the babies' preferences for higher pitched voices, they talk in high-pitched voices (Stern, 1985). In their speech and physical interactions with infants, caretakers repeat and so establish themes or patterns with minor variations. The variations keep the baby interested. But babies also seek regularity, or *invariants*. The play between *variants* and *invariants* is one aspect of the regulation of the level of excitation. *Variants* excite, and *invariants* soothe. In their interactions, a caretaker and baby establish a certain range in the level of excitation that is pleasurable to both. The caretaker does so by altering the balance between, on the one hand, variation and other exciting behaviors and, on the other hand, invariation or other soothing behaviors. The baby participates in constructing this range by visually or orally engaging the caretaker to increase the level of excitation and by turning away or otherwise disengaging from the relation when it is too stimulating (Stern, 1985).

The play of variants and invariants teaches the baby to recognize the differences between what remains the same about the other and the self and what changes. In other words, the infant can come to identify and organize a stable sense of the other and a stable sense of self (Stern, 1985).

FOUR SENSES OF THE CORE SELF

Stern infers that the second-phase baby integrates four senses of self into a "core self": "(1) *self-agency*...the sense of authorship of one's own actions... (2) *self-coherence*...a sense of being a nonfragmented, physical whole with boundaries and a locus of integrated action... (3) *self-affectivity*, experiencing patterned inner qualities of feeling (affects) that belong with other experiences of self; and (4) *self-history*...the sense...of a continuity with one's own past" (1985, p. 71). These "senses" remain outside of the infant's conscious awareness. The infant acts on the unconscious presupposition of a core self.

Self-agency emerges out of the integration of (1) "the sense of volition that precedes a motor act, (2) the proprioceptive feedback that does or does not occur during the act, and (3) the predictability of consequences that follow the act" (Stern, 1985, p. 76). By two months, most of the infant's behaviors are willed, rather than reflexive. Researchers infer that "motor plans" or "sensorimotor schemas" that link certain affects, intentions, and behaviors govern these willed behaviors (Stern, 1985, pp. 77–78). Observations indicate that, by two months, infants differentiate between their own willed behaviors and those movements, even of their own bodies, controlled by others. Contributing to the sense of agency is the fact that proprioceptive feedback accompanies one's own behaviors, but does not accompany others' behaviors. Finally, "self-initiated actions upon the self" result in felt and predictable consequences, while "actions of the self upon others" do not (Stern, 1985, pp. 80–81). The second-phase infant is able to discriminate between these patterns of consequences and so between the self and other (Stern, 1985).

Self-coherence integrates five "invariant properties of interpersonal experience" into a sense of the self as "a single, coherent, bounded physical entity" (Stern, 1985, p. 82). The second-phase infant is partially able to differentiate his or her caretaker as a separate *unity of locus* that exists in one space at one time and is the perceivable source of the caretaker's actions. This infant is also partially able to see *coherence of motion* in the caretaker, that all of the parts of the caretaker's body move together, as contrasted with a stationary background. The second-phase infant notices that *coherence of temporal structure* characterizes the caretaker's acts. For instance, when the caretaker speaks, her or his mouth moves in a synchronous relation to the sounds she or he emits. The baby perceives that *coherence of intensity structure* characterizes the caretaker's movements. For example, when the caretaker is angry, the loudness of her or his voice coheres with vigor of her or his movements. As she or he calms down, the voice lowers and the movements slow. Finally, the second-phase infant also sees *coherence of form*—for example, that the caretaker's face is the same through changes of expression, different movements, and when seen from different directions and different distances. Stern infers that the second phase infant is able to use these abilities, along with his or her sense of agency, to differentiate between the caretaker as a coherent other and his or her own self-coherence (1985).

Self-affectivity integrates into one category or vitality affect: "(1) the proprioceptive feedback from particular motor outflow patterns, to the face, respiration, and vocal apparatus; (2) internally patterned sensations of arousal or activation; and (3) emotion-specific qualities of feeling" (Stern, 1985, p. 89). For example,

> mother's making faces, grandmother's tickling, father's throwing the infant in the air, the babysitter's making sounds, and uncle's making the puppet talk may all be experiences of joy. What is common to all five "joys" is the constellation of three kinds of feedback: from the infant's face, from the activation profile, and from the quality of subjective feeling. It is that constellation that remains invariant across the various contexts and interacting others. Affects belong to the self, not the person who may elicit them. (Stern, 1985, p. 90)

Self-history or *memory* is necessary in the construction of a self that coheres over time. The second-phase baby demonstrates evidence of having three kinds of memory. When infants repeat the same voluntary patterns of physical responses to certain cues, they are exercising *motor memory*. When they recognize the sound of their mother's voice, the smell of her milk, and her face, they demonstrate *perceptual memory*. When they smile upon seeing a puppet that researchers had used to make them laugh a week earlier, they demonstrate *affective memory*. Stern infers that they are able to maintain a sense of the motor agency, perceptual coherence, and affectivity of the self over time (1985).

"Representations of Interactions that have been Generalized (RIGs)"

Infants experience these kinds of memory as integral aspects of *episodes,* short happenings "made of…sensations, perceptions, actions, thoughts, affects, and goals, which occur in some temporal, physical, and causal relationship" that leads the infant to experience them as cohering in a unit (Stern, 1985, p. 95). From a series of similar episodes, say of playing with a caretaker, an infant forms a *generalized* memory. From now on, the infant does not remember specific episodes of play with the caretaker, unless they differ in significant ways from generalized episodes, but only the abstracted experience. If the generalized memory is of an interaction, as is playing with a caretaker, the infant has formed what Stern calls a "Representation of Interactions that have been Generalized" or "RIG" (Stern, 1985, p. 97). RIGs integrate the motor, perceptual, affective, and memorial senses of self into an abstract unit or *representation* that is related to a unified abstraction or *representation* of the caretaker. In other words, through RIGs, infants construct a core self differentiated from a core other (Stern, 1985).

These differentiations assume and cannot occur apart from the ongoing relation between infant and caretaker. In this constitutive relation, the infant and caretaker construct—in addition to the differentiated self related to a differentiated other—other relational organizations, most importantly the reliance of the infant on the caretaker as "an other who regulates the infant's own self-experience," "a *self-regulating other*" (Stern, 1985, p. 102). For instance, in games such as peekaboo, the caretaker and infant together construct an experience the infant could not have alone. The caretaker modulates the infant's level of excitement or arousal. In other interactions, such as smiling and then laughing in response to each other, the caretaker regulates the infant's intensity of affect. Cuddling, holding each other, hugging, and looking at each other are experiences of security and comfort in which the infant relies on the other. The caretaker's response to an infant's behavior—for instance, banging a cup, signifying either anger or exuberance—determines which category affect the infant experiences in relation to this behavior. Through feeding, bedtime and napping rituals, and other responses to the child's needs, caretakers regulate the transitions in the infant's experiences of bodily states—for instance, from hunger to satiation—and states of consciousness—for instance, from wakefulness to sleep (Stern, 1985).

Stern emphasizes that these interactions in which infants rely on caretakers do not threaten infants' differentiation between self and other. In other words, by utilizing all the abilities so far described, infants know that their experiences are their own, and not the caretakers'. The infant experiences each interaction with a self-regulating other as an episode that includes: "(1) significant alterations in the infant's feeling state that seem to belong to the self even though they were mutually created by self with an other, (2) the other person, as seen, heard, and felt at the moment of the alteration, (3) an intact sense of a core self and core other against which all this occurs, and (4) a variety of contextual and situational events" (1985, pp.109–10). Repeated similar episodes with a self-regulating other form abstracted "representations of interactions that have been generalized or RIGs" (p. 110). Any single experienced attribute of such a RIG—a caretaker's behavior, an object, an infant's feeling—evokes the RIG, and the infant re-experiences or remembers the whole generalized interaction.

THE "EVOKED COMPANION"

Retrieval of RIGs with self-regulating others evoke the conscious or unconscious generalized and abstracted experience of being with this other in this kind of interaction—what Stern calls an "*evoked companion*" (1985, pp. 111–19). In a new, but similar, interaction with a caretaker, the infant uses the evoked companion to evaluate the interaction. Differences between the current interaction and the RIG result in modifications of the RIG and so of the evoked companion. The more experiences a RIG represents and generalizes, the less effect any new episode will have on it. In other words, unless a new episode is different enough to warrant classifying it as a new variation that modifies the RIG or as a different kind of interaction that evokes a different RIG, the infant's experience of the evoked companion will tend to determine how the infant experiences and responds to the current and actual other.

A baby who is alone, but who experiences a particular aspect of a RIG, can remember and experience the evoked companion associated with that RIG. For instance, a mother and daughter play regularly and joyfully with a rattle. The daughter, discovering the rattle in her mother's absence, shakes it. As it rattles, the baby joyfully laughs and plays in the same way she does when she plays with the mother. Stern (1985) speculates that the daughter experiences the evoked companion, even in the absence of the mother.

In the interactions between caretakers and children, the children are not the only ones who experience evoked companions. In the above example, the initial experience of playing with her baby likely evoked for the mother a RIG of her own mother's joyfully playing with her as a child. The evoked companion based on her own experiences of her mother shapes how she now experiences and responds to her daughter—in a similar way that her mother experienced and responded to her. The mother, in a sense, passes on to her child the evoked companion constructed with her mother. Stern's theory of the evoked companion helps to explain how families transmit personality traits, ways of interacting and behaving, and traditions from one generation to another (1985).

In the above example, the infant may experience the rattle as a personified object. According to Stern, in the second phase of infancy, babies distinguish persons from objects. As a caretaker, such as the mother in the example, plays with an object, such as a rattle, by making it speak and tease and tickle the child, such a toy takes on the attributes of persons and evokes in the infant feelings usually associated only with other persons. The toy becomes a means by which the caretaker regulates the child's experiences. When the caretaker is not there, the baby continues to play with the toy as if it were another person. "It has become, for the moment, a self-regulating person-thing, because like a self-regulating other it can dramatically alter experience of self" (1985, p. 122).

By the end of the second phase of infancy, caretakers and babies have differentiated core selves from core others. They have established ongoing relations in which they shape and regulate each other's experiences of self, others, and the world. They have built up evoked companions who provide selves with models for classifying and predicting their own and others' feelings, behaviors, and responses and who maintain the selves in a web of relations even when actual others are absent. And they have begun to incorporate inanimate objects into this social world. In summary, by the end of the second phase of infancy, the baby has joined in the social construction of reality.

Society, Self and Trust

Participation in society requires the construction of *trust*. Differentiation of self from other requires trustworthy caretakers who both are consistent and introduce optimal variations into their behaviors and responses. Infants rely on self-regulating others with whom they construct particular experiences, abilities, and evoked companions who support the solitary self. These self-regulating others introduce babies to their ability to imbue seemingly inanimate objects with the warmth and liveliness of persons.

Each baby constructs with his or her caretakers a particular web of trustworthy realities—in the self, others, and the world. A return to the first three examples introduced at the end of the discussion of the first phase illustrates this construction of trust.

Eric, the somewhat constitutionally bland baby, learns, in repeated interactions with his stimulating mother that construct her as an evoked companion, to trust her and others who are more exciting. With her, he comes to trust a more arousing world and his own ability, even when his mother is not there, to tolerate and enjoy such increased levels of stimulation.

In the poorer communities of poorer countries, parents and other caretakers necessarily focus on protecting children from the many physical dangers that surround them. Through repeated interactions with such physically protective caretakers, children have opportunities to learn to trust others, the community, and society, but do not have as many opportunities to learn to trust their own individual abilities and perceptions.

In patriarchal societies in which women are the primary caretakers of infants, girls tend to learn to trust their abilities to interact socially with others, while boys tend to learn to trust their abilities to manipulate objects. In each example the infant's interaction with primary caregivers has a definite impact on his or her ability to trust self and other.

Phase Three: Love

Somewhere between seven and nine months, the infant enters as a fully aware participant into what I have called the *spirit,* the register of relation. Until this point, the primary focus has been on how relations shaped the child's body and soul, who he or she is, and his or her abilities. In phase three, the focus shifts to the relations themselves, to how the child interacts with others, rather than how the interactions form the child.

In phase three, babies become able to recognize that other people have minds—intentions, points of view, and feelings—of their own; and that these internal states may be similar to or different from the baby's. In Stern's words, infants enter "a new *domain of intersubjective relatedness*" (1985, p. 125, emphasis original).

INTERSUBJECTIVITY

Trevarthan and Hubley (1978) define *intersubjectivity* as "a deliberately sought sharing of experiences about events and things" (Stern, 1985, p. 128). Researchers have found that phase-three infants share joint attention, intentions, and affective states (Stern, 1985).

When a nine-month-old infant's mother looks at something, the infant will follow the direction of her attention to its focus and then "look back at the mother...to confirm that they have arrived at the intended target"–in other words, "to validate...whether the focus of attention is being shared" (Stern, 1985, p. 129). When infants of the same age point at something, they again look back at the mother's face to see if she is looking at the same thing. The infant and mother share joint attention (Stern, 1985).

By nine months, infants also share intentions. For instance, an "infant reaches out a hand, palm up towards mother, and while making grasping movements and looking back and forth between hand and mother's face intones 'Eh! Eh!' with an imperative prosody (Dore, 1975). These acts...imply that the infant attributes an internal mental state to that person– namely, comprehension of the infant's intention and the capacity to intend to satisfy that intention" (Stern, 1985, p. 131). When year-old infants face something new about which they are uncertain–say "a bleeping, flashing robot like R2D2 from *Star Wars*" (Stern, 1985, p. 132)–they look at their mothers' faces to see how they are feeling. If a mother seems fearful, her baby will get upset. If she "smiles at the robot, the infant will too" (Stern, 1985, p. 132). The infants are able to perceive that their mother has her own feelings or affective states that the infants can share.

AFFECT ATTUNEMENT

Caretakers both encourage and confirm babies' emergent intersubjectivity through what Stern calls *affect attunement* (1985). For example:

- A nine-month-old girl becomes very excited about a toy and reaches for it. As she grabs it, she lets out an exuberant "aaaah!" and looks at her mother. Her mother looks back, scrunches up her shoulders, and performs a terrific shimmy with her upper body, like a go-go dancer. The shimmy lasts only about as long as her daughter's "aaaah!" but is equally excited, joyful, and intense (p. 140).
- A nine-month-old boy is sitting facing his mother. He has a rattle in his hand and is shaking it up and down with a display of interest and mild amusement. As mother watches, she begins to nod her head up and down, keeping a tight beat with her son's arm motions (p. 141).

Affect attunements are cross-modal matches of the intensity, time, or shape of the child's expression of feeling. In the first example, the mother matches her daughter's vocal expression with a physical movement of the same intensity and duration. In the second example, the mother matches her nods with the up-and-down shape and timing of her son's arm movements. The key feature of affect attunements is that they communicate the caretaker's sharing of the child's experience, the subjective feeling of the event (Stern, 1985).

Stern's research shows that infants perceive and respond to their caretakers' affective attunements. When a caretaker accurately matches the infant's vitality or category affect, the baby usually goes on with her or his activity as if the caretaker had done nothing. However, when the caretaker's response does not match the infant's feeling, the baby stops and looks at the caretaker, "as if to say, 'What's going on?'" (1985, p. 150).

LOVE AS INTERPERSONAL COMMUNION

Infants' participation in affective attunement is significant for two related reasons. First, affect attunement involves the nonverbal formation of metaphors and analogies. In the above examples, the first mother's shimmy and the second mother's nodding are metaphors of their children's experiences. Affect attunement thus prepares the infant for the use of symbols and language (Stern, 1985).

Second, Stern points out,

> It is clear that interpersonal communion, as created by attunement, will play an important role in the infant's coming to recognize that internal feeling states are forms of human experience that are shareable with other humans. The converse is also true: feeling states that are never attuned to will be experienced only alone, isolated from the interpersonal context of shareable experience. What is at stake here is nothing less than the shape of and extent of the shareable inner universe (1985, pp. 151–52).

A synonym for *interpersonal communion* is *love*. To love another is to know her or him from the inside, to share or commune with his or her experience, and to act on this shared perception. Third-phase babies and their caretakers together construct love.

As in the construction of hope and trust, the construction of love is specific to the particular child. As Stern states, what caretakers do and do not attune to determines which of the child's experiences he or she experiences as shareable or lovable (1985). A return to the last three examples discussed at the end of the discussion of phase one illustrates the construction of love.

Caretakers in poorer communities in the poorer tropical countries tend to attune to babies' expressions of needs for protection and comfort and not to babies' experiences of exercising individual abilities and initiatives. These babies tend to learn, then, that dependency on others and conforming to their expectations is lovable, while individuality and independence are not. When infants then enact these patterns of love with others, they both reflect and participate in constructing and maintaining the values of the society in which they live.

Caretakers in patriarchal societies tend to attune to girls who are engaged in social interactions and to boys who are manipulating objects and exploring the world. Girls in patriarchal societies tend to learn that when they engage in social interactions, caretakers affectively attune to or love them, while boys in the same societies tend to receive affective attunement or love when they manipulate objects or explore the world.

Mothers who perceive their babies to be "difficult" have difficulty affectively attuning to them. The babies feel isolated much of the time. As they grow older, they do not feel very lovable and have difficulty communing with others. They do not experience themselves as understanding others or others as understanding them. They do not attempt to communicate much because they have not experienced such communication from their caretakers. They become isolated and "difficult" children, the implication being that they are "difficult" to love.

Conclusion

By some time in the first half of the second year of life, babies have learned what they can hope for; what they can trust in themselves, others, and the world; and the extent and limits of love. Their interactions with their caretakers, others, and the world have decisively formed their bodies, contoured their souls, and directed how they relate to others in the realm of the spirit. Although later experiences may alter these lessons, this global orientation or faith remains as the primary foundation for how they will respond to life.

CHAPTER 6

The Toddler and the Community

Karen-Marie Yust

More than twenty years ago, Hebrew scripture scholar Walter Brueggemann wrote a little book for religious leaders and parents of infants and toddlers entitled *Belonging and Growing in the Christian Community*. His task was to guide faith communities and families in appropriate ways of forming very young children in faith. He counseled his readers, "Our nurturing task is to find ways of linking the big picture of [the church's] redemptive history with the immediate experiences of the child's daily life. Our hope is that the child will—over time—affirm that this is *my* story about *me*, and it is *our* story about *us*" (1979, p. 31). With these words, Brueggemann highlighted the importance of acknowledging the toddler's growing awareness of social structures and burgeoning language skills in the process of faith formation.

Five Assumptions for Faith Formation

Receive the Story

Brueggemann contended that five assumptions must inform parental and communal attempts to nurture faith. The first assumption is that infants and toddlers should be receiving the faith narrative incarnationally through the compassionate caring of parents and other adults. The issues of Erik Erikson's first psychosocial stage—trust versus mistrust—are the focal point of Brueggemann's concern. He reminds us that trust born of the experience that one's needs will be met consistently and lovingly is foundational to faith formation. Without this foundation laid in infancy, the toddler has a much less safe place from which to move into new engagements with the faith narrative.

Hear the Story

Brueggemann's second assumption is that very young children must hear the stories of their faith tradition and their own stories if they are to be fully transformed by faith. Parents and other significant adults must speak the language of faith—its stories, its music, and its rituals—so that the toddler hears this language as one of the familiar languages of his or her environment. Just as the acquisition of any language requires training the ear to the cadences of speech, being exposed to its vocabulary, and becoming familiar with its narrative conventions, so it is with religious language. Reading aloud the psalms, the creation stories, or the beatitudes—which are particularly rhythmic and linguistically repetitive—is the religious equivalent to reading nursery rhymes, Dr. Seuss books, and *Goodnight, Moon.* Other good religious texts are any that claim the attention of the adult doing the reading, for the adult's engagement with the text communicates itself to the toddler and helps the toddler know the text's power and themes experientially.

Parents and other significant adults must also invite the toddler to express his or her story, to communicate through sound and action the events of the day and the affective and structural components of the daily narrative. Sometimes adults elicit this story by narrating it themselves with the toddler's guidance, giving voice to experiences too frustrating, new, or complex for the toddler's limited vocabulary or cognitive comprehension. When parents verbalize the circumstances behind a tantrum or name a source of amazement (i.e., "You're angry because I won't let you throw the ball in the house" or "Isn't that amazing! A clown popped out of that box!"), they assist toddlers in hearing their own stories.

Celebrate the Story

It is not enough, however, for toddlers to simply receive the faith narrative incarnationally or to hear their own stories and the stories of their faith tradition expressed verbally. Toddlers also need opportunities to celebrate visibly and actively the intertwining of these two stories. Brueggemann notes that such celebrations "enrich our children with a very special historical imagination" that expands their sense of community across time and space (1979, p. 32). As Jean Piaget disclosed in his research on cognition in children, toddlers have very effective motor memory. They are able to remember concepts in action forms long before they can organize those concepts as logical thoughts alone. Their reasoning is based on perception and intuition. They record their activities and perceptions as a series of internal mental pictures like a slide show rather than putting the pieces together as a puzzle to form an integrated whole. Thus, children do not interpret religious celebrations in the same way as adults, nor do children understand the logic that informs the adult creation of a celebratory ritual such as a worship service. But toddlers intuit the purpose of religious rituals through their engagement with the affective aspects of the event, and they anticipate the repetition of processes their bodies and senses have encountered before, cued by their return to a familiar space and/or by the familiar sounds, sights, smells, rhythms, and emotions of the experience.

Tell the Story

In addition to celebrating the intersection of the toddler's personal story and the faith narrative, Brueggemann contends that faith formation requires toddlers to have opportunities to tell this integrated story in their own words and actions. Daniel Stern's extensive research into infant-caregiver interactive patterns has demonstrated that young children develop a sense of a verbal self by fifteen months (Stern, 1985). This verbal self involves both dialogical and coactive processes of communication. James Fowler has equated this emergent verbal self with the advent of symbolization. As young toddlers engage in regularized interactions that have become generalized (e.g., games such as peekaboo and ring-around-the-rosy), they build a repertoire of rituals that are familiar and predictable, yet newly constructed by the players each time. They also experience a deep connection with the other "player" that nevertheless reinforces a toddler's sense of distinctness as a bodily self, for the game is both mutual and physically interactive. The toddler's increasing physical ability to control his or her proximity to the other player, as well as the emerging ability to distinguish the boundaries between his or her own and other's actions—and thus "take turns" in an activity—also contributes to the satisfaction the toddler feels when engaging in ritual play (Sroufe, 1995, p. 197).

The toddler's familiarity with—and indeed, need for—such mutual and self-affirming rituals prepares the toddler to embrace similar rituals in the life of the religious community. Mary Ann Fowlkes has noted, "Children, because of their repertoire of natural patterns of ritual play, have the capacity to engage in religious prayers and worship cast in the same or similar patterns" (1989, p. 347). The dialogical aspects of worship, such as responsive readings, call and response singing, and exchanges of peace mimic the alternating participant games in which the toddler has found comfort, joy, amazement, and human companionship. The coactive singing of hymns and speaking of unison prayers and affirmations imitate the pattern of shared words and actions like those found in games like pattycake. When toddlers join or echo the "amen" at the end of a unison prayer and when they insist on the family ritual of holding hands and speaking words of blessing before every meal (even lunch at McDonald's!), they are telling their personal religious story to whoever is present to hear it.

Become History-Makers

Receiving, hearing, celebrating, and telling the religious story prepares toddlers to become persons who intentionally make the redemptive history of the tradition real. Brueggemann says, "In the process of maturing, the child may come to understand that she/he is not only a full participant in this history but a *history-maker*. This history-maker is one who can take initiative in speaking words and doing deeds which cause a redemptive kind of life to emerge in those around us" (1979, p. 32). Toddlers already are history-makers in unintentional ways through their bodily and social presence as incarnations of divine and human love and their ability to draw forth a nurturing love from their caregivers that imitates God's love for the world. They express awe and wonder in ways that often captivate adults and open adult eyes anew to the amazing beauty and fullness of the natural and social worlds. Brueggemann's concept of the history-maker, however, projects that toddlers who have opportunities to bring their personal story and their faith community's story into a dialogical and coactive relationship will become older children and adults who choose to engage in words and actions designed to encourage compassion and justice in their communities and in the world.

The Development of Autonomy

Self-Control

Part of the toddler's preparation for a more intentional role as a history-maker is the toddler's engagement in the normal developmental tasks of early childhood. Erikson identifies this stage as a time in which the toddler's burgeoning sense of autonomy is easily threatened. Each day involves crises that pit autonomy against shame and doubt, and the successful resolution of these crises is the developmental work of children between the ages of twelve and thirty-six months. Statements like "No!" and "Me do it!" are common ways that toddlers assert their desire for independence. Frustration is a common response when such assertions go unheeded by the adults who still control most of the child's world. Erikson noted that the negotiation between toddler autonomy and adult control of the toddler's world is freighted with lifelong implications. Children who are denied appropriate forms of independent action and thought doubt their ability to control themselves and fail to develop the foundations of personal responsibility. Instead of becoming intentional salvation history-makers, toddlers who doubt their self-control may develop a dependence on rigid authority structures to provide the moral framework within which they will operate as older children and adults. Children who are pushed to exhibit self-control before they are developmentally ready may succumb to feelings of shame deriving from their failure to meet adult expectations. They, too, will lack effective forms of self-control and perceptions of personal autonomy when they are older. Without a sense of personal autonomy, neither children nor adults can become the type of faithful history-makers identified by Brueggemann.

Erikson offers the example of bowel control and toilet training as an illustration of the psychosocial stage of autonomy versus shame and doubt. As toddlers gain the physical ability to control their sphincter muscles, they can begin to learn the concepts of holding on and letting go. However, bowel control and ideas about retention and release do not materialize overnight. Both the physical and psychosocial development necessary for toilet training and a healthy concept of an autonomous will occur over time. If adults demand that a child exercise bowel control before the child is physically able *and* psychosocially ready to choose such control, then the child likely will feel powerless to make appropriate choices and may (over time) give up attempts at self-regulation. If, on the other hand, adults neglect to offer age-appropriate guidance in the form of toilet training, then the child may experience shameful feelings when confronted by his or her failure to conform to societal norms. Such shame can lead to feelings of defeat and the same loss of self-regulatory initiative as that engendered by unrealistic adult expectations.

Individuation

Margaret Mahler describes this stage in different but related language. She focuses on the toddler's ability to separate physically from his or her caregivers and the role this physical separation plays in psychosocial individuation. Mahler notes that a toddler who feels confident about the love and support of a caregiver is comfortable exploring the world at a physical distance from the caregiver, although the toddler still prefers to keep the caregiver in sight. This visual connection is important because it allows the toddler to "check back" with the caregiver for reassurance even as the toddler ventures beyond the adult's physical embrace. If the caregiver prevents the toddler from using his or her developing locomotion skills to explore the world, the toddler has few opportunities to "practice" self-regulation and gain autonomy. Adults who are willing to step back physically and yet remain close emotionally permit toddlers to move out into the world and develop emotional competence.

Theological Implications

Some Christian theologians have picked up on the toddler's natural movement toward psychosocial autonomy as a metaphor for the nurturing relationship between the "Good" upheld by the religious community and the individual Christian. Søren Kierkegaard, writing about purity and free will, uses the example of a toddler's effort to learn to walk amidst the interplay of parental release, and toddler emotional development as a metaphor for faith formation. He notes,

> The loving mother teaches her child to walk alone. She is far enough from him so that she cannot actually support him, but she holds out her arms to him. She imitates his movements, and if he totters she swiftly bends as if to seize him, so that the child might believe that he is not walking alone...And yet, she does more.

> Her face beckons like a reward, an encouragement. Thus, the child walks alone with his eyes fixed on his mother's face, not on the difficulties in his way. He supports himself by the arms that do not hold him and constantly strives towards the refuge in his mother's embrace, little suspecting that in the very same moment that he is emphasizing his need of her, he is proving that he can do without her, because he is walking alone. (Kierkegaard, 1938, p. 85; quoted also in Sroufe, 1995, p. 205)

In capturing the interplay of dependence on the guidance of that which is good and desirable (signified by the mother) and the independent action of the self (signified by the toddler) in religious development, Kierkegaard– and social scientists such as Margaret Mahler and Alan Sroufe, who quote him–underscores the engagement of even very young children in the dynamics that mark faith formation. The human developmental process becomes the arena for practicing the "holding on" and "letting go" necessary for religious edification and maturation.

The religious community, therefore, can provide, through the interplay of its theological narratives with Erikson's developmental theory, a context that supports the toddler's development of appropriate autonomy. Both theologians (including Kierkegaard) and Erikson have identified the concept of "free will" as a pivotal concern of human development. Erikson defined free will as "the unbroken determination to exercise free choice as well as self-restraint, in spite of the unavoidable experience of shame and doubt..." (1964, p. 119). Religious anthropology (the term given to theological inquiry that focuses on the religious meaning of human life) traditionally has identified free will as the condition of human beings that allows them to decide freely whether or not they will accept the gracious gift of God's grace. When the community of faith encourages the appropriate development of the toddler's will, it also contributes to the toddler's ability to develop a personal story of sufficient ego strength that can encounter the salvation narrative and become an identifiable part of an integrated story of faith. Recall that Brueggemann's five assumptions for faith formation assume that young children have personal stories to "tell" and that their stories will be heard and celebrated by the religious community. The development of the young child's ability to share such stories requires that the religious community reinforce the child's sense of autonomy and free choice, a task that is consistent with the community's theological commitment to nurture a personal and freely chosen relationship with God.

Personal Authority

Several years ago while in seminary, I taught a group of two-year-olds during a weeklong vacation church school program. The theme for the week was the story of Moses. One of our daily activities was a toddler finger play that went, "God said to Pharaoh, 'Let my people go.' But Pharaoh said, 'No, no, no!'" During the first half of the finger play, the children and I would shake our fingers just like a chastising parent. Then we would switch to shaking our heads "no" during the second section. The children loved this finger play because it mimicked their real-life experiences, and many parents reported that their toddlers were still reciting this rhythm several months later. What I could not have anticipated was the lingering effect this activity would have on at least one of the children. Ten years later a former seminary colleague stopped me at a conference to say that his preteen son had been talking about a finger play he remembered from his toddler days and how the words had come back to him as an example of the times God sometimes expects different things from people than they want to give. My friend's son was reflecting on how easy it had been to be contrary when he was younger and how much more personal responsibility he had for making good choices as a twelve-year-old. A simple church school activity that had reinforced his toddler exploration of the word *no* in relation to authority figures had become a personal link with the salvation narrative that was informing his free choices as an older child and that likely will remain with him in adulthood.

This story also reinforces Rene Spitz's assertion that toddlers appreciate and use the word *no* as a way of identifying with those they consider aggressors against their autonomy (see Colarusso, 1992, p. 48). Spitz observed that the toddler's desire for closeness with adult caregivers conflicts with his or her craving for independence from those caregivers. At the same time, the toddler's increased mobility and accompanying curiosity about the world create numerous occasions when adults move to limit the toddler's explorations with the word *no*. The toddler, realizing that *no* is a term of limitation, adopts the same terminology in an attempt to limit the caregiver's authority over him or her. The move is thus one of imitation, wherein the toddler becomes like the adult caregiver, connected physically (through speech) and emotionally (through appreciation of the adult strategy) to the caregiver, and of differentiation, whereby the toddler rejects the caregiver's right to set limits. When my class of two-year-olds embraced the "no, no, no" finger play with delight, they were expressing their appreciation for the power of the word *no* to connect and distinguish them from the adults who provided them with security and love while also limiting their autonomy. They were demonstrating their awareness of the word *no* and its power as an important aspect of their personal narratives.

The Development of Religious Awareness

Innate Spirituality

That toddlers are just developing the autonomy and physical and social skills necessary to articulate their personal stories does not mean, however, that these children are only now becoming religiously aware. The theological concept of a humanity created in God's image encourages the presumption that the capacity for religious awareness is innate in human beings. To some extent this capacity is realized in the common sense of wonder that toddlers bring to their lived experience. Attentive to the amazing and mysterious nature of the world, toddlers experience what religious sociologist Peter Berger calls the "signals of transcendence" (Hay, Nye, & Murphy, 1996, p. 62). Yet conscious reflection on the causes or reasons for a wondrous experience is a learned response. Spiritual awareness, in contrast with spiritual experience, has to be "activated" or it may remain dormant for long periods–even most of a lifetime. Activating spiritual awareness requires that toddlers learn some mode of religious expression for their spiritual experiences. Adults who wish to encourage religious reflection must also assume that toddlers are capable of understanding religious concepts and practices on their own developmental level and that their understandings, although different from those of adults, are valuable. As Catholic theologian Karl Rahner has stated, "We conceive of an innate spiritual capacity in childhood, but recognize that this may focus in particular ways and take different and changing forms as the child's other capacities develop" (Hay et al., 1996, p. 60). Adults must also remember that the toddler's religious awareness is not static, but changes as the child develops, and that providing a safe and loving context for these changing expressions of faith is the goal of religious formation. Spiritual awareness depends in part on the acquisition of religious information, but it is even more dependent on the stirring of the imagination. It is the imagination that helps toddlers conceive of the world and of life as being potentially different from the way it is.

Language Acquisition and Religious Expression

Rabbi Howard Bogot has pointed out that "children are not only born with the basic liturgical ingredients–wonder, joy, love, drama, and natural spontaneity–but…they appreciate the opportunity to transform aspects of their world into personal as well as established declarations concerning God" (1988, p. 514). The toddler's transformative ability depends in part on the introduction of God-talk "that encourages the experimental in contrast to the definitional" and the telling of the faith narrative "in language forms that can stimulate dialogue and analysis" at the toddler's cognitive level (Bogot, 1988, pp. 510–11). The work of Swiss psychologist Jean Piaget suggests that toddlers actually bridge two stages of cognitive development. Younger toddlers (twelve to twenty-four months) operate at the level of sensorimotor or practical intelligence, whereas older toddlers (twenty-four to thirty-six months) have moved into the stage of preoperational or intuitive intelligence (which lasts until age seven or eight). The "language" of the younger toddler is a language of actions rather than verbal constructs; ideas about who the child is and how the world works are developed through physical experimentation. As the younger toddler builds a "logic of actions," he or she begins to "decenter from the self" and see himself or herself as an object among other objects (Piaget, 1967, p. 79). Younger toddlers also gain a concept of object permanence, contributing to their sense of security in and mastery of their world. They begin to walk and to label objects and their desires with words learned from their social environment. Their ability to use religious terminology and verbalize an awareness of God depends on their "overhearing" religious language in their primary social settings and "seeing" others apply this religious vocabulary in ways they can imitate.

The ability of young toddlers to learn religious language and practices through sensory immersion in a religious culture prior to verbal language acquisition was quite apparent in one of my parish ministry settings. This particular congregation had a live audiovisual feed of its worship service in its church nursery. Each week, the infants and young toddlers in the nursery "overheard" the music and spoken words of the liturgy and "saw" their community engage in the acts of worship. Those children who attended church frequently showed signs of having learned pieces of the sung liturgy. Young toddlers would sing snippets of congregational hymns with the same gusto as simple children's songs. They especially picked up the tunes and words to hymn refrains that contained multiple repetitions of simple phrases. They also would chime in on the last word of each line in a familiar hymn, and what they could not sing verbally they would hum. Parents reported that their almost-two-year-olds were as likely to sing a string of "alleluias" as "Twinkle, Twinkle, Little Star" when moved to sing during a shopping expedition or a long car ride. The practical intelligence of these children, combined with their social exposure to religious culture, was sufficient for them to learn and use–albeit without rational comprehension–the religious language of their faith community.

Intuitive Intelligence and Religious Enculturation

Sometime between eighteen and twenty-four months, toddlers move from Piaget's sensorimotor (practical) intelligence stage to the preoperational (intuitive) intelligence stage. Although older toddlers continue to learn through action, this stage is characterized by an egocentric perspective that presumes the entire world thinks as the toddler thinks. New information is sorted into the older toddler's existing mental categories, and alternative explanations for events and objects are rejected because they do not reflect the toddler's perspective. My youngest child, nearing his third birthday and just beginning to explore the alphabet, refused initially to accept that the lowercase *t* is a letter because he had been introduced to that same figure as the Christian sign for the cross. He also labeled the letter *W* an "upside over *M*" at that stage of cognitive development because he categorized *W* in terms of its visual similarity to his favorite letter (so chosen because it is the first letter of his name).

A favorite toddler pastime is naming the objects around them. Two-year-olds incessantly wonder "What is it?" and adult caregivers often have to name item after item as the child points each object out. Toddlers have good memories for these names, but their ability to remember does not indicate that they logically grasp the reasons for a particular label or the criteria by which labels are assigned to particular objects. If the first four-legged animal they ask to have named is labeled "dog," then every four-legged creature they encounter may be pronounced a "dog" as well, even if the creature happens to be a cat, cow, or horse. The introduction by adults of new label possibilities may or may not be accepted initially, depending on how well the toddler believes his or her existing categories are working. This, too, is an example of the toddler's assertion of free will over the way in which his or her psychosocial world is constructed.

Irreversibility and Religious Interpretation

Older toddlers are also bound by what Piaget identifies as "irreversibility." They observe objects and individuals in particular moments and do not interpret what they see in light of past states or actions. Piaget conducted a series of experiments in which young children were presented with two identical glasses (labeled A and B) filled with equal amounts of water. The children then were shown a taller and narrower glass (labeled C) and asked if the water amounts would remain the same if the water from glass A were poured into glass C and then glasses B and C were compared. Based on their observations of glasses A and B, the children believed the water amounts would be the same. However, when they actually saw the water in glass C, they believed that glass C contained more water than glass B because the water level in glass C was higher than that of glass B. Despite their earlier observation of glasses A and B and their earlier certainty that the amounts of water were equal, their last observation of two different water levels dominated their interpretation. They could not reason backward from what they were seeing to what they had observed before and logically alter their visual perception with foreknowledge.

This type of irreversible thinking actually assists toddlers in learning religious narratives, because toddlers are unconcerned with the moral dilemmas embedded in many religious texts. They appreciate the story of Noah and the ark because all the animals are safe from the flood. Young children do not struggle to resolve—as adults do—the logical tension between a theological doctrine of God's grace and the narrative claim that God once destroyed most of the world because of sin. Instead, they interpret religious texts through the lens of their own egocentric concerns and in terms of their own actions and feelings. If they are afraid of thunderstorms, they assume that the animals were afraid also and that Noah, who is presumed to be like the adults in their social world, had the job of providing comfort and reassurance. If they have experienced a boat ride, they presume that the population on the ark had the same experience as they did. Their intuitive logical perspective encourages them to create simple mental pictures of stories that coordinate with their simple mental images of their own experiences.

The Development of Moral Consciousness

Egocentrism

It is because toddlers do not yet think about or judge "right" from "wrong" that they are not included in Lawrence Kohlberg's stages of moral development. Prior to age four or five, in Kohlberg's schema, children are spontaneous actors and reactors; they do not engage in the cognitive practice of weighing the moral implications of their actions, even at what Kohlberg calls the "preconventional" level. Their egocentrism limits their ability to imagine a perspective other than their own, and they presume that their perspective is shared by others. It is in part the experience of conflict—in the form of adult or peer resistance to their demands and interpretations—that helps the very young child learn to see other viewpoints and to negotiate among multiple moral claims at a later age. Toddlers do not readily share their toys with one another because they cannot imagine a reason for sharing. They do not acquire a working concept of sharing as a "good" standard until they are preschoolers, and even then they make this moral judgment based on the physical consequences (punishment) or self-gratifying rewards (adult affirmation) they perceive are tied to sharing. Moral ideals traditionally linked to religious life, such as obedience, denying the self, and turning the other cheek, are also beyond the conceptual world of the toddler.

Awareness of Social Norms

However, toddlers do not exist outside the sphere of moral formation, even if they are not a part of that realm in Kohlberg's terms. The toddler's social community, particularly his or her adult caregivers, acts on him or her in ways that shapes the toddler's eventual perception of "right" and "wrong." Judy Dunn, using research data gathered by Jerome Kagan and others, has argued that children as young as eighteen months demonstrate a significant degree of understanding about the social norms and practices of their household (Kagan & Lamb, 1987, pp. 94–95). Kagan himself has noted that his studies of children in their second year show that young toddlers have "a preoccupation with objects that are broken, incomplete, dirty, or out of place," which indicates that even very young toddlers (thirteen to fifteen months) have some ability to recognize social norms and evaluate objects in relation to those norms (Kagan, 1981, p. 22). By the second half of the second year, the toddlers in Kagan's studies also demonstrated an ability to associate certain actions (such as the destruction of objects) with adult disapproval. Kagan concludes, then, that toddlers who are seventeen months or older have at least a limited capacity to create standards of behavior that we might categorize as precursors to moral judgments, in part because a seventeen-month-old child appears to have gained a tentative ability to infer causality.

> The child is said to have a standard for the destruction of property when he [or she] has a representation of classes of acts which violate the integrity of objects and are associated with adult disapproval. The ease with which the child associates signs of disapproval with actions suggests he [or she] is prepared to construct that link. (Kagan, 1981, p. 124)

Alan Sroufe, in his study of the emotional development of toddlers, has noted that even before the end of the second year of life, toddlers demonstrate negative emotions and/or anxiety about adult disapproval when engaging in acts they believe are inappropriate. In some cases, toddlers even correct themselves verbally as they consider committing a forbidden act (Sroufe, 1995, p. 198). Linking adult approval and disapproval with personal actions, then, prepares toddlers to evaluate those actions morally once they become capable of conceptualizing right and wrong.

Habituation

Thus, the toddler's social environment—its norms and its authority structure—becomes critical to the development of the child's moral judgment. The purpose of discipline in the toddler years becomes the development of habits (routine ways of acting) that support the community's social ideals. Drawing on the work of Emil Durkheim, Johannes A. Van der Ven contends that habituation then supports the development of self-regulation, an essential characteristic of moral formation. He notes that the best model of discipline is authoritative, incorporating both "high control" and "high support" from adult caregivers.

The parents set clear standards for the child and firmly reinforce these standards by using commands and sanctions when necessary. At the same time, however, they encourage the child's growing independence and individuality. This authoritative pattern is characterized by open communication, in which the parents carefully listen to the child and also express their own views. (1998, p. 49)

Because Van der Ven's authoritative discipline model is applicable to children from late infancy through adolescence, it requires some nuancing with regard to toddlers. Sanctions, in terms of punishments meted out for wrong behavior, are not appropriate until a child develops a sense of right and wrong, around ages four or five. Prior to this time, habits are cultivated by the patterning of desirable actions and the redirection of undesirable ones, as well as through the creation of contexts marked by some discernible order and predictable rituals. Also, the communication between adult caregiver and toddler depends as much or more on body language and emotional affect as verbal expression. Listening carefully involves attending to the ways in which toddlers are engaging the world and its challenges. Expressing one's views occurs in sensorimotor ways as well as in verbal address.

Emotional Constructs

Judy Dunn's research has indicated that households in which a parent initiates conversations about inner states and feelings, particularly the feelings of others in response to inappropriate behavior, result in the child's own articulation of and simple reflection on social and moral rules by the age of twenty-four months. Dunn demonstrates that both empathetic and teasing behaviors increase in the second and third years of life, suggesting that the toddler's increasing awareness of social norms and of emotional causality leads to both moral and immoral behavior. Just as the toddler uses the word *no* as both a connective and distancing device, the toddler treats his or her normative constructs as means for connection with the social community and for rejection of the community's authority. Furthermore, "[t]he data make clear that by twenty-four months children's verbal comments show some grasp of the notion of responsibility and blame in relation to feelings and to social rules" (Kagan & Lamb, 1987, p. 107). The toddler measures himself or herself in relation to social norms and may even feel some emotional distress when he or she breaks the rules, although this distress is related primarily to fear of adult disapproval. It is precisely this distress, however, that Kohlberg identifies as the primary motivator for "preconventional" moral judgments in four- and five-year-olds. The toddler's understanding of moral codes thus lays the groundwork for later moral judgments.

The Development of a God-concept

Personification

The significance of parent-child communication for toddler moral development begins but does not fully satisfy an exploration of the parent-child relationship and its impact on faith formation. Morality (moral action) is a significant aspect of faith, but it does not in itself constitute all there is to faith. Our attention to toddler faith formation also must include attention to the toddler's relationship with the Divine, God. Donald Ratcliff draws on the work of Ronald Goldman and Nancy Smith to demonstrate that parents mediate God to infants and toddlers through parental personification of the qualities typically associated with the Divine: omniscience, omnipotence, and omnipresence. Following Goldman, he suggests that it is "only later in the preschool and school years that children come to doubt these qualities in parents and eventually redirect them to a concept of God" (Ratcliff, 1992, p. 120). Antoine Vergote and Alvaro Tamayo conducted a cross-cultural study in which they determined that human representations of God (defined as mental devices for maintaining a relation with the Divine in its perceived concrete absence) frequently are bound up with specific and symbolic parental figures and relationships. Toddlers become capable of simple God representations at the same time that they begin to engage in pretend play, usually in the second year of life. These representations of the Divine draw on specific information about God provided to the toddler by adults (e.g., God is powerful, God takes care of us, God loves us) and interpreted by the toddler according to his or her interpretation of what that information means for some thing labeled "God." For the typical toddler, "God" appears to fit best into the same category as a primary adult caregiver, usually a parent. Thus, the child's earliest concept of God generally mimics that child's understanding of his or her parental figures. But toddlers attach little truth value to the word *God,* and indeed they cannot yet differentiate between God's nature or character and their assumptions about the nature and character of their primary caregivers. Although they can imagine something (someone) called "God," they cannot yet form beliefs about God's nature or existence because they do not begin to ask such questions about their concepts until sometime in their fourth year (Pratt & Garton, 1993, p. 20).

Transitional Objects

Ana Maria Rizzuto contends that the God-concept of toddlers is best described psychoanalytically as a "transitional object" concept. The idea of God functions for the toddler much like a security blanket, pacifier, or special stuffed animal. It is a comforting idea, allowing the toddler to imagine that someone is always with him or her and providing for his or her needs as the toddler expects and wants the primary caregivers to do. Often this concept takes on other characteristics of the toddler's world as the toddler grows older. In the "transitional space" of fantasy play, older toddlers and preschoolers create many imaginary characters and hypothesize about the looks, shapes, and sounds of other objects about which they have only heard. They draw on the resources of their material world to aid them in their imagining (Rizzuto, 1979). Out of this play, many preschool children describe their image of God as that of an old man with a white beard, suggesting that they have associated God and God's attributes with the North American depiction of Santa Claus. That God, like Santa Claus, seems to have positive magical qualities that no other person they know possesses heightens their interest in making connections between these two mythical figures.

Working from the same psychoanalytic perspective, D. W. Winnicott describes a theory of play in which one of the toddler stages involves the ability to be alone in the presence of another. He states, "The child is now playing on the basis of the assumption that the person who loves and who is therefore reliable is available and continues to be available when remembered after being forgotten" (Winnicott, 1971, pp. 47–48). This development also describes the older toddler's relationship with God as someone who can exist as a representation of the toddler's beloved caretakers and be called to mind when useful. The two-year-old who has heard a parent say each night at bedtime, "God is watching you while you sleep" likely will develop a concept of God as someone close by waiting to care of the toddler, just as the parent is in a nearby room prepared to do the same. So the toddler goes about the business of playing secure in the sense that "God" will be there if needed. That God may be mediated through the actions of loving adult caregivers rather than a particular person named "God" does not trouble the toddler. He or she presumes that someone named "God" could indeed step in to provide care if another person does not do so. In the absence of a concrete and soothing adult presence, the toddler can invoke the idea of God as a means of reassurance and self-soothing, much as the toddler might call to mind the image of a primary adult caregiver.

God as Ultimate Background Object

Nancy Smith suggests that this invocation is further enabled by the existence of God as an "Ultimate Background Object" in the psychological world of the infant and young toddler. Through the "existential experience of trust in the primary care-taker" the toddler experiences the world and the one responsible for order in the world as trustworthy (Ratcliff, 1992, p. 121). (Recall that this is the first assumption of Walter Brueggemann's system for nurturing faith, as well as the first stage of Erik Erikson's psychosocial theory.) As the child learns to distinguish the role and authority of the primary caregiver from the role and authority ascribed to God, the child reinterprets the experience of trust as a response to divine as well as human provision, just as the child redirects the qualities of omniscience, omnipotence, and omnipresence to God. Smith notes that "God" as the ultimate positive background object is often accompanied by a figure that personifies evil and functions as a negative ultimate background object. Some theological traditions name this personification "Satan" or "the Devil" and place this negative figure in conflict with God. A toddler who is introduced to this religious language likely will adopt the tradition's names for good and evil by the age of three. In traditions that do not utilize this language, this negative ultimate background object will receive its name from the negative cultural figures of the toddler's world, such as the "bogeyman," the "monster" hiding in the child's room, or a popular television anti-hero.

The Impact of Social Location

That toddlers borrow names for God and evil from the language of the culture around them offers just one more example of the way in which very young children are shaped by their environment as well as their genetic heritage. Behavioral research suggests that noticeable gender differences in play usually surface among four-year-olds, and often children of that age express a preference for playmates of the same sex (Segal, 1998). Likewise, children often do not make racial distinctions based on skin color until they are four or five. Parents and caregivers often assume that this means toddlers are immune to gendered and race-oriented acculturation. Such an assumption is false. Just as toddlers understand the language of their home long before they speak it, toddlers perceive the cultural values of their social location well before they can articulate those values. The toddler girl who frequently stands on a chair beside her father as he washes dishes learns through observation that housework is something fathers do, and when she engages in pretend play, she may pretend to be a father washing dishes. Because she does not yet associate fatherhood with biological sex, she has little difficulty imaging herself as the "daddy" working at the sink. When she is older and capable of making gender distinctions, she may even identify dishwashing as a "masculine" job based on her personal observation of human behavior.

The African American toddler boy who repeatedly watches cartoon videos in which the "good guys" with light-colored skin always beat the "bad guys" with dark-colored skin learns from this observation that light-skinned people are "good" and dark-skinned people are "bad." When he is older and aware of his own skin color, he will likely experience a tension between his sense of himself as good and his general observation that dark-colored skin belongs to "bad guys." This tension is akin to the powerlessness and shame that a toddler experiences when forced to exercise bowel control before he or she is ready.

The enduring strength of the assumptions toddlers make about the world based on their observations has became powerfully apparent to me through conversations I have had with preschool and early elementary children. When I began my last position as a parish pastor, I asked a group of children ages three to six what they thought about having me as their new minister. A five-year-old girl responded, "I'm glad you're a girl, because my mom said we might get a boy minister, and I don't think boys can be real ministers!" Several other children nodded in agreement. These children had grown up in a congregation led solely by female pastors; they considered female clergy the norm and were skeptical of male "imposters." Even their parents' assurances that men could be and were "real" ministers had not convinced them to set aside their personal observations.

A conversation with my oldest son when he was seven also illustrates the power of toddler perceptions. This child endured several painful medical tests in the month proceeding his third birthday, including a bone marrow biopsy. The day before his younger sister's third birthday, he turned to me at the dinner table and asked when his sister was going to have her "really big lab test." Surprised, I asked what he meant. "You know," he said, "that bone thing like I had." I discovered that he had defined his experience with the bone marrow biopsy as something normative for all children turning three years old. He assumed that all his friends had a similar experience in their background; when he realized that his experience had been unusual, he spent several weeks working through the meaning of this revelation for his own sense of self. The experiences of toddlers can prove to be long-lasting frameworks on which they construct their perceptions of reality.

Thus, the cultural and experiential messages received by toddlers create the norms against which they will, as older children, test and incorporate new information. As toddlers, they explore and reinforce these normative messages for themselves through imaginative play. Two- and three-year-olds engage in pretend play as a way of making sense out of the world they observe. They lack the ability to assess critically the circumstantial, gendered, or racial connotations of the images and behavior they observe and replicate in their play. Adult caregivers help toddlers develop healthy social norms when the adults provide examples of human interaction and identification that respect individual giftedness and encourage social connectedness.

Conclusion

Throughout all aspects of the toddler's development, the possibility for faithful transformation is evident in the ways human experience points even the very young child toward the Divine. But what is also evident is the dependence toddlers have on their adult caregivers and their religious community to supply the religious vocabulary and rituals necessary for articulating and enacting their God-given spiritual nature. Brueggemann's five assumptions about faith formation underscore the necessity of "religious enculturation," the immersion of persons within a ritual community that has a clearly defined narrative tradition and identity, coupled with a set of personal and social ethical norms. Toddlers who are immersed in regular Friday *Shabbat* services, daily family prayer before meals, weekly congregational singing, seasonal Advent candle lighting rituals, and/or a host of other common communal religious practices develop a sense of the holy and the Holy One that they can experience, embrace, and sometimes even name for now, and then reexperience, re-embrace, and rename as they develop.

That toddlers' expressions of faith are not identical with adult expressions does not make them any less people of faith. It simply means that we have to take into account the specific physical abilities, cognitive skills, emotional behaviors, and social interactions of toddlers in order to see the work of God in their lives. In this way, we play a role akin to that of God in the creation story of Genesis 1: We look at toddlers and see that they are good and faith-full because of the one who made them. And in doing so, we agree to assume our role as advocates of faith. It is not enough to entertain toddlers and other young children until they are old enough to engage in cognitive reflection and attain a spiritual awareness more recognizable to adults. We must create contexts, point the way, share the stories, and give directions that help toddlers express their spiritual experience in ways that transform who they are in the very real developmental stages in which they reside.

CHAPTER 7

The Oedipal Child and the Family Crucible

A Jungian Account

Terrill Gibson

How may we understand the landscape of the soul?
MARGOT WADDELL (POWELL, 1993, P. 171)

Ancient myth continually informs modern psychology and theology. Archaic narratives, formed no doubt through elaboration of individual dreams and community rituals, have remained amazingly vibrant across the millennia. No matter how much new data modern science generates, these mythic molds are plastic enough to absorb the novelty with dignity and meaning. This explains in great part why the best of pastoral care is narrative care. We have always been, and apparently always will be, most essentially a people of story and myth (Capps, 1993). One of these ancient stories has had enormous impact on the twentieth century and its self-understanding. Perhaps the most important story shaping culture in the modern era, the Oedipal myth was embraced by the Viennese psychiatrist Sigmund Freud. Freud gave the myth a bold new interpretation growing out of the contemporary psychological crisis of modern women and men. Modern pastoral care evolved from direct contact with this exhilarating new reading of the old tale when Freud and his then associate, Swiss psychiatrist Carl Gustav Jung, lectured together at Clark University in

Massachusetts in 1909. Many clergy were in that audience and were so compelled by this psychoanalytic hermeneutic that they immersed themselves in its fascinating frame. A whole new style of clinical pastoral care was the result–the modern pastoral care and psychotherapy movement (Hollifield, 1983; McLynn, 1996).

Some see Freud as a one-myth theorist, a monotheoretical analyst, and Jung as a poly-myth theorist, a polytheoretical analyst (Hillman, 1992; D. Miller, 1981). Freud believed that the Oedipal myth was a universally valid construct for the crucial incest-resolving juncture in human development. Others say this is a reductionistic selection from the great spectrum of ancient myths with their psychological insights into human origins and evolution. Jung tried to read the Oedipus myth as a polychromatic narrative, an explanatory image with many facets through which to shine the light of understanding.

I am a pastoral psychotherapist and Jungian analyst. My experience has me supporting polytheoretical narrative in pastoral care modeling. So in discussing Freud's historically crucial ideas about the Oedipal event in human psycho-spiritual development, I will be reading the myth in its much broader and earlier polytheoretical/polytheistic context. Furthermore, as a Jungian pastoral psychotherapist, I will be looking at ways to project Oedipal ideas into the prospective future. Although Jungian psychology appreciates and honors the backward glance of the classical Freudian worldview, it is most urgently attentive to the trajectory of future psycho-spiritual development–what Jung called individuation, and what the Protestant theology of his youth understood as sanctification.

Although the Oedipal event is classically assigned to children ages three to six developmentally, this chapter takes the decidedly Jungian view that the mythic reverberations and elaborations of this encounter are played out across the entire life cycle as a developmental line–anticipated in birthing and culminated in dying. The four orienting themes of this volume (physiological and cognitive changes, intrapsychic and interpersonal changes, moral and faith development issues, and social location) are addressed and integrated in both the stage chart (Figure 7, below) and subsequent sections that form the substance of this chapter. But first let us hear the Oedipal/Electral stories.

Oedipus and Electra

Incest is a genuine instinct.

C. G. Jung (1946/1966, p. 179)

It is now a fairly universal notion in psychoanalysis that the contemporary Oedipal developmental construct is sexist (Jonte-Pace, 2001). It tells only half the story, the patriarchal half. It needs at least the addition of Electra's ancient story to approach a more whole truth. Both stories are outlined here.

The Oedipal/Electral story is primarily about incest. Our culture has a distorted idea about incest. We all see the terrible harm to children who are physically and sexually abused by unaware parents. But we forget that there is an inevitable, necessary, positive incest in infancy, a soul-stimulating Desire awakened by the gleam in the "Other's Mothering/Fathering Eye" (Dodson & Gibson, 1997). The trick is for a conscious, boundaried parent to mediate that Desire in a healing way. The Oedipal/Electral story contains a blueprint for this developmental dexterity.

The Myth of Oedipus

Oedipus is a tragic tale of a man condemned and blessed by oracular wisdom. The Delphic oracle foresaw that Oedipus would tragically slay his father and incestuously marry his mother (both unconsciously–*unwittingly*) and that he would be rewarded for solving the riddle of the Sphinx (for full outline and sources, see Graves, 1980).

Queen Jocasta and King Laius had a son, Oedipus. The Delphic oracle warned King Laius that one day a son would kill him in retribution for Laius' criminal seduction of a young boy (Gee, 1991). Laius was alarmed by this intelligence, but flushed with Dionysus' wine, he bedded Jocasta and the fated son was conceived. Terrified, Laius had a slave take his infant son out to a wild place and abandon him to the elements. This compassionate slave, rather than carry out Laius' infanticidal instructions, found a goatherd on the exposed slopes of Mount Cithaeron and gave the child to his care.

Eventually, the Queen of Corinth, Periboea, wife of King Polybus, adopted Oedipus, "he-of-the-swollen-feet," so named by the Queen because Laius had the child's ankles cruelly mutilated with spikes. Oedipus grew up to be a strong, assertive prince. But he did not fit in in Corinth. He was envied and taunted by his peers. A drunkard at a party accused him of being adopted. Although the foster parents protectively repudiated this claim, Oedipus wondered if his gentle parents could really be his (R. Stein, 1973). Troubled, he went to Delphi to seek oracular help and was warned that if he returned home, he would slay his father and marry his mother. Tragically, he assumed that home was Corinth, so he did not return there.

Oedipus was driving his chariot down a narrow cleft out of Delphi at the same moment his birth father approached, going to the oracle for balm out of fear that his own augured death was near. King Laius' herald ordered the bold Oedipus to give way. There was a wild commotion at the crossroads. The brazen herald killed one of Oedipus' horses. Oedipus, in retaliation, slew him, then dragged the king from his chariot and slew him as well. The oracle's die was cast.

After the king's burial, Creon, brother of Jocasta, came to rule Thebes. Soon, the dreaded beast Sphinx approached, laying waste to the fields and communities of outer Thebes. The Sphinx could be stopped only if someone could answer the famous riddle of the muses of Mount Phicium: "What being, with only one voice, has sometimes two feet, sometimes three, sometimes four, and is weakest when it has the most?" (Graves, 1980, p. 10). Those who tendered wrong answers would be killed. Creon offered both the kingdom of Thebes and his sister in marriage to the man who could answer the Sphinx's confounding riddle and thus save the realm.

After many tried and failed, Oedipus arrived from afar and stepped forward to declare his certain answer to the riddle: The being is "[Hu]man because [s]he crawls on all fours as an infant, stands firmly on his [or her]two feet as a youth, and leans upon a staff in his [or her] old age" (Graves, 1980, p. 10). This was a wise developmental answer, for Oedipus knew that the query was about the wisdom learned in the life cycle from birth to death. Oedipus knew this answer deep in his own foot-mutilated, staff-dependent body. *We survive by the knowledge we have suffered into being.* In despair, the Sphinx declared her defeat and cast herself to her death from the citadel's towers.

Oedipus then, again fatefully and unwittingly, married Jocasta. He had three sons and a daughter, Antigone. Because of the unconscious patricide and incest, Thebes continued in crisis. There was plague and famine all around. The blind seer Teiresias, being given visions that the gods knew something was wrong and were demanding reparations, produced in the royal court of Thebes a letter from Queen Periboea, adoptive mother of Oedipus. In it was testimony from Menotes (who had exposed the infant Oedipus for King Laius) that the scars on the feet and ankles of Oedipus provided irrefutable evidence that he was the son of Jocasta and Laius.

Wholly undone, Oedipus grabbed the fastening brooches of his mother's gown and blinded himself. Jocasta hung herself. The sons were cursed by the father to an early, incest-damned death. Oedipus eventually fled or was driven out of Thebes, led on the arm of his daughter Antigone. Oedipus finished out his days in sanctuary under King Theseus of Athens. His sons became fractious, embroiling the middle Greek peninsula in their bloody triangle. From afar, Oedipus again cursed them to fail and die at kinsmen's hands, a curse fulfilled. Oedipus died in exile.

The Myth of Electra

> The gods are not altogether unkind. Some prayers are granted.
>
> MARY ZIMMERMAN (2002)

Electra is the daughter of King Agamemnon. Hers is an incest story typically "full of envy, jealously, and psychic pain." Agamemnon is an unconscious savage, snatching a child away from his wife's (Clytemnestra) breast so he can have intercourse her. He sacrifices another daughter, Iphigenia, to Artemis in return for a poached deer. Clytemnestra takes a lover for solace, but when Agamemnon returns from a military campaign with a new mistress, Cassandra, Clytemnestra plots and slays him in rage.

Electra is "shattered by his death." She is alone, for she protectively had arranged to have her younger brother Orestes sent away from court. She is "beset with sorrow on all sides," now that she has been "torn from her father and left with no man to defend her, to guard her rights and find a suitable husband to take his place as a loving guide and protector" (Powell, 1993, p. 156). Orestes in his maturity eventually returns and fulfills Electra's vow of vengeance by murdering their mother for her crime against their father.

Electra's father was, of course, a wounded brute—a core fact the Electral child cannot fully acknowledge because of the absolute abandonment it would represent. The Electra antagonist cannot see the loved object as hateful and destructive. If she did, there would be no hope or meaning to existence at all. To live, we require a loved object that loves back, even if in horribly distorted fantasy. Break that mirror of beloved and lover, and the heart is shattered.

In Mary Zimmerman's stunning stage adaptation of Ovid, there is a self-contained and gifted young woman, Myrrha. She resists every one of the powerful goddess Aphrodite's considerable inducements to surrender to her carnal, passionate self. Eventually, angered by this independence, the goddess fills every cell of Myrrha's body with an unholy desire for her own father, Cinyras. We are awed by the ferocity of the goddess's wrath as she shakes the fear-numbed body of Myrrha like a rag doll across the surface of the pond of unconscious being, the main scenery element of this primal, powerful piece.

Afterwards, young Myrrha is horrified by the new compulsions of her flesh and imagination. She thrashes, rages, and pleads in the pond for forgiveness and removal of the curse. But the passion grows apace. Myrrha's nurse notices her aberrant, pained behavior. She gently elicits the truth from her reluctant charge. Horrified, but seeing Myrrha's pain and resolve, the nurse helps concoct a liaison for Myrrha. The nurse tells Cinyras (in a patriarchal culture where multiple sexual relationships outside marriage were acceptable for men) that a young woman the age of his daughter wants intimacy with him if he is willing to be blindfolded during the encounter because of the young woman's shyness. Cinyras is aroused by this prospect and readily agrees.

Things go as planned. The union is ecstatic. Neither party is satisfied by one enactment. It goes on night after rapturous night until the father, in a moment of wild transport, rips off his mask to discover the horror of what has been happening. He is enraged and tries to throttle his daughter, stopping just short of her death. This tragic "Electral Victor," like the tragic Oedipal Victor, is mortified and gradually disappears—some say, as the myth goes, to become a tree, or a man (Adonis), or, most probable of all, an eternally suffering vapor in the great sea of the unconscious (Zimmerman, 2002).

This is the Electra complex, a mirror of the Oedipus complex. It is woman's complementary narrative of the inevitable incestuous wound. The death of innocence, self, vision, and hope in yet another flawed generation becomes sealed fate. The vapors will surely rise from the unconscious waters to infect the next generation's young unless someone wakes up to the hard developmental soul-work to be done.

Freud's Exegesis of the Oedipal Narrative

If the child is to become adult, then this move is achieved (in her/his unconscious fantasy) over the dead body of an adult.

D. W. Winnicott (Gee, 1991, p. 201)

The classical psychoanalytic adaptation of the Oedipal tale is succinct:

According to Freud's theory of the Oedipus complex the male child's sexual desire for his mother gradually reaches an intensity whereby he wants to get rid of his father so that he can have his mother for himself. At the same time he loves and admires his father so that he is thrown into a love/hate ambivalence. But because of his fear of castration [by the threatened father] the boy finally represses his sensuous desires for his mother, as well as his hate for his father. He does this through a process of identification with and introjection [literally a psychological swallowing] of the father or parents into the ego [the Freudian center of conscious personality]. This introjected parental authority establishes the kernel of the super-ego [the Freudian agency of moral control against the dark impulses–sexual and aggressive–of the instinctual unconscious–the id], which acts as a severe internal force that perpetuates the prohibition against incest. Ultimately, the super-ego becomes the carrier of other social values. Thus the resolution of the Oedipal complex is largely dependent on a strong super-ego, which is able to successfully repress the incest desire (Stein, 1973, pp. ix-x).

It is easy to see how Freud read backwards from his patients to the ancient Greek myth of Oedipus. Working with disturbed middle-aged adults filled with psychic symptoms such as panic attacks or crippling depressions, Freud would encourage these pained persons to tell dreams and free associate. From his work with hypnosis, Freud had discovered that the psyche (here, Jungian-defined as the full psycho-spiritual potential of a person) codes the meaning of a symptom in these symbolic dream and associative forms. The analyst, then, is a deep listener to and interpreter of this modern scripture of living symbolic/symptomatic pain. Pastoral care and its ancient care-of-souls traditions have been doing just this form of deep listening for millennia.

Freud saw the repetitive symbolic patterns apparent in male patients—the deep unconscious desire for Mother (Jocasta), the fear of Dad's envy and rage over this (Laius), and the tragic consequences if these desires are not repressed (castration-blindness and the withering of the family kingdom). For his women patients, Freud saw a mirrored story in Electra—the deep unconscious desire for Father (Agamemnon), the fear of Mother's envy and murderous rage over this (Clytemnestra), and the tragic consequences if these desires are not repressed (absolute abandonment and the withering of the family kingdom). For Freud, the pre-latency child (ages three to six) must learn to use super-ego muscle to force these forbidden incestuous impulses into submission, or suffer the ruinous psychological consequences. Freud's devastated adult patients and their chaotic inner lives and turmoil were the terrible wages of such failed repression.

Psycho-spiritually, we are all born into a tragic kingdom such as Thebes. All our families are fallen and have a developmental curse hanging over their heads. Given this universal condition of familial suffering, everyone would love to trade in his or her family for a newer model. There is pain and imperfection in every family structure. The eternal fantasy is that the fractured family around us is a mistaken family. We live with an idealized hope that our *real* family will come and claim us, redeem us from this undeserved affront to our innocence and grandiosity. Otto Rank, one of the original favored sons in Freud's inner circle, wrote elegantly of this universal theme (Rank, 1932/1959).Freud's Oedipus explores the paradoxical opposite of this same tension. If I cannot replace my family to eliminate this wound to primal suffering, why not merge with it? If Dad is a bad king and an inadequate lover, why not dispatch him and show him how to run an empire and treat a wife? Because a noble son cannot overtly murder the father and commit incest with the mother, why not make him the tragic victim at the crossroad of mistaken identity and murderous comedy of error? Because a noble daughter cannot overtly murder her mother, why not have her brother carry out this corrective vengeance?

Theology sees myth as the original sacred language, the primal science of divine image. Sacred story has fostered a virtual industry of thought in recent decades. Postmodernism has championed both the recovery and the transcendence of local narrative and image in a world gone globally mad. The ancestors knew the power of "speaking about gods through myth" (Burkert, 1987, p. 77). So Freud's putting mythic story on a pedestal was on target, even if his emphasis was idiosyncratic and partially erroneous. He knew the deep concentration of symbol, affect, and impact that genuine mythic language commands in our bodies and souls.

Oedipus is just a story—one story. As mentioned above, many feel psychoanalysis has been impoverished by this artificial and narrow selection from a complex ancient corpus of myth. But if the story is seen in a developmental context, as one of many mythic narrative jewels that illustrate the ascent of ego and soul up, through, within, and beyond the individual and family life cycle, it gains currency and power. What if, as Jung believed, myth is part of a transpersonal archetypal canon of psycho-spiritual truth and guidance? What if, to use a process theology metaphor, these mythic stories are ways the Divine lures us across life's arch to the greater good and whole (Cobb & Griffin, 1976)? What if these tales "align" our individuality to the "field" of the archetypally transcendent Other?

> ...[E]ach species follows its own archetypal and morphological currents in order to ensure a successful expression of innate form and substance. Alignment with these properties brings with it a symmetry between individual and field. This symmetry and alignment carries a powerful archetypal effect in that it works to collapse individual experience into morphological singularity. In other words, individual and independent experience is temporally superseded by the workings of transpersonal archetypal fields. (Conforti, 1999, p. 44)

The Oedipus myth, then, is a bridge that blends our individual existential triumphs and sufferings into the greater "morphological singularity" that Judeo-Christianity calls the realm of God. In fact, the core "riddle" of the Oedipal story is a developmental riddle, a narrative of the human sanctification process across the arch of the life cycle: "The answer is human because in infancy (wo-man) crawls on all fours; (wo-man) walks upright on two feet in maturity; and in old age (wo-man) is supported with a stick" (Gee, 1991, p. 195).

Myth is the language of destiny; it traces the imprint of called being in our psyches—individual and collective. It both constellates and remembers our vocation and constantly recalls us to vocation's path. Myth weaves together the subtle fabric of personal and communal meaning that moves us along from alpha to omega. Myth is the vessel of the soul; it carries the soul and protects it through the ardors of this vulnerable world. Myth and the soul live deep inside the body, for both ancient and modern theology tell us that the soul, the *imago dei,* lives deep within its fabric, for "my individual experience of the movements of a living pulse, a vital, ever-changing energy within my body, is what I understand as soul" (Stein, 1973, p. 13). Myth attempts to instruct the soul as it matures across both the individual and family life cycle (McGoldrick, 1980; Carter & McGoldrick, 1999). Myth shows us where the thresholds of soul-making passage lie. We must choose to enter or avoid them.

The Oedipal/Electral portal is one of those calling moments in the life cycle. It is more fundamentally related to our destiny than our pathology. It is an initiatory threshold built on our way, not the random detritus of developmental terrorism visited upon our infant innocence. The gateways of our psychological development across both the individual and family life cycle are indeed mysteries. These are little miracles of being, these rites of passage. When viewed at the right distance, the geometric expansion of personality and soul that occurs under the mythic pressure of these awesome thresholds of transition is amazing. A simple example would be the famous *Star Wars* film trilogy and its inherently Oedipal tale about the destruction and recreation of a soulful psycho-spirituality across three generations of a family's history (Kurtz, Lucas, & McCallum, 1977). The Oedipal complex is simply a current cultural cipher for one of these developmental doorways. Freud's ideas capture a little of the essence and awe of that passing, but nothing near its enormous panorama. The Oedipal/ Electral event is an accomplishment, not a disease. There is a developmental fable embedded in the Oedipus and the Electra stories. It is a fable whose universal aspects transcend the utilitarian narrowness and obsession that has characterized its psychotherapeutic and pastoral care use to date.

There are at least four major developmental movements and warnings woven into the deep text of the tale. An image of this developmental conversation appears below (Figure 7). The major themes are borrowed from Jung (*Uroborus*–the ancient circular image of the primal snake biting its tail) and Dante (*inferno, purgatorio, paradiso*–see Dante Alighieri, 1314/ 1909 and, especially, the beautifully illustrated Jungian text by Taylor & Findley, 1997). The addition of Fowler's (1981) and Erikson's (1950/1963) well-known categories are here for a rough orientation. Because they are so well known, nothing more will be said of them directly. They are simply friendly parallel star systems to help navigate these strange Oedipal seas.

The famous medieval poet Dante Alighieri was the first and still foremost theorist of spiritual development in the West. In his imaginal descent into the netherworld, guided first by the venerable Virgil and later by his beloved Beatrice, Dante outlines the developmental process the individual and family must suffer in realizing soul through this life journey. Dante has four basic themes that he learns in his travails through the dangerous gates of passage through hell, purgatory, and paradise: The pilgrim must always stay awake, stay calm, keep moving, and accept wise guidance. It is clear that Dante saw his inner passage as a mirror of the outer passage that happens over and over in life through each of these dangerous developmental portals from birth to death. And it is clear, in his images and reflections, that Dante saw the body and its divine Eros as central to the process of soul realization in this world and beyond. Traditional Western theology has been suspicious and fearful of Eros and body (Brock, 1988). Oedipus is nothing if not a tale of Eros and the body.

Along with the paradise lost/paradise re-gained gradient in the Oedipal myth is Edward Edinger's reminder of the ancient Greeks' tragic sense of mythic death and rebirth in their theater. Our most reliable source of the Oedipus myth is Sophocles' trilogy of plays on Oedipus (*Oedipus Rex, Antigone,* and *Oedipus at Colonus*). And embedded deep in Greek drama is a four-fold structure. First, there is the *agon*, or contest—here, in Oedipus-as-infant—for the generative Mother-paradise (against the stagnant Father-ruler). Then there is the inevitable defeat and undoing of the hero—the *pathos*, or passion (like the Holy Week passion of Christ in his suffering and defeat). Then there is *threnos*, or lamentation and restorative wandering for and by the Hero and his loss (like Christ's descent into hell). And finally, if consciousness is attained, there is *theophany,* or rebirth of spirit and a depth recognition of the Divine imprint to being—resurrection (Edinger, 1994, p. 125). The Oedipus tale encompasses all four quadrants of this mythic journey of soul-making across a lifetime.

Figure 7: Developmental Echoes of the Oedipal Event

ABODE OF SOUL	TERRAIN of SOUL JOURNEY	FOWLER CATEGORIES	ERIKSON CATEGORIES
Eden (conception to 18 months) Agon	*Uroboros*	Primal/Intuitive-Projective Faith	Oral-Sensory/ Muscular-Anal
Expulsion from Eden (18 months to puberty) Pathos	*Inferno*	Mythic-Literal Faith	Locomotor/ Latency
Beyond Eden (adolescence to middle age) Threnos	*Purgatorio*	Synthetic-Conventional/Faith	Adolescence/ Young Adulthood
Return to Eden (middle age to death) Theophany	*Paradiso*	Conjunctive/ Universalizing Faith	Middle Adulthood/ Maturity

Developmental Echoes of the Oedipal Event

Eden

Eden's Age: Conception to eighteen months
Eden's Task: To experience the magical incubating safety of empathic-merger with a good-enough parental guardian. By being born, the infant Hero has won the contest/*agon*—(s)he is the adored center of the world.

> I respect the wisdom of Eros, because it is like a divining rod in its movement directly to the quick of life.
>
> ROBERT STEIN (1973, P. 132)

All kingdoms (in the Judeo-Christian myths) remember those glorious halcyon days when all was prosperous and full of light. It is a time of innocence unsullied. It is Genesis, chapter 1. Everything is in perfect order and harmony. It is Camelot. Arthur is young and strong. Guinevere is beautiful and abundant.

Paradise is an unconscious place. There is no awareness of a snake in the garden and a Lancelot in the court. The snake image is felicitous. Jungians often talk of this stage as belonging to the Uroborus, the cosmic snake that bites its own tail, not knowing where mouth leaves off and anus begins—"the tail eater, which is said to beget, kill and devour itself" (Jung, 1946/1966, p. 242). This is like the infant discovering its own hand or mother's breast and putting it in its mouth. The infant does not know where it leaves off and the world begins. The infant is the world. The world is the infant.

The only way to grow is to suffer the trauma of separating and differentiating, of learning where mother's breast ends and one's hand begins. If the envelope of familial being that surrounds that painful emergence is too anxious or unconscious, deep psycho-spiritual havoc can be wrought. Melanie Klein says it is here, in this infant child's world, that we encounter "the archaic Oedipus complex, which [Klein] conjectured occurred as early as the oral stage of development (before twelve months) and was characterized by an unconscious infantile fantasy in which father's penis and internal babies dwelled inside mother's body" (Grotstein, 1997, p. 59). Already there is incestuous envy and brooding. The child wants what dad or mom already has—a penis and its children safe in mother's primal womb. The Electral child is greedy to possess the same womb, penis, and children in absolute safety.

No matter how mature the parent, limits have to be set on these brooding envies. Innocence inevitably suffers a defeat. The child feels abandoned and/or annihilated. If the parents are healthy enough, this is a short-term experience that their empathic love can contain and co-suffer with the infant until it feels more secure in its new isolation and independence. If the parents themselves are character-damaged from their own early-life wounding, the child can suffer a crippling personality disorder that will stalk him or her into adulthood and beyond. The degree of abandoned, anguished suffering the young Electra-Oedipus will endure is installed here. The developmental die is cast this young (Kohut, 1971, 1977).

The Inevitable Expulsion from Eden: The Oedipal Inferno

Expulsion from Eden Age: Eighteen months to puberty.

Expulsion from Eden Task: Within the safety of "the adopted home of Corinth," the child begins to suffer the pain of differentiation and master its attendant fears of abandonment, annihilation, and mutilation (both physical and psycho-spiritual). *Pathos,* tragedy, is the new unbidden central companion of the journey. The child sadly must experience and integrate the imperfections of this world, both inside and outside the developing personality. The child experiments sexually (masturbation, group-sex play) so as to gain Eros-connection and empowerment. The child swaps loyalties (under Oedipal-Electral fears) from one parent to the other (a cross-gendered swap usually, unless same-sex parents) as a way to broaden psycho-spiritual horizons and models of being).

> *Do you think that I have come to bring peace to the earth? No, I tell you,*
> *but rather division! From now on five in one household will be divided,*
> *three against two and two against three; they will be divided: father*
> *against son and son against father, mother against daughter and daughter*
> *against mother.*

LUKE 12:51–53A

The child Oedipus is really the victim in the Oedipal/Electral story. James Grotstein reminds us that the Sphinx is sphincter, "she who squeezes," and the Great Mother and the Great Father squeeze childhood innocence in these tragic tales (Grotstein, 1997, p. 57). Innocence is always squeezed in this world. We never stay in Eden. Capricious gods following arbitrary rules always expel us. No one ever gets to hold on to primal innocence. We all get thrown into the pit, the inferno of worldly suffering.

Jungian psychology is an oppositional psychology. In Jungian psychology, the great engine of life and creativity is the tension of opposites. What drives life forward is its fear of the backward. What animates life is the reality of death. What completes the masculine is the feminine (and vice versa). The heavens only exist in contrast to the earth. Dry requires moist; heat, cold.

In this view, *birth is a primal fusion that must eventually be dismembered so that the generative oppositions of the soul can be revealed.* We must become disloyal. We must betray this incestuous parent. Patients in their forties and fifties who have not accomplished this essential act of development arrive regularly in pastoral counselors' offices. The primordial union of parent and child, necessary for the initial absolute vulnerabilities of the neonate, must soon be severed by the autonomous questing and individuation of the infant, toddler, and child.

For Oedipus, this necessary disruption is cruelly precocious. He is emblematic of the "orphaned child motif…'an abandoned foundling.'" But beyond this classic association, Oedipus' dilemma is unique, for the usual "abandoned child" of mythic lore is "found alone in nature, as if born out of Mother Nature," but Oedipus' abandonment "through rejection by the parents, and especially rejection by the mother, is not a common hero motif." It is, indeed, uniquely anguishing. Oedipus' abandonment places him in "a special category" of suffering and tragic inheritance, "which brings him very close to modern [wo]man" (Stein, 1973, p. 66). Freud chose this illustrative story well for reasons he did not fully understand. Less about universal castration, the Oedipus story is a tale about universal abandonment, which seems to be an increasingly global psychic reality.

In the moving cinematic adaptation of John Irving's *Cider House Rules* (Blomquist & Holleran, 1999), the film's narrator begins by telling us that he was twice returned to the backwater Maine orphanage we are viewing on screen. The first time he was returned because he did not cry—presumably the adoptive parents were concerned about his lack of animation. The second time he was returned because of the severe abuse he suffered in the adoptive home. Within minutes I was gripped by the saga of this sad orphan now presented as a young adult working as the specially trained aid of the compassionate orphanage doctor, an ether-addicted curmudgeon of tragic soul. The cumulative effect of this young man's presence and the poignant children in this house of abandonment moves us so because it mirrors our personal abandonments so well.

This orphan was the Oedipal/Electral child not once but thrice abandoned by his biological and adoptive mothers. This is the "special category" of modern abandonment described above. This is the universal tragedy of development we all share. We all are Oedipus, not because we are all castrated but because we are all abandoned. We are all Electral orphans.

We must be abandoned in order to be found. This is a universal theme in cross-cultural myths and fairy tales. We cannot begin to evolve psycho-spiritually unless we have detached from our origins: "Abandonment is therefore a necessary condition, not just a concomitant symptom" (Jung, as quoted in Gee, 1991, p. 196).

Primal, original-time trauma can kill. It can kill unless its omnivorous invasion of innocence can be neutralized so that the tender tissues of the infant psyche can be anesthetized to the assault. Modern pastoral care is a merciful container and transformer of this primal abandonment grief.

Beyond Eden: The Unrequited Yearning of Purgatory

Purgatory Age: Puberty to mid-life.

Purgatory Task: To return to Thebes and claim the crown of adulthood by solving the developmental riddle of the Sphinx. To marry, propagate, and develop a career powerfully and successfully, but to also allow consciousness of a deep-gnawing sense of dissatisfaction and incompletion. To know, under the apparent surface of success, the lurking feelings of emptiness and unquenched soul-quest. A deep sorrowing, *threnos,* a lamentation, begins appearing in one's day and night dreams.

> I suggested the profounder meaning of the Oedipus story was that of human sacrifice and that it prefigured the crucifixion of Christ.
>
> JAMES GROTSTEIN (1997, P. 59)

> The people...found grace in the wilderness.
>
> JEREMIAH 31:2

There comes a ripe natural moment of development when ego must face the truth of its disembodied, unremembered traumas and pull them back into the orbit of conscious catharsis and integration. Freud saw it in the universal crisis of the Oedipal renunciation, which, if resolved, led to a capacity for symbolic internalization. Jung called it the moment of the inflated ego's sacrifice—the dismemberment of the "old King" or the old gods to begin the renewal of the human (Kalsched, 1996, p. 177). It is a time of seemingly endless struggle after meaning, a purgatory of recurrent pain. Many choose to deny or ignore this inevitable developmental crisis through resignation, self-deception, or addiction, but it is a gateway all must encounter and resolve if soul is to be fully realized in our lives.

Our lives happen on multiple levels all of the time. These deep-psychic processes are both simultaneous and sequential. That is their maddening complexity and paradox in our lives. Major developmental thresholds demand that all these various strands be brought into sharp image, body consciousness, and integration. It is this synergetic accumulation that gives us the energy burst and propulsion to move on to the next and deeper level of individuating dimensionality and soul-making in our lives.

A client described the increasingly poignant but cryptic communications of her aging, partly senile mother. One day the mother reported to my client's middle-aged brother, "The ghost told me to tell you what a fine job you and your sister are doing" (in managing the mother's care). Careful inquiry revealed that the "ghost" was the deceased father-husband. My client seemed puzzled a bit by this strange hallucinatory apparition. Then she handed me a sheaf of recent dreams. Near the top was a dream wherein she is:

> Riding in a car with my parents, my father driving, we enter a highway. There is a barrier at the curve of the entrance. My dad is driving fast and has to turn sharply to avoid the barrier by driving parallel to the barrier and the edge of the road. He sideswipes the barrier but avoids major damage. Almost immediately, we encounter another obstacle in the road. This time we go over it. Amazingly, we do that safely, again without major damage.

I simply replied, "It is not only your mother who is seeing this ghost." The deep image-narrative of personal and family myth is always trying to speak and lure us into transformed life. We can wake up to the Oedipal/Electral car wreck and avoid permanent soul injury if we get conscious in time and gently remove our parents from the driver's seat of our lives. For most of us, that moment cannot arrive until full mid-life. We simply are not psychically up to it before then (Dodson & Gibson, 1997, pp. 1–31).

The Return to Eden: Transformative Metabolism of the Disowned and Disavowed

Return to Eden Age: Mid-life to death.

Return to Eden Task: To wake up to and achieve one's full spiritual destiny. To remember infantile crimes—both committed against one's innocence and against others in retaliation. To blind oneself with remorse. To grieve the "curse, murder, incest, and disease" of the original Oedipal/Electral sin-wound. But then to "see" the deeper "beauty, blessing, love, and loyalty" of the deep narrative-*theophany* under the surface story of one's life (Hillman & Kerenyi, 1991).

> Understand that you are a second little world and that the sun and moon are within you, and also the stars.
>
> (JUNG, 1946/1966, P. 197)

Development is initiation; initiation is development. And psycho-spiritual development requires phase-appropriate failures and vanquishments as much as phase-appropriate successes and achievements. The emerging soul must experience optimal failure and frustration as well as optimal victory. This requires individuated parents who can inflict this wound of denial on their progeny as well as on their own possessive narcissisms. The Oedipal boy must be denied his mother. The Electral daughter must be denied her father.

The Oedipal/Electral crisis is an initiatory crisis. Men and woman need to become both poets and warriors, priests and prophets, if their sanctification-individuation is to be complete. At some core level, estrogen and testosterone are the same hormone; they are different faces of the same *quinta essentia,* a symbol for the essential element of the soul in the great medieval mystics. They just require a different gradient of activation through the life cycle. For most men, the first initiation, what I call the minor initiation, is to enter their young adulthood as warriors by seizing their destiny. The second, major initiation is in mid-life and requires a surrender of that destiny to the poetic voices and images of the soul.

The minor initiation for most women is to surrender to the destiny of the birthing poet. The major initiation for most women then is a mid-life initiation to seize their warrior entitlements. For both women and men, the Oedipal/Electral choreography proves profound, for in the myth is deep wisdom about when to surrender and when to seize in the systolic/diastolic rhythms of realizing soul across the loom of the life cycle. Framed thusly, the Electral/Oedipal event is a poignant moment of soul-making, a compassionate, paradoxical seizing and wounding of being in the service of being.

Grace Imathiu tells a one-line African folk tale: When two elephants fight, it is the grass that suffers (Imathiu, 2000). The Oedipal crisis is created by the inevitable dyadic struggles between culture and instinct. The human soul is the grass in between. At one level, this seems to be an overwhelming imbalance—a crucible of forces over which the soul will never prevail. But at another, deeper, level, if one escapes the dualistic envelope of Western empirical thinking, the soul has survived because it is the integrating, animating force of the cosmos. If the soul stays conscious and calm, it can speak to and calm these massive elephants of instinctual arousal:

My assumption (an ancient one) is that Nature, including human nature, contains within itself a directing intelligence (soul) which is the source of all knowledge concerning the nature of [wo]man's being and becoming. The rational mind needs to allow itself to be instructed by Nature, to use its imaginative activity to give the best possible expression to the instinctual-emotional-bodily roots of human desire. (Stein, 1973, p. xviii)

The Oedipal/Electral crisis is a crisis of imagination. The Oedipal event, and the even deeper universal incest taboo on which it is built, demands a sacrifice of the literal in exchange for the stimulation of the imaginal. It is the crucial juncture in human development when the soul gains its full voice and vision. By being denied literal action in the outer world, the soul discovers its inner presence in the narrative actions of deep imagination. The soul is really born in the grip of Oedipal/Electral passions.

I have been told that Jewish mystics believe that the real text of the Torah is hidden between the lines. I feel that is generally true about all things in life. The real juice is between the lines, between the walls. It is what anthropologist Victor Turner calls the liminal realm of ritual, the space between ordinary and sacred time (Turner, 1995). Before a community ritual enactment, all is ordinary, everyday, uninitiated time. Everyone knows the right clothes to wear, the politically correct things to say, the right gestures of social decorum. Once the community enters the ritual space, liminal time takes over. Everyone is naked or ritually clothed. All talk is sacredly magnificent or raw burlesque. It is absolutely dark or blindingly light. The soul is provoked and transported to other realms of terror and beauty. The person emerges transformed. The old social decorum is reestablished, but the liminally-affected see the subtle subtext richness of things they missed before.

This liminal space is also often taboo space. It is dangerous to see the hidden, shadow side of things. It is nice when life is kept in strict, clear categories of male-female, light-dark, hot-cold, moist-dry, parent-child, Eros-logos, good-evil. There is comfort in the boundaries, even if there is a gnawing dualism to it all. We would like to have things be seamlessly whole, but we know that's not the way this messy world is, so at least we can keep things stringently separated.

And perhaps the most dangerous mixing of all is the generations. Incest is the most universal taboo against imprudent mixing of primal matter. And the Oedipal/Electral complex field is about incest most of all. It is about a liminal zone that can either destroy ego or build it, depending on the conscious awareness of entry into its magical realms. All the individual and family life cycle is a progression through such liminal zones of taboo mixing—all of them incestuous in nature and all cumulatively influenced by the Oedipal/Electral primal drama.

Myth, when broadly screened, is *heilsgeschichte,* saving-history-story. Inside its narratives is the whole history of human suffering. Good duels with evil all the time. And when good is conscious, good and the innocence for which it advocates will defeat evil—by a very narrow margin to be sure— but evil will be vanquished until it re-constellates in the next developmental period, the next generation, the next *Aion* (in Judeo-Christian mystical traditions, the next New, Full Time).

Pastoral theology is a renegade theology. It is renegade to traditional, comfortable theologies of accommodation. It is the theology of the repressed returned to consciousness. And most urgently, it is a body theology. Pastoral theology trusts the body narratives the most and believes the body's theological proposition that what is core to life is close to Eros. Pastoral theology is erotic theology (Brock, 1988). Developmental pastoral psychology is body psychology—it maps the psyche as it engraves itself across the terrain of the changing body space.

And the Oedipal/Electral event is a messy body event if it is anything. Incest erupts in the genitals before it arrives in the brain. The Oedipal/ Electral trajectory is launched in infancy but propels us all throughout our lives. We revisit it at every major developmental punctuation—infancy, latency, adolescence, young adulthood, middle adulthood, ascendancy, old age, and death. Perhaps, in a developmental individuation well lived, we yearn more for the lost taboo parent/sibling at our death than we did at the breast. Perhaps it is just a more conscious, forgiving, and accepted yearning that is reinstalled in a body-and-soul-energizing way that makes it different from the unconscious torrent of despair that first marked the infantile eruption of such yearning in our being. Without incestuous longing, we would have had no real life. Its crisis was our first great teacher about the mysteries of Eros-mediated soul at the core of existence.

The Oedipal/Electral event reverberates across the whole life cycle. It intuits something of the essential mystery of that thin thread of Eros that connects our birth to our death, our masculine to our feminine, our light to our dark. It both starts much earlier than previously imagined and extends much longer than presumed by modern psychology. Much of its powerful, individuating conundrum cannot be faced with even moderate anxiety until middle life, when one finally has the courage to imagine terminating the affair with the contra-sexual parent (Dodson & Gibson, 1997, pp. 19– 22).

Ultimately, the Oedipus story is a redemption story. But like all redemption theologies, our redemption is always a qualified redemption that lasts only a brief developmental moment and then must be rediscovered and deepened at the next gate of individuation through which we pass (Jung, 1946/1966). We gain a little vision of paradise and then lose it again until the next developmental round, when we might be able to hold on to it a little bit longer.

There is a tendency to limit our myth to cartoon myth, to sound-bite myth. We remember but a miniscule portion of the full mythic tapestry. Usually this is the most dramatic, tragic aspect of myth. But in this severe foreshortening of perspective, we miss the broad canvas of myth. We forget that Faust did not wither in hell; he ascended to heaven, transformed by the rigors and travails of his journey of Self (J. Ingersoll, personal communication, April 11, 2000). We have done this with Oedipus, forgetting that ultimately it is a redemptive tale. The Oedipus who voluntarily enters the underworld at life's end is an Oedipus who has suffered through a profoundly deepened insight into his condition. He has individuated. He enters the underworld a soul-changed, conscious man. He didn't "for nothing" wander around all those years leaning on the shoulder of his daughter Antigone. Something soulful and precious was cooked up on that incestuous crutch.

In Sophocles' *Oedipus at Colonus,* during his final frail days, leaning on the guiding arm of his daughter Antigone, Oedipus enters the underworld of death in an ancient grove sacred to Demeter. He surrenders "in full confidence" to the guide of souls, Hermes. Oedipus is making his descent into the Deep Feminine Earth–the very force of Eros his rational, self-righteous, and unbalanced logos self had ignored for too long. In the end the body met the psyche, the mind the heart, the human the divine (Stein, 1973, pp. 76–77). In a very real way, we all must suffer the consequences of the Electral/Oedipal crisis our whole lives; there always must be a partial failure of our development way back then when we were young and vulnerable. It takes a lifetime to live out the meaning of that inevitable failure and to taste the fruits of its redemption. If we can wake up in our life journey and bear the numinous forces we are to encounter all along the way, we can become grateful for those raw soul-energies first awakened by that mad rush of incestuous, divine, Oedipal-Electral passion.

> There is a tide in the affairs of men [sic],
> Which, taken at the flood, leads on to fortune;
> Omitted, all the voyage of their life
> Is bound in shallows and miseries.
> On such a full sea are we now afloat;
> And we must take the current when it serves,
> Or lose our ventures.

WILLIAM SHAKESPEARE (*JULIUS CAESAR*, ACT 4, SCENE 3, LINES 242–48)

CHAPTER 8

Acculturation and Latency

Vivian Thompson

The latency age of children begins at age six and ends at age eleven. The beginning of latency is traced to a psychological event, the resolution of the Oedipal complex, with its end point being the onset of puberty. During the latency phase, great importance is placed on intellectual growth, competence, and a desire to be successful in age-appropriate tasks. Across time and across cultures, the primary task of latency-age children is to learn the skills that their society will require of them in adulthood, whether reading, writing, and arithmetic, or hunting, farming, and weaving (Colarusso, 1992; Erikson, 1950/1963). As the children's competence in their skills grows, they begin to see what their unique contribution to society could be.

The Oedipal phase is centered on the family of origin. The latency phase is the beginning of reaching outside of the family to school, peers, teachers, ministers, rabbis, community leaders, and various groups and organizations. The peer group at times becomes more important than the family of origin (Harris, 1998), even though the family of origin remains quite necessary for the development of this age group.

In the life of latency-age children, play is essential. Thinking of a child's play as meaningless or just a relaxing activity is not an accurate perception. As defined by Waelder, "play now may be characterized as a method of constantly working over and over, as it were, assimilating piecemeal an experience that was too large to be assimilated instantly at one swoop" (1964, pp. 217–18). Play therapist Garry Landreth notes: "Play is the child's symbolic language of self-expression and can reveal (1) what the child has experienced; (2) reactions to what was experienced; (3) feelings about what was experienced; (4) what the child wishes, wants, or needs; and (5) the child's perception of self" (1991, p. 15).

In later latency (age eight to eleven), games have rules and are taught to the children by their older peers who were in turn taught by their peers, so that games reflect the transmission of culture. The famous rhyme "ring-around-the-rosy" actually tells a story based on fact. Back when the black (bubonic) plague was around, a ring would appear around the rosy part of the boil-like spot, hence, "ring around the rosy." People smelled very badly when having this disease, so they carried posies (flowers) in their pockets to camouflage the smell, hence, "a pocket full of posies." When the people died, they would burn the corpses to ashes because the plague was contagious, hence "ashes, ashes." Then, "we all fall down," because so many died. In this way the seemingly innocent or nonsensical games of latency age children can persist as a form of tribal memory long after the historical events they commemorate have been forgotten (Day, 1989).

Psychiatrist Calvin Colarusso notes that although "the form of play does not change significantly after latency–adolescents and adults continue to play baseball, checkers, and Monopoly": the reasons for play continue to reflect "the major developmental preoccupations of each phase. For example, in midlife the normative anxiety about time limitation and personal death is momentarily mastered by the opportunity to conquer time through play. In tennis, there is always another game, another set, another match, and the opportunity to reverse time and begin anew" (1992, pp. 88, 89). Even in adulthood play remains an activity with significant implications for developmental tasks.

Interpersonal Changes

Children begin at the ages of six and seven to spend long hours playing with same-sex peer groups. Girls explore relationships through these long hours of play. Latency-age girls play jump rope, dolls, dress up, hopscotch, tag, hide-and-seek, and other age-appropriate games. They reach out to their own same-sex peer group in school and in organized activities such as Girl Scouts and Awana. They are beginning to acquire social skills. School-age girls were once thought to be less aggressive than boys, but it is now recognized that "their superior social intelligence enable(s) them to wage complicated battles with other girls aimed at damaging relationships or reputation" (Talbot, 2002, p. 26; Simmons, 2002). These same social skills can also be used to promote interpersonal and group harmony (Gilligan, 1982).

Girls practice the roles they will play as adults. They rehearse how they will dress for home, the office, dinner, and dancing. They play the role of mother and baby with their dolls (Barbie, Polly Pocket, American Girl dolls, and generic). Girls play out relationships with their doll families' being man and wife, grandma and grandpa, aunt and uncle, siblings, and best friends. Latency-age girls assimilate their understanding of gender roles from their families but also from their broader community and culture.

Boys at this age are also directed more toward the outward community as they begin to look beyond the family of origin. Boys are generally more physically aggressive than girls between the ages of six and eleven. Therefore, boys thrive on contact sports such as kickball, baseball, basketball, football, soccer, video games, and war games such as paintball. Boys enjoy organizational games such as T-ball and Little League, and organized activities such as the Boy Scouts and Awana.

Boys like to collect items such as Pokemon cards and cards of sports heroes. They enjoy matching wits with their peers over the various activities the Pokemon characters can do, as well as over the statistics of football, baseball, and basketball stars. Girls enjoy collecting stickers, pretty rocks, dolls, jewelry, and items that tell of their special interests such as Egyptology, anthropology, and compact discs (CDs) of their favorite music. They spend time with their girlfriends sharing these collections.

During the latency stage, boys and girls generally play and talk apart from one another. A boy in the third grade, age nine, could not stomach being placed between two girls in a circular reading group. Boys are repulsed at the sight of makeup and the colors pink and purple. They are very outspoken about not wanting anything to do with the opposite sex. They can be outwardly insensitive by running across the room to get away from anything seen as "feminine."

It is interesting to speculate about how young males come to appropriate these views. Is this attitude something they inherently feel, or is it part of the culture? Boys still grow up in homes where they are taught not to cry, that to play with dolls is to be a "sissy or a wuss," and that playing with makeup is a "weird" thing for a boy to do. These actions do not fit with the Western cultural ideal of what a manly boy does in his playtime.

It is my belief that the revulsion boys show toward girls is a learned behavior from our society. Given the freedom and safety to play in any way they wish in the play therapy room with just the therapist, boys frequently engage in play with dolls and testing out various kinds of makeup.

Girls are not so outwardly against being with boys. They do not overtly show their negative feelings as boys do. It is just that girls gravitate toward one another because their interests are the same, such as playing house and trying out roles as mother, sister, or baby. Grade-school-age girls may admit to their friends that they are attracted to certain boys while refusing to admit to this attraction in group settings.

Social Location

Having structure and being able to control that structure is important to latency-age children. This is why it is so important at this time to encourage participation in girls' clubs and boys' clubs, or similar same-gender groups, where the rules are all-powerful. Rules include how to become a member, what must and must not be done in order to remain a member, where and when the club will meet, who can and cannot belong. Rules serve to promote group harmony and contain aggressive tendencies for both boys and girls. This is all done for the sake of establishing structure and organization in children's lives.

Armed with the major skill of learning how to read, the child sees and hears through radio, television, newspapers, and magazines that the world is much different from what he or she imagined. Children learn that the world is a far larger, more disorganized, less predictable, and more frightening place than they ever suspected. Countries go to war; people move away, may be untrustworthy, and will probably be disappointing at times. The innocent and magical world of children begins to crumble, giving way to the harsh realities of adult life (Rubinstein, 1987).

A child wishes to grow up in a family with loving, kind parents. The child wants to believe that the parents are good and reasonable, and the child wants to love them. Moving out into the larger world of school and various peer groups, the youngster learns that parents are fallible and may not be part of the larger, more acceptable social group.

> [The child's] family may be the "wrong" color, "wrong" ethnic group, "wrong" religion, or may not have the "proper" socioeconomic status to satisfy the requisites of those "in the know." The child is exposed, perhaps for the first time…to prejudice and a devaluation of himself and his family. This can cause a great deal of distress and turmoil, calling into question a youngster's view of himself and his family. He must eventually come to terms with himself, with his position in the community of his peers, and with where he belongs in the larger society. (Rubinstein, 1987, p. 176) [*sic*, non-inclusive language]

In school, some young males have a tumultuous time. Because of boys' high energy, they may be disruptive or restless and may be labeled as having a conduct disorder. Most of these boys are really quite normal. Latency-age boys cannot sit still for hours without stimulating teaching, frequent breaks in schedule, and plenty of time to have other physical activities. This type of child may be misdiagnosed as having Attention Deficit Hyperactivity Disorder (ADHD) when he is just attempting to contain the energy of boys at this age.

Within the school experience, each girl and boy learns which behaviors are acceptable and which are not. In learning the peer group's mores and standards and learning how to accommodate to the group's expectations, the boy or girl practices fitting into the larger group or society. Each child learns which challenges he or she can confront and accept without causing physical harm and without experiencing guilt or moral discomfort.

Going off to school can be stressful to any child. The individualized attention and unconditional love received at home will not be offered at school. The child may feel overwhelmed by all of the new pressures and new faces he or she must now get to know. This will be the first occasion for the child to be scrutinized by an adult stranger (the teacher) who evaluates him or her on merits in relation to other children. The child will learn about achievements and competition and about assets and limitations in comparison with others.

Physiological Changes

A critical role is played out in latency peer relationships with regard to physical self-awareness. These are the years when sexual identity is usually formed. In early latency it is perfectly normal to see two six-year-olds, same sex or male and female, exploring each other's bodies. Peer physical discovery is not abusive when it is non-coercive and consensual between same-age children. Masturbation is also quite normal. Children need not be shamed by this behavior, but asked to please carry that out in the privacy of their own bedroom or bathroom.

As the latency-age child matures, physical growth is at best very uneven. Boys of eleven can be quite tall and tower over their classmates, making them suffer from low self-esteem and have feelings of being a misfit. Girls may begin developing breast buds at the age of nine, while their peers mostly have the straight bodies of typical nine-year-old girls.

As the latency-age child compares his/her body with that of his/her peers, real or imagined differences are magnified and distorted. Noses, legs, and arms are too long; bodies are too thin or too fat; and those perceived differences might make the child isolate and feel as if he/she does not fit in with his/her peers. These individual differences in maturation suggest that latency-age children have far more body image and self-esteem issues to confront than when they were in the earlier years of school—kindergarten and first and second grade.

Integration of the Superego

During the latency stage, which is divided into phases—early (five and a half to eight) and late (eight to ten or eleven)—many changes take place (Bornstein, 1951). A new psychic structure appears in the latency-age child—the *superego*. At this time, children introject the moral authority of their parents, and the new inner force—the superego—guards against the conscious desire and drive to manifest overt aggressive acts and sexual fantasies. In the conscious state, the healthy child is aware of himself and others, knows where he is in place and time, and has control over his actions.

As the child matures, the ego increasingly mediates between the conscious[1] and the unconscious[2] in the child's psyche. According to analytical (Jungian) psychology, the superego manifests itself when the child develops sufficient ego strength. The communication between the superego and the ego creates a balance that brings centeredness and calmness to the child, preventing him from acting on fantasies of sexual behavior or aggressive outbursts.

This process can best be examined in play therapy when the child builds stories in sand play during the session. The appearance of the mandala[3] in the sand play represents the emergence of the superego, an aspect of the Self, or the inner regulating system in the child. Jung, in his autobiography, *Memories, Dreams, and Reflections* (1963), recalled a time when he would draw a mandala, or circular drawing, every morning as a means of discerning his inner state. Only later did he discover the significance of the mandala as a symbol of formation, transformation, and wholeness in many religious traditions. One thinks of the Celtic cross or the circular sand paintings of Tibetan Buddhist monks.

The child reads stories, such as fairy tales, which instruct him/her about the many facets of the personality. Fairy tales also teach about the cultures of other lands and open the door for discussions about aggressive feelings and sexual impulses. Schaefer, Briesmeister, & Fitton (1984) note that storytelling can help a child communicate fears and anxieties to adults. Stories and games in which life challenges are appropriately resolved help provide the child with models that demonstrate effective ways of responding to a confusing world. This is true even in the case of superheroes that clearly have "special powers." Hero stories express the hope that the child who is sometimes unfairly treated by adults and bigger children will grow up to be strong, wise, and just. This is a wonderful age to expose children to biblical story–telling, encouraging them to identify with the male and female role models who demonstrate courage and forbearance in the face of adversity.

If the child is to progress in a normal developmental way, many issues must be addressed and mastered during the latency age. These issues center on sexual identity, integration of the superego, building emotionally intimate and supportive peer relationships, and mastery of new skills and talents. There are indications that perceived pressures to conform are stronger in the fifth and sixth grades than at later times, even though the importance of specific peer groups has not yet peaked (Gavin & Furman, 2000).

Depression and Latency

Children can experience depression and loneliness during latency age because of rejection by their peers. Rejected children tend to retain this status throughout elementary school. They are likely to have future adjustment problems and often require psychiatric treatment in adolescence or adulthood (Colarusso, 1992).

Hopefully, within the family, the child is loved and accepted. Classmates (and children outside school) won't automatically bestow this kind of familial affection. They won't bother to understand any quirks or preferences, and if a child has anything unusual about him that peers do not perceive as "normal," he or she may be ostracized or teased. In my clinical practice I have seen evidence of these psychologically damaging situations.

At age eleven, Jeff was a mere four-feet two-inches, a result of being born to two very short parents as well as having some digestive tract problems. In his same class was Gary, also eleven, who measured five-feet five-inches. All of the other boys in the class were closer in height to Gary. As a result, when recess occurred, Gary was always elected to be the captain of the basketball team, and Jeff was not wanted on anyone's team because of his small size. When Jeff was asked, "What do you do when you can't play basketball with your classmates?" he answered, "I just go play on the swings and cry."

In another case, nine-year-old Rebecca was extremely quiet and shy. When groups of nine-year-olds were placed together to put on the spring show, no one thought Rebecca had any ideas at all. If she did, none of the ideas would be "cool" enough for the school's spring show.

As a result, when Rebecca was brave enough to voice her idea, it was promptly discarded as being "stupid" because the idea came from her. Her peers even went so far as to send an e-mail to her on the computer stating, "You're stupid," and "You have a big problem!" Rebecca was forced to perform the "in" girls' idea in the spring show, and the whole incident left her depressed. Rebecca was very bright and full of imagination, but because of her debilitating shyness, her good points were not recognized.

Depression during the latency stage was the result in both of these cases. Clinical depression does exist in early childhood and the latency-age youngster (Schaefer et al., 1984). Fortunately, many child psychologists, psychiatrists, and other clinicians are beginning to acknowledge the presence of depression in young children and the role that depressive symptoms play in the child's development and behavior. Practitioners do encounter children who are experiencing psychologically real pain, which has debilitating effects on physical, emotional, social-interpersonal, and academic development.

Grief in Latency-Age Children

Acting-out behavior in latency-age children is often misunderstood and misdiagnosed. Acting out, often flagged as defiant or oppositional behavior, can result from a serious loss, whether that is the death of a parent, sibling, or pet; a best friend's moving away; divorce; or many other losses. Children do not grieve as adults do. Children grieve through irritability, hostility, and aggressive acting out toward peers or anyone who just happens to be there when the feelings of grief explode. Depression in children looks exactly like grieving symptoms and visa versa. This behavior is often misdiagnosed as Attention Deficit Hyperactivity Disorder or treated as if the child means to be hurting others. In reality, the child doing the acting out is hurting emotionally. This needs to be understood by teachers, parents, and other caregivers. In many instances, professional help is indicated.

Figure 8: The Therapeutic Process

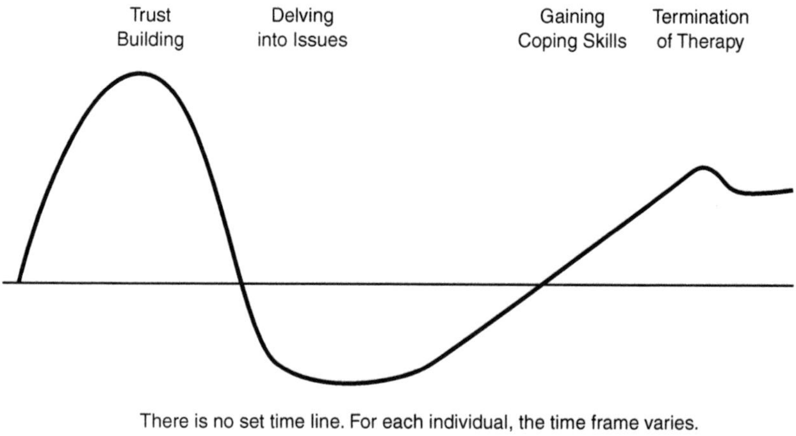

| Trust Building | Delving into Issues | | Gaining Coping Skills | Termination of Therapy |

There is no set time line. For each individual, the time frame varies.

Play therapy is an effective intervention for the treatment of childhood depression. It can put children in touch with the inner resources that all children have, and can help them master their unpleasant and sad feelings, help them overcome their resistance to verbal and nonverbal forms of expression, and move them toward resolution of their helplessness and hopelessness.

> According to Piaget (1962), play bridges the gap between concrete experience and abstract thought, and it is the symbolic function of play that is so important. In play, the child is dealing in a sensory-motor way with concrete objects which are symbols for something else the child has experienced directly or indirectly. Sometimes the connection is quite apparent, but at other times, the connection may be rather remote. In either case, play represents the attempt of children to organize their experiences and may be one of the few times in children's lives when they feel more in control of their lives and thus more secure (Landreth, 1991, p. 9).

Play therapists are trained to recognize children's play as a non-verbal, symbolic form of communication. (Play therapy is also useful for work with adults who may not be particularly verbal or have difficulty putting early childhood memories into words.) The play therapist's tools usually include a doll house, games, dress-up clothes, paints, and a variety of toys that are sorted by type–people, wild and domestic animals, machines, and so forth. There are two sand boxes, one dry and one wet, in which toys can be arranged. The play therapy sessions described below use a non-directive approach derived from the work of Carl Jung. Virginia Axline, in her classic *Play Therapy* (1947/1969), identifies eight basic principles of non-directive play therapy: (1) good rapport with the child, (2) acceptance, (3) permission, (4) attention to feelings, (5) respect for the child's innate problem-solving abilities, (6) willingness to follow the child's initiative, (7) patience, and (8) necessary limits (Axline, 1947/1969). The same basic principles apply to insight-oriented psychotherapy with adults, in which words are the primary tools of communication rather than toys.

The following case is an example of play therapy intervention. In all cases, the names have been changed to protect the confidentiality of the clients.

The Case of Janet

A seven-year-old girl, Janet, showed some symptoms of depression. She was having problems sleeping, and she was not eating very much at lunch or dinner. Breakfast consisted of a bowl of cereal.

Janet was the middle child of a blended family. Her mother was thirty years old. Mom had been married at the age of sixteen, and she had given birth to her first daughter, Colleen, at that early age. Colleen was seven when her mother divorced her father. Mom remarried one year later and gave birth to Janet when Colleen was nine years old. Because the mother was only sixteen when Colleen was born, there was more of a sibling rapport between the two of them rather than a mother and daughter relationship.

When Janet was four years old, Mom gave birth to Sharon and soon after went through her divorce from Janet's and Sharon's father. Then she was the single mother of three children, ages thirteen, four-and-a-half, and one year. She found that she had to work two jobs in order to keep a roof over her head and to feed and care for her family.

Mom began to lean on Colleen emotionally, and robbed her of her childhood, because she told Colleen about her multiple problems and her sense of being overwhelmed. Colleen became Mom's confidante; Sharon was the baby and therefore needed much attention. Janet developed the typical middle-child syndrome of being neglected.

Three years later, in her first session, Janet came into the playroom clutching a big stuffed rabbit and immediately announced her need of more nurturing from the mother through her play. During the first hour with me, she fed the stuffed rabbit carrots and lettuce, read it stories, played with it in the sand, and tucked it into bed.

After Janet's session, in my conversation with the mother, I questioned her about the amount of time she had to spend one-on-one with Janet. She confessed that it was very little, but at that point she could do nothing about it because she had to work both jobs to meet her family's needs. The father was not paying child support, so the mother could see no other way to make ends meet. The mother definitely felt anger toward the father for non-support; some of this anger was directed toward Janet.

Because nothing changed in the child's life, Janet continued to play out the theme of needing more nurturing from the mother. In her next session, she again brought in her rabbit, but safely placed it in the arms of a huge stuffed bear in the playroom. Then she began to make her play even more personal. She began playing with a doll that looked like an infant. She fed her a bottle, rocked her in the rocking chair, sang a lullaby to her, took her shopping at the mall, and even took her along to the grocery store. Then the evening came–she bathed the baby, read to her, and tucked her in for the night by putting her in the sandbox (mother Earth), leaving her safely with me (see Illustration 1).

Illustration 1: Baby Doll in Sand Tray

The mother continued to maintain that she just had no time to spare to be with Janet. It is important to note here that the mother was also a middle child in her family, so some of the mother's unresolved family-of-origin issues were surfacing. When I explained that Janet would be happy to just be with her when she went shopping at the mall or even to the grocery store, Mom replied that Colleen had taken over the duty of going to the grocery store, and that she very seldom went to the mall, because she didn't have any money to spend. The next time Janet came into the session, she made a picture of herself. It showed a little girl who was very, very sad with huge tears coming down her cheeks.

After this session, I spoke with the mother again, and the mother told me that Janet was really acting out at home. She quarreled all the time with Colleen and refused to obey her sixteen-year-old sister when Colleen was asked to babysit for Janet and younger Sharon. Janet refused to play with her baby sister and always had a temper tantrum at bedtime.

I repeated to the mother that Janet needed more one-on-one time with her. Without that, she would continue to act out. I also told the mother to take Janet to a psychiatrist to have her assessed for depression, because her drawing of herself suggested a *very* sad child.

The mother protested, saying she did not want to put Janet on any type of medication, so she did not follow through with the recommendation. I was certain that with the symptoms of having trouble sleeping and not eating well, in addition to the acting-out behavior, Janet was clearly telling us that she was depressed. The sadness was so obvious in the picture of herself as a little girl with huge tears. I also explained to the mother that the acting-out behavior, which looked very much like rage, was really sadness.

First, Janet was very sad because she didn't get the attention and nurturing she needed from her mother. Moreover, she was grieving the loss of her father through the divorce. She was still seeing her father, but on a very erratic basis, and this caused Janet great emotional pain. As the psychological pain continued and nothing was being done to change it, Janet's sadness turned to anger and rage, as expressed through her noncompliance with her older sister, Colleen, and also resulted in her sometimes being mean to her younger sister, Sharon.

Anger is a secondary emotion. It is deeply felt after some type of serious emotional pain that has been experienced. When working with a very angry client, I always keep in mind that beneath that anger is a very sad and extremely wounded psyche.

At this time, the mother decided to take her ex-husband, the father of Janet and Sharon, to court so that he would be ordered to pay child support. After the order came from the judge that support must be paid or a jail sentence would be issued, the father began to pay back support. As a result, the mother was able to quit her second job, and she now had more time for her three girls and herself.

At the next session, Janet showed the shift that had been made. She placed water in the wet sandbox to indicate that new life was coming into the mother and Janet was hopeful. The next time I saw her, Janet did the same thing; only this time she put even more water into the sand, indicating that her mother was continuing to exhibit even more new life and new energy. Janet was beginning to get more one-on-one time with her mother, and there was much less acting-out behavior at home as a result.

Then an interesting change occurred. During the next visit, Janet placed a bridge in the sand that was only a bit moist. There was also a little dead bird in the sand. In analytical psychology, the bridge is understood to symbolize a change in attitude. I wondered if this indicated a positive or a negative change in attitude. The mother reported that the acting-out behavior was increasing again, and she was very frustrated with Janet.

The mother, a very attractive woman in her mid-thirties with a dependency on men, had introduced a boyfriend into the family system. It was reported by Janet that the boyfriend was over at their house every night and also on weekends.

At the next visit, Janet placed three adult female dolls sitting on rocks with their feet in the water (see Illustration 2). Immediately across from the female dolls were three male dolls sitting on the sand with their feet in the water. The babies were cast aside, away from the adults, and appeared to be playing in the sand a great distant away from the adults. Janet showed her need for nurturing through the mother duck's holding the baby duck. Again, Janet felt that she no longer mattered to her mother.

Illustration 2: Female and Male Dolls in Water

When the mother became aware that Janet was having difficulty because she was taking a backseat to the mother's boyfriend, the mother became very defensive, arguing that she deserved to go on with her life in this manner. The mother had taken her stand, and Janet was hurt and angry again. Thus, the acting-out behavior returned.

In Janet's next session, she had toy soldiers in the dry sandbox. There was a very clean line of separation, and they were clearly fighting. Janet indicated that she had been having arguments with her mother about the boyfriend's being over too often. The positive point in this scenario was that Janet was finally directing her anger directly toward her mother instead of taking her anger out on her sisters.

In the following visit, Janet made a large red spider with huge legs and wanted to give it to her mother. She also wanted to tell her mother that the spider was supposed to represent her (the mother) and that the spider was mean. Again, there was progress because Janet could finally direct the anger where it belonged, toward the mother. But the mother was not responding to Janet's anger by giving her more attention. In fact, she continued to defend her right to spend time on her social life instead of responding to the needs of her child.

At this point, as a therapist, I needed to make a decision. Without the mother's cooperation, Janet would want to continue to regress to the point where she had missed the earlier developmental bonding with her mother. She would not smoothly move on, as she needed to do. However, I had seen this mother respond before to the need for more time with Janet, so I believed she would again. I knew from working with her that she genuinely cared about her children and truly wanted to be a good mother. If the mother did not respond, I felt that Janet had to be supported through this period in her young life, so the therapy continued.

It was no surprise that in the next session Janet took all of the domestic animals off the shelves, and all the wild animals as well. She spent the entire time putting the mothers together with their babies: a mother elephant with a baby elephant, a mother lion with a baby lion, a mother hippopotamus with her baby, a mother pig with a baby pig, a mother dog with a puppy, a mother turtle with a baby turtle, and on and on.

When she had them all paired up, she had them talk to each other about their day, and how they were feeling, and what they would do when they spent time together. Again, she played out needing simple plans, but they would take time. The plans included taking a walk together and talking, going on a picnic and bringing their favorite foods, going swimming and afterwards being in the sun conversing together. I once again went to the mother and told her that she needed to spend more time at home with Janet, baking cookies, coloring together, and talking more during the bedtime ritual before Janet went to sleep at night.

This time, the mother responded by saying that she would spend more time at home but that she did not want to give up the relationship with her boyfriend. The adults decided that more of their time as a couple needed to be spent at home with the three girls, interacting with them.

This was closer to what Janet needed, but not quite on target. In the next session, she made a picture that was clearly divided down the middle. On the left were the mother, her boyfriend, older sister Colleen, and younger sister Sharon sitting around on chairs and sofas watching television. In the other half of the picture, she placed herself and other babies in a nursery room being attended by her grandmother. Developmentally, she had regressed back to the toddler stage, where she would need a lot of rocking, stroking, and holding from the mother. She was not getting her needs met just because the mother was in the next room watching television.

Having conveyed to the mother that she was doing better by staying home more but that she still needed to be more attentive to just Janet, the mother became very thoughtful. Janet had been performing well in school but continued being argumentative with her mother, and at times with her sisters. The temper tantrums at bedtime were most frustrating. The mother wanted this to stop, so she began thinking of ways to meet Janet's needs.

Janet knew that her mother was contemplating change. During the next session in the playroom, Janet spent the whole time cooking food. This was a metaphor for ideas bubbling up to consciousness from the unconscious, about how the relationship between Janet and her mother might begin to evolve and change.

The mother began by asking her boyfriend not to come over on the weeknights. He complied, freeing the mother to spend Monday through Thursday evenings with her three girls. The time spent with the three children began to slowly change. While the girls played together, the mother would not participate but would watch the children play together with their animals and watch their imaginary stories being played out.

Janet next made a scene in the sand in which all of the younger horses were running around in a field and the mother horse was standing outside the sandbox, but she was watching and playing very close attention to them. It is significant at this point that the mother began a new position professionally, which brought much more income into the family. The mother visibly relaxed. Because she now had more money and more time, she was much more pleasant for her children to be around.

Janet made a strong ego statement the next time she came into the playroom. She took off her shoes and made footprints in the sand. This was stating that she now knew who she was. Her ego was gaining enough strength so that she could stand on her own two feet if she needed to do so. Clearly, she had moved out of the toddler stage psychologically.

In the following session, Janet had all of the baby horses going in a counterclockwise direction, but the mother horse had turned 180 degrees and was now facing her children. She was also included in the sandbox, meaning that she and her children were getting more of what they needed from her, especially Janet. The mother's attitude and understanding of Janet made a 180-degree turn.

When we met again, Janet created a scene in which the mother energy was present in the form of many trees. The tree is often a metaphor for the mother because it shades us, gives us protection, and, if it is a fruit tree, feeds us. The other piece in the scene of trees was the presence of two covered wagons being pulled by horses that were a team. Janet displayed happiness in the session because she now felt that she and her mother were pulling in the same direction and working together instead of being at odds, as they had earlier appeared in the scenes with soldiers fighting each other.

The mother was making time in her life to give one-on-one attention to each of her children. Colleen, the teenager, was most happy when she and her mother went shopping in the mall and had lunch together. Sharon was happy to swing on swings, to have mom watch her as she played in the sandbox in the park, or as they went down the slides. The bedtime ritual of a bath, reading, and singing was important to her also. Janet was enjoying the fact that the mother let her have friends come over on weekends to spend the night. Being of latency age, her peers were very important to her. Even better, the mother was actually playing with her and her friends through board games, baking cookies, and reading stories together. Janet still enjoyed taking walks and talking with her mother, and she loved going along for frequent trips to the grocery store because she was able to pick out some of her favorite foods.

A shift also appeared in the life of the mother. Now that she had a position that paid her adequately and she was more invested in quality time with her children, her need for a boyfriend ended. She was smart enough to know that working full-time, running a household, and being the mother of three was more than enough for her. Therefore, she wisely broke off the relationship with the boyfriend. Janet was feeling so nurtured now that she planted a garden in the sand at the next visit, meaning that she not only had enough food to feed herself but she could also produce enough food/energy to give to others.

The mother continued to be a stable person at home and in her job. It is significant that when she was emotionally available for her children, she in turn was fed emotionally.

In her last session, Janet began by making a circle (mandala) with leaves. She then placed rocks, a very strong foundation, inside the circle. She placed the mother turtle in the center and the baby turtles, which stood for herself and her siblings, around on the other rocks. It was significant that when she placed the mother in the center, it also signified that she was able to access the mother within herself when she needed to be nurtured. She now had enough strength to care for herself emotionally if the need existed (see p. 198 for Illustration 3).

This whole process took a little over one year in play therapy and included the following healing elements:

- The child's expressing herself through stories in the sand tray
- The presence, full attention, and acceptance by the therapist
- Constant communication with the parent
- The mother's willingness to grow and change.

Children of latency age show remarkable resilience when their emotional needs are recognized and met by their parents, peers, and adult mentors.

Illustration 3: Circle of Leaves with Turtles in Sand Tray

The Case of Tim

As stated earlier, latency is an age in which peer relationships are of utmost importance. In the next case of Tim, age nine, this was very problematic. Tim had no friends, and he was very hurt and angry.

Tim's mother died when he was six years old. His father remarried shortly afterward, and Tim was not ready for his mother to be replaced that soon. His maternal grandparents lived nearby, and the grandmother began having Tim spend a lot of his time with them. The father knew that Tim was having trouble accepting the new stepmother, so he allowed Tim to stay with the grandparents a lot of the time. In the long run this did not benefit Tim.

Tim was very bright, especially in the area of computers. He read everything he could get his hands on about computers, so his knowledge grew quickly. The grandmother allowed him to spend long hours on the computer and even purchased updated versions of computers and software as needed. Tim became isolated and seemed to be able to relate only in computer language and to computers.

At school, he was having multiple problems. Because he was so one-dimensional, he could not relate well to peers who were collecting baseball cards and talking about the local sports teams, as well as playing computer games. Tim became the butt of jokes from his peers because he was sensitive and his temper was easily triggered. He came home daily with reports from the teachers that he had once again initiated a fistfight. He also was not respectful to his teachers, so he would yell at them when he was confronted about his behavior. Tim was a loner, and he was becoming more and more negligent of his schoolwork. His grades were falling to the D and F category, and he was in danger of failing.

When the family brought Tim to me, the father, stepmother, maternal grandmother, grandfather, and Tim presented themselves. It became immediately clear that the maternal grandmother and father were at odds with each other. The grandmother wanted to continue to hover over Tim and meet his every wish regarding computers. The father wanted Tim at home where he belonged so that he could get to know his stepmother and have chores and responsibilities like other nine-year-olds who earned an allowance. Tim was torn between wanting to be with his father and continuing to be given everything he asked for at his grandmother's house.

In the playroom, Tim constantly worried about not having any friends. He made sand tray after sand tray using symbols of isolation. He made a tree standing alone in the middle of the sand tray, a lone camel crossing the desert by itself, a dog curled up in a ball sleeping alone, and then a boy (himself) playing alone on his bicycle, and similar scenes.

Tim not only continued to have problems with fighting at school but he was fighting with his father as well. When Tim was asked to take out the trash, he adamantly refused. His father punished him by taking everything out of his bedroom that he played with, leaving only his bed. There were not even lights to read by. Tim would run to his grandmother, and she would have sympathy for him and take him into her home again.

In our family sessions, it became obvious that the stepmother was quite fond of Tim and that she disciplined him with love. It was recommended that Tim be made to stay at home with his father and stepmother. He could no longer run away from his life by going to his grandmother's. The degree of anger at home and at school was not normal.

Latency-age children cannot be allowed to yell at their teachers and refuse to do simple chores at home. This is the age when responsibility to the family of origin and to authorities at school needs to develop. If responsibility and respect are not learned in the latency stage, the laziness and disrespect may continue into adolescence and adulthood. Tim's behavior continued to leave him with no peer friendships at school, so his grades continued to drop. The maternal grandmother started to push for home-schooling because Tim could then do all of his lessons on the computer. The maternal grandmother wanted to be the home-schooling teacher.

As the therapist, I knew of Tim's great loneliness and need for peer relationships. We also talked frequently about his mother so that the unfinished grief could be completed and would no longer be a component of his anger. I pushed strongly for Tim to be kept in the public school setting, because only by facing his problems with peers, teachers, and grades could he possibly overcome them. I could see home-schooling only isolating him more from a social life and feeding into his addiction to the computer.

The grandmother said she would see that Tim socialized by taking him to gym classes at the local YMCA and encouraging him to become involved in neighborhood baseball and basketball teams. Amid protests from the stepmother and me, the father acquiesced to the maternal grandmother and allowed her to begin home-schooling Tim.

When last we spoke, Tim was still a loner, still addicted to the computer, and had become very skillful at manipulating his grandmother into letting him do nearly anything he wanted to do. Now his whole education was in question. This is an example of how the family system colluded to keep a nine-year-old from going through a developmental stage where he could have learned to get along with the various peer groups present at school. In adulthood, I suspect Tim will continue to be very isolated and friendless. He will certainly end up working with computers, but this could result in an unfulfilled life without support from friends and family.

The Case of Jill

In another case, Jill, age eight, was refusing to go to school. She was in second grade and reportedly was well liked by teachers and her peers. This was not her perception, however. She viewed herself as being fat (which she was not) and ugly (she was truly pretty). Her perception was her reality, so she could not imagine anyone liking her as a friend. Her mother would reluctantly allow Jill to stay home from school when she complained in the mornings about not wanting to go because she did not feel well.

When Jill came into the playroom, it became evident that she had created a fantasy world for herself. She was obsessed with drawing cartoon characters. She would make up names for these characters and would carry on a conversation with them. In the sand, she would only make scenes with figures from *The Little Mermaid, The Wizard of Oz, The Lion King,* and *Beauty and the Beast.*

I talked with the mother about her daughter's creating her own fantasy world. We talked about the developmental needs of an eight-year-old girl and how Jill's needs were not being met by keeping her home from school. The mother was adding to the problem by allowing Jill to play at home and watch television; therefore, she was having fun, making school even less desirable.

The father and mother had divorced right after the mother became pregnant with Jill. Jill's father had moved to Arizona, so Jill did not even know him because she had no contact with him. This lack made it all the more important for Jill to be successful with her life at school, because she needed the peer support. It was clear that Jill was not going to make the effort to go to school as long as her mother allowed her to stay home.

Her mother and I talked about how she could not permit Jill to stay at home any longer, because she was getting behind in school. We developed a plan where Jill would receive a sticker of her choosing to place on a calendar each day she went to school. At the end of two days of success, Jill could choose a reward such as an ice-cream cone or a nickel for her bank. We gradually increased the number of days she would go to school before receiving a reward. Finally, after five days of successfully going to school, Jill could choose between seeing a movie or having a friend over to spend the night. At first she would choose the movie because it was safer. However, as a result of going to school on a regular basis, she did begin to make friends with girls her own age. Soon she began choosing to have a friend over to spend the night on a regular basis. Her group of friends grew to the point that Jill was able to invite seven girls to her birthday party.

Jill truly wanted to go to school and be a part of the peer group. However, she had convinced herself that she was unlovable. When the mother became the strong disciplinarian she needed to be by making Jill go to school, Jill's perception of herself changed. As a result of being made to go to school every day, she began to see that the other girls really liked her, and she did indeed fit in.

In the playroom, Jill's play became more realistic in that she began to do what eight-year-old girls typically do. They play with dolls and make up fantasy stories about being grown up. They love to paint with pink and purple colors and to sprinkle glitter on the paint. They enjoy making animals out of pipe cleaners. They experiment with makeup to fantasize about the way they may look someday. This is the form that Jill's play took. She was a much happier child after she began going to school and interacting with her peer group on a regular basis.

Latency-Age Moral Development

The moral development of latency-age children is strongly influenced by the family of origin, but is also formed by the moral values of their peers. They learn through play with their peers how to address their emotions such as grief, joy, disappointment, rejection, love, and so forth.

Children possess an inner strength and are resilient. They bounce back. Attempting to explain that they are the product of their home environment seems to be far too simplistic and does not account for the differences and variability in children raised in the same environment. How do we account for some children who seem invulnerable to what would appear to be devastating circumstances in their lives? Some children experience regular beatings by unloving and insensitive parents, but are not beaten down psychologically in the process. Some children are reared in poverty but grow up rich in spirit and outlook on life. Some children have alcoholic parents but unlike so called co-dependent brothers and sisters are themselves independent and well adjusted. Some children are reared by emotionally disturbed parents and are themselves quite successful and well adjusted as teenagers and adults. A possible explanation seems to be in the integration that has occurred within individuals as they have interacted with their environment. (Landreth, 1991, pp. 51–52)

The attitudes and values of peers and significant adults such as coaches and teachers add a most important component to the superego and at the same time provide an environment and a safe container for the discharge of sexual and aggressive tendencies through discussion and group activities. Acceptance by the same peer group is one of the best gauges of psychological health during latency, and rejection is a frequent indication of pathology and a very common presenting symptom (Colarusso, 1992).

Latency-age children also learn to understand the concept of discipline in a more advanced way. A latency-age child expects the punishment to be fair, such as being grounded from going outside in proportion to the number of poor grades he or she brings home. As he or she grows older, he or she can begin to understand the concept of negotiation. If the child refuses to help his or her mother with household chores, mother will not drive the child and his or her friends to the movies.

The peer group, in addition to family and community values, is a significant influence in the child's moral development. Within the dynamics of the group, children learn how to play and get along with one another. They must make up rules, learn to give and take among themselves, and take into account one another's shortcomings and intentions. The family, extended family, community leaders, and teachers play a most important role in helping the child gain the experience to make a moral judgment, through stories and imagination as well as in real-life situations. Grade-school-age children will tend to follow the lead of influential others, but more independent thinking begins to appear as they approach adolescence.

When the elementary school years come to an end and the skills learned there are attained, the latency-age child is now ready to try out new physical and mental skills. This is when interest in playing an instrument, mastering a new hobby such as building radio-controlled airplanes, or becoming an expert swimmer/diver may emerge. All of these together form a well-rounded individual who will enjoy life during adolescence and into adulthood, thanks to good work habits, a positive self-concept, and a sense of fairness in relation to the needs of others.

Faith Development

Spiritual development usually begins to find individual expression at six years of age. (See chapter 6 for toddler faith development in family and faith community contexts.) A child interfaces with different people in numerous situations over time. Until age five-and-a-half to eight years, the child has accepted the mores and values of his or her parents. During the years of eight to eleven, he or she begins to examine this parental belief system. By interacting with other adults and peers, the child gradually formulates ideas of right and wrong, learning to examine the subtleties of a person's intent and to make evaluations about a situation and its circumstances.

Latency-age Jewish children will put on the yarmulke (if they are boys) and attend Shabbat services at the synagogue or temple on Friday evening. They look forward to holidays such as Purim and Hanukkah and practice the eating rituals of their elders. The typical latency-age Jewish girl or boy growing up in a religiously observant family would not even think of marrying someone outside of his or her same religious group because children of this age are strongly influenced by the beliefs of parents, peers, and their immediate community. Jewish children who are less consistently influenced by their heritage are more likely to question the practices of their faith group when these come in conflict with the lifestyles of their Gentile peers.

Protestant children observe Good Friday and perhaps go to the sunrise services on Easter Sunday morning if that has been the practice of their parents and extended family. They observe the birth of Christ on December 25 without question. They recognize the norms of their faith group as modeled by adults; these may include specific prohibitions as well as familiar forms of corporate worship. Children who have attended church regularly with their parents assimilate the worldview of their faith group as part of their sense of identity. But they may also begin to reflect on the views of their faith group as they are exposed to a variety of faiths.

Catholic children are taught to pray to Mary and the various saints. In *Angela's Ashes* by Frank McCourt (1996), little Frank prayed to St. Francis of Assisi when he was in trouble, just as his mother did. He also believed that an angel lived on the seventh step of the stairway in their home because his father told him it was so. Little Frank frequently prayed to this angel. As Frank, the son, entered late latency (age eight to eleven), he began to question the validity of the angel's being on the seventh step of the stairs. He also questioned whether St. Francis of Assisi truly heard his prayers.

During latency, children have opportunities to visit the homes of their peers. They see the differences in the moral values of each household. So, in late latency, they begin to question whether what they have been taught is truly the only way to worship God. Even though children begin to question the teachings of their faith at this stage, it is very difficult to give up the practice of their religion without feeling a lot of guilt. So they tend to continue to live according to the religious teachings of their parents because they want so much of what they learned at the age of five-and-one-half to be true. To give up these teachings and beliefs would create great insecurity. So the answers to faith questions go largely unresolved at the latency stage. But as the latency-age child grows toward adolescence, he or she must be given the freedom to make up his or her own mind about his or her belief system, his or her moral standards, and spirituality.

Summary

It is with bittersweet emotions that parents ready their child for the first day of school. Although most children have attended preschool or kindergarten, grades one through six will demand new roles and new expectations.

Although the child will return during these years for emotional support from the parents, his/her life now becomes much more complex. The child's energies are now directed outside the home. In the greater outside world, if he/she is to be successful, evidence of maturation in emotions and intellect will be expected.

Latency-age children must deal with a variety of new situations both inside and outside the classroom. The child will come to realize that some peers may want her/him as a friend or a team member, while others may avoid him or her for reasons that are not easily understood. Children of this age must reevaluate ideas they had earlier taken for granted about their family of origin. Perhaps this will be the first time an objective look has been taken at the family, and the child's ideas may begin to change.

The six- to eleven-year-old child learns about achievement and competition, strengths and weaknesses, and cooperation with others. The child takes on new values and tries out new roles in the home, in the classroom, at a play group, in community worship, and in other settings. He or she tries these new roles and moves from the family's being the center of his/her personal universe toward the ever-widening world.

Children of the same age together learn culturally selected skills for living. The peer group becomes all-important and even a regulator for self-behaviors. The latency-age child learns about new heroes and villains and value systems that are totally different from those at home. Within all of these new experiences, the child develops intellectual, personal, and social skills that will strongly determine his/her path throughout life.

Notes

[1]Regarding consciousness, Jung notes: "For indeed our consciousness does not create itself—it wells up from unknown depths. In childhood it awakens gradually and all through life it wakes each morning out of the depths of sleep from an unconscious condition. It is like a child that is born daily out of the primordial womb of the unconscious" (Jung 1930/1969).

[2]Jung defines the unconscious as follows: "This consists of everything we do not know…The unknown falls into two groups of objects: those which are outside and can be experienced by the senses, and those which are inside and are experienced immediately. The first group comprises the unknown in the outer world, the second the unknown in the inner world. We call this latter territory the unconscious" (Jung, 1951a/1959).

[3]Mandala (Sanskrit "circle") is a basic form that can be found in nature. Mandalas are circular designs scratched into rocks, estimated to be as much as 25,000 to 30,000 years old (Jung, 1979).

CHAPTER 9

Early Adolescence

Venturing toward a Different World

Ronald Nydam

Introduction

One recent spring, a twelve-year-old boy captured *CNN Headline News* when he was intercepted by a police officer in a field near his middle school, marching with a shotgun toward his classmates. He was on a mission, a plan to search and destroy at least some of the people who had upset him. The officer intercepted him, only to be met with shotgun fire. He returned fire, and both were wounded in the shoot-out. In the end, the school was wounded, students were wounded, teachers were wounded, parents were wounded, and the community was wounded. Without knowing the many and complicated reasons why this early adolescent acted in such a destructive way, questions arise from this report that may be useful in guiding us into today's world of boys-becoming-men. The adventures of early teen development sometimes turn toward tragedy in ways that harm us all, taking joy away from living. In this story of youth and violence, why a boy? Why twelve years old? What was he thinking? What was he feeling? Why so violent an action? Why are schools no longer safe places? Where was God in this story?

Ashley is thirteen. Although it is still early in the spring, she spends her weekends on the Jersey shore in her two-piece bathing suit, enjoying the sunshine, her friends, and the looks that come her way. At times she seems rather unaware of herself, then, at other times, quite aware of herself as high-school boys show up and stand close by, eyeing her. At six o'clock in the morning she gets up by her own alarm clock and prepares herself for a bus ride to school. This means eating an early breakfast on her own, having barely enough time in front of the mirror grooming for the day, and starting a load of wash as she leaves for the bus stop. She and her younger sister live with their father, with their every-other-weekend mother only a mile way. Ashley is unusually responsible, pulling good grades, and making life work as well as it can. But her affect is rather flat, unemotional. She handles herself well, both with peers and with adults. She hopes to be either a veterinarian or a pediatrician someday—interesting choices. There are questions that come to mind in thinking about her experience. What happened to her childhood, to the days when kids lay on the grass and wondered what animals the clouds looked like? What of her body awareness and her comfort with being the object of boys' attention? What is it like to be a thirteen-year-old adolescent girl in America today? Chores may be beneficial for the developing teen, but what about this silent self-reliance? To whom does she turn for nurture and advice? How does she put herself together? What values determine her self-esteem? In what or whom does she believe beyond herself?

Changing Times: The Societal Context of Adolescence

Adolescence is a social construction. It is a culturally bound, very Western phenomenon (Hine, 1999). And it is being both squeezed and extended. Adolescence, for the twenty-two million teens in America today, is life in the "in-between," between childhood and adulthood. In other cultures, in other worlds, it does not exist. In some villages in sub-Saharan Africa, children move through a variety of rites of passage into adulthood and upon puberty take on adult privilege and adult responsibility. At age fifteen they are functional adults. In Western industrial society, where basic education now takes students into their early twenties and where nearly 50 percent of students return to live at home after college, the delay of adulthood has placed teens in the unusual time warp of an *extended* adolescence where they are neither child nor adult, where they are called on to postpone gratification, including sexual gratification, in order to prepare adequately for adult living in Western society. And now this period of in-between time is being *shortened* in the sense that there is less time for growing up. Church youth programs, which only a few years ago focused on high-school teens, are nearly universally reaching downward in age to include the middle-school student. The buying power of early teens guides consumer marketing. Families like Ashley's break up and demand more maturity of the children. With cyberspace in place, options for education, entertainment, and electronic connection are on the edge of limitless. Many adult options, in all senses of the word, are available to very young people. There is simply less time to be a child-becoming-adult in Western culture.

But adolescence is also being *extended* in that, for a variety of reasons, teens start dating later; young adults live at home longer, including the "new" after-college group; and marriages are occurring later, around age twenty-seven now. So the stretch of adolescence, squeezed as it is toward earlier separation, is a longer period of time. The pressure to be grown up, self-reliant, and rather independent is like a relentless wave in the ocean gathering strength from its own momentum. It makes for difficult swimming.

Parenting in the Matrix of Human Development

It may be the case that the contradictory demands of early independence and extended adolescence make for the development of different human beings today. At least in American society, the changes that have occurred in parenting over the past two hundred years have been so significant that the children of today's culture may be rather distinctive, more so than for earlier generational shifts. In the middle of the eighteenth century, with the commencement of the Industrial Revolution, families left the farm, where work relationships had kept parents and children together, and came to the city, where fathers formed a work force *away* from wives and children. In the middle of this past century, when the voices of women began to be heard and they began to pursue careers within a more equitable range of occupational opportunities, they also left the home, leaving parenting responsibilities as tasks and relationships shared with mates or delegated to extended family members and day-care providers. To whatever degree today's children are less parented by their parents, *they may become different human beings,* different from their parents in ways that have to do with variations in attachment to them.

The developmental theories that have guided our understandings of childhood and adolescence see growth and development as movement along a continuum between the early symbiotic connections between parents and child toward a more differentiated connection with parents as maturity increases. The goal of adulthood in Western society is a fully differentiated self, able to manage life with appropriate dependence, including assistance and care from others. And one of the goals of adolescence is differentiating–learning how to be a self, no longer needing parents, on the way to maturity. Although societal expectations are different for boys and for girls, especially in terms of dependence-independence and emotional self-awareness, still there is a way in which each must be on his or her own. The fully differentiated person can love deeply and maintain intimacy, can be relatively non-anxious in the midst of chaos, and can be realistic and accepting of human limitations.

Optimal development assumes the *presence* of parents as helpful resources who *optimally frustrate* their children toward healthy functioning. They are there! D. W. Winnicott, for example, speaks of the "good enough mother" (not necessarily the infant's own mother) whose presence allows for a child's development toward object constancy, the belief that the parent is available, believed to be present even when the child is "waiting" in the church nursery (1953/1971, p. 10). *It is the steady reliable presence of the parent, the primary caregiver, who facilitates this growth in trust in the availability of parents when they are needed.* Transitional objects such as "blankies" and teddy bears, according to Winnicott, are internalized and discarded (not grieved) as parents remain present to children *so that they can learn to leave them.* He describes the "intermediate area," or intersubjective space between parent and child, as the psychic place of personal formation (1953/1971, p. 11). The proximity of parents is always taken as a critical variable in healthy human development (Barna, 1995; Hersch, 1998).

But what if, in the general population of Western society, parents are *less available* to their children, both early on and later in development? What if mothers or fathers live a mile away and make an every-other-weekend connection? What happens when parents are further from home and further away from their children, both physically and emotionally, as these children seek to mature? *What kinds of persons do these children become?* How do day-care provision, latchkey afternoons home alone, pagers and cell phones, and personal computers umbilically linked to the Internet, so common in middle-class America, change the nature of the person the child in our culture becomes? Children are sent to school with low-grade fevers because they are not sick enough to stay home, given the difficulties of managing their care in the face of a busy workday. Single mothers, for example, are caught in the impossible bind of serving as both parent and provider; when something has to give, sometimes children pay the price. There are both moments of success to be celebrated and moments of despair to be managed without enough parental support. Self-reliance is less a developmental phase-appropriate achievement and more a narcissistic defense, a simple necessity for many young teens today. Young teens are parented by alarm clocks.

Peership in the Matrix of Teen Development

And, despite all the best of efforts of parents to be parents, what about the strength of peership in terms of the formation of young people? At approximately age eleven, peers become more powerful than parents in terms of influence. That is to say, having friends becomes a priority, and listening to them, going along with the peer crowd, becomes a powerful tug. Acceptance by classmates and the *ability* to have some friends matter the most. (Judith Harris argues this point in *The Nurture Assumption* [1998] in which she nearly dismisses the role of parents in teen life.) The persons that early teens choose for friendship are most likely others with whom they have in common certain life experiences and specific attitudes toward life, their parents, their teachers, and their daily chores and assignments. Normally, they choose those who understand them, who appreciate their attitudes and perspectives on things. Happy teens find happy friends. Angry teens "hang with" other angry teens, finding a mirror of themselves in another. Although the dynamics of parental relationships may have much to do with the initial formation of such attractions to peers, *these relationships develop their own strength as significant forces in the formation of young persons.* This translates into more momentum for the rolling waters of teen development, sometimes even pressing for the wave to crest and spill itself over in whitecaps of tension and confusion.

Culture and the Swirl of Values

Added to this swirl of winds and waves is the strength of the current that is culture–the strong moving water pulling the masses along. With rural life nearly gone in our culture, with parents heavily involved in the urban workforce, and with peers as an increasing source of nurture, *the culture of our day has even more to say about whom young people become.* The influence that comes from the consumer marketplace–from various styles of music, from hours of television viewing, from roaming in the malls– may be so pervasive that even the best parenting is still rivaled by the subliminal parenting that the culture does in terms of rewarding image and appearance, reinforcing interpersonal smoothness at the cost of depth, and setting forth material success as the great goal of successful living in America. And young teens, caught in the riptides between parents and peers and culture, sometimes cry for depth of meaning in a world they experience as shallow. Were the waters deeper, the currents would be more manageable. Still waters run deeper in terms of spiritual strength, but the shallow waters of Western culture's often superficial living leave some teens ready to check out or even give up on life. Many teens take their lives every year in America, at earlier ages than just a few years ago (K. Williams, 1995). In Nigeria, where poverty and malnutrition are constant and where two of the usual seven children in a family die because of this, teen suicide is not heard of. Why the difference? And how much of the answer may have to do with child-friendly African culture and child-less-than-friendly American culture (Curran, 1984)?

Confident Caring

Nevertheless, despite the myriad of challenges that today's young teens may face, *parenting teens can be as much of a delight as parenting in earlier years.* It may sound rather contrary to the concerns already expressed, but it is a myth that adolescence *must* be difficult, explosive, and a time of turmoil, unresolvable conflict, and inevitable rebellion. Empathic parents can at times "join the resistance," riding the wave of teen development together if they have an understanding of what might be going on. One father, when approached by his fourteen-year-old son about getting his ear pierced for a ring, simply said, "Okay, but if you do, I do!" The son smiled and wondered about a different way to define himself. Certainly puberty sets the stage for new struggles in relating to early teens; parents are often fearful of what these teenage years will bring in terms of painful conflict. Fears about teen sexual intercourse and possible pregnancy, for example, silently guide parental decisions. But the expectation that things will not go well is sometimes self-fulfilling. *Parenting out of anxiety and fear is qualitatively different from parenting out of confidence.*

Children-becoming-adults negotiate the waters of growth the best they can, one navigational decision at a time. Indeed, they face lots of choices, more than many of us present-day adults who remember black-and-white television and only four or five network channels. And as well, both peers and culture may be more influential variables in development today than in our days gone by. But these changes in family life, teen friendships, and current culture need not feed a disparaging view of teenagers and a corresponding need to control them or to let them be until they "get through" adolescence. Calling adolescence a "phase," for example, may be a less-than-subtle method to block our own useful curiosity about what life is like for them, creating distance in order to quell *our* anxiety about managing their experience. An empathic appreciation of their developmental struggles is critical to good child rearing and can result in an enjoyable, playful, sometimes painful, deeply enriching ride for families on the curl of the wave.

This chapter seeks an empathic understanding of early teen (ages twelve to fifteen) development. First, issues of *reality assessment* will be introduced as vital to perceptions of self, others, and the world. The paramount importance of *sexuality* will be explored, as managing puberty is the central theme of early teen experience. Issues concerning *teen identity* will be identified, although this becomes of primary importance in middle and late adolescence, the subject of the next chapter. Male and female *emotional maturation* for early teens will be addressed separately, as they are quite distinct in our culture and deserving of individual examination. And *issues of faith* will be explored, particularly as these relate to a shift from atonement to meaning as a central spiritual theme for early-adolescent faith.

Psychological Development and the Capacity to Assess Reality

The early adolescent is becoming a person who is capable of increasing levels of abstraction (Piaget's *formal operational thinking*), able to get and ponder and critically reflect on the cognitive construct we call an idea. Part of early teen life includes this kind of new reflection—critical assessment and logical evaluation—of the ideas and beliefs of others, especially parents and friends, so as to decide what is "me" and what is "not me" (Colarusso, 1992). The world of ideas, of thoughts, and of fantasies becomes the new place in which the early teen begins to live. Recent studies suggest that brain development continues into a person's twenties (Begley, 2000). With puberty, a spurt of new brain cells and neural connections develop, allowing for further mastery of auditory, visual, and tactile signals. In adolescence the brain reorganizes itself, pruning extraneous neural functions and consolidating frontal lobe functions (self-control, judgment, and emotional regulation). It appears that what is employed the most grows best well into later adolescence.

Although the boundary between fantasy and reality is thought to be well defined in early childhood, for early teens it may now be the case *less* so than is thought. It may, in fact, be a challenge to early teens to continue to discern what exactly is *real* in their experience. That is, they may not know about reality–specifically emotional reality–the way we would think that early teens do. By emotional reality, I mean an accurate read of the emotional experience of other persons, the capacity to become empathic. They may not have figured out how others experience life in a manner that parallels their own difficulties. One fourteen-year-old ninth grader reported of her peers, in the Colorado high school where her fellow student had just gunned down a state trooper, "Everyone here thinks they are in a movie!" This comment is informative in that it points to an *altered reality* in which some adolescents are not sufficiently aware of the realities around them: that bullets really kill forever, that shooting is bloody, that others have feelings and lives that can be deeply hurt. *This observation points not to characterological pathology but to compromised, unfinished development to which parents and society must attend.* Children need to play in the wonderland of fantasy. Imagination is their work; such play is their developmental task (Winnicott, 1968/1971). But with parents less proximate, they may have more difficulty sorting out what is real. Early teens may still be children; their fantasies and distortions may still be guiding their decisions.

The Skin Horse in *The Velveteen Rabbit* understood the problem:

"What is REAL?" asked the Rabbit one day, when they were lying side by side near the nursery fender, before Nana came to tidy the room. "Does it mean having things that buzz inside you and a stick-out handle?"

"Real is not how you are made," said the Skin Horse. "It's a thing that happens to you. When a child loves you for a long time, not just to play with but REALLY loves you, then you become Real."

"Does it hurt?" asked the Rabbit.

"Sometimes," said the Skin Horse, for he was always truthful. "When you are real you don't mind being hurt."

"Does it happen all at once, like being wound up," he asked, "or bit by bit?"

"It doesn't happen all at once," said the Skin Horse. "You become. It takes a long time. That's why it doesn't often happen to people who break easily, or have sharp edges, or who have to be carefully kept. Generally, by the time you are Real, most of your hair has been loved off, and your eyes drop out and you get lose in the joints and very shabby. But these things don't matter at all, because once you are Real, you can't be ugly, except to people who don't understand." (M. Williams, 1975, pp. 12–13)

Reality, as the Velveteen Rabbit learned, has to do with being rubbed. It takes shape as others mirror and affirm our experience in such a fashion that life becomes understandable, predictable. Reality has to do with our expectations of what will happen next to us, just as the sun comes up and the sun goes down, day after day. We feel real when our lives are noticed, acknowledged, understood. When we cry and a parent responds to our sadness, we know that our pain is real and that we are real as well. We are usefully mirrored. In relation to others, we learn about their reality as they become real to us, sharing their stories and life experience in close proximity. And we develop *a sturdy sense of reality* when our lives are sufficiently experienced with others who love, affirm, rub, contact us in ways that give us confidence about what to expect next. But for some early teens who have been too alone, the boundaries between fantasy and reality stay fuzzy, without clear perceptions of either self or other, with fantasies about the nature of living still in place, vestiges of childhood. They may remain too much in Winnicott's "potential space" (1971, p. 109). To restate Winnicott's observations about early object constancy in terms of adolescence:

> The [child's] confidence in the [parent's] reliability, and therefore in that of other people and things, makes possible a separating-out of the not-me from the me. At the same time, however, it can be said that separation is avoided by the filling in of the potential space with creative playing, with the use of symbols, and with all that eventually adds up to a cultural life. (Winnicott, 1971, p. 109).

Only when the ability to distinguish me from not-me, reality from fantasy, is flawed could an ordinary twelve-year-old boy start shooting at a police officer or a classmate or a teacher or a parent without sufficient awareness of the harm involved. Violent video games do not create killers, but they do facilitate a compromised appreciation for the nature of human suffering when violence does occur. Altered reality is not reality. It may leave older children and early teens "inside a movie" where they are unable to see and sense the real consequences of their behavior. Teens who attempt suicide, for example, often report a regressed way of thinking in which they believe that they would only go away for a short while, that their deaths would not be permanent. Just as an expired goldfish is flushed away, only to be replaced by parents the next day, so older children and early teens may be in a state of mind where there is less than a firm grip on reality, where magical thinking remains (Nydam, 1989).

Relinquished and adopted teens,[1] for example, often run into unusual difficulties with reality. They manage a compromised reality when their relinquishments and birth parent stories are not acknowledged, when both society at large as well as adoptive families do not openly discuss or allow information about the birth parent side of their beginnings (Nydam, 1999). They report "not feeling fully real" because they do not know these stories. When the truth about the why of their relinquishments, the health and well-being or difficulties of their birth parents, the nature of their ancestries, their ethnic origins, and their medical histories are kept from them, they are often unable to be or feel fully real. Birthdays are often odd experiences for adoptees, who report being unsure about what to celebrate and feeling ambivalent, wondering about the unacknowledged parents who gave them life. They are then kept from the necessary grieving that needs to happen when a break in attachment occurs. They struggle with identity, especially in early and middle adolescence when identity formation becomes central. Relinquished and adopted adolescents are substantially overrepresented in the clinical population, meaning that they have understandable and usual difficulties navigating teenage years.[2]

When basic truths about life are not affirmed, not "rubbed" by proximity to others, when both the joys and the struggles of growing up are not acknowledged, then a sense of reality may be less than fully present. Conversely, in search and reunion with birth parents, adult adoptees often report that they "finally feel real" in a manner that brings relief. When "ghost parents" become real, when the internal experience of adoptees is externally affirmed, then the human heart is restored to fullness in living. But not without the tears of mourning.

Bobby, age eleven, finally came for pastoral psychotherapy, red-haired and freckled and grumpy. He had been kicked out of summer camp for starting fights with fellow campers. Although not carrying a shotgun, he was still the kind of boy who was quite unaware of the feelings of others. He had punched his way through fifth and sixth grade, and now it was catching up to him. His blond-haired and blue-eyed adoptive parents were at the end of their rope, wondering how to be helpful to their son. Neither care nor structured discipline seemed to have an effect on Bobby.

Bobby was tough, successfully withstanding any efforts on his parents' part to facilitate change. His first report was that it was "a stupid camp anyway!" If, in truth, he did not care and if, in truth, he had no pangs of conscience about hurting others, then, yes, maybe he was on his way to characterological difficulties, a "hardness of heart" that would disallow significant healthy attachment to anyone. His parents became increasingly fearful when Bobby's anger turned on his younger relinquished and adopted brother, who was "taking it," but not without suffering. At age eleven, Bobby's life was in crisis.

After several sessions of pastoral psychotherapy, some on the floor together looking at football cards, I took initiative, in effect "leading the client," and asked about any thoughts or concerns he might have about his birth parents about whom he knew nothing. The play stopped. He began to weep and pulled his t-shirt up over his face to cover his eyes and wipe his tears, saying, "I worry about her all the time. I don't know if she is okay. I don't know her." An emotional and personal reality close to his heart had never been asked about, affirmed, "rubbed" by another. His birth story reality remained in a "ghost kingdom"[3] where the real was yet unreal, where birth parents were ghost parents, where his suffering was surreal and unacknowledged. Bobby's life experience, especially after age seven or eight, when the capacity for conceptualization gives new meaning to existence of ghost birth parents, was humanly depressed, struggling with unknown and unacknowledged grieving. His adoptive parents, who were to be the source of nurture and care for his partially broken heart, were not available to Bobby in the place where he hurt the most. This compromised attachment to his parents left him stuck, paralyzed in the midst of his sadness. His choice of slugging people was his normal early-adolescent way of communicating his internal frustration. When the *reality* of his birth parents was acknowledged, when they became real, then his development could once again proceed toward greater maturity.

Getting a useful grip on reality, especially emotional reality both in self and in others, does not come automatically. It is the result of a process of thousands of ongoing internalizations of the truth about self and others that happens within the context of intimate human interactions. However, when important matters such as relinquishment are not discussed, when inner experience goes unmirrored, when, instead, young people spend much of their waking hours plugged in to headphones, when they spend many hours online with Internet friends, when they live in too much home isolation, then a clear picture of reality, especially as this relates to their own feelings and to the consequences of their actions, becomes an image just beyond their reach. They become early teens at risk of not appreciating the nature of reality, of not understanding how their behavior affects others, of honestly not knowing what they are doing.

Physiological Change—Early Teen Sexuality

If adventure is defined as a combination of excitement and fear, then adolescence is adventure, especially as this relates to physical development. Changes in body and deepening awareness of emotions and of the sexual impulse make for what may be a tumultuous ride. For early teens fear may come first. The physical changes that occur when puberty "happens" are significant, perhaps more so than at any other transition in life. Body contours change, body hair appears, breasts begin to develop, genitalia enlarge, wet dreams confuse and excite the night, and menstrual flow begins.

It is a time of both unavoidable awkwardness and possible delight. These spurts of early-adolescent growth are unpredictable, uneven, and out of personal control as the body "takes over" in its press toward physical maturity. For some, these physical changes occur earlier and earlier. Girls-becoming-women begin menstruation earlier than ever, as early as age nine. Theories about why this is the case include better nutrition than even fifty years ago, growth hormones in food, and more exposure to light with electricity making our days of light significantly longer (Pipher, 1994). For boys, who begin puberty later than girls, the awkwardness and embarrassment of spontaneous erections make for unsteady sailing in early adolescence. And, of course, along with these many changes comes the occurrence of the pimple, as acne becomes for some a major assault on good appearance. No wonder that there are dips in self-esteem and a sense of uncertainty as these physical transformations come to center stage. These are the challenges that can create fear, as the next day seems so uncertain. What will happen next? One of the major developmental goals of early adolescence is managing and accepting these bodily transformations.

But puberty can also be exciting. When parents and friends are supportive, encouraging, and next to the young teen, open and honestly celebrative themselves, then puberty can be a rite of passage that is experienced as any of life's transitions can be—as a blessing. As early adolescents become pubescent, the *meaning and power of human sexuality within the family take on special significance.* If parents are comfortable with their own sexuality, if they are able to enjoy being sexual, resolved in their commitment of fidelity to each other, and appropriately private about their times of intimacy, then sexuality for the next generation can be viewed as another blessing from God. As puberty commences, early teens can internalize a sense of acceptance and pleasure in their bodily transformations. And all goes well. The first menstrual flow is anticipated, even celebrated—never a shocking surprise. When it happens, mothers and fathers quietly nod affirmation to their daughter-becoming-woman. Erections and nocturnal emissions are expected and managed with minimum embarrassment; sons have some sense about what is happening to them when their voices crack and facial hair begins to grow. Body exploration, including the "discovery" of masturbation and the power and pleasure of sexual gratification, proceeds with curiosity and excitement in a fashion that is relatively free of inner conflict and anxiety for pubescent sons and daughters because their parents are able to affirm physical changes, steadying the rudder in fast-running tides. In this case, amid the riptide of conflicting messages between parents and peers and culture in our very sexualized society, parental mirroring can be especially meaningful to ameliorate the natural fears and concerns that early teens experience.

But it is often the case that parents are not able to stay calm. Freud's very useful contribution to psychological understanding, despite his gross reductionism, is his guiding principle that the libidinal impulse is powerful and overwhelming. He believed that managing the sexual impulse is critical for civilized community. Much of behavioral choosing has to do with the wise and necessary management of our sexuality, often below levels of awareness. Dealing with anxiety about sexuality becomes the challenge for both parents and teenage children. Unfortunately, anxiety begets anxiety, and so the unresolved discomfort of parents is internalized by children, leaving them in the inevitable bind that when they become aware of their male and female sexuality, including the sexual impulse of attraction, it feels as if something is "wrong." This is the essence of a neurotic conflict–when something that is *normal,* the experience of sexuality (or of any normal emotion such as sadness, anger, guilt, or fear), is disallowed and even disavowed. Today, for example, adolescents may be described in surveys as "sexually active," intending to mean that they are having sexual intercourse. But this also suggests that, if intercourse does not occur because it is immoral and unwise for teens who are not ready for such depth of intimacy, then teens ought to be "inactive." This idea may solve the problem of parental and societal fear, but it communicates negatively to teens who *should* be sexually active when the phrase is taken to mean that they are enjoying their gender, their sexual attractions, exploring their own bodies, and in developmentally useful ways playing with themselves and with others whom they find attractive. In some evangelical Christian communities, teens are encouraged to never date, never kiss, never do much of anything sexual until they are at an age for marriage, as if age by itself could prepare them for intimate relationships (Harris, 1997). This is abstinence for the sake of parental and communal calm. But it certainly puts teens at a disadvantage in terms of normal human development. Avoiding sexuality altogether is a costly defense. The deeper waters still flow and will at times pull teens under.

Family values and attitudes that surround sexuality come to the fore when children commence puberty. The power of sexuality in the family system plays out in relating to early teens. This is of particular importance for sons and daughters who turn to their parents, at least initially, for encouragement and support when having acne lowers self-esteem, when perspiring is surprising, when hair is never right, when breasts are not yet developing, or when genitals are not yet maturing. An encouraging word from an empathic parent can make a tremendous difference. However, this is precisely the moment in developmental time when unfortunate breaks in attachment may occur *because of the dawn of sexuality.* Puberty is often problematic *for parents.* When, for example, daughters begin wearing their first brassiere, when their bodylines begin to curve, when their menstrual flow begins and they start to become women, fathers sometimes leave. Their own discomfort about their daughters becoming sexual nudges them away, as if staying near has unacceptable incestuous intent. Developing daughters are distanced, wondering why their fathers no longer hug or hold or touch in ways that were healthy and affirming only months before. Although the etiology of eating disorders is complicated, one variable to be considered is the dynamic of needing to create a body acceptable for parental affirmation. When fathers withdraw from early-adolescent daughters, daughters may be left wondering why puberty has made them somehow unacceptable. Human sexuality is not simply about the press toward intercourse, as profound and pronounced as that may be. It is also about God-imaging relationality, finding self in another, intimate connecting, tenderly entering and receiving a different human heart.

Social Location and Cultural Contaminants

In *Reviving Ophelia: Saving the Selves of Adolescent Girls,* Mary Pipher writes that America is a girl-poisoning, girl-destroying culture (1994). Today's parents are frequently in opposition with the culture in terms of teaching values and raising their daughters to become happy, useful adults. Pipher outlines the manner in which, early in adolescence, girls are called on to sacrifice their authentic selves and trade spontaneity and honesty for disorientation and depression. She describes them as saplings in a hurricane, attempting to manage three significant variables. First, at the level of development, early-adolescent girls are asking normal questions of self, what they think, how they feel about their bodies, what they believe their place may be in the universe. Second, Western girl-unfriendly culture pressures them into gender specific secondary roles in society, with a primary expectation of thinness. Third, they are called to separate from parents and go it alone, more than is wise or necessary. As a result, Pipher writes,

> Girls today...are coming of age in a more dangerous, sexualized and media-saturated culture. They face incredible pressures to be beautiful and sophisticated, which in junior high means using chemicals and being sexual. As they navigate a more dangerous world, girls are less protected. (1994, p. 13)

The expectations of gender for adolescent girls are seen by Pipher as overwhelming—too much of a load to manage without significant cost. Something new is happening, she writes, which disables them, demanding a sacrifice of self that they may spend a lifetime seeking to restore. Again,

> In early adolescence, studies show that girls' IQ scores drop and their math and science scores plummet. They lose their resiliency and optimism and become less curious and inclined to take risks. They lose their assertive, energetic and "tomboyish" personalities and become more deferential, self-critical and depressed. They report great unhappiness with their own bodies. (1994, p. 18)

For Pipher the developmental issue for girls is "power envy," the desire to have equal advantage in terms of the use of talents and pursuit of ambitions. This envy is managed by (defensive) conforming, withdrawal, depression, and anger—all responses to the cultural defeat of the selves of adolescent daughters. But open expression of anger is disallowed for girls; they are left to learn how to express anger indirectly. Women who express anger are judged; men who express anger are admired. Our societal expectation of girls-becoming-women is that they surrender a fully developed sense of true self and adopt a contrived identity that reflects these cultural demands. Pipher believes that our culture is the primary thief of the authentic selves of teenage daughters, disallowing their ability to flourish in life. This is in contrast to Alice Miller (1981), who regards parents as primarily accountable for demanding the self-sacrifice of talented children for their own narcissistic indulgence as parents. Adolescent girls are left struggling with the impossibility of trying to adapt to lethal cultural norms for their lives, never getting to know themselves well at deeper levels of awareness. They are not simply waving to us in concern; they are sometimes frantic, drowning in their early life difficulties and sorrows (Pipher, 1994).

Depending on how accurate Pipher's assessment is, it becomes quite understandable that many young girls struggle daily with bulimia, anorexia nervosa, or compulsive eating. They are responding to messages they hear in early adolescence—from parents, from peers, from culture—that they *should* be different, thinner, smarter, better than they really are. With regard to body image, they learn that they *are* their bodies, and thus, their bodies must be right. This body narcissism lends to preoccupation with food and may possibly explain the ease with which Ashley, at age thirteen, stands on the beach nearly naked. Her presentation of herself may not be as much an issue of sexuality, of being provocative, as it is an issue of appearance, of being noticed. Appearance is simply a way to be seen for many adolescent girls. Alcohol and drug use in earlier years takes the edge off of personal disappointment in terms of being physically imperfect. And sexual acting out may be a way to make the challenge of becoming sexual matter *less,* be *less* formidable, by denying and minimizing its importance.

When young people face desperate feelings *without* the needed resources to manage them, they may understandably withdraw, even to the point of "checking out" in the manner that many Generation Xers have done. Suicide, the ultimate withdrawal, which demonstrates murderous rage, is increasingly a choice for young teens. As many as one third of these may be related to further difficulties with gender identity. Hart notes that while 2 to 3 percent of the population is clearly gay or lesbian, approximately 10 to 15 percent of the population may be bisexual (1990). Managing and integrating these same-sex attractions may be too much to do for adolescents already pressed to their own developmental limits.

Although boys succeed three times more than girls in suicide attempts–they typically use firearms–girls are *four times* more likely to attempt suicide (Nydam, 1989). They usually use pills, which may be a cry of ambivalence about ending the suffering of living. Staying empathic to the struggles of early teen girls requires a significant stretching on the part of parents and other care providers in order for them to appreciate the reality that they *are* understood, that there is a way through troubled waters, and that smoother sailing is ahead.

For early-adolescent boys, one might think, things ought to be better. It would appear that if, as Pipher suggests, young girls are at a disadvantage, then boys would be at an advantage. Male gender carries automatic privilege in a patriarchal society such as ours. So perhaps theirs would be an easier passage through the currents of early adolescence. But not so, according to Kindlon and Thompson, two child psychologists who wrote *Raising Cain: Protecting the Emotional Life of Boys* (1999). They contend that boys-becoming-men are significantly limited in their early development because of the "emotional miseducation" that boys receive in our culture. Specifically, they mean:

> We build emotional literacy, first, by being able to identify and name our emotions; second, by recognizing the emotional content of voice and facial expression, or body language; and third, by understanding the situations or reactions that produce emotional states...Lacking an emotional education, a boy meets the pressures of adolescence and that singularly cruel peer culture with the only responses he has learned and practiced–and that he knows are socially acceptable–the typically "manly" responses of anger, aggression, and emotional withdrawal. (1999, p. 5)

Turned away from their inner lives by both parental and societal expectations, boys-becoming-men are "unversed in the subtleties of emotional language and expression and threatened by emotional complexity" in a way that young girls are not. Accordingly, they are left to manage the difficulties of growing up with a "limited emotional repertoire." These authors debunk the myth that aggression is about high testosterone levels, as if biology were the determinant for the inordinate amount of violence among boys (all the way from harsh language to murder and suicide). They suggest, instead, that basic human emotions are discouraged and denied by both parents and society so that a wider range of emotions including sadness, shame, and fear are disallowed in their development. Specifically, young men in our culture are taught to see the softer side of human experience as feminine and therefore unacceptable. "The culture of cruelty teaches boys that, in the male realm, feminine qualities are loathsome; to the degree that a boy buys into that belief, and loathes the qualities of tenderness and vulnerability in himself, he grows to hate parts of himself and girls as well" (1999, p. 210). Homophobia results; it is the stepchild of a patriarchal society that only acknowledges the "masculine"– the strong, the hard, the aggressive–as good for men. Kindlon and Thompson write that "the fear of homosexuality imposes a touch taboo that isolates boys physically from the comfort of touch and sexualizes any touching that does come their way"(1999, p. 81). Harsh discipline sets the stage for more aggression as an internalized response on the part of boys and early teenage men. All of this leaves early teens who are male struggling in emotional isolation, swimming alone amid the sharks of rage and aggression.

The most significant result of this emotional miseducation is the absence of empathy. Because their emotional antennae are directed away from sensing emotions both in themselves and in others, they are left at a disadvantage in terms of comprehending and understanding the emotions of self and others. *The foundation for empathic connection is poorly formed.* They remain unaware of the lived experience of others. Firing a shotgun at a police officer or a classmate becomes more possible, less forbidding, because basic empathic awareness is lacking.

The unusually high incidence of violence in American society is explained by this appreciation of the difficulties of men in terms of "living into" the experience of others. Early teen males, most vulnerable to these influences, will only grow and change by experiencing the very warmth and nurture that they felt the need to reject. They are caught in the bind of disallowing what they need in order to maintain the image of masculinity that society requests. Just as Cain rose up to slay his brother in a moment of envy around pleasing God (Gen. 4:1–16), so many young brothers with poor impulse control act and react in violence and rage, which betray them. Their anger becomes a cover in our male child–unfriendly society for inner pain, guilt and shame, and unexpressed grief. They can only tread water so long in the riptide of anger and aggression, and then they start to sink.

Faith Development—Redemption as Meaning

Early teens, the focus of concern in this chapter, are spiritually pressed to find meaning in their lives. To the degree that they have been more isolated and less parented, as has been suggested, superego structures, which are the internalization of parental values, are less in place. Accordingly, they have fewer difficulties with "pangs of conscience" in terms of moral judgments on behavior–both their own and that of others–and more difficulties with inner emptiness. When caught in some kind of misbehavior, they are more inclined to feel embarrassed than guilty. Embarrassment is an issue of shame, of failed self-perception and poor self-presentation. It is a narcissistic issue. With understandably more concern for self (latchkey children come home and fend for themselves), their primary concern is about injuries to the self. Guilt, a response to falling short of a superego ideal, has more to do with others in terms of violating the moral code of others, first of all that of their parents. Guilt is object-relational, other-related, including one's relationship to God, however God might be conceived. Guilt has to do with making a mistake; shame has to do with *being* a mistake. In *The Depleted Self: Sin in a Narcissistic Age,* Donald Capps suggests that today's early teens have more shame and less guilt, and therefore their redemption has more to do with healing the narcissistic injuries that they sustain (1993).

More than twenty years ago James Fowler defined faith as "a coat against nakedness" (1981), which turns out to be a very useful way to think about the theological issues that the young face today. Emotional vulnerability, for both early-adolescent boys and girls, cries out for a system of belief, a way to make sense of human experience that will guide them through stormy waters. Their own values will form around the effectiveness of these beliefs in terms of their capacity to uphold them as they begin to face further questions about the nature of reality, about their own identity, and about the manner in which parents, peers, and culture have meaning for them. Again, questions of right and wrong, about the importance of moral imperatives such as telling the truth, keeping commitments, respecting others, and caring for people, may all be secondary to their primary concern for spiritual survival methods such as finding acceptance, having friends, and wanting to get up in the morning. Existential meaning is primary. The day must matter; they must matter, or else life becomes drained of its significance.

The ongoing search for adequate mirroring may dominate the lives of early adolescents as they work to find their way toward themselves, in terms of deeper self-understanding and identity formation; toward others, in terms of the needed balance between object relations and self-objects (internalized people and things); and, most importantly, toward God, the metaphysical power or being that upholds all of life. Like adults, young teens truly believe in God when they *experience* God in ways that give their lives significance. *They are less interested in the offer of atonement; they are more interested in the offer of relationship, including divine relationship.* The content of their beliefs about God are both personal and varied; what matters to them is that they believe something. The current code word *spirituality* captures this religious value. The term is used in a postmodern, relativistic way. "God is whatever works for you" (Leland, 2000). The use of this term suggests the need to have a cosmic connection, a transcendent *imago* that steadies the course as young people navigate teenage living. Early adolescence is the search for the Spirit of God in ways that give youth hope by offering them vital participation in a world that is both overwhelming and understimulating; they can move toward calmer water only when they sense the divine rudder steering them through the passage toward a different world.

Notes

[1]Relinquishment and adoption are best understood as two separate events in the lives of adoptees. Relinquishment refers to the break in bonding to birth parents. Its effects on development may be lifelong in terms of how the adoptee constructs a sense of self and negotiates relationships. Adoption refers to the new attachment to adoptive parents and also influences lifelong development in a variety of ways. They are best *both stated* in reference to adoptees, as adoption has been unfairly blamed for the normal human struggles that accompany relinquishment. See *Adoptees Come of Age* (Nydam, 1999), especially pages 12–15.

[2]Two percent of Anglo-American children are relinquished and adopted; 25 to 30 percent of teen clinical populations are relinquished and adopted. But interestingly, only 2 percent of adult clinical populations are relinquished and adopted. Once the struggles of identity formation in adolescence are managed, adoptees return to more normal functioning (Nydam, 1999, pp. 65–67).

[3]Betty Jean Lifton writes of the "ghost kingdom" in which relinquished and adopted persons live, where they reify and manage the "ghosts" of birth parents, birth siblings, by-birth siblings never born to infertile adoptive parents, and the myriad of images and fantasies about what life might have been like had relinquishment not occurred (Lifton, 1994).

CHAPTER 10

Identity in Middle and Late Adolescence

Alice M. Graham

I see you seeing me:
I see the me you think you see.
You see you according to me:
You see the you you think I see.

JAMES FOWLER (1981, P. 153)

In the course of my pastoral counseling practice with males and females in the late-adolescent phase, I hear consistent themes: Am I good enough to be an adult? Am I competent enough? Will adulthood be good for me? Will I be better at adulthood than my parents? Can I be successful in the adult world? Can I be as good as my parents? Do I want to be an adult, really?

Obviously, the young people whom I see in my practice are actively expressing concerns, or someone has noticed a marked resistance to applying to colleges, finding a job, finishing high school, or asking a date to the senior prom. For these young people, there is a general absence of forward movement that would inspire confidence in their ability to manage themselves as adults. So if they agree to come for counseling, in my experience, adolescents are usually despairing of any possibility of a positive outcome for their lives. In addition to overwhelming internal distress, the young man or woman often must also defend against confused messages from significant adults.

This is a period for parents and teachers when their ambivalence in letting go of the fledgling adult is evident. The parental rules and guidelines established for the teenager may not be consistent with the child's maturity, or preparatory for increased independent functioning. On the one hand, parents have the clear expectation that the adolescent behave like an adult, and at the same time, they may harbor the profound fear that their son or daughter is unable to behave like an adult. Parents fear that their failure to raise a child who has the capacity to become a competent adult is a reflection of their inadequate parenting. These parental fears may be projected onto the child, further confusing the teenager, who is then emotionally caught between conflicting messages.

Many parents are unaware of the transitional nature of late adolescence, expecting the older teen to "just grow up" without providing appropriate emotional support for this transitional phase. Older teens require a quality of support that holds firmly and yet is sufficiently flexible to be responsive to the teen's push toward more and more autonomy. In another family context, this late-adolescent period may be a time of finally enjoying their teenager after several years of early-adolescent turbulence. Both parent and child may have finally accommodated the developmental angst of early adolescence. So at a time when stress between parent and child is easing, parents are faced with the process of letting the child go. In addition, parents face dealing with the loss of the child to adulthood, including any related emotional benefits they have derived from the parenting process.

> We all know intellectually that this is a time for our children to separate and assert their independence. But long after they have become taller or stronger than we are, our primal protective feelings are easily unleashed. We carry images in our heads of the curly haired toddler, the gap-toothed 6-year-old, and times when a caress or a hug could make their world all better. As they get older the problems they face have increasingly greater consequences. The stakes get higher. The mature, rational part of us wants them to solve their own problems and believes they can, but another part of us wants to stay connected, be in control, feel needed, and protect them from the pain we know they will face. (Coburn & Treeger, 1997, p. 6)

The seventeen- to twenty-year-old must deal with contradictory emotional messages from parental figures and their own internal swirl of anxieties. At times, it seems impossible to sort out the entangled sources of anxieties frustrating the young person who is struggling to make major life decisions.

Encounters with late-stage adolescents outside of my practice suggest that the range of issues that I have seen as a therapist reflect what is occurring in most adolescents. In order to defend against the anxiety consistent with such a major transition time, these young people may exhibit a good bit of bravado and confidence about their movement into the challenging world of adulthood. They may verbalize more readiness than they internally feel. Some young people spend their energy weaving elaborate scenarios about their lives in the future. High-school and college-age youth can become quite grandiose in their futuristic conceptions. The capacity for denial of seemingly obvious realities coupled with an often noble idealism serves to fortify their commitment to forward movement. In most instances, they will be facing a host of shifting expectations as they move toward a new academic community, work community, and/or relational community. They are leaving the familiar world of high school, with its easy access to their friendship network; they are losing their role as child in the family, church, and larger community. In a period that brings so many losses, grief, anticipations, and a myriad of unknowns, very few persons can escape some confrontation with fear, apprehension, and doubt about one's ability to negotiate the demands and responsibilities of adult life. During this period, it is often only with an exaggerated sense of possibility that the fledgling finds the courage to move forward.

Physiological and Cognitive Changes

In this "entryway" period to adulthood, the adolescent has consolidated the physiological changes of early adolescence and evolved into a familiar patterned relationship with his or her body. The capacity for memory, abstract thought, ability to learn, and problem solve are in place. Cognitively, the ability to think abstractly opens the way to critical assessment of their own ideas and the ideas of others. Superego processes may be altered in response to new configurations of experience. The increased capacity to test assumptions and construct theories supports the idealistic thrust toward social change (Colarusso, 1992).

The late-adolescent male is at his peak in sexual capability and overall biological vigor. The young woman will reach her sexual peak at a later point; by late adolescence her menstrual cycles will have stabilized, and her particular cyclical pattern will have been accommodated. Both genders will be aware of a pull toward deeper levels of intimacy as a way to know themselves and be known more fully in response to their fully matured sexual capabilities. For males and females, some acceptance of physical capacities as confirmed by school athletic experiences and peers has occurred. This self-acceptance may reflect a resignation to physical realities rather than a positive accommodation. The overweight, clumsy thirteen-year-old may have evolved into a sturdy, intimidating football player; or the tall, thin, angular twelve-year-old may have become the agile basketball player. For another late-stage adolescent, the dreams of being the star of the soccer team may have dissolved in the face of poor hand-eye coordination, weight issues, or a range of other physical limitations.

Resignation to physical limitations may combine with other faulty resolutions at earlier stages of development, resulting in a body image more reflective of distorted resolutions than of a reality-based valuing of the body self.

> Because body growth is uneven and uncontrollable, it is accompanied, even in the most beautiful girl or handsome boy, with periodic losses in self-esteem and injured narcissism. As the adolescent compares his or her body with that of peers and adults, real or imagined differences are magnified and distorted. Legs, arms, and noses are too long; pimples too gross and obvious; and in private thought or conversation with best friends, breasts and penises are too small—or too big. (Colarusso, 1992, p. 92)

In the absence of any overt trauma, the body relationship reflects the cumulative accommodations of earlier stages.

In this stage, some workable resolution with the body self must occur in order to move forward into the work world and adult relationships. This accommodation solidifies, for the time being, issues of shame and fear related to the body self. The African American college student may adopt Afrocentric dress to contain and defend against fear and shame absorbed from the culture at large. The white college student may adopt some countercultural way of being to ward off parental "demons" of conformism and conservatism. The short person may focus their energy on intellectual achievements in order to deflect attention from a small stature. The Asian-born student may become meticulously "Western" in order to fit in, rationalizing this as necessary for readiness to successfully enter the Western work world. Whatever body conflicts remain from earlier adolescence are to be contained and emotionally obscured for the sake of forward movement. In my experience as a therapist, only those body issues that impede forward movement can be effectively addressed while a young person is struggling with moving into adulthood. For example, a successful high school "jock" tends to resist considering the future limitations of his athletic abilities in terms of long-term life goals. The beautiful adolescent finding validation in a budding modeling career may be unwilling to take seriously concerns about broader preparation for her life. So whatever has contributed to identity validation will be understood as the vehicle for continuing successful functioning in the adult world.

In the face of traumas such as rape, physical abuse, serious injury, or debilitating illness, there will be a decisive impact on the young person's relationship with his or her body self. Such incidents will have a critical impact on the person's ability to resolve the developmental tasks of this period. The body self as the repository for all previous resolutions is critical to the emerging life plan. For instance, a young woman who had been studying ballet since the age of five years discovers that she has a knee injury that cannot be repaired. She must radically change her expectations of her body as the primary vehicle of future aspirations, not to mention the identity issues with which she will struggle in order to move into the next phase of development. Body assaults are a disruptive, disturbing intrusion into a relatively new solidification of body image, which is in itself an accommodation. An athletic jock who sustains a serious sports injury must radically reevaluate life plans and construct a new self-concept, perhaps, in direct contradiction to the one that seemed to be a given. Athletes or musicians who must face the fact that their skills are not sufficient to obtain the dreamed-of scholarship may turn against their body selves as the cause of their inability to move on with their life script. Eating disorders are another expression of the body's being used to manage internal conflicts that threaten continuing emotional development. A wide range of issues involving weight, physical appearance, and physical abilities contribute to shaping an adolescent's views about what is possible in the future. These self-assessments are often distorted through unrealistic comparisons with standards of perfection absorbed from the media, parental projections, and limited life experience.

Intrapsychic and Interpersonal Changes

The late-stage adolescent is confronted with the impulse to flourish. The impulse to get on with life, to take charge, to move more toward an unfolding sense of what it means to become an adult characterizes this phase of development. Whether this impulse to become is empowering or intimidating for the individual depends on a wide range of internal and interpersonal factors. How are people in his community of relationships responding to his efforts to "try on" adult behaviors? What about her is being affirmed, and what is not being affirmed? Internally, there is a need for validation of understandings, wants, and dreams. Externalizing these needs gives tremendous power to being seen and named in a particular way by the external world. In the process of being seen as a young adult, the adolescent is cueing the world about his or expectations and is being cued by the external world about what is possible. Effective reciprocal cueing affirms the solidifying identity and encourages the emerging adult.

For example, an eighteen-year-old boy is startled to realize that in his white family no one ever refers to skin color when describing persons of color. He is both curious about this as an aspect of whiteness—his whiteness—and angered by the absence of support for stating what he thinks ought to be a simple descriptive detail. He is confused by an awareness of his unwitting participation in this familial pattern and challenged and threatened by what it would mean to his internal sense of self to deviate from family and communal norms. This internal dilemma is further complicated by a realization that it means something that his therapist is African American and that he is white. What is the "right" meaning of behaviors, and who is the person in relation to the "right" meanings? Fowler (1981) would see these as the typical questions of Stage 3–synthetic-conventional faith that are quite dependent on one's relational context. Variations on this kind of experience affect the developing adolescent as he/she moves through the many communities of people that frame and participate in his/her world. These realizations of contradictions, understandings, and puzzlings are integral to the process of "composing a me." The adolescent may be plagued by questions such as "Which parts of me that you see are me? Which parts do I not want to be me? Which parts of the me that you see have to be me?" This is very different from the early-stage adolescent, who is asking, "Is there a 'me?'"

The seventeen- to twenty-year-old is creating a self in the midst of a sea of projections–his or her own and others'. Some of the received projections feel good and are affirming, while others are off-putting and disturbing. The increasing degree of independent functioning typical of late adolescence has gradually moved individuals into an ever-more-complex network of relationships drawn from their family, school, peers, work, and other communities that envelop their lives. Many young people are negotiating the competing demands of the work and school communities with peers and with the home community. They are confronted with the often conflicting expectations of these communities as they struggle to define a personal identity effective for realizing their future goals. There is the illusory sense or expectation that the composing of this identity is primarily the result of his or her own personal effort. In reality, at this stage the core identity has already been shaped and influenced by a host of historical and developmental factors. It is this illusion of self-creation that provides the energy for self-composition.

A seventeen-year-old declares that the world created by her parents is a false world that has only minimal redeeming qualities. The young woman, having initiated the process of individuation, proceeds to re-create herself along lines that feel more "like her." In opposition to the falsity of her parents' lives, she will be a "good" person. These initial steps into individuation leave the individual's functioning in the world shaped by her parental community, albeit in a negative relationship with that world. It is this writer's contention that this very illusion of self-creation lays the foundation for more profound reality-based re-creations in later stages of adulthood. The impulse to flourish of this stage is to declare that I can be a person who is free from overt parental influence. I can create the self that "I" am to be.

> The spirit, restless with its limited successes and its corresponding failure to liberate itself without entailing further entrapment, now breaks free in the strange new powers of adolescence. (Loder, 1998, p. 204)

Losses of relationships, failures in efforts to achieve particular goals, and frustrations in realizing one's hopes for the self during the adolescent phase can serve to inhibit, constrict, or extinguish the impulse to flourish. For instance, a bright nineteen-year-old college junior, unable to formulate a life plan from her own range of interests, fell into despair about her ability to move forward with her life. Following the parental script in most respects thus far, she felt completely stymied about how to use her intellectual acumen and her undeveloped imaginative self to see herself into the future. This was particularly confusing because, up to this point, her self-concept of being self-initiating and autonomous was a major factor in her success. Due to a particular set of circumstances, her developmental options had been limited to the academic arena until college. Feeling herself both privileged and underprivileged in reaction to the many projections of hopes and expectations, hers and others, she deemed herself inadequate and unable to assume adult status. Hidden within her despair was a secret sense that she was different in some important ways from her family. This secret, if acknowledged, would initiate for her the overwhelming process of individuation; that is, the process of self-definition necessary for movement at this stage. Having been able to avoid conscious awareness of her own distinct identity, through a complex combination of social and relational circumstances and intrapsychic development, she felt unable to move forward in developing a more personalized life plan.

A struggle for self-definition can develop for youth who are at odds with their families due to differences in personality—the dilemma of an introverted child growing up in an extroverted household, for example (Keirsey, 1998). The difficulties inherent in the late-adolescent task of self-definition are exacerbated in the case of an adopted person if essential information about the young person's origins and birth family has not been disclosed (cf. Brock & Parker, 2001; Nydam, 1999).

Equally problematic is the case of youth who are overly conformist in late adolescence and therefore fail to initiate a separate identity that is not dependent on their immediate family and community. Another young woman chose to continue the parental script because it was too overwhelming not to remain within it. She could only tolerate minor personalized deviations at this stage. Some persons will choose not to move at all, delaying for a time the intrapsychic work of self-definition. They may opt to delay college or take a year off in order to be freed sufficiently from parental and community projections to develop a greater sense of identity.

Erik Erikson suggests that every culture devises ways for its young people to take a moratorium in ways that are keeping with the society's values (1968). For instance, a study year abroad, a cross-country camping trek, doing manual labor—all are ways to create sufficient space for their emergence. This willingness to step out of a given pattern of expectations may in itself be the initiation of significant work of individuation. Unfortunately, self-negating responses to the impulse to flourish can occur.

Erikson recognizes that attempts to delay or avoid movement through an emotional time-out can fail, resulting in persons committing themselves to a path that is ultimately self-destructive. Increased experimentation with drugs and other risk-taking behaviors involving reckless driving, sex, and violence may serve to distract from overwhelming internal conflicts. In the older adolescent, these destructive involvements may camouflage fears about the ability to survive the future. Girls may suppress their future-oriented strivings by losing themselves in a premature committed relationship that avoids the anxiety and sense of isolation that accompanies the demands of self-definition. As a result of socialization patterns in our culture, girls may have more difficulty with individuation, looking to escape the process by fusing with another person. This avoidance through fusion with another may be culturally sanctioned with a fabulous wedding celebrated by family and community.

Both males and females may avoid the challenges of self-definition by following the traditional socialization pathways historically offered by the culture as represented in their local community. Each may opt for seeing their futures only through the lens of gender-specific roles, ignoring aspirations that cannot be easily affirmed by others. Some boys may get caught up in ill-conceived, machismo-fueled enterprises to prove themselves male enough to outwit the "system"—in reality, they are also avoiding the tension that comes with the process of composing one's life. The impulse to flourish may be extinguished by any number of negative sociological factors, such as severe academic deficiencies, poor social skills, oppressive poverty, impoverished relational networks, and overwhelming chaos in the adolescent's current life. Any of these factors alone or in combination may result in the loss of the capacity to form a positive compelling vision of the self for the future.

> The greater danger to the human spirit in this is not from the adolescent but from the sociocultural side: the fear of nonconformity on the part of the status quo society will not so much redirect or transform the human spirit, but if possible, suppress or break it so it will conform without complaint. (Loder, 1998, p. 205)

Without a socially affirmed vision that supports the impulse to flourish, there is often not sufficient psychic energy or relational support available to the individual to move forward. This may account for the fact that so few adults move beyond the "Stage 3" faith that first emerges in adolescence (Fowler, 1981). Yet in every generation there are numerous examples of persons who, despite the absence of social affirmation, relational support, or socially affirmed vision, were able to glean a meaningful framework for their existence that supported forward movement.

Moral and Faith Development

In late adolescence the capacity for abstract reasoning allows young people to critically assess and logically evaluate their ideas and the ideas of others. God can be conceptualized as a spirit. So a God that was experienced anthropomorphically, as an old gray-haired man with a beard, can now be understood as a being that cannot be seen and is everywhere. For adolescents, the qualities ascribed to God are a derivative of how they understand the self in relation to the significant others in their life. The religious beliefs of a relative or friend with whom they felt really loved and understood may be the source of their faith. Conversely, those caretakers who were emotionally abusive to them may result in a rejection of all things religious. Early prolonged periods of inconsistent care may be internalized to the point where it is inconceivable that anything not tangible and concrete could be trusted. Their understanding of faith and morality emerges from the cumulative body of meaning derived from the overall pattern of relational experiences encountered on their developmental path. Utilizing Erikson's understanding of human development, we can say that through the resolution of crises in each of the developmental stages preceding adolescence the young person has internalized the meaning that he or she has for the external world. These meanings can provide clear categories of right and wrong. These categories can then reinforce the person's ability to know who and what he or she is to be about.

> The end of my childhood coincided with my marriage at eighteen to another boy whom I wanted to marry, I think now, not just because he reminded me of my father, but because at some dim level he also seemed to offer me a way out from under the burden of my unworthiness of my mother's love and sacrifices. He believed entirely in what I learned as a child about the importance of sacrifice for women. Wives sacrifice; husbands receive. If I could prove my love to him by the sacrifices I could make; if I could become the one sacrificing rather than the one sacrificed for, I would no longer be unworthy. I would be an adult woman. I would be free. My sacrifices would quench my burning anger and raging guilt. (Bondi, 1995, p. 133)

The older adolescent relies heavily on external authority for understanding and applying faith to life choices. For older adolescents, it is critical for them to feel valued and to feel that their behavioral choices are consistent with those of someone who values them. For this valuing to contribute to forward movement, it must have non-negating meaning for the adolescent. The Bondi quote cited above illustrates the kind of temporary resolution that the older adolescent can make in an effort to comply with familial, communal, and religious norms and values. In virtually every case in which the author has been involved with adolescents, it was important to the progress of therapy for the adolescent to identify a person who valued him or her in ways that were meaningful to the teen. Bondi found this in her boy-husband and the model drawn from her mother's life. This is one reason why conversion experiences can be so intense at this stage. Public conversion experiences are communal and usually provide a community to support and encourage the converted. Conversion offers a clear way to be and provides specific ways to be accepted by God. These ways are usually concrete and actionable. However, if the anxieties around developmental issues are too great, then young people may substitute consuming religiosity for appropriate wrestling with the conflicts and contradictions inherent in their expanding awareness of the complexity of adult demands and expectations (cf. A. Freud, 1936/1966).

One young woman from a sheltered background in a small town found herself adrift as a college freshman on an urban campus. She had minimal skills in negotiating conflicting demands and expectations, her own and those of others. In order to escape the profound confusion she experienced in not knowing what was right and wrong for her in this diverse context of values, she took refuge in the religiosity of a cult-like church congregation. Within this congregation she found validation of her fears about the confusing "evil" forces dominating the world outside the congregation. Here, she could regain a sense of safety that was reminiscent of her childhood and avoid the internal distress that college life presented. Learning languages in preparation for a career in international diplomacy became irrelevant. Her religious commitment to God was her singular focus. The demand that she heard from congregational leadership was that God should be the constant daily focus of her attention through continuous prayer and meditation. In this situation, her appropriation of the "faith" excluded any attention to her urges toward sexual intimacy, clarifying her identity amid relational complexity, composing a concept of self useful to her in the adult world, and the academic preparation needed to realize her aspirations. Consumed with religious fervor, she effectively avoided the "evil" forces that threatened to destabilize her and retreated from the perplexing cacophony of internal and external messages.

In a rather paradoxical way, this young woman's preoccupation with becoming a *perfect* follower of Christ provided the cry for help that let school officials know that she was in serious emotional trouble. Her religious preoccupation resulted in failing classes, insomnia, loss of appetite, and major depressive episodes. Having distanced herself emotionally and relationally from the home community from which she had brought a sturdy but limiting construct of meanings for herself and her relationship to God, she felt betrayed by her urges toward greater freedom to be a fuller self. The self-definition and moral standard drawn from her historical experiences were not sufficiently encompassing to support her in the significantly more complex world that she had very enthusiastically entered.

The work of psychotherapy was to provide a transitional experience in which to rework her self-concept, integrating the historical inputs, the learning from her religious absorption period, and responses to the rich stimuli of the urban campus and to reclaim her enthusiasm for her ability to compose a life for herself. Through the re-working of her experiences, she had the benefit of a more reality-based self-assessment.

In late adolescence there is a need for external validation of one's standard of behavior and a need to believe that there are clear and predictive standards for living life. Many late-stage adolescents opt out of mainstream religion and attach their "faith" to what seems to work in developing a conceptual framework for their lives. The reward for a "right" conceptual frame is tangible progress toward one's goals and visions for the self. Religious faith can provide a useful guideline and boundary for the development of a non-destructive standard of behavior. It can bind anxiety that could impede forward movement through metaphors that give existential meaning to suffering, isolation, alienation, and loneliness. It is the work of later stages–the "demythologizing" of Fowler's Stage 4 individuative-reflective faith, for example–to unravel the false aspects of the utilitarian function of faith.

Ethnicity

Ethnicity for a significant percentage of Americans is an everyday fact of life. For European Americans, ethnicity is gradually becoming a meaningful aspect of their daily reality as well. During earlier stages of adolescence, the individual has to cope with the cultural diversity that is present in home, school, and work communities. Each of these communities may have different degrees of acceptance as well as appreciation for differing cultural groups. If the adolescent is a member of the ethnic group that is dominant in the home community, he or she brings to this stage of development a sense of a cultural home. He has probably internalized what it means to be a member of the cultural tribe, and that is a core aspect of his identity. Obviously, if his ethnic group is devalued in the larger community–for instance, at school or work–then the task of this stage includes overcoming the devaluation in order to honor his own urges and aspirations.

> One of the most difficult tasks for all Black families, irrespective of socioeconomic level, is that of educating their children about the realities of racism in this country, while concomitantly teaching them to strive to "be all that they can be." The task is not an easy one. A parent must help a child develop a sense of self and of his "Blackness." (Boyd-Franklin, 1989, p. 25)

Parents face the daunting challenge of conveying to adolescents a sense of possibility from a context in which they have experienced dehumanizing treatment.

The ability to overcome negative stereotypes is directly tied to the aggressiveness of the devaluation. Inequities in unemployment and job discrimination ascribed to race and ethnicity can negate the adolescent's capacity to visualize a positive future. If an inordinate amount of psychic energy must be utilized in defending the self against devaluing systems through which the person must negotiate, then the individual may abort the journey in order save a diminishing spirit. Another option is to absorb the aggression into one's core identity and use that anger as the energy for propelling oneself forward into adulthood. Persons may settle for lesser dreams because the emotional cost is too high for the "real" dream. Ethnic/racial minority persons under the pressure of family and community may settle for what is both familiar and non-threatening for their relational network. A variation of this resolution is adoption of a double life. The person develops a false self to present to the work world and a secret true self for engagement with the home and/or private world. This is an attempt to protect what feels essential to the self and the relational fabric that sustains the internal life.

> I suffered a bruising adolescent education. I don't mean to over dramatize: There was, in these teenage banalities, usually something humorous and nothing particularly tragic. But in each of these realms, I came to feel I was not normal and obtusely, I ascribed the difficulties of that age not to my age but to my color. I came to suspect that there was an order to things, an order that I, as someone Chinese, could perceive but not quite crack. I responded not by exploding in rebellion but by dedicating myself, quietly and sometimes angrily, to learning the order as best I could. I was never ashamed of being Chinese; I was, in fact, rather proud to be linked to a great civilization. But I was angry that my difference should matter now. And if it had to matter, I did not want it to defeat me. (Liu, 1998, p. 17)

Exposure to ethnic and racial discrimination is devastating to the soul whether it is systemic or occasional. As Liu indicates, there is a sense of not fully belonging that must be overcome so that what does not make sense (discrimination) will not prevent minority youth from receiving the rewards of the society. In the absence of strong communal support affirming the person, it is difficult for any individual to move forward into adulthood without the spirit's being deeply damaged. And when the absence of support is based on ethnicity, race, or other physical reality, then the individual must develop a strategy to compensate for the devaluing projections. The strategy can involve an aggressive commitment to achievement in order to prove her value to the external world. An alternative strategy could involve a refusal to engage the next developmental phase or, to quote Liu, to be in exploding rebellion against all that the devaluing culture represents.

The accommodationist strategy—working hard to prove oneself worthy—contains the rage and self-hatred for being the unacceptable other. The need to compensate for who one is racially, ethnically, or physically forces a distorted identity that may constrain possibilities for fuller development in later stages. The contained rage and self-hatred can have a devastating impact on the person's ability to enjoy subsequent successes. The pattern of the accommodation at this stage indicates the possible direction of potentially destructive themes that will extend into adulthood. These thematic patterns will carry the self-hatred and rage about that self-hatred into adult choices about work and relationships. The core issues of rage and self-hatred may not become accessible until some degree of achievement in the adult work and social world is realized. The young person who is supported in redirecting his response to racially motivated devaluation into a positive commitment to self-development is growing the emotional and spiritual muscle for engaging life more fully in later stages. In my experience, persons who confront ethnic and racial discrimination at this stage, if they achieve significant success in later stages of development, do so fueled by their rage and strong faith in an ultimate plan for their existence. There is a deep belief in an ultimate underlying power and plan that is propelling them forward. Their future is redeemed in the presence of faith.

Summary

Middle- and late-adolescents, empowered by a fully developed body and a critically conscious mind, have a strong impulse to thrive as they move toward independence in adulthood. Yet despite their general air of self-assurance, high-school and college-age youth still require the emotional support of family, community, and beneficent adult mentors to affirm both their present abilities and their future potential.

Life goals are still being elaborated at this stage and may need to be revised in light of new discoveries or changing circumstances. The demands of individuation can be avoided or postponed through early marriage, passive conformity to familial and societal expectations, or defensive uses of religiosity. Racism, sexism, and economic deprivation can cause the idealism of adolescence to go underground or can thwart it altogether. Middle and late adolescence is a time of both peril and promise. If all goes well, young people can find enduring sources of identity, meaning, and faith through fidelity to a vision of the self they are called to be.

CHAPTER 11

The Differentiation of Self and Faith in Young Adulthood

Launching, Coupling, and Becoming Parents

Bonnie Cushing
Monica McGoldrick

A Systems Perspective—This Chapter in Context

A primary goal of counseling individuals who are in their twenties and thirties is to help them recognize and honor their own uniqueness while remaining connected to others. The work requires developing a taste for authenticity and a tolerance for difference. It focuses on connections–on the many webs that exist between people, life themes, and beliefs. *Family systems therapy* takes a multigenerational view of human development and sees time as being cyclic (as compared to linear), with overlapping stages and revisiting of unresolved issues throughout the lifecycle.

Our particular formulation of development is also grounded in the understanding that (1) in our society race, gender, ethnicity, class, religion, and sexual orientation count in ways that give advantages to some and disadvantage others; and (2) individual lives can never be separated from their larger contexts. Because of these perspectives, it has been a challenge for us to organize our thinking into the discrete categories of physiological, cognitive, intrapsychic, interpersonal, social, moral, and spiritual development for the purposes of this book. These categories are entwined in the complex ways we shape one another throughout the course of our life cycle. We have tried to explore the two pivotal decades of the twenties and thirties in as orderly a fashion as possible without compromising this overarching vision of interconnection, and we hope the reader will follow us, remembering that phases are never as simple as the schema we present.

A Time of Generativity

There are great differences in the pathways people take through the life-cycle phases of young adulthood, coupling and parenting, depending on factors that include individual and familial characteristics and one's location in the larger culture. But in general, these developmental phases are concerned with generativity in terms of work, partnering, and having children (Carter & McGoldrick, 1999; Korin, McGoldrick, & Watson, 2002). During these phases adults are expected to begin to function without the physical or financial support of their parents; they begin not only to care for themselves but also to take responsibility for the care of others.

Developing a Self in Context

In every society gender, class, culture, and race form a basic structure within which individuals learn what behaviors, beliefs, values, and ways of expressing emotion and relating to others they will be expected to demonstrate throughout life (see chap. 8). Each generation is different, as cultures evolve through time, influenced by the social, economic, and political history of their era, making their worldview different from that of those born in other times (Cohler, Hosteler, & Boxer, 1998; Elder, 1998). The gender, class, and cultural structure of any society profoundly influences the parameters of a child's evolving ability to empathize, share, negotiate, and communicate. It prescribes his or her way of thinking for self and of being emotionally connected to others.

Healthy development requires establishing a solid sense of our unique selves in the context of our connections to others and our spiritual connection to the universe, including our concept of God—the force beyond our own personal will or lives. Connecting to others becomes a challenge when they are different from us, and defining a self becomes a challenge when our self-definitions differ from those to whom we are connected—our family, our community, and our society. This type of *differentiation of self*—defined by Murray Bowen (1978) as a state of self-knowledge and self-definition that does not rely on the acceptance or rejection of others—is a quintessential task of young adulthood.

Because our society so quickly assigns roles and expectations based on gender, culture, class, and race, children's competences are obviously not simply milestones that they reach individually, but rather accomplishments that evolve within a complex web of racial, cultural, and familial contexts.

A child's acquisition of cognitive, communicative, physical, emotional, and social skills is necessarily circumscribed by the particular social context in which he or she is raised. Thus, our evaluation of these abilities can only be meaningful if these constraints are taken into account.

Making Room for Others

Racial, religious, and other kinds of prejudice are learned emotionally in childhood and are very hard to eradicate later, even if one's intellectual beliefs change (Goleman, 1997). Indeed, the most challenging aspect of development involves the negotiation of our interface with others who are different from ourselves: men from women, young from old, black from white, wealthy from poor, heterosexual from homosexual, Jew from Muslim or Christian. Our level of maturity on this crucial dimension will depend on how these differences and connections were dealt with within our family of origin, within our communities, within our culture of origin, and within our society as a whole (McGoldrick & Carter, 1999). It is our belief that children are best able to develop their full potential—emotionally, intellectually, physically, and spiritually—when they are exposed in positive ways to diversity and encouraged to embrace it. Children who are the least restricted by rigid gender, cultural, or class role constraints seem likely to develop the most evolved sense of a connected self (Almeida, Woods, & Messineo, 1998).

We may think of a core spiritual task of the young adult life-cycle phase as involving making room for the "Other." This task manifests itself in many forms throughout our lives, requiring us to expand our horizon and open our hearts. In its archetypal form it appears as the Stranger, the Unfamiliar, or the Mysterious. In our twenties and thirties, many take on the challenge of making room in our lives for a partner, for children, and in a broader sense, for diversity within our communities. In the process of exploring these challenges, we hope to also highlight the importance of not only *making* room for others in one's life but also *keeping* room for one's family-of-origin, culture-of-origin, and faith-of-origin as resources for personal development and spiritual growth.

It is at this phase of life that one begins to develop a mature consciousness of intimacy, by beginning to understand in an adult way where the other is coming from, to empathize with the other's experience, to forgive others and oneself for limitations, and to accept the realities and limitations of one's personal history (especially one's parents and ancestors) as preparation for taking on the role of nurturing and giving to others.

Making Room for Spirituality

It is the concept of God (Yahweh, Jesus Christ, the One, the Spirit, etc.) that helps us to stay with this ongoing process of making room. This Spirit enables us to endure in the face of ambiguity and contradiction. It is that which drives us to connect with others and comforts us in times of suffering. God is experienced through the medium of authentic relationship–to oneself, to others, to the continuity of all life. It is what makes our remaining open to the Other possible, by providing the inspiration and the perseverance necessary to remain connected in the face of difference. Spirituality both includes and transcends human experience, connecting the human to a greater power or being (Maslow, 1998).

Faith of Origin and the Differentiation of Faith

Every person grows up in with a particular relationship to the spiritual aspects of our existence and must at some point in life, usually during young adulthood, transform his or her spiritual beliefs from accepted wisdom to personal commitment (see Fowler's stage of *individuative-reflective* faith, 1981, p. 174). Spiritual beliefs and practices include, but are not limited to, the family's religion, because every family has a faith of origin, whether they are aware of it or not. This faith-of-origin spectrum may range from an orthodox observance of a particular religious culture, to a hybrid of various religious traditions, all the way through to atheism. Spiritual beliefs and practices influence a family's conduct in its everyday life, where it locates itself in the world and in history, and how it responds to injustice.

Faith of origin can never be completely separated from a family's culture, for it is through the medium of culture that spirituality is embodied and expressed. Spirituality includes both form and content, both what is expressed and the acts of expression themselves. The forms of worship one practiced throughout childhood–receiving the Host, lighting Sabbath candles, chanting before an altar, and so forth; the foods associated with ritual meals; the music accompanying sacred events–all retain power beyond their original intent. They come to mean home itself.

One's faith of origin is also shaped to a large degree by the position the family's race, ethnicity, class, and lifestyle holds in the larger society, and to what degree their faith traditions are visible and valued in that society. Issues of class, economic status, and sexual orientation have a profound impact on the need for, access to, and creative expression of, matters of faith. Each family member's experience of his or her faith of origin can also be greatly influenced by gender and birth position, as specific roles and expectations within different faith traditions are frequently assigned based on these characteristics. Public institutions in North America do not generally acknowledge the importance of Islamic, Buddhist, or Jewish sacred days by closing or celebrating, but major Christian holidays enjoy this recognition, albeit in a secularized form. This public privileging of Christianity over other traditions can have a lasting impact on all of us in terms of the kind of "faith-esteem" we develop from childhood and how confident or unsafe we may feel in expressing our spiritual beliefs. In addition, in many faith traditions females are less highly valued than males and have less access to leadership opportunities in worship. This will also influence a woman's "faith-esteem" and her relationship to the Divine.

Continuity versus Innovation

Most parents continue to provide the sites for celebration of family life-cycle events and family and religious holidays. Although church attendance has dropped in recent years, both Americans and Canadians continue to utilize religious institutions for rites of passage (E. J. Miller, 2000). Most parents hope that their children will continue to enact the values of the family in their choice of hometown, work, friends, partners, religious practices, and cultural style. Young adult children may respond to these normative expectations of loyalty by either complying with parental urging at the expense of their own discernment process, devaluing their parents' wisdom, or isolating themselves from contact to avoid conflict or criticism (Fulmer, 1999).

Encouraging young adults to begin a personal examination of their faith of origin and supporting them in beginning the differentiation of their faith can be particularly helpful at this juncture in the family's lifecycle. Severing the connection to one's faith of origin as a means of reactively distancing from one's family of origin serves only to intensify unresolved emotional sensitivities and yearnings. Such attempts not only fail to accomplish the task of differentiation but can also result in a bankruptcy of spirit, blocking access to the rich reserves of resilience that faith can offer.

A personal relationship to a mentor—teacher, pastor, rabbi, therapist, spiritual director, employer, and the like—can be pivotal for the young adult at this phase. Although usually idealized, and therefore possibly dangerous in terms of potential exploitation, the ability to connect to a mentor or mentors can serve as a bridge between immersion in family worldviews and greater self-definition. The mentor relationship can represent a developmental achievement that holds spiritual potential in the transference of wisdom and the offering of respect between generations (Fulmer, 1999; Bly, 1997).

Cognitive Challenges

The nature and focus of learning can shift significantly in young adulthood to include management of material things and "business" relationships. Increasingly, one needs to be computer and culturally literate, in addition to other forms of literacy, in order to succeed. In this new millennium, there is more to know—and, perhaps, a more urgent mandate to know it—than ever before.

Whether all of this knowledge and consuming provides more or less opportunity to develop spiritually depends on one's perspectives and traditions. Some say that the "material plane" is a distraction; others would argue that it is the very stage on which the spiritual plays itself out. Regardless of the perspective, the complexity of today's world poses a challenge that is both exhilarating and stressful for the young adult.

Supporting Body and Soul through Work

Contemporary society, with its economic uncertainty, its requirement of protracted education and skill training, and the acceptability of late or no marriage or childbearing, tends more and more to keep young adults in an adolescent or barely post-adolescent mode until they are in their thirties. "The 1990 census revealed that 21 percent of 25 year olds were living with one or both parents, up from 15 percent in 1970" (Mogelonsky, 1996, p. 29). A larger percentage of men return home after their first departure than women. Some believe this is due to the fact that young men returning home do not lose as much autonomy as young women do, because daughters tend to be drawn into more domestic and caretaking responsibilities (Fulmer, 1999). At any rate, this trend of prolonged "economic adolescence" (Sum, Fogg, & Taggert, 1996) is a common reality in today's society.

Young men have always been expected to work to support first themselves and then their families, but in the last four decades more women of all social classes have joined the workforce to increase their future independence from men, answer a real need to supplement their husband's income, be the sole provider for self or family, and/or find personal fulfillment. So for both sexes one of the primary tasks of young adulthood is to find work for which others will pay (Fulmer, 1999). Many adolescent interests must be considerably transformed to become a job or career. If young adults cannot find a salable interest, they risk having to do work they do not find meaningful. A sense that work—which probably will take more of their time than any other single activity in life—is making a contribution to the common good is integral to the health and well-being of individuals and, certainly, communities. This search for meaningful work may involve many false starts, disappointments, and sobering experiences for young adults; may cause much anxiety for their families; and may be increasingly at odds with our society's focus on the importance of money.

The inability to engage in meaningful work that successfully supports one's self and family—in both material and spiritual terms—has profound implications for the later phases of one's lifecycle and the legacies that are passed on to the next generation. There is great peril in attending to material needs at the expense of the spiritual ones (Lerner, 1996). Entering into our current world of employment, where one's success is more often than not measured by how much wealth and power are accumulated, sets up young adults for possible physical, emotional, social, and spiritual "bankruptcy" in their middle to late adulthood.

This has particular significance for those in our society who are greatly limited by race, gender, class, and sexual orientation as to what opportunities are available. For instance, by age thirty, one out of every three black males is already dead, on probation, on parole, or in prison (Roberts, 1994). Young black males who are able and ready to work find themselves increasingly shut out of meaningful jobs because they lack the necessary education, technical skills, or training. This lack of stable wage earning for young black men creates, in turn, a problem for young black women in this phase, who find a severely diminished pool of marital prospects. Taken together, the massive obstacles of racism and poverty impede the forward development of young adults of color at this phase and may derail potentially productive people into the underclass, from which escape becomes harder as the life cycle continues.

Developing a Relationship with Money

It is in the young adulthood phase of the life cycle that one's relationship to money begins to solidify. This, of course, is greatly influenced by the race, ethnicity, culture, and class of one's family of origin as well as the unique family scripts surrounding money that have been handed down through the generations. The roles of inheritance, migration, and events such as war, economic depression, slavery, and persecution, either past or present, can also play a significant part in a family's financial attitudes and practices. These legacies, along with the limitations placed by racism, sexism, and other societal constructs, influence the ways young adults will view, spend, and save money as they do—or do not—become fiscally independent.

Despite recent gains, many women will experience less of a sense of competency and entitlement than men regarding money, due to rigid gender dictates that have socialized women to be dependent and focused on the care of others, not self. Given this, it is no surprise that economic inequities exist between men and women, with women and children being much more likely, worldwide, to live in poverty. Significant economic inequities also exist based on race and ethnicity, maintaining a class structure that continues to benefit some at the expense of others. Many believe that this system remains in place at great spiritual cost to all classes.

The spiritual dimension of money and how individual, communal, and global resources are used and shared could fill volumes in and of itself. Most faith traditions address this issue in various ways. Tithing, charitable acts, service, and social action are all practices espoused by different religious communities. Some traditions ask followers to denounce material prosperity or to view the pursuit of money as antithetical to spiritual pursuits.

How young adults begin to formulate and resolve their relationship to money will be directly linked to their degree of differentiation from their family of origin and faith of origin, as well as the economic reality that their social status affords them. The spiritual significance of individuals and families mindfully dealing with money has implications for global welfare.

Young Adult Sexuality

The current generation of young adults has more sex and knows more about sex than previous generations did. The number of sexual partners through one's lifetime has increased in recent years, while the age at sexual maturation and at first intercourse has decreased (Seidman & Reider, 1994). At the same time, anxieties about AIDS, herpes, and other sexually transmitted diseases are of continual concern to young adults today.

How young adults experience their sexuality depends on many factors, including their gender, class, ethnicity, religion, sexual orientation, history of sexual abuse, physical appearance, and health. The degree to which an individual conforms to the cultural stereotypes—either a young, sexually-obsessed, powerful, slim, physically strong and capable, dominant heterosexual male or a young, monogamous, skinny and sculpted, modest, and submissive heterosexual female—will greatly determine how affirmed or denied he or she feels in America's society, not just sexually but in every way. By the time they reach young adulthood, women and men have been well schooled in the requirements of traditional gender roles by their families, public institutions, and the media. Men are pressed to suppress aspects of themselves considered "feminine"—being emotionally available, expressive, and nurturing—and strive for power and control in all relationships (Green, 1998). Women are pressed to sacrifice their own needs in the service of their relationships and be grateful for whatever level of recognition and care they get in return. Other cultures have variations on these traditional norms, but nearly all provide but a narrow window to acceptability through which one can escape judgment. It is in this climate that people today evolve their sexual selves and form sexual unions with others. It is also in this climate that sexual harassment, violence, discrimination, abuse, and exploitation flourish. Gender stereotypes are distortions that limit both men and women in developing their full potential, spiritually and otherwise. Because a positive spirituality stresses the interdependence of all beings and demands that people be both accountable for themselves and accountable to others, the ability to connect, express, and act on both the "masculine" and "feminine" aspects of ourselves is essential for the differentiation of faith. This differentiation is necessary for the full development of any personal spiritual practice.

Biologically speaking, men's and women's sexual drives and needs shift throughout the life cycle—and, in most cases, rarely align with each other at the same time. For the young adult man, whose sexual drive can "peak" in his early twenties, being capable of impregnating becomes more of a focus as he begins to start a family. Later in his life the issue of virility may reemerge, as the specter of his mortality becomes more prominent.

For the young adult woman, sexual desire may peak in her thirties and beyond. Female sexuality can expand to include pregnancy, labor, delivery, and nursing, and rarely does a woman bear children without altering the texture of her sexuality forever. Her "biological clock"–which mandates procreation–can begin to tick in her twenties, and for some this clock can become an insistent alarm if unfulfilled by her mid-thirties. There is still a strong social stigma attached to a woman who remains childless, especially if it's a conscious choice or if her culture views childbearing as a woman's spiritual destiny.

Because men and women are on different "sexual schedules" throughout their young adulthood, heterosexual partnering provides a spiritual opportunity in this phase for the individual to transcend self in order to include Other. For gays and lesbians, young adulthood can bring the spiritual challenge of self-acceptance and fulfillment or denial of one's sexual authenticity. Many gay and lesbian young adults must also contend with parental disapproval, as well as face condemnation from the faith traditions they were raised in and continue to practice.

Becoming Part of a Couple

What distinguishes the choice of sexual partners in adolescence and post-adolescence from the choice of partners in young adulthood is the growing wish for a "home" and family of one's own. For many, it is in this phase that the search for a gratifying relationship begins in earnest. Romantic partners are now measured not only by whether they are fun and appealing but also by how well they will fit with the young adult's wishes for an ideal family.

During courtship, the young adult tends to idealize his or her partner and avoid looking at the enormous and long-range difficulties of establishing and maintaining an intimate relationship. It is important for individuals to be able to shift their emotional investment from the fantasized "perfect" love of early young adulthood to a real person who is available and ready to partner. This difficult transition requires wisdom and is often imperfectly made in this phase of the life cycle (Fulmer, 1999).

To complicate matters further, couples often seek to complete themselves in each other to the degree that they have failed to resolve their relationships with their parents (Bowen, 1978). If the work of differentiation from one's family of origin has not progressed very far for partners prior to the couple's involvement, they may have more difficulties later on in their relationship (McGoldrick, 1999). Many, however, have pointed to the potential for loving partners to challenge and support each other through this lifelong process of self-development as one of the spiritual dimensions of coupling (Pinkola-Estes, 1992; R. Johnson, 1994).

Marriage is more than the joining of two people. It is the joining of two enormously complex systems. Marriage symbolizes a change in status among all family members and generations and requires that the couple negotiate new relationships as a twosome, and renegotiate relationships singularly, with many other subsystems: parents, siblings, grandparents, nieces and nephews, and friends (McGoldrick, 1999). Couples deal with their families in many different ways. In general, women tend to move closer to their families of origin after marriage; men may become more distant, shifting their primary tie to the new nuclear family. Some partners find marriage the only way to separate. Conversely, enmeshment with the family of origin may continue even after marriage. Others cut off from their families completely. Another pattern involves continued contact but with ongoing conflicts and tensions that periodically emerge at times of stress and transition. The ideal situation, and the one that is rarely found, occurs when both partners have become independent of their families before marriage and at the same time maintain close, caring ties.

An ever-increasing proportion of young adults are living together before marriage or even living with several partners before deciding to marry. In 1970, the average age of marriage in the United States was twenty-one for women and twenty-three for men. Now it is twenty-five for women and over twenty-six for men. Divorce statistics show that those who marry at an age that falls outside the normative range (between twenty and thirty) have more trouble making the transition to marriage, although it appears overall that it is better to marry later rather than earlier. In addition to cultural or class issues, which may make earlier marriage a norm among certain cultural groups or working-class families, those who marry early are often responding to family of origin stresses that will make the process of coupling more difficult to achieve (McGoldrick, 1999).

It is important to recognize that not all young adults follow the same pathways regarding romance. Some marry in later phases of their life; some elect to live together without ever obtaining a marriage license or religious blessing; some choose to live alone throughout their lives. Gays and lesbians are often not free to marry under the law, even if they so desire.

In any case, all couples must renegotiate a great many issues they have previously defined individually or in their families of origin, such as when and how to eat, sleep, talk, have sex, fight, work, relax, and worship. The power aspects of how these things get negotiated, and the power inequities that continue to persist between many heterosexual couples, are highly likely to be obscured by the couple themselves, the extended family, and others in the society (Almeida et al., 1998; Carter, 1999). Some research has shown that it is the partner who makes more money and has more status and recognition in the greater community (usually the man) who tends to control the relationship decisions (Blumstein & Schwartz, 1983). Frequently, the wife is expected to somehow join the identity of her husband, thus increasing her difficulty in differentiating and maintaining her separate identity. This traditional arrangement makes it much harder for men to show any vulnerability and thus to engage in intimate relationships.

Decisions must be made about which family traditions and rituals to retain and which ones couples will develop for themselves. Struggles over how to perform rituals and holiday celebrations are a lens through which couples can learn about each other's family of origin, and become the crucible for working out loyalties to extended family and current differentiated beliefs and identities (Imber-Black & Roberts, 1998). Although this is true to some degree with all couples, it is particularly true of religious, class, ethnic, or racial intermarriages.

The struggles of intermarried couples can be viewed as a spiritual practice wherein each partner tries to balance power and cultural visibility in the relationship–the practice of making room for him- or herself while making room for the other. The frequency of marriage between partners from widely different cultural backgrounds is accelerating. The physical distance from families of origin, the changing role of women, and the diminishing role community plays in supporting families all have a profound impact on contemporary couples and make the issue of defining their spiritual resources and values ever more important. Spirituality can help extended families stay connected and can help couples counter the sense of isolation they may feel in today's world.

The marriage ritual, or wedding, is generally the largest ceremony organized by the family and can be highly reflective of family process (McGoldrick, 1999). It is often the time when the differences in class and economic status between the partners' families begin to emerge both overtly and covertly, as the financial aspects of the wedding–which can be substantial in today's society–are decided and executed.

Generally, the more responsibility young adults can take for arranging their wedding ritual to reflect their changing position in their families and the joining of the two systems, the more auspicious it will be for their future relationship (McGoldrick, 1999). It is an opportunity for the couple to recognize that their marriage is a life event not just for them, but also for their families. At its best, a wedding celebrates the cultures and faiths of origin of both partners, reflecting the young couple's unique values and facilitating this family transition by marking the changes in status of family members and shifts in family organization (McGoldrick, 1999).

For gay and lesbian couples, these transitions can be both simpler and more difficult (Laird & Green, 1996; Marshall, 1997). On the one hand, it appears to be an advantage for gays and lesbians that they are less bound by the constricting rigidities of traditional gender roles. On the other hand, the stigmatizing of homosexual couples by our society means that their relationships are often not validated by their families, communities, and faith traditions, and they must cope with prejudice on a daily basis. Because gays and lesbians are still denied federal and most religious recognition of their relationships (Glaser, 1996), many families are not given the same opportunities available to heterosexual couples to mark and process this transition or to receive the concrete benefits and emotional support they need throughout their lives together. For many gay and lesbian young adults, coupled or single, the marginalization they experience can make it even harder to find, or found, a spiritual home. Despite these obstacles, gay and lesbian families and spiritual communities are able to persist and thrive in today's world.

Becoming a Parent

Parenthood is often described as a transformational experience, paralleled only by one's own birth and death. It has been symbolized as a bridge, a portal, a threshold through which no one passes unchanged. And this is true not only for biological parents but also for adoptive parents, stepparents, foster parents, and surrogate parents (aunts, uncles, mentors, etc.). The potential for spiritual development through the process of parenting is considerable.

There is, however, much more mythology and romantic fantasy around the transition to parenthood than there is realistic expectation. The basic assumption that motherhood—and, by extension, parenthood—is an automatic leap ahead in status, joy, and fulfillment is rarely questioned.

When couples become parents, there tends to be a shift of power (even for the previously relatively "equal" heterosexual couple) back toward the traditional arrangement of breadwinner father and domestic mother. Suddenly, or insidiously, the husband is earning and managing all or most of the money while there is unequal participation from him in the work at home. Despite the glowing image of mother and child depicted by culture and media, the major research on the transition to parenthood indicates that it is accompanied by a general decrease in marital satisfaction and a lowering of self-esteem for women (Cowen et al., 1985; Entwistle & Doering, 1981). The traditional family has often not only encouraged but even required dysfunctional patterns, such as the overresponsibility of mothers for their children and the complementary underresponsibility or disengagement of fathers (Avis, 1985).

This over- and under-responsibility has had a limiting effect on the spiritual development of both genders. Our culture, strongly influenced by the male-dominated psychoanalytic tradition, has given extraordinary importance to the mother/child relationship in the earliest years of life, to the exclusion of other relationships in the family or to later developmental phases (Lewis, Feiring, & Kotsonis, 1984). The psychoanalytic model sometimes promotes the view of human development as a primarily painful process in which mother and child are viewed as potential adversaries. Such assumptions lead to a psychological determinism that sees mothers as all-powerful and blames them for whatever goes wrong. Mothers today have inherited expectations of mythic proportions to be all-giving and all-knowing (Chodorow & Contratto, 1982). Taking on stakes that high can make spiritual growth extremely difficult for mothers. Given the biological vulnerability women experience throughout the pregnancy, labor, delivery, and postpartum phases of earliest motherhood—and, usually, the innate receptivity that accompanies such vulnerability—this model of "mother-accountable-only" parenting can significantly impede growth for women at, perhaps, one of the most spiritually fertile times of their lives.

And what happens to the opportunities for growth available to fathers at this critical juncture, given the mythology they, too, inherit from our culture's basically patriarchal paradigm? Generally, they are pushed to the periphery of an extremely powerful spiritual experience and subtly instructed that the most valuable contribution they can make at this point is to contend with the larger world and leave mother and child to their tasks. Research has shown that if men's capacity for nurturing is activated when their child is an infant, they continue to feel competent to be involved in their children's lives (Gerston, 1993). This "competency to be involved" can be integral to spiritual development; lacking a sense of one's interaction competence can, and does, greatly impede men in their relational and spiritual lives. Parenting roles in North America are changing, albeit very slowly. More and more women are beginning to maintain an identity beyond their roles of wife and mother, and men are participating in household work and childcare in greater numbers and to a larger degree than any previous American generation (Kimmel, 1996).

The complex web of systems that a child is born or adopted into has much accommodating to do to bring this new family member into their fold. Many families mark the event with a religious ritual: a christening, bris, or naming ceremony, usually followed by a party for family and friends. As with other family transition rituals, issues about how and where the event is celebrated and who gets invited reflect the ongoing extended-family process (Carter, 1999). Indications as to how fully the parents have negotiated what faith tradition(s) their child will be initiated and raised in emerge at birth, if not in pregnancy or before. This is a key time to deepen faith differentiation work, or to begin it, if it has yet to be explored. The value of clarifying, transforming, or reclaiming aspects of one's faith of origin is particularly profound at this time, when the mysteries of new life are made manifest.

The young adult parent can expect to inherit major unresolved multigenerational patterns, triangles, ghosts, and taboo issues. This is a wonderful stage to engage young adults in doing deep family work. One of the greatest spiritual gifts of parenting is that it gives people the power and strength to do things for their children's sake that they would not attempt for themselves (Carter, 1999). It is truly amazing to witness what people become willing to face as they rise to the "occasion" of parenting.

Perhaps what we experience in the beginning phase of parenthood is our initial encounter with mortality. Many new parents come to the emotional, if not intellectual, realization that they (and their children) are vulnerable to death in those early days, months, and years—and this realization can deepen their relationship to life and their commitment to protect and nurture its miraculous gifts. Confronting one's own mortality can be one of the most powerful spiritual encounters available to human beings. Through having children, facing a medical crisis, or losing a relative or friend, it is usually in the phase of young adulthood that one meets this ultimate "Other" for the first time.

Many young adults who desire biological children must struggle to do so, or accept that they won't be able to. Infertility affects approximately one of four couples in America today (Cooper-Hibert, 1998). The intensity of the negative experience of infertility can be easily overlooked by family and friends, but it is reported by those directly affected as one of the most stressful life experiences they have encountered (Kedem, Mikulincer, Nathanson, & Bartov, 1990). There is always the danger that couples will identify themselves as damaged, isolating themselves socially and becoming depressed. This is especially likely when couples belong to ethnicities that particularly focus on the importance of children or fundamentalist religions that expect couples to produce many children (Carter, 1999). This marginalization can add suffering to the couple's already acute sense of bereavement. Technological advancements in the field of fertility have presented both solutions and new dilemmas for contemporary couples.

Many families among us are also crushed by the poverty, discrimination, and abuse that can be by-products of the racism, sexism, classism, and heterosexism in our society. Other pathways to parenthood— such as international and interracial adoption, single parenting, and gay and lesbian parenting—leave some families to struggle alone with social stigma without the supports that every family needs to prosper, both physically and spiritually. Parents in current minority groups are only too aware of the potential harm to their children of being stigmatized. In addition to the myriad of parenting tasks all people face, they also have to track the potential negative impact on their children's self-esteem, sense of competency, and positive group identification that society's marginalization presents them with. For many families these extra burdens must be faced with limited resources and minimal, if any, support.

Conclusion

Young adulthood is a time when "the development of a core self, a strong, yet pliable identity...bestows life's most precious gift—the ability to relate to both self and others with true intimacy" (Borysenko, 1996, p. 76). During the phases of young adulthood—from launching to coupling to parenting—one begins to care for oneself, deal with one's own and others' sexuality, search for meaningful work, and negotiate and renegotiate relationships to parents, peers, and communities. New parents will be transformed by the task of parenting the next generation. It is the time when one begins to care for others and, one hopes, to develop one's ability to respect and advocate for those less fortunate, or help oneself, one's children, and one's community in the face of injustice (McGoldrick & Carter, 1999).

Despite all the complexities and difficulties of contemporary life, the desire to create family–in whatever form it may appear–and the joy and transcendence this desire offers through the medium of human connection, continues to inspire us. This connection not only exists between people presently living, but also reaches back to those who have come before and forward to those who will follow after.

Differentiating our self and our faith allows release from the judgment of others while, at the same time, supporting the development of self-definition and personal discernment. Our ever-evolving differentiated faith can provide the strength to make room for the Other–be it aspects of ourselves we previously disowned, a partner, a child, or a stranger. It can also provide the means through which we can creatively express and celebrate this very spiritual capacity.

The dimensions of living we have explored in this chapter–physiological, cognitive, intraphysic, interpersonal, social, moral, and spiritual–are intricately woven together to form a tapestry whose very fibers are spiritual in nature. Just as we cannot separate the spirit from the flesh, we cannot separate these dimensions from one another, or from their ultimate source.

CHAPTER 12

The Middle Years

Russell Haden Davis

The transition from young to middle adulthood, unlike the transition from latency to puberty, is a gradual one. No clear indicators mark the passage from being in one's twenties and thirties to being in one's forties and fifties. Nor are there clear and discrete markers of the passage from midlife to late adulthood. In fact, from a subjective point of view, a recent survey shows that nearly 33 percent of Americans in their seventies consider themselves middle-aged as do 22 percent of those eighty or older (Elias, 2000). Considering the fact that the over-eighty group is the fastest-growing segment of the American population, we may well be facing a change in the definition of middle age.

The identifying characteristics of the middle years are both discrete in certain respects and on a continuum with both young adulthood and late adulthood in other respects. Part of the task of this chapter is to identify where middle development shares characteristics with earlier and later times, and where the accent is different. Many of the differences between earlier and later stages are ones of quantity rather than quality. That is, in this developmental epoch in comparison to earlier ones, the differences are in the realm of more and less, rather than of radically different human experiences. This is especially true of factors such as social and cultural location or intellectual and cognitive functioning. This chapter considers those aspects of the experience of middle age that set it apart from developmental issues of young adulthood.

To set the stage for the themes of this chapter, Loder (1998) points out that two of the world's great masterpieces of literature begin at the midpoint of life. Dante begins *The Divine Comedy* with a description of a midlife crisis. In the middle of the journey of life, he said, he found himself in a dark forest and had lost sight of the straight path. At the time that Dante wrote this, he was thirty-five years old, midway in the biblical lifespan of three score and ten years. The experience of being lost, in dark woods, and in unfamiliar territory is a significant part of the experience of the middle years for many people (Alighieri, 1314/1909; J. Jones, 1991).

In a similar vein, Goethe's Faust finds that although he has thoroughly studied philosophy, medicine, and law, he believes himself no wiser than the poorest fool. In midlife, he comes to feel that his life is wasted despite his finest achievements. His pact with Mephistopheles is a desperate attempt to salvage a life. The experiences of both Dante's traveler and Goethe's Faust are part of the terrain of those who, as Jung says, have crossed the meridian of the zenith of the sun and now find themselves in the afternoon (Goethe, 1808/1995).

The afternoon of life can be charted by the following themes: physiological and cognitive changes, intrapsychic and interpersonal changes, changes in moral and faith development, and the influence on midlife development of social location.

Physiological and Cognitive Changes in Middle Life

In the middle years, a number of physiological and cognitive changes take place. Because the physiological changes often are the primary force in motivating cognitive changes, we will consider the two together for the most part.

Physiological Changes in Middle Life

In the middle years, many physiological changes occur that are experienced as the deterioration and/or diminishment of bodily functioning. These have a significant impact on intrapsychic life (our thoughts, feelings, and emotions), on interpersonal life (our relationships), and on spiritual life (our faith, values, and ways of making meaning).

As persons move from their twenties and thirties into their forties and fifties, physiological changes due to aging and lifestyle—sometimes called "physical retrogression" (Colarusso, 1992, p. 163)—pick up speed and become a powerful force in mental life. The impact of such changes begins even earlier for professional athletes and others whose identity and livelihood depend on maximum physical performance. Physiological changes have significant impact on our thoughts and emotions and on our sense of who we are. Mind and spirit are deeply affected by body.

Midlife physiological changes, unlike those in puberty, are usually relatively slow in their onset and often develop without sharp physiological markers. Changes in physical appearance, bodily functioning, and performance and the onset of somatic distress are all part of the midlife picture. Most, if not all, of these changes affect the way we think and feel about our body and our sense of self. That is, the physiological changes of the middle years alter our self-image and self-esteem.

BODILY APPEARANCE

Changes in bodily appearance, although common in the middle years, vary to a certain extent from person to person. Some variations in the types and extent of bodily changes are affected by gender, race, and ethnic group; even here, enormous individual differences exist within groups.

Midlife alterations in physical appearance, due to aging and the accumulated effects of lifestyle, include changes in a number of possible areas. Changes in bodily weight and proportion are common. Changes in skin texture, tone, and elasticity show up as wrinkles, sagging, spots, blemishes, and altered vein appearance. Changes in hair color and density include graying, thinning, and partial or complete baldness. Muscle tone and postural changes often appear as rounded or sagging shoulders and curvature of the spine. Occasionally, the middle years will see the shrinking of bodily height, although this is more common in older adults.

Bodily appearance, and attempts to maintain it and improve it, serve different psychological functions and have different personal meanings in middle age than in adolescence and young adulthood.

> *The appearance of one's body in midlife takes on a different significance.* Efforts to remain trim and fit are not made to develop a sense of identity or to separate and individuate, but to maintain health and youthfulness and to deter the effects of aging. The struggle is to retain body integrity in the face of anxieties about aging, the vulnerabilities of failing health, and the potential loss of independence. (Goin, 1990, p. 524)

BODILY FUNCTIONING

Changes in bodily function due to aging and the accumulated effects of lifestyle also vary somewhat from person to person and by gender, race, and ethnic group. Again, as with changes in bodily appearance, individual differences exist widely within a group or category.

In the years from forty to sixty, alteration and/or deterioration of vision, teeth, hormonal balance, reflexes, reaction times, stamina, muscle strength and flexibility, and sexual functioning are common. Those without visual problems before the age of forty are likely to develop presbyopia. Sufferers of "elder vision" may make jokes about their arms not being long enough to read. Complaints about the need to wear reading glasses are not uncommon.

The Change of Life in Women

The middle years for women usually bring an end to the capacity for childbearing. Hormonal changes, especially decreased estrogen production, bring about the cessation of menses (menopause) and create the experience of "hot flashes." Other subjective phenomena associated widely with menopause, at least in caricature, occur only in a minority of women and are ancillary to the hormonal changes of menopause itself.

According to Sheehy (1995) menopause is as individual as a fingerprint. No two women have the same experience of menopause. Every experience, however, deserves respect, a medical dialogue, and loving support as needed. At least a dozen books on menopause are recommended by women's health centers around the country; a list of these can be found in Sheehy (1995).

Thoughts, feelings, and emotions vary widely among women about the impending cessation of reproductive ability. The complex of ideas and emotions accompanying the realization that reproductive time is running out is known as "the biological clock." The ticking down of the clock may lead to strong feelings about having children, even for those who did not formerly choose to bear offspring. Feeling-filled questions arise: Do I want to have children? Do I have enough children? What if something happened to one of my children? Do I have all the children of a certain gender that I want? Men may also raise similar emotion-laden questions.

The Change of Life in Men

Is there a male hormonal change in midlife for men, a counterpart to menopause? An increasing number of medical research studies are exploring the possibility. For many men, the physiological issue is occasional or chronic erectile dysfunction and the accompanying psychological realities that go with impotence. Studies show that up to one half of American men over forty years old have been subject to impotence to varying degrees (Sheehy, 1995). The popularity of the drug Viagra (and related humor) attests to the importance of recovery from impotence for both men and their partners.

Sexual and Reproductive Function Changes in Both Men and Women

Changes in sexual functioning are often different for men and women. Whereas men may experience a peak of sexual interest in the first half of life, women may find their zenith of sexual interest in the middle years. At a time when men are experiencing a decline, women are often at a peak of sexual interest and maturity. Some couples experience these differences in timing of sexual interest as being "out of sync," and will feel frustrated or angry as a result. Changes in both the ability to perform sexually and the ability to have children have enormous impact on self-image, self-esteem, and self-definition. A man who experiences decreasing sexual interest and potency, a woman who is reaching the end of her childbearing years–both may experience lowered self-esteem. Both will need to redefine themselves as sexual and procreative beings. A woman, however, who finds herself more sexually alive in the middle years will also create a new sense of self.

Cognitive Changes in Middle Life

As a result of the physiological changes in the middle years, coupled with other experiences to be described in this section, individuals undergo significant cognitive changes. These cognitive alterations include changes in awareness of self, other, environment, and community. I will begin by addressing these in terms of existential issues in middle life. As such, the existential issues lead to a lived-philosophical reorientation–a change in orientation that is at the same time both cognitive and deeply emotional.

EXISTENTIAL ISSUES IN MIDDLE LIFE

Physiological changes in middle life raise certain lived-philosophical issues for most people. The existential themes are time and death. The individual undergoing the changes of middle life often has a foreshortened sense of time and a deep awareness of the possibility of one's own death. The lived experience of these existential and philosophical issues has a direct bearing on the nature of religious, moral, and spiritual development in the middle years.

Many of the issues that existential philosophers, theologians, and psychologists address in their writings are faced by the individual at midlife in an extremely personal and experiential way. It is almost as if middle and late adulthood are the human laboratory in which existentialism is grounded. The preeminent issues are death (one's own death), finitude, time, anxiety, dread, nothingness (and the threat thereof), and courage in the face of a threat to personal nonbeing.[1]

In the middle years, personal confrontations with the issues of finitude are brought about by one or more of the following:

- The physiological changes of aging described above
- Caring for aging and ailing parents and coming to terms with their dying and/or death
- The serious illness and/or death of one's contemporaries
- The birth of grandchildren, nieces, and nephews combined with the realization that one may not be alive when they reach one's current age
- One's own confrontation with a life-threatening or incapacitating illness and/or injury
- The death of a child
- The death of a pet who, psychologically, is a surrogate child

TIME AND DEATH

In the middle years, the conceptual experience of time may change from a sense of time-since-I-was-born to a sense of "how much time is left, and did it mean anything anyway?" (Loder, 1998, p. 283). The focus on time limitation and the awareness of one's own potential death often leads to a personal evaluation of and preoccupation with the meaning of one's own life.

Many engage in an ongoing life review and reassessment, leading to judgments about the success or failure of one's life, as did Goethe's Faust. Depending on the degree of consciousness of and intentionality about life review, the reevaluation may lead to resolutions about how one wants to live the rest of life. In such ongoing review, many people experience a shift in their values about what is most important and, at times, make a decision to live life differently. Such review is often precipitated by a crisis that brings personal mortality into focus. Some, in response to crisis and review, decide to pursue abandoned dreams from the past—further education, a new career, the simplification of life, a shift in focus from material values to relational one.

Some gender differences seem typical of the shift in values that may accompany midlife existential reassessment, at least in the contemporary culture of the United States. The current generation of midlifers who, when they were younger were subject to different formative values, have experienced a shift in what it means to be a man or to be a woman. Consequently, many middle-aged men today are shifting from focusing on work and careers to savoring and building relationships. On the other hand, many middle-aged women today, who spent years focused on relationships, are turning to new values of career, work, and self-fulfillment. In the case of both men and women who have had careers for many years, the existential crises of midlife may leave them hungry for experiences of life and ways of living that were formerly neglected or abandoned.

For some, the existential encounter with time and death leads to a revitalized life; for others, the life path leads toward stagnation and self-absorption. For most, encountering one's finitude involves significant existential anxiety and/or massive attempts to deny or escape the awareness of anxiety and fear.

DIALECTICAL COGNITION

According to Fowler (1981), midlife cognition moves beyond the dichotomizing cognition of young adulthood. Dichotomizing logic tends to see things as "either/or." Dialectical knowing is the type of cognition that may emerge in the middle years.

> In dialogical knowing the known is invited to speak its own word in its own language. In dialogical knowing the multiplex structure

of the world is invited to disclose itself. In a mutual "speaking" and "hearing," knower and known converse in an I-Thou relationship. (Fowler, 1981, p. 185)

According to Fowler, a knower capable of dialogue is required for dialectical knowing. The individual must possess sufficient self-certainty to grant the initiative to the other.

Loder, building on Fowler, says that it is important to recognize that although the human spirit has struggled with negation from very early in life, in midlife "negation places its stamp on the form and pattern of intelligence" (1998, p. 292). Negation, in this context, refers to thought and experiential processes concerned with death, nonbeing, suffering, and loss. Loder sees negation as potentially transformative. To reach the capacity for dialogical thinking, one must have experienced suffering, loss, responsibility, failure, and "the grief that is an inevitable part of having made irreversible commitments of life's energy" (Loder, 1998, p. 291). Irreversible commitments always involve loss—loss of the ability to live out other commitments, other potentialities. And loss, inevitably, is accompanied by grief. In young adulthood, grief results from the loss implied in choice—the loss of omnipotentiality (the ability to be all things). In middle life, the grief and loss are more retrospective. We remember with sorrow what we might have become or could have been had we not made certain choices. For example, a person who chooses a certain mate (for better, for worse, until death do us part) necessarily loses other potential mates. A man or a woman who chooses to go into ministry loses other career possibilities. Loder notes that, in midlife,

> ...because the dark side of development can no longer be ignored, it is the incredible resilience of the human spirit that comes forward to create coherence and meaning when the disappearance of the ego is clearly inevitable. At the cognitive level, dialectic and paradox prevail as the ultimately irrepressible human spirit seeks a comprehensive and meaningful solution. (1998, p. 292)

Intrapsychic and Interpersonal Changes

The intrapsychic (inward) and interpersonal (relational) changes of midlife spring directly from the physiological, cognitive, and existential issues just discussed. These midlife changes, according to Colarusso, deserve to be called developmental changes, even though no new psychic structures are formed in adulthood.

> [T]he *awareness* of the adult experience of aging and the *preoccupation* with time limitation and personal death which accompanies it (mid-life) are increasingly powerful conscious and unconscious intrapsychic influences which grow in intensity as the young adult

passes through middle age into late adulthood. They stimulate the psyche to new levels of complexity. (1992, p. 118)

That is to say, the aging process in the body and the concomitant changes to psychic structures are the adult equivalents of earlier development, which featured physical and psychological growth and the formation of psychic structures (such as ego, id, and superego).

The developmental theme for interpersonal relationships is different in midlife from that in young adulthood. The young adult is developing the capacity for intimacy, especially with friends and lovers, colleagues, and, for many, a mate. The midlife adult is focused on maintaining intimate relationships with people of the same age group—that is, with a mate, with friends, and with colleagues. The midlife adult is also developing the capacity for new kinds of relationships with those younger and older. That is, the adult in midlife is involved with the generative task of caring and guiding the next generations (including children and grandchildren) and with caring for the older generation.

Maintaining intimacy with a spouse or significant other, to the extent the relationship involves sexual lovemaking, requires coming to terms with the physiological changes in one's own body and that of the beloved as well as coming to terms with changes in cognition and self-esteem of both self and other. Many couples find that marriage enrichment workshops help them develop new paths to intimacy in midlife. Allowing more time for foreplay, sharing and developing a deeper fantasy life, and other techniques can contribute to continued sexual enjoyment as our bodies age.

Meaning-Making and Interpersonal Relationships

The developmental theory of Robert Kegan (1982) is especially helpful in understanding interpersonal relationships throughout life, including midlife. Kegan calls his approach "neo-Piagetian" and "constructive-developmental." In his theory, a person is a constructor of meaning; the construction of meaning evolves throughout life in alternating periods of stability and instability, in alternating movements toward independence or inclusion. Kegan is concerned with tracing the development throughout the life-spiral of the human activity of constructing meaning. Meaning-making involves a relationship—between the individual and the environment, and between the individual and other persons (object relations).

In adulthood, Kegan sees two different styles of meaning-making: the interpersonal and the institutional. The person in "interpersonal" meaning-making feels as if "I am my relationships." Such persons yearn for relationships, connections, and inclusion. They fear exclusion, autonomy, disapproval, and loss of relationships (and, secretly, of being engulfed by the other). The person embedded in "institutional" meaning-making favors autonomy, self-regulation, and self-nourishment. The person fears loss of boundaries, loss of control (especially self-control), and loss of the sense of being distinct (and, secretly, of being utterly alone).

Kegan thinks that it is not uncommon for one partner in a marriage to be embedded in interpersonal meaning-making and the other to be caught up in institutional meaning-making. For the former, love is the preeminent value; for the latter, work. Such differences in meaning-making can lead to the experience of "being on different planets."

Several things are important for the current discussion. One is that the upheavals that many couples experience in marriage may be a consequence of the differences in their styles of meaning-making and also a consequence of one or both partners shifting from one style of making-meaning to another. This is particularly likely when the age difference between partners is pronounced, but it can also be influenced by the diverse priorities gender roles typically elicit from men and women. When counseling couples in what Harville Hendrix calls the "power struggle" phase of a marriage or new relationship, ministers and psychotherapists need to remain neutral with respect to competing value systems (except in cases where there is threat of harm). Couple relationships can grow in depth of intimacy and commitment if partners are encouraged to develop, through focused dialogue, a new appreciation and tolerance for the differences that appear to divide them (Hendrix, 1988, 1992).

Kegan feels that the loss of the widespread experience of genuine community and extended family prevalent in preindustrial America leaves couples without the support they need during adult development. Without broad community support as we or our partner change styles of meaning-making, we may be tempted to run away from home. Adults who run away do not usually return home when it gets dark, as they might have done as children.

> Without these supports during times of adult development, left to ourselves, we often negotiate our transitions by separating ourselves not only from our old meaning but from the actual person who (and commitments which) have come to stand for those meanings. (Kegan, 1982, pp. 217–18)

Ministers would do well to read Kegan in depth (especially chapters 7 to 9) and to explore how their parish and congregation can become a supportive, caring community that nourishes young, middle, and old through the shifting styles of making-meaning most adults experience.

Although Kegan does not discuss fully a style of making meaning beyond the institutional, he provides a number of hints as to what might be next. Kegan speaks, for instance, of moving from a definition of self as only my relationships or only my work to a more open and dialectical process involving contextualization. Such a position would involve openness to contradiction, paradox, and dialectical thinking (both/and rather than either/or). And he says that the "choices for adulthood need not be between a form of intimacy at the expense of identity, or an identity at the expense of intimacy" (Kegan, 1982, p. 253). In this way, Kegan's views sound similar to Fowler's description of dialectical knowing. The bottom line is that Kegan envisions development beyond autonomy and the other sacred values of the institutional balance.

Social Location

One important issue for a chapter on middle adulthood is cultural context.[2] Although the existence of adulthood is universal, the exploration of what it means to be an adult is a specifically American phenomenon, and a relatively recent one at that. "Indeed, no precise equivalent of the Anglo-American term 'adulthood'" to indicate "a distinct stage in the cycle of life…[exists]…in any other European language" (Malia, 1978, pp. 173–74).

Issues of gender are also important for an understanding of midlife development. Sheehy believes that the "fundamental steps of expansion that will open a person, over time, to the full flowering of his or her individuality are the same for both genders" (Sheehy, 1976, p. 22). The tempo of development, however, "is not synchronized in the two sexes;" that is, "men and women are rarely in the same place struggling with the same questions at the same age" (Sheehy, 1976, p. 22). Jung, in discussing changes in values in the afternoon of life, notes that men typically turn from a work orientation to a relationship orientation, whereas women may do the opposite, especially if work and career were not their focus in the morning of life.

The work of Carol Gilligan (1982) is particularly instructive concerning gender and development. Her discussion of women who choose to have abortions, including those who so choose because of rape, raises important issues for the development of women and the meanings of generativity in such women. Although Gilligan's examples in her chapter "Crisis and Transition" are drawn from young adults, such issues are important wherever they occur in the life cycle. The choice for abortion, however, for a woman who has no children but is still early in the childbearing years may have quite different meanings than for a woman who is near the end of the fertile years.

Many psychological theorists have noted that middle-aged women are often highly invested as caregivers. Gilligan (1982), however, points out that when the issue of women's rights are added to women's care, then a previously neglected focus on self-care may come to the forefront and change a woman's judgment to a positive valuation of love of self.

Gilligan also notes that normative views of maturity, especially traditional ones, have devalued many of the virtues in which women excel: attachment, relationships, nurture, and interdependence. In a society that has valued independence, career, tough-mindedness, and independence, the values held by women have previously been considered inferior. This has caused difficulty not only for women, but also for men when, in midlife, they are pulled to values previously denigrated.

Moral and Faith Development

Each of the sections in this chapter is interdependent. Just as when we discussed physiological changes in midlife we referred to the psychological, emotional, and spiritual concomitants, so also in this section on moral and faith development we stay connected to the themes raised in other sections.

In the first section, physiological and cognitive changes, we spoke at length about the existential issues that arise in midlife. These existential issues are closely connected with a theological understanding of the development of courage in midlife.

Courage and Existential Anxiety

The existential issues raised by the physiological process of aging, especially those of time and death, lead to anxiety. Paul Tillich defines anxiety, theologically understood, as

> the state in which a being is aware of its possible nonbeing...It is not the realization of universal transitoriness, not even the experience of the death of others, but the impression of these events on the always latent awareness of our own having to die that produces anxiety. Anxiety is finitude, experienced as one's own finitude (1952, p. 35).

Tillich undertakes a classification of anxiety. Basic anxiety that stems from the threat of nonbeing cannot be eliminated, but is inherent in the very nature of our existence. But anxiety also takes the form of anxiousness about fate and death, about emptiness and meaninglessness, and about guilt and condemnation. The solution of anxiety is not its elimination, but rather courage. Tillich defines courage as "self-affirmation of being in the face of nonbeing" (1952, p. 155).

Such courage, however, does not have its source in human affirmation. Rather, courage needs the "power of being" (1952, p. 155). Such courage, which Tillich calls "the courage to be," is "rooted in the God who appears when God has disappeared in the anxiety of doubt" (1952, p. 190). Obviously, Tillich is engaged here in the dialectical thinking described by Fowler and Loder.

Conjunctive Faith

Dialogical knowing and dialectical thinking, which develop best in midlife, have theological implications. Fowler calls the faith that springs from dialogical knowing "conjunctive faith" (1981, pp. 184–98). For Fowler, faith goes through stages of development from infancy to adulthood. In the stage of faith development that Fowler calls "conjunctive faith," when approaching God and others, the individual seeks first to understand, then to be understood. One desires earnestly to know the other deeply. Concerns about self and the needs of existence take second place to a desire to know the other thoroughly, to be an I to a Thou.

Conjunctive faith (1) is "ready for closeness to that which is different and threatening to self and outlook (including new depths of experience in spirituality and religious revelation)"; (2) has a commitment to justice "freed from the confines of tribe, class, religious community or nation"; (3) wishes to foster the possibility of "others generating identity and meaning"; and (4) is attracted by the "possibility (and imperative) of an inclusive community of being" (Fowler, 1981, p. 198). Inclusive communities are known more by whom they include than whom they exclude. Inclusive communities have few enemies and few scapegoats. Their goal is universal love lived out in concrete, daily relationships and realities.

Obviously, conjunctive faith is an achievement of some in midlife, but is not automatically bestowed with middle age.

Generativity and Stagnation

Religious, psychological, and spiritual existence in midlife can be characterized by a developing ratio of generativity and stagnation. To understand this, we will look at the psychosocial and psychoanalytic theory of Erik Erikson.

Erik Erikson's earliest intellectual influence was Søren Kierkegaard. His mother read Kierkegaard's works to him when he was a baby and a child. Later, Erikson came under the influence of Sigmund Freud and trained with Anna Freud. Erikson developed a developmental theory that extended the psychoanalytic theory of development. Freud's formal theory of development ended with adolescence. Erikson proposed that we develop throughout life and that eight stages of development comprise the life cycle. The middle years are ones in which the individual, in relationship to self and society, develops his or her own unique place on the continuum between the polarities of generativity and stagnation. Erikson thought that each of us arrives at a ratio, a relative balance in which generativity and stagnation both exist, and in which one predominates in personality to a greater or lesser degree.

GENERATIVITY

Generativity is first and foremost procreation, the bringing into the world of new beings. Generativity, by extension, is also productivity and creativity, new products and new ideas. The major value that develops, where generativity has a relative victory over stagnation, is interest in establishing (through genitality and genes) the next generation. Generativity is expressed through having children and through other forms of altruistic concern and creativity, which are symbolic forms of parenting. Generativity presupposes intimacy, sharing partnerships, and divided/shared/collaborative labor. Generativity is expressed in parenting, in teaching the next generation, in producing that leads to a legacy, and in curing and caring (Erikson, 1950/1963).

Caring, which is the virtue that Erikson associates with generativity, is "the widening concern for what has been generated by love, necessity, or accident" (1964, p. 131). Erikson, who is quite interested in cross-cultural understandings, amplifies his meaning of care by turning to Hindu religion. In Hindu thought, care means a number of things: restraint (to be care-ful), charity (to take care of), and compassion (to care for) (1982).

Charity (to take care of) is the care of persons, creative products, and ideas. Such care is conservation. The ethic of care that generativity implies is a more universal form of care—not simply care-in-order-to-survive, but care-as-vital-development (Erikson, 1982).

Generativity, then, is a stage in the development of the ego when the welfare of future generations takes the forefront. The generative person expresses the "courage to be" through love of the future and of the yet-to-be-born children of the future. Thus, generative persons are deeply interested in religion, law, theater, technology, ideology, marriage, and family, which are all institutions that support the Eriksonian virtues and ego strengths of hope, will, purpose, competence, fidelity, and love (Loder, 1998).

Finally, generativity is a synthesis between personal and interpersonal insights and public responsibility. Generativity is a rapprochement between developing individuals and those social and cultural institutions that foster positive human development (Loder, 1998).

STAGNATION

Having children or wanting children is not proof of generativity. Parents who are filled with excessive self-love are not generative. Parents for whom their children are merely an extension of themselves—their hopes, dreams, aspirations, and ambitions—are not generative. Parents who lack a faith in the human family and who fail to welcome a child into a trusted community are not generative. These parents, then, are on the road to stagnation. Stagnation often expresses itself as an excessive need for pseudo-intimacy (Erikson, 1964). Stagnation, the opposite of generativity, is found in authoritarianism, which Erikson sees as an "ungenerous and ungenerative use of sheer power" (1982, p. 70).

The demands imposed by aging are intended to "make us stop and take notice, to turn inward so we can turn outward in a new way with new resources." Failure to engage in personal reassessment "means entrenchment in established roles and overcompensation" when old resources no longer work (Loder, 1998, p. 285).

> "Generativity versus Stagnation" means that there is a decisive hiatus in the middle years. Middlescence, like adolescence, is a major developmental turning point. Powerful forces gathering strength and associations through the course of a lifetime make one resist change. (Loder, 1998, p. 286)

Gandhi and Generativity

Erikson, to illustrate his various theories of the life cycle, wrote three psychohistories, or psychological biographies, one each of (1) Luther (late adolescence and young adulthood) (1962), (2) Jefferson (the interplay of individual and national identity) (1974), and (3) Gandhi (generativity and middle life) (1969).

Erikson (1969) sees Gandhi as a religious actualist, like Luther. The essence of religious actualism for Luther was fourfold: (1) Christ comes today; (2) God's way is what makes us move; (3) we must always be reborn, renewed, regenerated; and (4) to do enough means nothing else than always to begin again.

The Hindu concept of the life cycle, according to Erikson, "allots a time for the learning of eternal concerns in youth, and for the experience of near-nothingness at the end of life, while it reserves the middle of life a time dedicated to the 'maintenance of the world.'" In the middle of life a person must "forget death for the sake of the newborn individual and the coming generation" (Erikson, 1969, p. 399).

In a chapter called "Homo Religiosus," Erikson writes:

> At the time of the Ahmedabad strike, Gandhi was forty-eight years old: middle-aged mahatma, indeed. That the very next year he emerged as the father of his country only lends greater importance to the fact that the middle span of life is under the dominance of the universal human need and strength which I have come to subsume under the term *generativity*. I have said that in this stage a man and a woman must have defined for themselves what and whom they have come to care for, what they care to do well, how they plan to take care of what they have started and created. But it is clear that the great leader creates for himself and for many others new choices and new cares. These he derives from a mighty drivenness, an intense and yet flexible energy, a shocking originality, and a capacity to impose on his time what most concerns him—which he does so convincingly that his time believes this concern to have emanated "naturally" from ripe necessities. (1969, p. 395)

Middle aged religious leaders such as Gandhi "create concerns greater than he and his followers can really promise to take care of in their lifetimes" (Erikson, 1969, p. 400). Gandhi, whom Erikson sees as both father and mother to India, was compelling in enrolling others in his generative concerns, not only for the future of India, but for oppressed people in other parts of the world.

An equally great man, Martin Luther King Jr., picked up and carried forward Gandhi's generative legacy of passive resistance and nonviolence, to galvanize the conscience and actions of this nation. And King, like Gandhi, began a liberation movement that has changed our society, but also is not yet completed.

Generativity as Personal Legacy

Generativity in many ways is concerned with legacy. Gandhi is certainly an excellent example of the generativity of an international religious leader. His legacy was large: freeing India from British rule. But Gandhi was concerned with all people. He was concerned about the impact of his actions on the British and offered apology to them. And he insisted that India deal with its own sins of domination and oppression, especially the caste system.

A secular example of generative legacy on a large scale is the wildlife conservation projects of Ted Turner. Whatever we may think of Turner the cable TV and media tycoon, Turner is clearly generating a legacy—not in the media, but in environmental conservation. Turner is the largest individual landowner in the United States, with holdings of 1.7 million acres in nine states. On Turner's ranches, rare and endangered species of wildlife, native grasses, and animals that others might consider lowly, such as rattlesnake, coyote, and prairie dog, are given equal protection. Turner tries to recreate land as it was before the arrival of white pioneers; that is, he prefers largely unfenced open land stocked with bison rather than cattle. Turner has assembled the largest buffalo herds in North America as well as herds of elk, bighorn sheep, and rare California condors. When Turner dies, the ranches will go into a preservation trust. And when the last Turner dies, the lands will become part of the Turner foundation. His goal is to protect the lands and their wildlife "as long as the water flows and the wind blows and the grass grows" (O'Driscoll, 2000, p. 1A).

Whether you agree with Turner's project is not important. It illustrates well the legacy created by a generative project. Each of us, however, has a different calling. Our calling, our vocation indeed, must be the thing that shapes our generative actions and determines what legacy we wish to create.

The Religious Function of Middle Age

For Carl Gustav Jung, the second half of life (beginning around age forty) has a deeply spiritual purpose. Jung divides human growth and development into four quarters, which he likens to the daily course of the sun: (1) dawn and early morning (infancy and childhood); (2) mid-morning (adolescence and young adulthood); (3) afternoon (the middle years); and (4) dusk (very old age).

The afternoon of life marks the beginning of midlife and of what Jung refers to as the second half of life. Life at the midpoint begins to be beset by problems. Jung thinks that problems are a gift to us because they press us to greater consciousness and to a more profound spiritual life. The task of the first half of life is developing a strong sense of personal self (ego) and pursuing personal achievements: money, a family, and a place in society. The task of the second half of life, and especially of the afternoon of life, is *individuation* (Jung, 1946/1969). Jung defines individuation as the coming-to-be of the Self (with a capital *S* to distinguish it from *self* used as a synonym for ego). Jung understands the Self to be the archetypal imprint of the *imago dei,* the image of God. So the task of the middle years, for Jung, is to move from ego-centricity to God-centeredness.[3] The religious task of the second half of life, in becoming God-centered, requires, paradoxically, not an ascent but a descent into the inner life. In many ways, the contemplative life is what is needed for the midlife transit.

Many people who reach the middle years still try to cling to the values and ways of acting that sustained them in the first half of life. But Jung notes that whoever "carries over into the afternoon the law of the morning...must pay for it with damage to the soul" (1930/1969, p. 400). "Aging people should know that their lives are not mounting and expanding, but that an inexorable inner process enforces the contraction of life...For the aging person it is a duty and a necessity to devote serious attention to himself," to the development of the inner life (1946/1969, p. 399).

> After having lavished its light upon the world, the sun withdraws it rays in order to illuminate itself. Instead of doing likewise, many old people prefer to be hypochondriacs, niggards, pedants, applauders of the past or else eternal adolescents—all lamentable substitutes for the illumination of the self, but inevitable consequences of the delusion that the second half of life must be governed by the principles of the first. (1946/1969, p. 399)

Jung understands that for many, the afternoon brings a reversal of values. "At the stroke of noon, the descent begins. And the descent means the reversal of all the ideals and values that were cherished in the morning" (1946/1969, p. 397). For example, those who have put family and relationships first may suddenly become interested in the life of the mind and in business. And those who have put work ahead of relationships may find themselves yearning for greater love and intimacy.

Jung laments that there are no schools for people over forty years old (1930/1969). In the past, religion had always been such a school. There one learned how to face death. A belief in a life after death with God provides a goal for the second half of life–to prepare oneself for immortality. Death, in that view, is something to be welcomed, for it provides a transition to a new life with God. Jung remarks, "It happens sometimes that I must say to an older patient: 'Your picture of God or your idea of immortality is atrophied, consequently your psychic metabolism is out of gear'" (1946/ 1969, p. 403). Jung, therefore, finds religious belief, when it is a living faith, to be health-inducing.

> I am convinced that it is hygienic…to discover in death a goal toward which one can strive, and that shrinking away from it is something unhealthy and abnormal which robs the second half of life of its purpose. I therefore consider that all religions with a supramundane goal are eminently reasonable from the point of view of psychic hygiene. (1946/1969, p. 402)

Development Tasks

Living through the years of middle life and making the passage to late adulthood require that a number of developmental tasks be undertaken. Adult developmental tasks are "the psychological response to major life experiences (such as work, achievement, parenthood, grandparenthood, death of loved ones, and retirement) which produce intrapsychic changes as the result of actual occurrence or psychological consideration by all person in a particular age group" (Colarusso, 1992, p. 120).

The major tasks of the middle years are as follows.

- Mourning the lost body of youth and responding to the accompanying narcissistic injuries
- Coming to terms with the cognitive changes related to a changed perspective on time and a personal, existential awareness of death
- Securing a positive ratio of generativity over stagnation in order to enter late adulthood with a sense of integrity rather than despair
- Moving from self-centeredness to God-centeredness through contemplation and individual development so that, at sunset, we may embrace death as a passage to eternal life with the Creator and all redeemed creation.

Summary

In this chapter on midlife, we have examined the major changes that occur during the middle years. The changes experienced in middle age are quite comprehensive. Our body changes. Our ways of thinking change. Our feelings about who we are change. Our ways of relating to self and others changes, as does our faith and our relationship with God. We change also in our understanding of our existence in society. Because we are an interrelated whole, a change in one part affects all our other parts. And if we are able to have more generativity than stagnation, more creativity than negativity, then we will find ourselves growing and developing in our abilities to love, to care, to provide for, and to leave a legacy for future generations.

Notes

[1] The writings of Kierkegaard, Nietzsche, Heidegger, Camus, Sartre, and Tillich are excellent among the theologians and philosophers. Among the psychological theorists, the writings of Ludwig Binswanger, Medard Boss, Viktor Frankl, and Rollo May are instructive.

[2] For excellent material on social and cultural location (including gender and ethnicity), the reader is encouraged to re-read chapters 11 and 13. In chapter 11, the sections on developing a self in context, on making room for others, and on work and money are especially important for an understanding of midlife development. And the material in chapter 13 on social location and the family also applies to persons in the middle years.

[3] Jung, when writing as a depth psychologist, prefers to refer to the Self rather than to God. That is, he prefers to use psychological rather than religious or theological language.

Faith and Development in Late Adulthood

K. Brynolf Lyon

So teach us to count our days that we may gain a wise heart.
PSALM 90:12

Throughout most of human history, the period of life we now think of as late adulthood was experienced only by a few. Even in the United States as late as 1900, only about 4 percent of the population was sixty-five years of age or older. Life expectancy at birth was forty-seven years. The great demographic transition of the last century, characterized by lower fertility and mortality rates, initiated remarkable increases in the number and percentage of older adults in nearly every country throughout the world. In the United States, for example, the percentage of older adults more than tripled over the past one hundred years, to constitute nearly 13 percent of the population by the century's end. Life expectancy at birth is now seventy-nine years for women and seventy-two years for men (Administration on Aging, 1999). To put this another way, in 1900 in this country less than half of children born survived to the period of life we are discussing in this chapter, whereas roughly 80 percent of the children born today will do so (Kramarow, Lentzner, Rooks, Weeks, & Saydah, 1999). While this increase occurred earlier in the so-called "developed" countries, many "less developed" countries are now experiencing a rate of growth in their late adulthood populations even greater than that in their more "developed" counterparts (U.S. Census Bureau, 1995).

Much is hidden as well as revealed, of course, in this quantitative data. Certainly, they help us appreciate the sheer length of life now afforded increasing numbers of people. Yet what it means to grow old—what the physical, emotional, and spiritual challenges and opportunities of late adulthood are—remains opaque in the face of such statistics. The particularity of the aging subject (his or her biography, culture, race, gender, sexual orientation, and location within the political economy) and the influence of that particularity on the course of life in late adulthood may be obscured by the force of the larger trends. It is the purpose of this chapter to move somewhat closer to the aging subject and the developmental and contextual factors that give shape to this period of life.

Bodies and Cognition in Late Adulthood

Older adulthood is frequently associated with cognitive and physical impairment. To grow old, it is thought, is to suffer bodily decay and the diminishing of cognitive abilities. Although there are certainly forms of cognitive and physical impairment that accompany late adulthood, these processes of decline are significantly more diverse and normally arise later in this period of life than often thought. We now distinguish, for example, between the young-old (sixty-five years of age to seventy-four years of age) and the old-old (those seventy-five years of age and above) to account for these differences. Thus, while some cognitive and physical decline characterizes nearly all persons in late adulthood (and, indeed, late middle age), its more debilitating expressions are being pushed further back in the life course.

There is significant disagreement about what to make of bodily and cognitive change and decline in late adulthood. Most prominently, the issue of whether these processes are functions of aging per se or secondary to discrete health conditions is a matter of some dispute. If the former is the case, then bodily and cognitive change and decline are simply an expression of our finitude, and while some expressions of it will be treatable, it is not eradicable. If the latter is the case, these processes are not intrinsic to the aging process and will be increasingly less prevalent as medical advances develop more sophisticated treatments for the discrete conditions. Certainly, modern medicine has already found ways to delay and/or treat a variety of conditions formerly thought internal to growing older. And it is quite clear that historic and current differences among groups of people in the social conditions of health (economic well-being, access to and utilization of medical care, and cultural values that support the flourishing of persons) account for a great deal of the differences between genders, races, and ethnicities on these matters. Yet whatever one makes of the larger debate, at least for the foreseeable future certain forms of bodily and cognitive decline and negatively-valenced change will continue to be a normally expectable aspect of the aging process.

Cognitive and Intellectual Functioning

Studies of development in middle and late adulthood show that there is a variable progression of cognitive and intellectual functioning through these periods of life. At a broad level, in healthy populations, the efficiency and flexibility of cognitive operations (fluid intelligence) begins to decline for most persons during late middle age, whereas the contents or products of cognitive operations (crystallized intelligence) generally remain stable until the mid-seventies (Salthouse, 1998; Schaie, 1996). As we age, therefore, we tend to process information more slowly, though our ability to make use of what we have learned stays relatively constant until very late in life. Even with regard to this widely recognized pattern of cognitive change in adulthood, however, we must be cautious in interpreting it. There is, for example, as much if not more variation in cognitive functioning within the older adult population itself as there is between older adults and younger adults (Salthouse, 1998).

Most older adults state that their memories do not function as well as they did in earlier life. Indeed, concerns about memory loss with aging are prominent for many people. As with cognitive functioning in general, however, the research on memory and aging produces a dual pattern. Although very little difference exists between relatively healthy younger and older adults in simple recall tasks, there are significant decrements in "working memory" for those in late adulthood. The ability to both store and process information simultaneously, in other words, tends to decline with age. Indeed, it is likely that the decline in fluid intelligence and working memory with age are interrelated (Salthouse, 1998; Smith, 1996).

Recent studies also suggest an important difference in the style of cognitive functioning in everyday problem solving between persons in late adulthood and those in younger cohorts. The two cognitive styles have been referred to as the bottom-up approach and the top-down approach. In the face of everyday problem-solving tasks, younger adults are more likely to engage in extensive information searches, use inductive reasoning, and use more formalistic, abstract thinking. Older adults, on the other hand, tend to make decisions about everyday problems with less information than younger adults, based on previously acquired experiential knowledge and decision-making procedural strategies developed over their lifetime (Willis, 1996).

Although not an expectable aspect of aging for most people, the prevalence of cognitive-impairing dementias of older adulthood (Alzheimer's disease and vascular dementia) does accelerate rapidly from about 1 percent of persons in their early sixties to some 30 percent of persons in their nineties. In terms of cognitive functioning, such conditions bring about significant impairment in memory, judgement, and reasoning. Dementia patients also frequently experience significant behavioral changes such as increased anxiety, aggressiveness, suspiciousness, and depression (Butler et al., 1998). The symptomology and course of dementias produce significant stress and caregiving demands among and within family members. As Janie Long has noted, the families of dementia patients frequently face multiple challenges: "communication problems, financial and legal concerns, the question of institutionalization, the issue of power and the renegotiation of roles, dealing with grief, and unresolved family-of-origin issues" (1997, p. 220).

Bodies and Health

The graying or loss of hair, wrinkling of the skin, diminishing of eyesight and hearing, decline in muscular strength, and bone loss are common features of the aging body (Whitbourne, 1998). Likewise, the prevalence of chronic health conditions such as heart disease, cancer, stroke, arthritis, and diabetes increases with age. Even among noninstitutionalized older adults, some 80 percent report at least one chronic condition (Kramarow et al., 1999). Compared to younger cohorts, older adults are three times more likely to be limited in their daily activities by a health condition. They have more and longer hospital visits and spend almost twice as much in out-of-pocket health care costs as younger persons (Administration on Aging, 1999). The decline of the body and bodily functions are significant features of late adulthood.

It is easy in the face of such statistics to lose sight of the fact that older adults remain healthier longer into late adulthood than ever before. Many of the chronic health conditions of early late adulthood do not, for example, produce significant physical limitation. Indeed, three-fourths of persons over sixty-five in this country report their health as good. Thus, though bodily changes and decline are undeniable features of late adulthood, the onset, effects, and personal meanings of those changes vary widely.

One locus of this variation is found in gender and racial differences in this country. For example, although women live longer on average and have lower rates of hospitalization than men, they are more likely to suffer from disabilities and chronic health conditions requiring ongoing medical care. Men tend to die earlier and faster once they become ill. Women are more likely than men, therefore, to live both alone and in institutions. Racial differences are also significant. African American men and women have significantly shorter life expectancies than their white, Hispanic, and Asian American counterparts and are more likely to experience disabling conditions. Yet interestingly, at age eighty-five, African American life expectancy exceeds that of whites (Kramarow et al., 1999).

Given the physical challenges faced by many older adults, it is often assumed that the majority of such persons require long-term institutional care. However, less than 5 percent of persons over the age of sixty-five in the United States are in nursing homes. The majority of older adults live in a family setting. Nonetheless, the percentage of persons requiring nursing-home care increases dramatically with age, to nearly 20 percent of persons eighty-five years of age and older. Although even these numbers may seem relatively small, the majority of older adults will eventually require some caregiver assistance with activities of daily living (Administration on Aging, 1999).

The significance of bodily decline and change in late adulthood for our emotional and spiritual lives is twofold. First, such losses can place important adaptive demands on persons. The sheer narcissistic injury of bodily decline, change, or dysfunction can be troubling. Hearing impairments, the diminishing of visual acuity, and bodily fragility can produce significant emotional distress. Likewise, the emotional correlates of the realities of caregiving arrangements necessary to sustain the aging self in such circumstances are powerful features of this period of life for many persons. These challenges of late adulthood associated with the body are set, of course, in the context of the person's larger biography of life themes and the ways in which that life history has gifted and impoverished the self in dealing with these issues. The conflicts and emotional shadings one has experienced, for example, in the face of issues of dependency, autonomy, and interdependency are frequently re-evoked and restated in the face of the physical diminishment and bodily changes that accompany late adulthood.

Second, however, the body (and *our* body) is mediated to us in part by the social and cultural environment in which we live. The social valuation of bodies becomes a mirror in which we see and experience ourselves (de Beauvoir, 1973; Woodward, 1986, 1991). Given the idealization of youth (both culturally and through those more archaic wishes and fantasies that function within us throughout our lives), aging often produces a disjunction between our bodies and our sense of who we are. Older adulthood, in particular, can produce an alienation from our bodies: a sense that who we are is somehow not who we see reflected in the mirror, that our self-identity is different from what our bodies seem to reflect back to us. The body can seem, to varying degrees, fundamentally or significantly "other," producing the challenge of integrating our experience of our bodies and our sense of self or adaptively altering the character of our investment in our bodily selves. The meaning of cognitive and physical change and decline in late adulthood both shapes and is shaped by intrapsychic and interpersonal development.

Intrapsychic and Interpersonal Changes

Jean was an eighty-one-year-old white woman who had been referred to counseling by her daughter Betty. Her husband had died some two years earlier, soon after they had moved from their family home to the city where Betty lived. The move was precipitated both by her husband's declining health and by the onset of Alzheimer's disease in Jean. Betty had encouraged the move, wanting to care for her parents in the face of their health conditions. Jean had initially resisted the move, not wanting to be a burden to her daughter. Struggling now with the losses of her husband, familiar surroundings, and long-time friends and with the early stages of the decaying of her own sense of personal coherence and continuity, Jean was deeply depressed and angry. An assertive and successful businesswoman throughout her life, she was terrified by the changes taking place within and around her. I sat with her during our first meeting, struggling with my own anxieties about the terrors that she faced and that I would come increasingly to face vicariously with her.

While Jean's story is not representative of the older adulthood population as a whole, in many respects, the intrapsychic and interpersonal changes of late adulthood do frequently involve loss and grief. The physical and cognitive changes noted earlier can create losses of certain functional abilities that may well precipitate changes or stresses in the sense of self. The ability of the self to move around in the world, for example, may change with aging, and this change can certainly affect one's sense of self-esteem and emotional vitality. Likewise, such losses eventually require, for many persons, an increased dependence on others, and this dependency, as I noted above, can re-evoke the dense and complex intrapsychic dynamics of dependency in early life. The losses of late adulthood, however, are not simply those connected with one's own physical and cognitive functioning. Friends die or move away; neighborhoods change; and, for most married women, their husbands die well before they do. The issue of widowhood requires special mention in this regard.

Although the extension of the life span has pushed the experience of widowhood later into late adulthood for most persons, it remains an expectable loss of our later years. Some 70 percent of women and some 22 percent of men over sixty-five are widowed in this country. Most men who are widowed will live some six years after the death of their wife, while women will live approximately fifteen years. A significant period of life, especially for women, will take place as a widow (O'Bryant & Hannson, 1996). Most studies suggest that older adults (and particularly older women) experiencing this kind of bereavement are as resilient as younger persons in coping with the loss. Indeed, it appears that some younger women and younger families are more at-risk for a poor outcome in bereavement of a spouse than older women (Parkes, 1996). Nonetheless, the loss of a spouse in late adulthood produces an array of complex adaptive demands: changes in social roles, in the sense of identity, and in family interaction.

It has sometimes been imagined that the array of losses older adults must face leads inevitably to more sadness, anger, shame, and guilt. The picture is more complex than this. Studies of emotional development suggest that even though the intensity and frequency of positive affects decrease slightly in late adulthood, the intensity and frequency of negative affects do not increase simply as a function of age (Filipp, 1996). In other words, even though expressions of emotional enthusiasm and vitality decline somewhat with aging, older adults as a group are not more enveloped than younger persons by negative feelings. Having said this, however, it must be noted that more older adults are likely to suffer from clinically significant depressive symptoms than younger adults. Until very late in old age (when the trend begins to reverse), older women exhibit depressive symptoms with three times the frequency of older men (Kasl-Godley, Gatz, & Fiske, 1998).

In a somewhat larger framework, one of the earliest gerontological debates in this country concerned how older adults best cope with the challenges of old age. Disengagement theory, for example, held that the well-being of older adults is promoted by their withdrawal from, or decreasing their participation in, social activities. The idea was that such withdrawal helps the individual prepare for death by loosening their emotional bonds with others. Other early gerontologists argued that exactly the opposite was the case. What is sometimes called "activity theory" held that well-being in late adulthood is best promoted by remaining actively engaged in the world. Contemporary research, however, seems to point toward a far more complex picture than either of these rather stark alternatives suggest. While the extent or range of the social network in which older adults are embedded may decrease slightly with age, older adults actively nurture relationships that provide emotional support. It has been suggested in this regard that younger adults seek more instrumentally-significant relationships while older adults seek more intrinsically-meaningful ones—that is, that the desire for emotional intimacy increases with age (Filipp, 1996). To what extent this is due to changes internal to aging or to the fact that most older adults are women—and women of all ages are more likely than men to have friendships rooted in emotional sharing—is uncertain (Cavanaugh, 1998).

Robert Galatzer-Levy and Bertram Cohler (1993) have suggested in this regard that the ability to use current relationships and memories of earlier life events as sources of soothing and emotional vitality is crucial to emotional health in later adulthood. This provides a somewhat different angle of vision on the issues noted above. In other words, the issue is not the quantity of relationships or their intrinsic or instrumental character, but rather their function within the aging self as means of maintaining a sense of personal coherence and meaningfulness in the midst of the losses and changes of later life. Memories, they note, may even come to have as strong if not stronger role than current relationships in this process for some older adults.

Several persons have attempted to situate the issues of loss and grief in late adulthood in the context of broader challenges of psychosocial development in this period of life. The theories of Erik Erikson and David Gutmann are especially prominent. Erik Erikson, for example, argued that the intrapsychic and interpersonal changes of late adulthood must be seen in the context of the larger life cycle. He suggested that a particular nexus of psychosocial issues or adaptive challenges characterizes each stage of life. Erikson described the "nuclear crisis" of late adulthood as that of integrity versus despair. He described the essential challenge in this way:

> Burdened by physical limitations and confronting a personal future that may seem more inescapably finite than ever before, those nearing the end of the life cycle find themselves struggling to accept the inalterability of the past and the unknowability of the future, to acknowledge possible mistakes and omissions, and to balance consequent despair with the sense of overall integrity that is essential to carrying on. (1982, p. 56)

By integrity, Erikson meant "a sense of coherence and wholeness" in the face of the threats in late adulthood to the linkages (psychological, physical, and socio-cultural) that have held one's life together. Despair, on the other hand, referred to the sense of being overwhelmed by lost opportunities, guilt over deeds done, and hopelessness about the future. In Erikson's perspective, the central psychosocial challenge of late adulthood restates and transforms the earliest issues of life: the complexities of hope and trust in the midst of an uncertain self-world relationship (1982).

In this context, Robert Butler has suggested that older adults face the task of "life review." The life review process, in Butler's perspective, occurs as older adults face the physical and social losses of later adulthood. Past experiences are either increasingly brought to mind or are worked through in a less consciously aware manner. It is a means of attempting to reintegrate one's biography in the face of impending physical dissolution. The often-noted reminiscence of older adults, Butler suggests, is a natural process of preparing and healing that may lead either to a strengthened sense of self or to depression (1998).

In a somewhat different vein, the anthropologist and psychoanalyst David Gutmann (1987, 1997) has argued that the psychosocial challenges of later adulthood are tied not only to issues of loss but also to new opportunities for emotional growth. Gutmann, drawing on his extensive cross-cultural studies and on Carl Jung's theory of stages of life, suggests that late adulthood brings its own unique opportunity for emotional development. As a consequence of psychological changes accompanying the empty nest in middle age and retirement in late adulthood, previously repressed or dissociated aspects of the personality begin to emerge. The requirements of generativity (both vocationally and parentally), in other words, often necessitate that certain aspects of ourselves be repressed or otherwise kept at bay in the service of the demands of production and reproduction. With the easing of those demands, older adults may begin to experience those dimensions of their emotional lives that were set aside. In traditional and patriarchal cultures, for example, women find more aggressive and assertive aspects of themselves emerging outside the context of caregiving, while older men often find more relationally nurturing and receptive aspects of themselves coming to the fore.

Nonetheless, it should be noted that most studies of the developmental trajectory of personality traits across adulthood suggest continuity. In other words, apart from situations of brain disease that may precipitate dramatic personality change, most older adults will be like who they have been like throughout their adult lives. Broad stability in personality across adulthood rather than change tends to be the pattern for most persons (Costa, Yang, & McCrae, 1998). There is a saying that, as we age, we become more like ourselves—and this appears to be true. This conclusion need not be seen as contradictory to the theories cited earlier. It only requires that we recognize what we ought to anticipate in any case: that most persons resolve whatever developmental or environmental challenges they face in adulthood in favor of continuity with their enduring dispositions.

The works of Galatzer-Levy and Cohler, Erikson, Butler, and Gutmann are all psychosocial theories; that is, they all point in the direction of the influence of historical, social, and cultural factors in intrapsychic and interpersonal development in late adulthood. It is to those issues that we must now turn more directly.

Social Location and the Family

Differentiating between the effects of shared historical experience within a generation and factors intrinsic to aging itself in the psychological dynamics of late adulthood is extremely difficult. Shared historical experience within a generation (what is called the "cohort effect") has been shown to powerfully shape our emotional lives (Galatzer-Levy & Cohler, 1993). The shared experience of large cultural and social events (such as the Great Depression) and, more generally, the shared experience of the educational, economic, political, and cultural systems of a particular historical period within a country or community significantly influence us. These shared experiences are likely to shape persons in such a way that certain kinds of common themes, struggles, and strengths will appear in late adulthood that are not due to universal factors intrinsic to the aging process itself but rather to cohort effects between generations. To understand the psychological and emotional dynamics of late adulthood, therefore, requires understanding the social and cultural history through which older adults have lived.

In so-called traditional (or tribal) societies, elders frequently occupied an important cultural role as mediators between the sacred and the secular spheres of existence. Older men in particular were mediators of the boundary between the mythic realm and the world of production and reproduction—as teachers and upholders of the sacred myths and rituals containing the more mundane work of everyday life. As Gutmann (1997) has argued, this transfer of social power (from the secular to the sacred realm) served to locate older males securely within the cultural geography of the community and to bind the narcissistic energies that might otherwise have been released with removal from the realm of production. In other words, older males were encouraged away from self-preoccupation and the diminishment of their self-esteem by being drawn back into the cultural work of the community at its sacred/secular boundary. Although often written in quite different social contexts, much of historic Christian theology has seen older adults in a similar vein: as persons who, given their long experience in the faith, have an important role in the community as models or exemplars of Christian life (Lyon, 1985).

The peculiarly modern notion of old age as a period of retirement arose as a result of social, economic, and political factors within industrialized nations (Graebner, 1980; Quadagno, 1988). Although the idea of universal retirement based on government-sponsored pensions has wide appeal, a consequence has been the dislocation of older adults (and particularly older males) within the traditional cultural geography of the community. The social meaning of late adulthood has come to be defined more by where it is not located (in the world of production and reproduction) than by any substantive, socially legitimated sense of where it *is* located. It is not surprising, therefore, that the social meaning of late adulthood is increasingly colonized by the more narcissistic images of a consumer society. Older adults, though they do not produce, can buy, invest, and tend to the development and enjoyment of their individual selves (Cole, 1992; Lyon, 1994).

The paradigmatic older adult in this image is a male who has had a relatively traditional (in the modern sense) career path. The power of patriarchy is made clear in this image given that the vast majority of older adults are, in fact, women. Although increasing numbers of women have entered the job market since the 1950s in this country, they are paid less than their male counterparts and are more likely than males to occupy jobs that do not provide a private pension. Consequently, though poverty rates have declined substantially over the past several decades for the older adulthood population as a whole, older women are significantly more likely than males to be at or below the poverty line. Indeed, some 51 percent of women over eighty-five live at or near poverty levels (V. Richardson, 1999). The percentage is still higher than this for older African American women. Even the decision to retire is powerfully affected by gender issues. Women, for example, are far more likely than men to make the decision to retire based on the caregiving needs of an ill spouse or elderly parent and, therefore, are more likely to struggle with the emotional, moral, and spiritual demands of such caregiving (V. Richardson, 1999; Lopata, 1996; Brody, 1990).

The above realities of late adulthood, however, point us not only toward recognizing the embeddedness of the aging self in the political economy, but also toward recognizing the challenges and opportunities of the ongoing embeddedness of the aging self in family context. Popular stereotypes suggest that older adults are cut off from their families, having little contact with their wider kinship network, and primarily recipients of care from younger generations. The reality, however, is that most older adults maintain significant contact with, and are important sources of assistance to, their children and siblings (Hargrave & Hanna, 1997). Gerontological research has clearly shown that older adults do not simply constitute a caregiving demand on younger generations, but in fact remain "continuing sources of socialization, caregiving, and financial support for younger generations" (Cohler & Altergott, 1996, p. 61). Although the forms of such contact are different from those that dominated earlier historical periods, intergenerational interdependency remains a reality for most persons. Indeed, one of the most significant facts about the family life of late adulthood today is not the disconnection of the generations, but rather the emergence of greater numbers of generations within a family living at the same time. Thus, more than ever before, there is a likelihood that three, four, or five generations within a family will experience one another in one form or another.

Think, for example, about the family role of grandparents today. Some 75 percent of older adults in the United States are grandparents. Most older adults who are grandparents prefer to be involved in their grandchildren's lives somewhat episodically, rather than continuously. Nonetheless, studies show that grandparents continue to serve important symbolic and socializing roles for younger generations (as living connections to the longer family history of their grandchildren). In addition, older adults frequently provide emotional, financial, and child care support, particularly in times of severe economic need, illness, and divorce (Robertson, 1996). While the life-cycle timing of grandparenthood varies widely (some become grandparents well before they are in late adulthood), the experience of grandparenthood remains a salient emotional experience for many older adults. As a grandparent, the dynamic joys and conflicts of their own parenting (and of their own being parented as children) are often re-evoked as they experience the parenting relationships of their children and grandchildren.

A second significant fact about the family life of late adulthood today, however, is its increasingly negotiable character. Whereas in previous eras, most intergenerational relations were governed by ethnically diverse, socially legitimated values determining the relationship of the generations to one another, we now face a situation where they are (or must be) increasingly negotiated within the family itself. Two aspects of this are important to note. On the one hand, largely as a product of changing family forms (consequent to increases in divorce, blended families, and gay and lesbian partnerships), the relationship between older and younger generations often falls outside of the traditional values governing those relationships. What, for example, is the relationship between grandparents and their adult child's stepchildren or between elderly parents and their adult child's same-sex partner? Such relationships must be negotiated within the family, because traditional cultural values do not cover those situations.

On the other hand, while family relationships must increasingly be negotiated within the individual family, ethnic and racial variations of intergenerational relationships remain an important fact today. Though many white families are dominated by the values of self-reliance and independence, for example, Asian American, African American, and Hispanic families tend to construct and draw on a much wider kin network (C. L. Johnson, 1996; Markides & Mindal, 1987). This active embeddedness within a wider kin network carries with it significantly different expectations, resources, and challenges for the aging self than that which tends to be the case for whites. Different family structures and kin networks interact with economic, political, and social realities to produce quite different experiences of aging.

The social location of the aging subject, in other words, is a significant variable in the experience of aging. Some social locations remain largely invisible or obscured to the images of late adulthood that tend to dominate our perception. The experiences of older lesbians (Fulmer, Shenk, & Eastland, 1999) and elderly urban African American poor often remain outside of the ways we think about late adulthood. On the other hand, other kinds of skewed understanding arise less from the invisibility of certain groups than from the way in which we construe their social location. As Helena Znaniecka Lopata (1996) has observed, for example, a great deal of gerontological research remains tied to patriarchal models of male-female relationships. Thus, she argues, much of the creativity of the aging of women today (their rearranging of life events and becoming less dependent on men, their distinctive styles of managing widowhood) is lost to view.

Religious and Spiritual Dimensions of Aging

Ruby and John were a sixty-seven-year-old African American couple in a Christian education class I taught on aging and faith at a metropolitan church several years ago. John suffered from emphysema and came to class every Sunday with his oxygen tank. Ruby was a robust woman, spending increasing time caring for her husband while still working as a clerk at a local grocery store. Lifelong church members, they said they had moved from a more theologically conservative church to a more liberal one during the civil rights struggles of the 1960s. They spoke of how God had been with them throughout the whole of their lives: in the midst of early struggles in their marriage; through the evils of American racism; at the times of the drug addiction and eventual shooting-death of their eldest son; in the marriage, divorce, and remarriage of their daughter; and even now, as John faced declining health and as Ruby both resented and cherished caring for him. Ruby said, "God has held us up in our times of trouble and in our times of blessing. And I know He will help us finish what He has begun in us."

How might we better understand the course of faith and spirituality in late adulthood? What does it mean to grow old in faith? Interpretations of the religious and spiritual dimensions of late adulthood have occurred from two broad perspectives: (1) human science investigations of the extent, functions, and trajectories of spirituality or religious beliefs and practices in late adulthood; and (2) theological or philosophical studies of the significance and meaning of late adulthood from the perspective of a particular faith tradition or philosophical stance. Each of these perspectives has its own set of questions, interests, and concerns. The first, for example, generally arises out of psychology or sociology and is governed by the research methodologies of those disciplines. They often intend to address something more (or other) than a particular faith community and are interested in exploring the human-ward side of religion or spirituality in late life. The second perspective arises from within either particular faith communities or particular philosophical perspectives and is an effort to explore the meaning of late adulthood from the perspective of the symbols, images, and beliefs of that community. I offer below a brief overview of the work of each perspective.

People draw on religious beliefs and practices in many different ways to many different ends. This is as true of older adults as anyone else. Thus, we ought to be suspicious of the oft-heard claim that adults become more religious as they reach older adulthood or that religious beliefs and practices necessarily increase the emotional or physical well-being of the elderly. Indeed, there is significant research data suggesting several important things in this regard. First, religious belief tends to remain relatively stable over adulthood. On the one hand, this means that even though participation in religious institutions may decline in the last period of life (particularly due to ill health), religious belief remains salient for older adults. On the other hand, religious belief does not generally increase with age. Second, the current generation of older women tends to find religious activities more meaningful than older men do, and older women draw on their faith more fully. Third, people do not tend to "turn to religion" with aging. In other words, if someone hasn't been religious in younger years, it is unlikely they will become religious in late adulthood. The ways that we have found larger meaning and significance in our younger years tend to be the ways we will seek it in our later years. Fourth, religious beliefs and practices have a variable impact on emotional well-being. Some beliefs and practices support or increase well-being for some people, whereas other beliefs and practices are detrimental to the well-being of some people (for a summary of all the above data, see McFadden, 1996). As we should anticipate, the role or function of religious belief and practice in late adulthood does not present a uniform picture. This variability should not obscure the fact, however, that many people, like Ruby and John, are able to draw on religion in later adulthood as a means of maintaining a sense of personal coherence and meaningfulness (Galatzer-Levy & Cohler, 1993).

Another way many social scientists have sought to address the question of the relationship of aging and faith is to look less at "religion" and more at "spirituality." Although what spirituality refers to varies considerably in this literature, it generally has reference to something that the researcher considers more fundamental or intrinsic to the person than institutional religion—for example, transcendence, unitive modes of knowing, the search for meaning, or wisdom. While this variation in the definition of spirituality makes this literature impossible to summarize in a short space (the works of McFadden, 1996, and Thomas & Eisenhandler, 1999, provide useful overviews), I will illustrate this perspective through the work of Lawrence Kohlberg and Lars Tornstam.

Several years ago, well-known psychologist of moral development Lawrence Kohlberg suggested the possibility of a final stage of development that may emerge in late adulthood. This developmental possibility is not, Kohlberg argued, a more advanced stage of moral thinking, but rather the emergence of religious questions that ground or structure moral thinking itself: What, finally, is life about? How ought we to die? As Kohlberg put it:

> It represents, in a sense, a shift from figure to ground. In despair we are the self seen from the distance of the cosmic or infinite. In the state of mind [I am referring to here, however], we identify ourselves with the cosmic or infinite perspective itself; we value life from its standpoint. At such a time, what is ordinarily background becomes foreground…We sense the unity…associated with a structure of ontological and moral conviction (1981, p. 345).

In a related vein, Swedish sociologist Lars Tornstam has argued that development in late adulthood is characterized by a process of "gerotranscendence." In his words, "Simply put, gerotranscendence is a shift in metaperspective from a materialistic and pragmatic view of the world to a more cosmic and transcendent one, normally accompanied by an increase in life satisfaction" (1999, p. 178). Tornstam, in other words, is suggesting that the process of development in late adulthood carries with it an opening to a new way for the aging self to situate itself in the world. As we age, he argues, we face a developmental challenge to see ourselves in relation to a broader, more inclusive frame of reference with lessened self-centeredness, one more appreciative of the mysteries of life and that re-locates ourselves in a longer temporal order. For Tornstam, gerotranscendence is not an inevitability in later adulthood, but rather a developmental possibility, with multiple paths to and through it. In ways consistent with but extending the perspectives of Erikson and Gutmann, Tornstam has attempted to study empirically the nature and emergence of gerotranscendence in older adults.

A second perspective on these issues emerges from philosophical and theological explorations of aging. This literature is, again, exceedingly broad and diverse, defying easy summarization (helpful overviews include Kimble & McFadden, 1995; Manheimer, 1999; McKee, 1982). Nonetheless, it is clear that the experience of the aging self raises a variety of questions with which most religious communities have been deeply concerned. What does it mean that we grow old and die? How are we to live in the face of bodily change and decline? What are we to make of the opportunities for growth and deepening that occur with aging? As our lives draw inexorably to a close and the possibilities for reparation and justice foreshorten, what are we to make of our failures and triumphs; the injustices we have experienced and perpetrated; the guilt, shame, joy, and delight we continue to know? What ought to be the relationship between younger and older generations? What happens to us after we die? A brief illustration must again suffice.

In Christian traditions, the spirituality of aging has tended to be seen in the light of four claims. First, God remains with older adults in the same way God is with us throughout our lives: as One who blesses, justifies, and redeems. No period of life, in other words, exists apart from God's nourishing, rectifying, and merciful presence. God's love embraces us, and God's grace upholds us in the face of our lives' failures. We need not be crushed under the weight of the shortcomings of our past, for it is God's compassion, and not our own effort, that authors the final word about our lives. Consequently, second, later adulthood is a period not only of loss but also of possibilities for growth in faith. Although the historic Christian traditions have been ever mindful of the realities of certain kinds of decline and decay that can accompany old age, they have also resisted defining late adulthood simply in terms of loss. Rather, even in the very midst of loss, certain kinds of growth can occur. This does not diminish or minimize the reality of loss itself, but rather suggests that loss is not all there is. The possibility for growth in piety, or spirituality, or faith remains ever-present. Third, older adults are specially called in this regard to serve as teachers and witnesses of faith to younger generations. Whether through meditation, example, or direct service, older adults are thought to have an important religious and moral role in the ongoing formation of younger generations in the faith. Finally, fourth, the experience of old age has been seen as contextualized by belief in the resurrection. Although our life in this world ends with death, our death is not the final thing about us. God redeems our lives from final meaninglessness, and our present experience is nurtured through hope in the resurrection of our bodies in Jesus Christ (Lyon, 1985, 1988).

Conclusion

Can the historic claims of the Christian faith regarding aging provide compelling resources for us today? Certainly, to retrieve the tradition appropriately cannot simply mean to repeat it. As I have argued elsewhere, much of the historic Christian tradition's understanding of aging was rooted in a dualistic understanding of nature and spirit, body and soul that can no longer be maintained. Likewise, Carrie Doehring (1999) has suggested that this understanding of late adulthood is skewed by its being permeated with male, patriarchal values. Thus, while these resources of belief from the historic Christian tradition remain important, the challenge of discerning the meaning and call of late adulthood is ever new to each generation. Faithful aging, as Carroll Saussy (1998) has recently observed, emerges in the meeting of the particularity of one's own aging and the experiences of others with the beliefs and practices of faith. As the challenges and opportunities of old age change (through medical advance, political and economic change, and the fortunes of communal existence) and as our understanding of the meaning of faith itself is transformed and restated, the need presents itself to understand afresh the meaning of our life journeys in light of the faith.

CHAPTER 14

The Wages of Dying

Catastrophe Transformed

In memoriam: Barry Ulanov (1918–2000)

Claude Barbre

It's time to prepare myself—as a friend said—
"Not to be here." It will happen. One day
The dish will lie empty on the brown table.

Toward dusk, someone will say, "Today
Some rooms were busy, but this room was not.
The gold knob shone alone in the dark."

No breath, no poems, no dish. And this small change
Will go unnoticed by the snow, the squirrels
Searching for old acorns. What to do with

All these joys? Someone says, "You take them."
(ROBERT BLY, 1998, "SUNDAY: WHAT TO DO WITH OBJECTS," P. 89)

Introduction

About death, the poet Philips Larkin said, "Most things don't happen. This one will" (Larkin, 1955, p. 23). Larkin's ironic pronouncement serves as a blunt rejoinder to the characteristic human dependence on wish fulfillment and denial of death. Even though human beings strive to convince

285

themselves that they will live forever, the certainty of death is a phenomenon that embraces all of life. In contrast, while Robert Bly's quiet meditation lifts to consciousness the inevitability of loss and death, there is a clear awareness that ultimate change does not mean eradication. Here is a hope and illumination that earthly joys will not be annihilated, but can be taken with us, somehow transmuted—a promise and imperative spoken from a mysterious and unnamed Other/other. From this perspective, life changes and continues. The "terror of things left" in the aftermath of death (Boll, 1965) is tempered by Bly's remarkable interrogative about joy. In their own way these poets voice an age-old adage: Each of us is faced in every moment with the possibility and inevitability of our own death and with the death of our loved ones. How we respond to this "unanswerable certainty" (Gilkey, 1988, p. 32) affects us in the very fabric of our collective and individual days. Our life provides a background to the meanings of death, just as the meanings of death serve as a background to those of life (Ross, 1997). The problem of death is therefore confronted and understood by religious and philosophical conceptions within the context of life.

A haiku by Basho reads, "Nearing autumn's close / my neighbor, now / what is it that he does?" (Meltzer, 1984, p. 152). Nearing life's close, with us throughout life, how do we live with the awareness of our mutability? Psychoanalyst Otto Rank argues that such a question is the major motivator of our creative and cultural world (1932/1975). Each of society's images of death reveals the level of independence of its individuals, their personal relatedness, self-reliance, and aliveness. Human experience, lived consciously, is an expression of ultimate reality and must creatively express a paradoxical nature. As we consider our own mortality, the "wilder shore of dying" (Broyard, 1992, p. 53) underscores the conditional nature of human life and awakens an eloquence of being alive. The experience of life with Death's companion presence draws us deeper into mystery's center.

In many religions, especially Christian mystical traditions, a person in the state of beatific vision both merges—attains union—with God, yet maintains individuality—some degree of separateness—as the culmination of all his or her actions in the presence of God. Is Death something of this experience? Does this not suggest a paradox of self, a unity at once connected to transcendent reality yet separate and of the world? How can we come to understand and prepare for such ultimate things, abide in the valley of not knowing when considering the kingdom of death? Philosopher of religion John Hick joins our meditation with his own interrogatives:

> Is the death of the body the extinction of the person? or does [s]he survive as a continuing consciousness? or as a resurrected person? with a spiritual body? in perpetuity or for a limited period? Will [s]he be born again to live another earthly life? Is there time or

timelessness beyond death? Is the individual absorbed back into some great spiritual reality, like a drop returning to the ocean? (1976, p. 21, inclusive language added)

Hick concludes, "We shall not be able to refrain from speculating about death until we can refrain from speculating about life, for one is inseparable from the other" (1976, p. 21).

We experience the presence of death from the very beginning of life. The infant's earliest imagery is directed toward connections with the other, and with a sense of the movement and integrity of his or her own body. This is associated with a positive sense of life and vitality. Death imagery is associated with a threat toward the integrity of the person in terms of stasis and disintegration (N. Walsh, 1996). The experience of birth is the infant's first encounter with such threats and gives rise to his or her death imagery. As Noel Walsh points out, "Birth has two powerful components: extrusion and emergence. Extrusion is the biological separation from the mother. The infant's body is passively forced through the birth canal to the outer word with all its new stimuli and sensations, and the cutting of the umbilical cord is its final separation from its former lifetime" (1996, p. 46).

Birth is bound with the experience of loss and separation, and also with the positive imagery of emergence, the first experience of individuation, autonomy, movement, vitality, and a new form of existence. "Our lives are filled with countless little intimations of death," writes Russian Orthodox philosopher Nicholas Berdiaev, "and when human feelings wane and disappear, this is an experience of death. When we part with a person, a house, a garden, an animal, and have the feeling that we may never see them again, this is an experience of death" (Berdiaev, 1931/1960, p. 251, cited by Guroian, 1996, p. 22). This tension between the double experience of death in life, life in death, introduces us to the major themes of this chapter: death viewed from the standpoint of human growth and development, and the lived responses of human beings to death, culturally and individually.

Letting In, Letting Go: Approaching Death

Pastoral theologian Charles Gerkin remarks that death and dying constitute "a process of narrowing, inexorably and unrelentingly moving the life cycle of the individual toward death. Instead of building up, life begins to contract" (1979, p. 95). Approaching death, the concept of self must now be adjusted to these narrowing realistic possibilities. Withdrawal from one activity after another becomes inevitable; life must be simplified. Aging tends to bring a decreasing range of abilities and, in the end, a decreasing intensity, except in the manner of a natural clinging to those connections that remain (Gerkin, 1979). As Gerkin notes, "In all life-giving and life-preserving responses there is mingled an impulse, however faint, of refusal, in virtue of which no creature needs to be taught about death" (1979, p. 97).

Freud argued that, in addition to our urge for self-preservation, we experience a "death instinct" inherent in organic life: to return to an earlier state of being that the pressure of external factors had forced us to abandon (S. Freud, 1920g/1955). In contrast to Freud's emphasis on instinctual oppositions, Otto Rank posits an existential view—namely, that to be born includes the need to be responsible for our own separate existence and survival. In this separateness we experience our mutability, our finiteness and vulnerability. We come to know of death, to fear the loss of our hard-won individuality, and to perceive the connection between birth and death (Menaker, 1982, p. 64). As Rank notes,

> There is in the individual a primal fear, which manifests itself now as fear of life, another time as fear of death. The fear in birth, which we have designated as fear of life, seems to me actually the fear of having to live as an isolated individual—a fear of separation from the whole—although it may appear later as fear of the loss of this dearly bought individuality, as fear of death, of being dissolved again into the whole...There is included in the fear problem itself a primary ambivalence which must be assumed, and not derived through the opposition of life and death instincts. (Rank, 1936/ 1972, p. 25)

Separation is one of the fundamental life principles, and our lives are continuous separations in which we "even in the last separation, death, must leave behind, must resign developmental phases of our own ego" (Rank, 1936/1972, p. 45). A dilemma is clear: Self-awareness of our mutability is one of the most powerful psychological forces in us. The self-actualization so necessary to each person can only be attained through separation, which symbolizes death. The creative impulse responds to an inevitable duality in life itself: a movement toward individuation on the one hand and a need to remain part of a larger whole on the other. The more we become self-conscious of our unique personality, the greater the urge to eternalize it. The tension between mortality and the wish for immortality is part of the life process. We seek to resolve this tension ultimately through utilizing our creative will to establish new relationships—connections that may somehow transcend our own mortality.

Rank believes that religious forms and social institutions serve as communal immortalities. We strive for the abrogation of individuality and for likeness, unity, and oneness with the all, as much as we do for separateness and autonomy. We seek to transcend mortality through the search for immortality. This search for solutions to the inevitability of death leads us, thinks Rank, to creative strivings, such as the creation of a child and the promise of a new generation that will carry our projections. We may seek to transcend mortality by connecting ourselves to a group, cause, or ideology that extends beyond the self. These connections are seen as surviving the self. This reaching out for something bigger originates in the individual need for expansion beyond the self, one's environment, even life itself. In this sense the individual is not just striving for survival, "but is reaching for some kind of 'beyond,' be it in terms of another person, a group, a cause, a faith to which he can submit" (Rank, 1958, p. 16). Thus, each human is "born beyond psychology and he dies beyond it but he can live beyond it only through vital experiences of his own—in religious terms, through revelation, conversion or rebirth" (Rank, 1958, p. 16). This reaching out includes artistic creation as a means toward individual immortality. Rank is clear that no matter how one attempts to deny the difference in oneself or others, to make everyone equal and the same, the uniqueness of each life will prevail.

Throughout history the attempt to deal with death anxiety is revealed in myth and legends, in religion, and in the artistic products of creative individuals with whom the collective world can identify. As psychoanalyst Esther Menaker says, summarizing Rank's thinking:

> Paradoxically, the fear of death and its counterpart, the wish for immortality, lead to the fullest expression of life in the form of the creative expression of the will. That is not to say that the wish for immortality is the *cause* of creative action and its consequent product, but rather it motivates and mobilizes the striving for the expression of individuality which is a given and is there at the outset. (Menaker, 1982, p. 47)

C. G. Jung describes his view about confronting death:

> From the middle of life onward, only he remains vitally alive who is ready to *die with life*. For in the secret hour of life's midday the parabola is reversed, death is born. The second half of life does not signify ascent, unfolding, increase, exuberance, but death, since the end is its goal. The negation of life's fulfillment is synonymous with the refusal to accept its ending. Both mean not wanting to live, and not wanting to live is identical with not wanting to die. Waxing and waning make one curve. (Jung, 1934/1969, p. 407)

About Jung's view, Robert Brooke remarks that although Jung tended to situate death as a dimension of the second half of life, his position is rather more subtle: "When Jung says that not wanting to live is identical with not wanting to die, and that waxing and waning make one curve, he is not only, or even primarily, referring to the arc from youth to old age but to a "curve" that is given within each moment or image itself" (Brooke, 1991, p. 89). Each moment of life is filled with the potential that we may encounter a kind of dying into life, as an acorn breaks to become an oak, or a seed cracks to become the wheat. In fact, Jung said elsewhere, if you are lucky, you will live yourself out of life (Jung, 1934/1969, p. 407).

In terms of old age, Jung notes that when death is near, the previous setting of boundaries often loosens, leading to a process of letting go of the ego's dominance. This penultimate stage of life is attained when death is accepted, the past honored, limits drawn, and the ego allowed to become relative. Jungian analyst James Hillman considers the physical symptoms that life brings as we begin to leave it, and he searches those symptoms for their role in our character. For example, instead of seeing insomnia as "waking in the night," Hillman encourages the aged to "wake *to* the night," suggesting that the many night anxieties "belong to the underside of the world, which becomes personally available to you through the ordeal of nighttime awakenings" (1999, p. 77). In addition, he underscores that the muddled agitations, and the spontaneous appearances of images in old age, are "intentions of the soul"–that is, these recollections are "a subtle hint that the soul is letting go of the weight it has been carrying, preparing to lift off more easily" (Hillman, 1999, p. 93). As we age, we come apart to leave and also to join. Hillman says it well:

> Perhaps we must come apart in order to depart so that we can appreciate what has been carrying us along for so many years–those faithful kidneys, those stalwart joints, giving uncomplaining service. Before the body becomes a corpse in a casket it seems to have a lot to say to the soul. It begins to act up, break down, and speak out. (1999, p. 102)

The final years of life mean encountering and honoring the Self, what Jung and others have called "the God within us" or *imago dei*–the most complete expression of our wholeness, which is also our unique idiom (Wulff, 1997; Palmer, 1997). A good example of this relationship is found in the Christian narratives when Paul the apostle says "...it is no longer I who live, but it is Christ who lives in me" (Gal. 2:20). Here we find an expression of two centers of the personality, anticipating Jung's contemporary description that the psyche contains a lesser center called the ego, the center of conscious personality–the subject "I" with which we are most certain and identified–and a center of personality that is larger than the ego, which he calls the Self (Sanford, 1979, p. 34). Jung believed that a well-lived life is one in which the dialogue between the ego and Self lead us to a greater potential of personality. Thus, a lived life knows death well. Facing death, reviewing the past, drawing limits, letting go of the ego, allowing creative emptiness, finding inspiration, verifying meaning–all these final stage-appropriate tasks suggest the achievement of living and accepting death as a part of life (Callanan & Kelley, 1992).

A good example of discovering life in death is found in James Hillman's etymology of the word *graves* (1999, p. 69). Hillman designates four distinct meanings of the word: *gravity,* the mysterious physical force that draws all things down to the core of the earth; *gravitas,* the Roman word for weighty seriousness; the *grave* of the cemetery, where the body is laid to final rest; and *gravid,* meaning "pregnant" (as we once said, "heavy with child"). Hillman suggests that these four meanings can fuse, so that worries about the grave of death, about the weighty seriousness and implacable downward demand of death's reality, can also lead us to new life. Thus, the downward pull of aging that leads us to serious matters and an anxious focus on the cemetery must not displace the depths of *gravitas* and the invisible pregnancy that the aged are meant to bear. "We old ones are the weight bearers," says Hillman, "and our nature grows us downward" (1999, p. 69). Hence, the author reminds us that the underworld beneath the grave can be entered long before the actual grave in the actual cemetery. So many of the great mythical figures–Ulysses, Aeneas, Inanna, Hercules, Psyche, Orpheus, Persephone, Dionysus–descended and gained a knowledge that deepened their characters. He suggests that to be "an elder, benefactor, conservator, and mentor, calls for a learning about shadows, an instruction from the 'dead'–that is, from what has gone before." As Hillman notes, the "dead" come back as ancestors, especially in times of crisis, when we are at a loss. Then the dead "awaken," offering a deeper knowledge and support: "They have already fallen; they know the pits, hence their enormous resources. They do not have to return as literal voices and visions, for they are already palpable in whatever is pulling us down, whenever we can't keep up. They are the force in the psyche's gravity" (1999, p. 69). Hillman decouples death from aging and instead restores the ancient link between older age and the uniqueness of each person.

Gender and Death

Carol Gilligan (1982), a former student of Eric Erikson's, "claimed that many so-called stages of the life cycle are based on male experience and that a separate development chart for women would be helpful" (Welchman, 2000, p. 124; L. J. Friedman, 1999). Marjorie Shultz points out such gender differences in her article "Death Does Us Part" (1999). As Shultz says, "Death is certain but not equal. Women live longer than men. They are more likely to be diagnosed with breast cancer, osteoporosis and Alzheimer's disease. First heart attacks are more often fatal in women than in men. Inequitable pay and lower pension and social security benefits cause more elderly women than men to live in poverty, making access to health care more difficult for them" (Shultz, 1999, p. 72). In addition, gender is a central factor in the controversial debate regarding a patient's right to choose death instead of suffering. Advanced directives, or living wills, will not be honored by physicians in more instances with women than with men. Miles and August report than often when a controversial medical decision is evaluated by the courts, incompetency claims refer to female patients as "childlike," treating expressions of women's views as "unreflective or emotional" (Miles and August, 1990, p. 88, cited by Shultz). Shultz adds that "courts view women as vulnerable and dependent on medical care, whereas when men express earlier preferences for termination of treatment, courts see failure to implement male patients' choices as assaultive" (Shultz, 1999, p. 73). In sum, Miles and August's suggestion that women are often denied status as autonomous moral agents in death decisions is disturbing.

Shultz points out that assisted suicide reveals a different gender-specific pattern than advance directives. For example, women constitute a significant majority of persons assisted to death by Dr. Jack Kevorkian. Shultz finds a number of reasons for this. First, "it is more difficult for women to have their views heard in medical settings, and they find it difficult to receive effective treatment from a mainstream medical profession still dominated by men" (Shultz, 1999, p. 74). Second, Shultz reminds us that "women's social roles as caregivers may (legitimately?) make them concerned about a burdening family when they themselves become sick" (1999, p. 74). Third, women are also generally more willing to seek help than men are. Fourth, women attempt suicide more frequently than men, although they are considerably less successful at completing it. In short, pervasive sexism in society and in the health care system leads to the devaluation of women's lives, over- or under-treating women, stereotyping, and differences in access to health care arising from differences in wealth.

Overall, gender differences affect the way cultures engage death. We see this dynamic in pregnancy exclusions to right-to-die statutes. As Shultz suggests, these divergences raise an even more chilling prospect about the future of a socially conscious health care system, because group ideology can reflect economic privileges. She concludes, "Women will more frequently be the victims of this new form of ignoring patients' choices, because of their larger numbers in the elderly population, their more limited means, their less aggressive insistence on personal rights, and, particularly, society's tendency to treat them as less competent moral agents. If so, gender injustices will intensify even in death" (1999, p. 75). Shultz alerts us to the need to recognize and honor gender diversity in regard to death issues.

Stages of Dying

While there are gender differences in regard to the phenomenon of death, Dr. Kübler-Ross's work designates five recognizable stages that characterize the death process for humanity in general, though individuals vary considerably in the way in which they proceed through these stages (Kübler-Ross, 1981). The first stage involves *denial* and an effort to isolate the thoughts and feelings related to the threat of death. Stage two is characterized by feelings of *anger* that may be focused or diffused and displaced on various persons and structures in the environment. A third stage finds the person bargaining with the illness—*bargaining* for time, for favor from God or from persons close to the patient. Stage four Dr. Kübler-Ross calls *depression,* a time when the terminally ill can no longer deny the illness, and the bargaining function no longer wards off the painful awareness of impending death. The result is the overpowering feeling of loss and defeat. Only as this stage is worked through can the person enter the fifth stage of genuine *acceptance* of death.

Jungian analyst Edward Edinger employs two terms from the language of alchemy and mythology to describe the dying process: *mortificatio* and *putrefactio.* These phases are overlapping ones and refer to different aspects of the same phenomenon. *Mortificatio,* says Edinger, means "killing," and thus conveys the experience of death as torment and annihilation. In alchemy, to describe a chemical process as mortification "is a complete projection of a psychological image. This did in fact happen. The material in a flask was personified, and the operations performed on it were thought of as torture" (Edinger, 1987, p. 148). *Mortificatio* is the most negative operation in alchemy, and its hallmark is the opposite of light, the darkness. It has to do with night, defeat, torture, mutilation, catastrophe, death, and rotting. However, these images of darkness also lead to more positive dynamics such as growth, resurrection, and rebirth. In psychological terms, to speak positively of black means being aware of one's shadow, an other, and this means that the law of opposites is at work, an intense awareness of one side constellating its contrary. As the apostle Paul said, "for if you live according to the flesh, you will die; but if by the Spirit you put to death the deeds of the body, you will live" (Rom. 8:13). Out of the blackness comes the light—the curve of life's waxing and waning.

Putrefactio is "rotting," the decomposition that breaks down dead organic bodies. The effects of seeing the decomposition of a human corpse might also be projected into the alchemical process. As Paracelsus writes, "Putrefaction is of so great efficacy that it blots out the old nature and transmutes everything into another new nature, and bears another new fruit. All living things die in it, all dead things decay, and then all these dead things regain life" (Edinger, 1987, p. 148). Edinger underscores that the biblical reference most frequently connected with *putrefactio* is the passage from the gospel of John, "Very truly, I tell you, unless a grain of wheat falls into the earth and dies, it remains just a single grain; but if it dies, it bears much fruit. Those who love their life lose it, and those who hate their life in this world will keep it for eternal life" (Jn. 12:24–25). The image of death and burial has always been associated with the planting of seeds and their germination. Germination and decay, light changing to darkness, death and rebirth—all point to *mortificatio* and *putrefactio.*

The archetype of the wounded healer, prevalent in world cultures, is connected to the death process. For instance, another term for the process of *mortificatio* is *nigredo. Nigredo* often is referred to as "corvus" or "crow or raven." The crow appears in Greek mythology in the birth of Asklepios,the god of healing. His mother was Coronis, the crow maiden, who, while pregnant with Asklepios by Apollo, had intercourse with Ischys. This infidelity was reported to Apollo by the crow, which was turned from white to black for bringing bad news. Coronis was killed for her crime, but the infant Asklepios was detached from her womb while she was on the funeral pyre. Out of catastrophe came birth and hope. In short, the birth of healing power from the *nigredo* belongs to the archetype of the wounded healer. This term, inferring beginnings, is connected to the term *caput corvi,* or head of the raven, a conception associated with *caput mortuum,* or dead head. The term *head* is associated with top, or beginning, the start of creativity. This understanding is suggested in Hillman's etymology of grave (ending) and *gravid* (birth). As Edinger says, the confrontation with death means that a physical change occurs: "The dead, worthless residue is the stuff of the *nigredo* phase. The fact that it is called a 'caput' or 'head' indicates a paradoxical reversal of opposites. The worthless becomes the most precious, and the last becomes first. This is a lesson that we each must learn again and again. It is the psyche that we find in the worthless, despised place" (Edinger, 1987, p. 148). These powerful images from mythology and alchemy inaugurate the moment of death in the individual and cultural imagination.

The Angel of Death: The Double Archetype as Immortal Self

In traditional religious imagery, the inner space of awareness is also called the soul:

> Following the Arab philosopher Avicenna, many Western spiri-
> tual teachers imagined the soul as having two eyes. One eye peered
> into the eternal, and one eye peered into the temporal. This made
> the spiritual identity of the human person a boundary reality, join-
> ing spirit and flesh, heaven and earth, the eternal and the tempo-
> ral. In ancient categories, humans are neither angels (pure spirits)
> nor animals (pure matter). They are the intermingling and flow of
> spirit and matter. (Shea, 2000, p. 98)

Therefore, Shea concludes, "on the one hand, the soul is the primordial connectedness of the human person with the Sacred, or Spirit, or God, or with whatever other words denote Ultimate Reality. On the other hand, soul points to the connection of the human person with the mind-body organism and through that organism with the entire world" (2000, p. 99). We will see that the notion of the divided soul, paradoxically connected simultaneously to the eternal and the temporal, finds completion in the unifying image of the Angel of Death.

Beginning with anthropology as the starting place for theology, Friedrich Schleiermacher underscored that theological statements can never allude to anything other than humanity's own feeling; thus, confusion of man's finitude with infinity is inevitable (McKelway, 1964). Although sympathetic to Schleiermacher's idealism, liberal theologian Paul Tillich, in contrast, emphasized a unity of all being, which enables human beings to transcend this noetic circle. As McKelway notes, Tillich's concept of the symbolic power of language, which follows from that unity, "allows him to say that finite theological statements may nonetheless have a real relation to their infinite object" (McKelway, 1964, p. 20). We can say the same about symbolic representations in art and archetypal depictions. As art historian John Russell remarked, "When art is made new, we are made new in it. We have a sense of solidarity with our own time, and psychic energies shared and redoubled...Art is there to tell us where we are, and it is also there to tell us who we are" (1974, p. 13). The Angel of Death representation in art and the imagination conveys a belief that our existential situation is open to discovery and transformation, and the essential connection between the divine and human takes on an ontological character, namely, the relationship between the finitude of humanity and the infinitude of God.

The poet Jean Cocteau wrote: "I will tell you the greatest secret...Mirrors are the doors through which Death comes and goes. Besides, look at yourself in the mirror throughout your life and you will see Death at work like bees in a glass hive" (Meltzer, 1984, p. 75). If we think of the Angel of Death as the self-representation of the experiencing subject that is the mirror image of the relationship to life, we see the double archetype at work. Phenomena that exist psychologically, says Jung, are of two types: Psychological existence is *subjective* if it occurs to only one person, one experiencing subject, but it is *objective* if the same pattern of experience can be corroborated in the spontaneous experience of a great variety of people, particularly when these individuals come from different cultural backgrounds. He describes such patterns as collective in that they are part of the common structures of human nature. These universal patterns of the collective psyche he called "archetypes." The archetypes of the collective unconscious appear to each person in a unique, if not eccentric, way because they are clothed in material from our personal history, our own unconscious. The archetypes serve as a structure that gives form to our unique experiences.

When the double configuration appears, we should indeed take notice, for this is the archetype of death, change, and transformation. Something is going to happen. Whenever patients in psychotherapy bring a dream image of a doubling motif, this usually inaugurates a transitional encounter in their lives. In fact, the root word *twin* has the same etymology as "twine" and "twilight." The Angel of Death appears in cultural depictions as this doubling or twinning presence, often wrapped around dying figures like a lover in the dance macabre, or juxtaposed to the dying as a reflection of the same face, signifying both life and death mirroring each to each. Esther

Menaker informs us that the *doppelganger* is a word compounded with the German verb "to go," literally "double-goer," and therefore conveys a more active quality than the English noun *double* can convey (Menaker, 1982, p. 91). The presence of the double connotes movement that seeks to mirror. Perhaps this helps us understand the image of guardian angels in mythology that mirror us as we move throughout life.

Death emanates from this ageless image of doubling. In English folklore it is believed that the apparitional doubles of those who will die that year can be seen at midnight on St. Mark's Eve—sometimes seen by the person due to die. Vampires are understood as the "living dead," a doubling of a once-living person, since the original of the double has been completely eliminated. Vampires are the "Xerox copies, separated from the original" (Lash, 1993, p. 17)—thus, the vampire has no shadow or mirror image. Kafka's beetle in *Metamorphosis* can be seen as a metamorphic twin. Robert Louis Stevenson's *Dr. Jekyll and Mr. Hyde* depicts the two sides of a self. From religious history, the belief of Docetism claimed that the human Christ was actually a double that underwent crucifixion. In Gnosticism we learn about the Demiurge, who is the fallen projection of the Supreme Being, the shadow of the original deity. From philosophy, Plato's writing in *Symposium* of the two souls seeking to unite into a lost wholeness, the one becoming the other, is also indicative of this archetype. According to the Homeric conceptions, humanity has a twofold existence: a perceptible presence, and an invisible image, which only death sets free. Thus, the double archetype is associated with the nature of the soul, and this is expressed collectively in the Chinese *hun,* the Egyptian *ba,* the Indian *jvian*—examples of life forces that strive toward God in some religions, and to rebirth in others.

In Christianity we see the soul as the pneumatic body resurrected into life "in Christ." These examples clearly suggest that the soul has a bipolarity, both earthly and transcendent. In fact, the Angel of Death has been called "Lord of the Twins" and has been associated with Eros and Strife, Isis and Osiris, the archangels Michael and Sari-el, also called "Princes of the Presence" (Lash, 1993, p. 23). In the film *Wings of Desire* (Dauman & Wender, 1988), we see angels wanting to become human—a wonderful suggestion of doubling forces twinning desire and division, love and loss. The paradoxical relationship of the human to the divine—a doubling in itself—is illustrated in medieval theology, which viewed angels as filling the gap between God and humankind. Angels Michael and Sari-el both have histories of fallenness and redemption, and both have been given the distinction at one time or another as the Angel of Death—illustrative of our theme of the double because they have experienced this middle space between humanity and God.

From a psychological perspective, Otto Rank argues that our fear of death does not result only from the natural love of life. Rather, it is the love for the personality peculiar to each one of us that is discovered as each person's conscious possession: the love of self. Thus, self-love is an inseparable element of our being, and the thought of losing ourselves in death is so anxiety-producing that we create images of new life and the hope of continuing development after death in order to assuage the fear of eradication and nothingness. Rank underscores that primitive narcissism is primarily threatened by the threat of death and destruction of the self, thus initiating throughout histories and cultures the concept of the soul, of an image as closely similar as possible to the physical self–a shadow, or double of the self (Rank, 1932/1971). Hence, the idea of death can be denied by a duplication of the self incorporated in the shadow or in the reflected image. This kind of duplication of the self is illustrated in the Angel of Death archetype, an imaginative representation of our relation to ourselves as well as to our beliefs in life after death.

Earlier in his life Jung himself commented on the image of roots brought to vitality with the acknowledgement of death:

> Life has always seemed to me like a plant that lives on its rhizome. Its true life is invisible, hidden in the rhizome. The part that appears above ground lasts only a single summer. Then it withers away–an ephemeral apparition. When we think of the unending growth and decay of life and civilization, we cannot escape the impression of absolute nullity. Yet I have never lost a sense of something that lives and endures underneath the eternal flux. What we see is the blossom, which passes. The rhizome remains (Jung, 1963, p. 4).

The struggle toward wholeness viewed from our human limitations is drawn by the potential within, the very essence of individuation. Toward the end his life, Barry Ulanov, scholar of art, literature, and religion, shared a dream that captures well the potential for completeness and wholeness as we move toward death. His dream is described by his wife, Jungian analyst and theologian Ann Ulanov:

> "A new fragment was found in Jerusalem," Barry dreamt. "Some knew that it was in Jesus' handwriting." It read: "The answer to all your questions is YES!" "That verb," Barry commented, "is a copula; Yahweh is who is, the Is who is with you." (Ulanov, 2001a, p. 14)

The image of the Angel of Death conveys the coming together of the "Is who is with you," an image that reflects our innermost life–that is, the relationship to death is the mirror image of the relationship to life, what Rank called "the double as immortal self." The image of the Angel of Death, then, is ultimately the reflection of the individual's being drawn into completeness, the YES of ultimate reality.

The Angel of Death archetype is an intriguing, archetypal image that can be explored from psychological and religious perspectives. Psychologically, it is natural and necessary that individuals and cultures create images of death in order to integrate and accept mortality as the central fact and common denominator of human existence. Death imagery expresses the experience of ambivalence in our relationship to death. The more successful death imagery is as an aid to integrating this ambivalence, the more clearly it brings to consciousness the interrelationship of paired opposites of this paradox–life and death. Jung's dream of the rhizome, Rank's double, Ulanov's Jerusalem–all are good examples of archetypal imagery, particular and universal, born of the collective unconscious, tailored to our unique form and clothed in material from each personal history. Throughout life, when we can tolerate and contain such oppositions, the image of the Divine as messenger is potentially present.

Theologically, our images of death are often structured by the relationship between the central paradox of human nature as created in the image of the divine nature. On the one hand, death is seen as a completion or perfection of our absolutely unique individuality, yet on the other hand, death is perceived as a dissolution into a collective, undifferentiated, ego-less state. Death imagery bridges this paradox and ambiguity. The ego attains a state of completion or, entering into an absolute stage of reality, ceases to exist as an individual ego. The Angel of Death, then, is a mediator or bridging image between existence and what is perceived as non-existence, or between the individual and the transcendent. This point of view often depicts the Death Angel as a mediator, or double, or paraclete. For instance, in Manichaeism, "the soul of every dead person immediately gazes on the image of its completeness. As soon as the soul has left the body, it catches sight of its savior and redeemer. The soul ascends together with the image of his or her perfectedness, and other angels follow" (von Franz, 1984/1986, p. 74). In such belief structures, the mediator is a light figure, an outer image of the cosmic spirit. The soul merges with this realm of light. In many ways this imaginative description reflects theologian Karl Rahner's view that "after our deaths we become all-cosmic and pass into the *material prima* of the universe, where we encounter the Lord of the World" (Murphy, 1988, p. 14). From this perspective, human nature always stands in a relationship to divine nature: Perhaps this is why we find angels in all capacities through life in manifold beliefs and experiences.

Catastrophe Transformed

Theologian George Florovsky sums up the Christian realism about human mutability when he writes that "death is catastrophe for man'" and asserts that this is the foundational principle of Christian anthropology (Florovsky, 1976, p. 111, cited by Guroian, 1996, p. 44). Carl Jung adds this assertion: "[D]eath is indeed a fearful piece of brutality; there is no sense in pretending otherwise. It is brutal not only as a physical event but far more so psychically: a human being is torn away from us, and what remains is the icy stillness of death" (Jung, 1963, p. 314). At the same time, Florovsky holds fast to the belief that death signifies the need for salvation—"this in contrast to both the standard demythologized secular view of death as the inevitable and ordinary end of personal existence and the dominant therapeutic view that we should accept death as perfectly natural and reconcile ourselves to our place in nature's cycle of birth, death, and new birth" (Guroian, 1996, p. 42). Indeed, human nature, he thought, is a unity of physical and spiritual existence. Human beings obviously have a biological nature like that of all other living things. Yet, thinks Florovsky, "human beings are also persons created in the image and likeness of God, loved by God as such, and destined by God to immortality. We are conscious and self-conscious beings who...realize the fullness of our own identity only in loving relationships with others. When death destroys these relationships, we are diminished" (Guroian, p. 23). About death's destructiveness, the philosopher Wittgenstein describes it thus: "As in death...the world does not change, but ceases. Death is not an event in life. Death is not lived through" (Wittgenstein, 1922/1990, cited by Smart, 1964, p. 182).

Christian ethicist Andrew McGill speaks of another kind of diminishment paid by the wages of sin and the domination of death in our lives. This identity-in-sin means "not to live from God, not to honor God as the constant source of our being, not to be thankful to God as the one who constantly gives us ourselves" (McGill, 1987, p. 52). Thus, sin is to refuse to live out of the reality that a person constantly receives from God. In this perspective of sin, death occurs when the boundary that designates our reality from everything else in the world is totally emptied of everything within it. As McGill says,

> Death is when our bodies dissolve into the ground or into the air, when our possessions pass to others, when our deeds and our names are forgotten, when nothing exists as belonging to us and thus as giving content, as giving reality, to our identity—so far as we see our identity as wholly in terms of a reality which we can have and which we can securely label with our own name, we live under the dominion of death. (1987, p. 53)

Accordingly, we live in terror of death, of having our life experience of reality taken from us. This terror leads to incremental denial and controls our lives. Sinful identity, a life diminished by death, means living to discover that all our having is eventually and totally defeated. We struggle to emerge into what Jung calls "a lived life" and take hold of it passionately. There is a failure to come forth into the world. We are estranged from a quality of being that can fully experience ourselves and others. We find ourselves unable to fully love. Although we may get along with people all right, something feels missing. Preoccupations with what we are not receiving from the external world eclipse the potential for giving from our creative, innermost spirit. We fear and dread the good in our lives instead of inviting it in. The potential of individuation found in the metaphor of unfolding to a larger Self is obstructed and in danger of perishing by degree. Our sense of destiny becomes a kind of fatalism. "If only" we say, as we live "as if." We live in terror of death, under its dominion of dispossession. Our whole being is dominated by this terror.

According to Augustine and all the great Christian writers, death not only

> threatens to destroy our very *humanitas,* to tear asunder the personal unity of body and soul, but also rips apart the social fabric of our lives. Death violates both the dead and the living. A being created for immortality stares into the abyss of nothingness and recoils because love will not abide desolation and nothingness. Much more than the prospect of my own personal extinction is at stake, finally. As we have seen, the Christian belief in the resurrection is not merely a selfish assurance that the "I" will not perish. Jesus says that in his Father's house are many rooms (John 14:2). Love is the foundation and mortar of that many-roomed house. "Those who love me will keep my word, and my Father will love them, and we will come to them and make our home with them" (Jn. 14:23, RSV). (Guroian, 1996, p. 27)

Transforming Love

At a memorial service celebrating the remarkable life of Barry Ulanov, Ann Ulanov spoke about the "tearing asunder" of death's impact, the ceasing of worlds juxtaposed to new foundations built by love:

> Barry would say, Just when you are expecting A,B,C, in comes Q! The new part that came up at the end for Barry was a level of animal fear in the face of death. The illness was shocking in its swiftness. Barry was a sophisticated man. We talked many times about death and its booster-shot effect on living life to the fullest. This past winter we talked again about death, his death. He had written two books about death. But up came another part, not a sophisticated, educated one, but a young part. On an animal level he consented, withdrawing from food and drink the last weeks of his life except for tiny bits. But on a human level he felt, as he said, "I'm losing my country," which he was as he made the transition from this life to the next. This time, he said, he could not write about death; now it is time for the experience. He worked on it

and something slowly shifted, from fear facing him like a wall to a passageway that led somewhere.

Barry found his way through the fear, not rising above it, and not submerged by it. But the way surprised us both. I came into his room at Sloan Kettering the day before we were to leave, saying, I've been foraging with the nurse's help, and held up my prize to take home: an efficient pad for the bed. Barry usually did not encourage this thieving lapse in my superego. But this time he flashed me a big wide grin, saying, "I love you."

It hit us. We saw that it was his loving–love moving through him–that would dissipate the fear. He was a man much loved by others. But we saw it was the power of loving back, or loving first, or loving forth and back that answered the fear and pain. It was loving that responded to the animal recoil in the face of leaving this country...Barry loved what Augustine wrote about God saying to us: "He who believes in me goes into me; He that goes into me has me." Barry made the going and now he has God and God has him. (Ulanov, 2001a, p. 13–14)

These words in a time of devastating loss both acknowledge the catastrophe of death and also the radical experience of that catastrophe transformed by love. We are also reminded that too often the presence of our "death fears" may reflect a despair about love, which, in turn, generates despair about life. Such a struggle is intimately connected to how we view death. The ways in which we wage war against death in our society ironically make us accomplices in our own spiritual brokenness and suffering. Too often, we remove death from the moral sphere of the home and transfer it to the technological environment of the modern hospital. Ethicist Vigen Guroian asks whether this development is the natural result of changes in society and medical technology:

[W]hatever the motives and inducements involved, it remains the case that our elaborate technologies often separate people from those whose love they need most of all when they are dying. And it is not only the dying who are deprived by this mechanization of medicine and institutionalization of death. Consciously or subconsciously, we all begin to anticipate in fear the same isolation and abandonment when our turn comes. We lose faith in love. (1996, p. 14)

Ulanov's words return us to that faith in love, to a faith in each other and God. The poet Galway Kinnell transforms the ancient adage, "the wages of sin is death," into a wisdom that says "the wages of dying is love" as he sees in his daughter's eyes "the angel of all mortal things" (Kinnell, 1982, p. 115). This idea, love's dependence on death, like the dying of the ego into the Self, is found clearly in Kinnell's "The Poetics of the Physical World";

> It is through something radiant in our lives that we have been able to dream of paradise, that we have been able to invent the realm of eternity. But there is another kind of glory in our lives which derives precisely from our inability to enter that paradise or to experience eternity. That we last only for a time, that everyone and everything around us last only for a time, that we know this, radiates a thrilling, tragic light on all our loves, all our relationships, even on those moments when the world, through its poetry becomes capable of spurning time and death (Nelson, 1987, p. 222).

A statement attributed to Karl Barth that "God is not timeless, but timely," resonates in both Ulanov's and Kinnell's vision that this moment when time and timelessness meet includes the presence of love that changes life and death. Indeed, the angel of all mortal things, the Angel of Death, lifts us out of time but at one's ownmost time, as both a preserver of this paradox as well as its initiate.

A dramatic example of this collective yet singular event is found in a poem by the playwright Ron Havern (personal communication, March 8, 1995) written the day of his death:

> I am the self who sees you;
> I am the self you dimly see,
> The self that shades the soul
> From too much light.
> The self that reminds us
> Of our origins.
> The self who has the power
> To carry us back to the source,
> The vast ocean of love
> We call God.
> Angel of Death, lead us into love;
> Drown us in love;
> Melt us in love;
> But be our gentle
> Brother and Sister.

How caring yet utterly consuming this Angel is perceived and experienced—both feared and hoped for—its expression so much like a psalmist engaging God with imperatives and petitions while encouraging mercy for all of us even in the denouement of life! Havern introduces the relationship to death as the mirror image of the relationship to life. It is ultimately the reflection of the individual being drawn into oblivion, drawn toward a totality that introduces a possibility for wholeness, healing, and hope. The Angel of Death can be viewed as the fulfillment of this healing completion when we experience a greater love that brings us to the mystery of who we must ultimately become.

To wonder about one's death is to encounter a subjective consciousness, a self-image of the self as an ego separate from the objective world. For example, a five-year-old boy had been talking to his parents about death—something he had just discovered. He asked his parents if they would miss him, and they said yes, very much, and they told him how much they loved him. He said that was good, then after a long pause, said sadly, "You know, I think I would miss myself!" Indeed, as we grow and develop, our self-image is accompanied by the development of a second self, often depicted as both the soul of the person and his or her reflection found in the Angel who meets us at the moment of death. When these moments of presence take place in an experience of love, individuals can see more clearly the chain of relatedness that connects them to one another. A self-perpetuation takes place in our internalization of the other who finds a kind of immortality through the legacies of its living presence in us. The wages of dying become that loving presence. Esther Menaker captures beautifully this notion of immortality:

> While belief in a personal immortality is a matter of faith and lies beyond the realm of our certain knowledge, there is an aspect of immortality that exists within the province of psychology…the individual self is structured by the internalization of emotional experience with significant others—preferably with those who we have admired and to whom we have been attached. These memory images are transmuted to harmonize with the original, constitutionally given nature of the self to form a cohesive whole. Thus, the "other" lives on—is immortalized—within ourselves. (1995, p. 151)

She concludes, "One can even say, in these terms, that the spiritual dimension in human life is the memory of love" (p. 151). James Hillman suggests that what is left after death "is an idiosyncratic image, especially the one presented in later years, and not the moral precepts that you tried to uphold under the mistaken name of 'character.' One's remaining image, that unique way of being and doing, left in the minds of others, continues to act upon them" (Hillman, 1999, p. 202). Hillman's conclusion resonates with Menaker's abiding theme:

> We are left as traces, lasting in our very thinness like the scarcely visible lines on a Chinese silkscreen, microlayers of pigment and carbon, which can yet portray the substantial profundities of a face. Lasting no longer than a little melody, a unique composition of disharmonious notes, yet echoing long after we are gone. This

is the thinness of our aesthetic reality, this old, very dear image
that is left and lasts. (Hillman, 1999, p. 202)

"Death is the last great union of the inner world-opposites," says von
Franz, "the sacred marriage of resurrection" (von Franz, 1984/1986, p. 47).
It is like ancient Merlin's dying moment in the Grail legend, his
disappearance into the union of spirit and stone, where his stone grave "is
at the same time also a nuptial couch and the vessel of the *unio mystica* with
the godhead" (E. Jung & von Franz, 1970, p. 390). C. S. Lewis writes of this
sacred marriage of love and loss in reference to his wife's death: "We are
'taken out of ourselves' by the loved one while she is here. Then comes the
tragic figure of the dance in which we must learn to be still taken out of
ourselves though the bodily presence is withdrawn, to love the very Her,
and not fall back to loving our past, or our memory, or our sorrow, or our
relief from sorrow, or our own love" (1976, p. 56).

How can we find the courage, the illumination, the spirit to love in this
new way? Andrew McGill offers the example of Jesus of Nazareth as a
model for this transformation. He underscores that the center of Jesus'
reality is not within Jesus himself. Everything that happens to him,
everything that is done by him, including his death, is displaced to another
context. He lives from beyond himself, always revealing that which is
beyond himself in what McGill calls an *ecstatic identity.* The death of identity
to an I-Thou correspondence is also a kind of death. Living-to-God is thus
as "living always related to God, living always open to God, in the act of
receiving oneself from God" (1987, p. 51). As McGill says, "Living an ecstatic
identity, then, is the new kind of identity, the new way of being...It is a
new kind of human nature which shows itself in a just and devout life,
which gives us a new mind and new morality" (p. 51). McGill describes
this new life:

> When we have this sense of ourselves as what we constantly re-
> ceive from God's free giving, what do we experience when we
> experience ourselves? *We experience love.* We experience this love
> primarily in terms of receiving ourselves and being ourselves. And
> when we experience ourselves as a gift, as a free joyful, and con-
> tinual gift, we are filled with that feeling which Paul placed first of
> all in the new life—the feeling of gratitude and love. (1987, p. 51)

Such an identity conceived in love consecrates our ordinary life, draws
us to a profound encounter with death as transformative rather than
envisioned and only a destructive assault on life itself. Indeed, the wages of
death, or rather the wages paid from this fear and dread of limitation, are a
life whose inner law is death. This is the essence of domination. In the New
Testament, the force of Satan is the power of domination. But part of the
new identity, in Jesus, says McGill, is the identity that is constantly being
received, which depends on being convinced that God is not interested in

dominating but in nourishing. The difference between the God of Jesus Christ and the god of Satan, then, is between a god whose power nourishes and a god whose power dominates. How is Jesus' death different from the usual death, which is the wages of sin? In Jesus' death, death goes all the way: "It destroys not just the actual possession of being, but the roots of the possessiveness. Or more accurately, in the death of Jesus the way of sinful identity is shown to be what it is: a pretense, a lie, an impossibility. Fear of death increases the possession. We thus measure our lives by only looking at ourselves" (McGill, 1987, p. 56). Resurrection, then, is not a possession, but a restoration of life against death. It is glimpsed in this life when "our personal illumination feeds out of and into a shared vision of life with others" (Ulanov & Ulanov, 1991, p. 160).

Conclusion

A poem fragment by Paul Celan acts as an envoi:

Only there did you wholly enter the name that is yours,
sure-footed stepped into yourself,
freely the hammers swung in the bell frame of your silence,
the listened for reached you,
what is dead put its arm round you also
and the three of you walked through the evening
(1972/2002, p. 45).

Reading Celan's poem challenges us to confront what Ann Ulanov calls "the blast of divine otherness in whatever form it takes" (Ulanov, 1997, p. 297). Our approach to these challenges is to posit ways in which to build a relationship to the Divine: "Something is there that we did not know was there. Something is happening inside us and we must come to terms with it" (Ulanov, 1997, p. 297). We must find ways of bridging the gap between the ego and the ordering force of the unconscious. In doing so, "this gap between the known and unknown, the personal and the impersonal, the individual and community, the language of feelings and words in contrast to the communication of instincts, affects, and images, may become transformed into a space of conversation and engagement between the self and other" (Ulanov, 1997, p. 297). This is the numinous space of Celan's "only there," the emergence of a paradoxical place where the infinite and finite meet. Such a place is indicative of transformation, whether it be the *temenos* of a consulting room, or as British psychoanalyst D. W. Winnicott so beautifully described it, a play of words and worlds where we create what we discover and find with joy and wonder what we have created (Winnicott, 1971). This is also the numinous encounter personified by the Angel of Death.

Celan's poem begins with a feeling that the persona's search has come to a culmination ("persona" being the mask we use to face the world).

Although the arrival of a long-awaited moment has come at last, the moment also marks a profound beginning: "Only there did you wholly enter the name that is yours." It is as if the persona has been carrying another name for a long time, a name that has never belonged to him or her. There is a sense of relief and fulfillment in coming to this place, an arrival that is particular and "wholly," suggesting both wholeness and the sacred. The moment connotes a place that is entered into like a place of worship or initiatory experience, a sacred space that is embodied and forever essential to life itself.

The poem begins in a turning, an active embrace of receiving and letting go. Celan is well known for this openness and mystery of unidentified personal pronouns—the "you" and "yours"—as if we are being addressed by an alter ego or a deity or only the amorphous unknowable "other" to whom all Celan's poems make their way (Hamburger, 1972/2002, pp. xxxii–iii). Here, it is no different: A presence enters the poem from the start without any introduction or identification. An experience of being that we listened for reaches back to us, and also reaches us, as if also journeying to find us. It is in the meeting of the known and unknown, in that place of paradox and potential, that we are given a sense of self drawn from both the soul and the numinous "you" that addresses us, naming us. It becomes, like the poem itself, a passage through the unutterable, because "it has passed through it and come out on the other side" (Hamburger, 1972/2002, p. xxxiii). Such a moment not only grants us the sure-footed energy of self-blessing, it calls us to lock arms with what is shadowy and death-dealing and other. In doing so it acknowledges that the transcendent and liminal encounter ("the listened for reached you") is also ordinary. As the widening evening advances, it surprises us with the freeing of an inner great carillon, inside the very silence no longer confining and anonymous, but now alive with the dangers and possibilities of the open road.

We, too, must start out into the evening in order to arrive at the moment where we may enter the name that is palpable and alive. Recognizing the importance of the other, a force at once beyond our understanding yet intimately familiar, will confer a tremendous sense of humanity on us, like bell hammers released and swinging between the finite and the infinite. This humanity includes a "third" that walks with us confidently into the approaching night, whose name is the essential we also embody. It joins us as we turn to acknowledge our pain and suffering. It appears as we experience with all our senses its presence, and we are no longer afraid of it nor of death's greeting because we have found both transcendence and immanence in the paradoxical space of our being. This is the place where psyche and soul meet, where something dances, something declares itself. This is the unidentified Someone who says about joy as we confront the catastrophe of death: "Take it with you." Here, the "angel of all mortal things" annunciates individual immortality, not only according to religious beliefs in a cosmic paradise but also by proclaiming a doubling infinitum into this world, this place, our lives.

We can take our joys with us *now*, even in the face of death. We can choose Being and be transfigured along with the experience of ordinary things. We can look inward to find not only a growing individual, seeking relationships with others, but also wonder and wisdom in becoming a mirroring presence, providing others with nourishment for their own development and self-transcendence, even at the moment of death.

References and Bibliography

Abrams, R., Casserly, T. E., & Nodiff, B. (2000). *Boomer basics: Everything that you need to know about the issues facing you, your children, and your parents*. New York: McGraw-Hill.

Ackerman, N. (1958). *Psychodynamics of Family Life: Diagnosis and Treatment of Family Relationships*. New York: Basic Books.

Adams, G. (2000). *Adolescent development: The essential readings*. Malden, MA: Blackwell.

Administration on Aging. (1999). *Profile of older Americans: 1999*. Washington, DC: Administration on Aging.

Ainsworth, M. D. S., Blehar, M. C., Waters, E., & Wall, S. (1978). *Patterns of attachment: A psychological study of the strange situation*. Hillsdale, NJ: Erlbaum.

Alighieri, Dante. (1314/1909). *The divine comedy* (H. W. Longfellow, Trans.). New York: Begelow. (Original work published ca. 1314–1324)

Allman, L. R., & Jaffee, D. T. (Eds.). (1982). *Readings in adult psychology: Contemporary perspectives* (2nd ed.). New York: Harper & Row.

Almeida, R. (Ed.). (1998). *Transformations of gender and race: Family and developmental perspectives*. New York: Haworth Press.

Almeida, R., Woods, R., & Messineo, T. (1998). Child development: Intersectionality of race, gender, class, and culture. In R. Almeida (Ed.), *Transformations of gender and race: Family and developmental perspectives* (pp. 23–47). New York: Haworth Press.

Alsup, J. (1975). *Post-resurrection appearance stories*. London: The Society for Promoting Christian Knowledge.

Altman, N. (1995). *The analyst in the inner city: Race, class, and culture through a psychoanalytic lens*. Hillsdale, NJ: Analytic Press.

Anderson, B. (1983). *Imagined communities: Reflections on the origin and spread of nationalism*. London: Verso Books.

Anderson, H., & Johnson, S. (1994). *Regarding children*. Minneapolis, MN: Fortress Press.

Armistead, M. K. (1995). *God-images in the healing process*. Minneapolis, MN: Fortress Press.

Ashbrook, J. B. (1996). *Minding the soul: Pastoral counseling as remembering*. Minneapolis, MN: Fortress Press.

Ashbrook, J. B., & Albright, C. R. (1997). *The humanizing brain: Where religion and neuroscience meet*. Cleveland, OH: Pilgrim Press.

Ashton, P. (1975). Cross-cultural Piagetian research: An experimental perspective. *Harvard Educational Review, 45,* 475–506.

Atwood, G., & Stolorow, R. (1979/1993). *Faces in a cloud: Intersubjectivity in personality theory.* Northvale, NJ: Jason Aronson.

Atwood, G., & Stolorow, R. (1984). *Structures of subjectivity: Explorations in psychoanalytic phenomenology.* Hillsdale, NJ: Analytic Press.

Augustine. (400/2001). (R. Warner, Ed.) *Confessions of St. Augustine.* New York: Signet Classics.

Avis, J. M. (1985). The politics of functional family therapy: A feminist critique. *Journal of Marital and Family Therapy, 11,* 127–38.

Axline, V. (1947/1969). *Play therapy.* New York: Ballantine Books. (Original work published 1947)

Bakan, D. (1958). *Sigmund Freud and the Jewish mystical tradition.* Princeton, NJ: Van Nostrand.

Barbre, C. (1997). Enter the name that is yours: The essential we embody. *Union Seminary Quarterly Review, 51*(3–4), 144–65.

Barbre, C. (1999). The death of Oedipus: A reconstructive, theological reflection. *Gender and Psychoanalysis, 4*(4), 517–48.

Barker, P. (1992). *Basic family therapy* (3rd ed.). New York: Oxford University Press.

Barna, G. (1995). *Generation next: What you need to know about today's youth.* Ventura, CA: Regal Books.

Barth, K. (1928). *The word of God and the word of man* (D. Horton, Trans.). Boston: Pilgrim Press.

Basch, M. (1988). *Understanding psychotherapy: The science behind the art.* New York: Basic Books.

Bateson, G., & Bateson, M. C. (1987). *Angels fear: Towards an epistemology of mind.* New York: Macmillan.

Becker, E. (1973). *The denial of death.* New York: Free Press.

Beebe, B., & Lachmann, E. M. (1988). The contribution of mother-infant mutual influence to the origins of self and object relations. *Psychoanalytic Psychology, 5,* 305–37.

Beels, C. (2001). *A different story: The rise of narrative in psychotherapy.* Phoenix, AZ: Zeig, Tucker, & Theissen.

Begley, S. (2000, May 8). Mind expansion: Inside the teenage brain. *Newsweek,* 68.

Belenky, M. F., Clinchy, B. M., Goldberger, N. R., & Tarule, J. M. (1986). *Women's ways of knowing: The development of self, voice, and mind.* New York: Basic Books.

Bellah, R. (1985). *Habits of the heart: Individualism and commitment in American life.* Berkeley, CA: University of California Press.

Benhabib, S. (1995). Complexity, interdependence, community. In M. Nussbaum & J. Glover (Eds.), *Women, culture, and development* (pp. 235–55). Oxford, UK: Clarendon.

Berchmans, R. (2001). *A study of Lonergan's self-transcending subject and Kegan's evolving self: A framework for Christian anthropology.* Lewiston, NY: Mellen Press.

Berdiaev, N. (1931/1960). *The destiny of man* (N. Duddington, Trans.). New York: Harper & Row. (Original work published 1931)

Berger, P. L., & Luckmann, T. (1966). *The social construction of reality.* New York: Doubleday.

Bick, E. (1968). The experience of the skin in early object relations. *International Journal of Psycho-Analysis, 49,* 484–86.

Billingsley, A. (2000, February). *Changes in the African American family structure since 1960.* Paper presented at the Conference on Black Families, National Council of Churches, Atlanta, GA.

Bion, W. R. (1959). *Experiences in groups.* London: Tavistock.

Birren, J. E., & Shaie, K. W. (Eds.). (1996). *Handbook of the psychology of aging* (4th ed.). San Diego, CA: Academic Press.

Bittner, G. (1991). Against religious headbirths: A psychoanalytic critique. In J. Fowler, K. Nipkow, & F. Schweitzer (Eds.), *Stages of faith and religious development: Implications for church, education, and society* (pp. 180–91). New York: Crossroad.

Blanck, G., & Blanck, R. (1974). *Ego psychology: Theory and practice.* New York: Columbia University Press.

Blieszner, R., & Bedford, V. H. (Eds.). (1996). *Aging and the family: Theory and research.* Westport, CT: Praeger.

Blomquist, A. C., & Holleran, L. (Co-producers), & Hallstrom, L. (Director). (1999). *Cider House Rules* [Motion Picture]. (Available from Film Colony/Miramax, Los Angeles, Calif.)

Bluebond-Langner, M. (1978). *The private worlds of dying children.* Princeton, NJ: Princeton University Press.

Blumstein, P., & Schwartz, P. (1983). *American couples: Money, work and sex.* New York: William Morrow.

Bly, R. (1997). *The sibling society.* New York: Vintage.

Bly, R. (1998). A week of poems at Bennington: Sunday–what to do with objects. In J. Hollander & D. Lehman (Eds.), *The best American poetry 1998* (p. 89). New York: Scribner.

Bogot, H. (1988). Making God accessible: A parenting program. *Religious Education, 83,* 510–17.

Bolen, J. S. (2001, April 5 & 6). We are spiritual beings on a human path. *Healing: Body, soul & community.* Fourth annual Spirituality and Psychotherapy lectures at Christian Theological Seminary, Indianapolis, IN.

Boll, H. (1965). *The clown.* New York: McGraw-Hill.

Bollas, C. (1985). *The shadow of the object.* London: Free Associations.

Bollas, C. (2002). *Free Association: Ideas in psychoanalysis.* Cambridge, UK: Icon Books.

Bondi, R. (1995). *Memories of God.* Nashville, TN: Abingdon Press.

Bornstein, B. (1951). On latency. *Psychoanalytic Study of the Child, 5,* 279–86.

Borysenko, J. (1993). *Fire in the soul.* New York: Warren Books.

312   *Human Development and Faith*

Borysenko, J. (1996). *A women's book of life: The biology, psychology and spirituality of the feminine lifecycle.* New York: Riverhead Books.

Boszormenyi-Nagy, I., & Spark, G. (1973). *Invisible Loyalties: Reciprocity in Intergenerational Family Therapy.* Hagerstown: Harper & Row.

Bowen, M. (1978). *Family therapy in clinical practice.* New York: Jason Aronson.

Bowlby, J. (1988). *A secure base: Parent-child attachment and healthy human development.* New York: Basic Books

Bowlby, J. (1999). *Attachment* (2nd ed., Vol. 1). In *Attachment and Loss* (3 Vols.). New York: Basic Books.

Bowman, B. W. (1998). *Dying, grieving, faith, and family: A pastoral care approach.* Binghamton, NY: Haworth Pastoral Press.

Bowman, P. J. (1989). Research perspectives on black men: Role strain and adaptation across the black male adult life cycle. In R. Jones (Ed.), *Black adult development and aging* (pp. 117–50). Berkeley, CA: Cobb & Henry.

Bowser, B. (1989). Generational effects: Impact of culture, economy and community across generations. In R. Jones (Ed.), *Black adult development and aging* (pp. 3–30). Berkeley, CA: Cobb & Henry.

Boyd-Franklin, N. (1989). *Black families in therapy: A multisystems approach.* New York: Guilford Press.

Breger, L. (2000). *Freud: Darkness in the midst of vision.* New York: Wiley & Sons.

Bregman, L. (1999). *Beyond silence and denial.* Louisville, KY: Westminster John Knox Press.

Brock, R. N. (1988). *Journeys by heart: A christology of erotic power.* New York: Crossroad.

Brock, R. N., & Parker, R. A. (2001). *Proverbs of ashes: Violence, redemptive suffering and the search for what saves us.* Boston: Beacon Press.

Brody, E. (1990). *Women in the middle: Their parent-care years.* New York: Springer.

Bromberg, P. (1998). *Standing in the spaces: Essays on clinical process, trauma, and dissociation.* Hillsdale, NJ: Analytic Press.

Brooke, R. (1991). *Jung and phenomenology.* New York: Routledge.

Broughton, J. (1983). Women's rationality and men's virtues: A critique of gender dualism in Gilligan's theory of moral development. *Social Research, 50,* 597–642.

Broughton, J. (Ed.). (1987). *Critical theories of psychological development.* New York: Plenum Press.

Brown, L. M., & Gilligan, C. (1992). *Meeting at the crossroads: Women's and girls' development.* Cambridge, MA: Harvard University Press.

Brown, R. (1966–1970). The gospel according to John. In *Anchor Bible* (Vols. 29 & 29a). Garden City, NJ: Doubleday.

Brown, R., & Meier, J. (1958). *Antioch and Rome.* New York: Paulist Press.

Browning, D. (1987). *Religious thought and the modern psychologies: A critical conversation in the theology of culture.* Philadelphia: Fortress Press.

Browning, D. (1997). Can psychology escape religion? Should it? *International Journal for the Psychology of Religion, 7*(1), 1–12.

Broyard, A. (1992). *Intoxicated by my illness.* New York: Fawcett Columbine.

Brueggemann, W. (1979). *Belonging and growing in the Christian community.* Crawfordsville, IN: General Assembly Mission Board, Presbyterian Church in the United States.

Buber, M. (1936/1970). *I and thou* (W. Kaufman, Trans.). New York: Scribner. (Original work published 1936)

Buck-Morss, S. (1987). Piaget, Adorno and dialectical operations. In J. Broughton (Ed.), *Critical theories of psychological development* (pp. 245–74). New York: Plenum Press.

Burkert, W. (1987). *Ancient mystery cults.* Cambridge, MA: Harvard University Press.

Burman, E. (1994). *Deconstructing developmental psychology.* New York: Routledge.

Butler, L. (2000). *A loving home: Caring for African American marriage and families.* Cleveland, OH: Pilgrim Press.

Butler, R. N. (1982). The life review: Interpretation of reminiscence in the aged. In L. R. Allman & D. T. Jaffee (Eds.), *Readings in adult psychology: Contemporary perspectives* (2nd ed., pp. 368–78). New York: Harper & Row.

Butler, R. N., Lewis, M., & Sunderland, T. (1998). *Aging and mental health: Positive psychosocial and biomedical approaches* (5th ed.). New York: Merrill.

Buttrick, G. (1962). *The interpreter's dictionary of the Bible.* Nashville, TN: Abingdon Press.

Caffrey, S., & Mundy, G. (Eds). (1995). *The sociology of crime and deviance: Selected issues.* New York: New York University Press.

Callanan, M., & Kelley, P. (1992). *Final gifts: Understanding the special awareness, needs and communications of the dying.* New York: Bantam.

Campbell, J. (1996). *The hero with a thousand faces.* New York: MJF Books.

Capps, D. (1983). *Life cycle theory and pastoral care.* In D. Browning (Ed.), Theology and Pastoral Care Series. Philadelphia: Fortress Press.

Capps, D. (1987). *Deadly sins and saving virtues.* Philadelphia: Fortress Press.

Capps, D. (1993). *The depleted self: Sin in a narcissistic age.* Minneapolis, MN: Fortress Press.

Capps, D. (1993). *The poet's gift: Toward the renewal of pastoral care.* Nashville, TN: Westminster John Knox Press.

Capra, F. (1976). *The tao of physics.* Boulder, CO: Shambhala.

Cardwell, S. (1965). *The MMPI as a predictor of success among seminary students.* Unpublished master's thesis, Butler University, Indianapolis, IN.

Carter, B. (1999). Becoming parents. In B. Carter & M. McGoldrick (Eds.), *The expanded family life cycle: Individual, family and social perspectives* (3rd ed., pp. 249–73). Boston: Allyn & Bacon.

Carter, B., & McGoldrick, M. (Eds.). (1989). *The changing family life cycle: A framework for family therapy* (2nd ed.). Boston: Allyn & Bacon.

Carter, B., & McGoldrick, M. (Eds.). (1999). *The expanded family life cycle: Individual, family and social perspectives* (3rd ed.). Boston: Allyn & Bacon.

Cavanaugh, J. C. (1998). Friendships and social networks among older people. In I. H. Nordus, G. R. VandenBos, S. Berg, & P. Fromholt (Eds.), *Clinical Geropsychology* (pp. 137–40). Washington, DC: American Psychological Association Press.

Celan, P. (1972/2002). Count the almonds (M. Hamburger, Trans.). In M. Hamburger (Ed.), *Poems of Paul Celan* (Rev. ed., p. 45). New York: Persea Books. (Original work published 1972)

Childs, B. (Ed.). (1994). *The treasure of earthen vessels: Explorations in theological anthropology in honor of James N. Lapsley.* Louisville, KY: Westminster John Knox Press.

Chodorow, N., & Contratto, S. (1982). The fantasy of the perfect mother. In B. Thorne (Ed.), *Rethinking the family: Some feminist questions* (pp. 54–71). New York: Longman.

Chopp, R. (1995). *Saving work: Feminist practices of theological education.* Louisville, KY: Westminster John Knox Press.

Cixous, H. (1994). *The Hélène Cixous reader* (S. Sellers, Ed.). London: Routledge.

Cixous, H., & Clement, C. (1975/1986). *The newly born woman* (B. Wing, Trans.). Minneapolis, MN: University of Minnesota Press. (Original work published 1975)

Clinebell, H. (1990). *Understanding and counseling the alcoholic through religion and psychotherapy.* Nashville, TN: Abingdon Press.

Cobb, J. B., Jr., & Griffin, D. R. (1976). *Process theology: An introductory exposition.* Philadelphia: Westminster Press.

Coburn, K. L., & Treeger, M. (1997). *Letting go.* New York: Harper Collins.

Cohler, B. (1998). Psychoanalysis and the life course: Development and intervention. In I. H. Nordus, G. R. VandenBos, S. Berg, & P. Fromholt (Eds.), *Clinical Geropsychology* (pp. 61–78). Washington, DC: American Psychological Association Press.

Cohler, B., & Altergott, K. (1996). The family of the second half of life: Connecting theories and findings. In R. Blieszner & V. H. Bedford (Eds.), *Aging and the family: Theory and research* (pp. 307–31). Westport, CT: Praeger.

Cohler, B., Hosteler, A. J., & Boxer, A. (1998). Generativity, social context, and lived experience: Narratives of gay men in middle adulthood. In D. McAdams & E. de St. Aubin (Eds.), *Generativity and adult development: Psychosocial perspective on caring and contributing to the next generation* (pp. 265–309). Washington, DC: American Psychological Association Press.

Colarusso, C. A. (1992). *Child and adult development: A psychoanalytic introduction for Americans.* New York: Plenum Press.

Cole, T. (1992). *The journey of life: A cultural history of aging in America.* New York: Cambridge University Press.

Coles, R. (1967). *Children of Crisis* (Vol. 1). Boston: Atlantic-Little, Brown.

Coles, R. (1992). *Anna Freud: The dream of psychoanalysis.* Reading, MA: Addison-Wesley.

Conforti, M. (1999). *Field, form, and fate: Patterns in mind, nature, and psyche.* Dallas, TX: Spring.

Coontz, S. (1997). *The way we really are: Coming to terms with America's changing families.* New York: Basic Books.

Cooper-Hibert, B. (1998). *Infertility and involuntary childlessness: Helping couples cope.* New York: W. W. Norton.

Cooper-White, P. (1995). *The cry of Tamar: Violence against women and the church's response.* Minneapolis, MN: Fortress Press.

Cooper-White, P. (2000). Opening the eyes: Understanding the impact of trauma on development. In J. Stevenson-Moessner (Ed.), *In her own time: Women and developmental issues in pastoral care* (pp. 87–101). Minneapolis, MN: Fortress Press.

Corbett, L. (1996). *The religious function of the psyche.* New York: Routledge.

Costa, P. T., Yang, J., & McCrae, R. R. (1998). Aging and personality traits: Generalizations and clinical implications. In I. H. Nordus, G. R. VandenBos, S. Berg, & P. Fromholt (Eds.), *Clinical geropsychology* (pp. 33–48). Washington, DC: American Psychological Association Press.

Couture. P. (1991). *Blessed are the poor? Women's poverty, family policy, and practical theology.* Nashville, TN: Abingdon Press.

Couture, P., & Hunter, R. (Eds.). (1995). *Pastoral care and social conflict.* Nashville, TN: Abingdon Press.

Cowen, C. P., Cowan, P. A., Heming, G., Garrett, E., Coysh, W. S., Curtis-Boles, H., & Boles, III, A. J. (1985). Transitions to parenthood: His, hers and theirs. *Journal of Family Issues, 6*(4), 451–81.

Crain, W. (2000). *Theories of development: Concepts and applications* (4th ed.). Upper Saddle River, NJ: Prentice Hall.

Cross, S. E., & Madson, L. (1997). Models of the self: Self-construals and gender. *Psychological Bulletin, 122,* 5–37.

Crossan. J. (1994). *Jesus.* San Francisco: Harper Collins.

Curran, H. V. (1984). *Nigerian children: Developmental perspectives.* Boston: Routledge & Kegan Paul.

Daloz, L. A. P., Keen, C., Keen, J. P., & Parks, S. D. (1996). *Common fire: Leading lives of commitment in a complex world.* Boston: Beacon Press.

Damasio, A. (1994). *Descartes' error: Emotion, reason, and the human brain.* New York: Putnam.

Damasio, A. (1999). *The feeling of what happens: Body and emotion in the making of consciousness.* New York: Harcourt.

Dauman, A., & Wender, W. (Producer & Director). (1988). *Wings of Desire* [Motion Picture]. (Available from Orion Classics)

Davies, J. M. (1988). Multiple perspectives on multiplicity. *Psychoanalytic Dialogues, 8*(2), 195–206.

Davies, J. M., & Frawley, M. G. (1994). *Treating the adult survivor of childhood sexual abuse.* New York: Basic Books.

Day, J. (1989). *The black death.* New York: Bookwright Press.

de Beauvoir, S. (1973). *The coming of age.* New York: Warner.

DeMarinis, V. (1998–1999). The body's sacred containing: An emerging dialogue between feminist studies and ritual studies for pastoral psychotherapy. *Journal of Supervision and Training for Ministry, 18,* 86–93.

Derrett, J. D. M. (1982). *The anastasis: The resurrection of Jesus as an historical event.* Shipston-on-Stour, Warwickshire, UK: P. Drinkwater.

Descartes, R. (1641/1992). *Meditations on first philosophy* (G. Heffernan, Trans.). South Bend, IN: University of Notre Dame Press. (Original work published 1641)

Diamond, R., Meyers, M., Kezur, D., Scharf, C., & Weinshel, M. (1999). *Couple therapy for infertility.* New York: Guilford Press.

Dinnerstein, D. (1976). *The mermaid and the minotaur.* New York: Harper & Row.

Dodson, L., & Gibson, T. (Eds.). (1997). *Psyche and family.* Wilmette, IL: Chiron.

Doehring, C. (1999). A method of feminist pastoral theology. In B. J. Miller-McLemore & B. L. Gill-Austern (Eds.), *Feminist and womanist pastoral theology* (pp. 95–111). Nashville, TN: Abingdon Press.

Dore, J. (1975). Holophrases, speech acts and language universals. *Journal of Child Language, 2,* 21–40.

Dourley, J. (1981). *The psyche as sacrament: A comparative study of C. G. Jung and Paul Tillich.* Toronto, Canada: Inner City Books.

Dourley, J. (1984). *The illness that we are.* Toronto, Canada: Inner City Books.

DuBois, W. E. B. (1903/1961). *The souls of Black Folk* (Reprint ed.). Greenwich, CT: Fawcett. (Original work published 1903)

Duska, R., & Whelan, M. (1975). *Moral development: A guide to Piaget and Kohlberg.* New York: Paulist Press.

Dykstra, C. (1981). *Vision and character: A Christian educator's alternative to Kohlberg.* New York: Paulist Press.

Dykstra C., & Parks, S. (1986). *Faith development and Fowler.* Birmingham, AL: Religious Education Press.

Edinger, E. (1972). *Ego and archetype: Individuation and the religious function of the psyche.* New York: Penguin.

Edinger, E. F. (1985), *Anatomy of the psyche: Alchemical symbolism in psychotherapy.* Peru, IL: Open Court.

Edinger, E. F. (1987). *The Christian archetype: A Jungian commentary on the life of Christ.* Toronto, Canada: Inner City Books.

Edinger, E. F. (1994). *The eternal drama: The inner meaning of Greek mythology.* Boston: Shambhala.

Eiesland, N. L. (1994). *The disabled God: Toward a liberatory theology of disability.* Nashville, TN: Abingdon Press.

Eigen, M. (1981). The area of faith in Winnicott, Lacan and Bion. *International Journal of Psychoanalysis, 62,* 413–33.

Eigen, M. (1998). *The psychoanalytic mystic.* New York: Free Association Books.

Eisendrath, P., & Dawson, T. (1997). *Cambridge companion to Jung.* New York: Cambridge University Press.

Elder, G. H., Jr. (1998). *Children of the great depression* (Reprint ed.). New York: Harper Collins.

Elder, G. H., Jr., Modell, J., & Parke, R. D. (Eds.). (1994). *Children in time and place: Developmental and historical insights.* New York: Cambridge University Press.

Elias, M. (2000, August 3). "Middle Age" stretches toward 80: The swelling tide of octogenarians presents the challenge of a lifetime to science, society. *USA Today,* p. D1.

Entwistle, S. G., & Doering, D. R. (1981). *The first birth: A family turning point.* Baltimore: Johns Hopkins University Press.

Erikson, E. H. (1950/1963). *Childhood and society* (2nd ed.). New York: W. W. Norton. (Original work published 1950)

Erikson, E. H. (1962). *Young man Luther: A study in psychoanalysis and history.* New York: W. W. Norton.

Erikson, E. H. (1964). *Insight and responsibility: Lectures on the ethical implications of psychoanalytic insight.* New York: W. W. Norton.

Erikson, E. H. (1968). *Identity: Youth and crisis.* New York: W. W. Norton.

Erikson, E. H. (1969). *Gandhi's Truth: On the origins of militant nonviolence.* New York: W. W. Norton.

Erikson, E. H. (1974). *Dimensions of a new identity: The 1973 Jefferson Lectures in the humanities.* New York: W. W. Norton.

Erikson, E. H. (Ed.). (1978). *Adulthood.* New York: W. W. Norton.

Erikson, E. H. (1980). *Identity and the life cycle.* New York: W. W. Norton.

Erikson, E. H. (1982). *The life cycle completed: A review.* New York: W. W. Norton.

Erikson, E. H. (1997). *The life cycled completed: Extended version with new chapters on the ninth stage of development by Joan Erikson.* New York: W. W. Norton.

Erikson, E. H., Erikson, J., & Kivnick, H. (1986). *Vital involvement in old age.* New York: W. W. Norton.

Fairbairn, W. R. D. (1952). *Psychoanalytic studies of the personality.* Boston: Routledge.

Filipp, S. (1996). Motivation and emotion. In J. E. Birren & K. W. Schaie (Eds.), *Handbook of the psychology of aging* (4th ed., pp. 218–35). San Diego, CA: Academic Press.

Fine, R. (1987). *The development of Freud's thought.* Northvale, NJ: Jason Aronson.

Flax, J. (1990). *Thinking fragments: Psychoanalysis, feminism, and postmodernism in the contemporary West.* Berkeley, CA: University of California Press.

Fliegal, Z. (1986). Women's development in analytical theory: Six decades of controversy. In J. Alpert (Ed.), *Psychoanalysis and women: Contemporary reappraisals* (pp. 3–32). Hillsdale, NJ: Analytic Press.

Florovsky, G. (1976). *Creation and redemption* (Vol. 3). *The collected works of Georges Florovsky.* Belmont, MA: Nordland.

Fogarty, H. W. (1987). *Approaches to the process of personal transformation: The spiritual exercises of Ignatius Loyola and Jung's method of active imagination.* Unpublished doctoral dissertation, Union Theological Seminary, New York, NY.

Foucault, M. (1980). *Power/knowledge.* New York: Pantheon.

Foucault, M. (1988). *Madness and civilization: A history of insanity in the age of reason.* New York: Vintage.

Foucault, M. (1994). *The birth of the clinic: An archaeology of medical perception.* New York: Vintage.

Fowler, J. (1981). *Stages of faith: The psychology of human development and the quest for meaning.* San Francisco: Harper & Row.

Fowler, J. (1987). *Faith development and pastoral care.* Philadelphia: Fortress Press.

Fowler, J. (1996). *Faithful change: The personal and public challenges of postmodern life.* Nashville, TN: Abingdon Press.

Fowler, J., Nipkow, K., & Schweitzer, F. (Eds.). (1991). *Stages of faith and religious development: Implications for church, education, and society.* New York: Crossroad.

Fowlkes, M. (1989). Roots of ritual in social interactive episodes during the first three years of life: Implications for bonding in the faith community. *Religious Education, 84,* 338–48.

Fox, G. (1694/1976). *The journal of George Fox* (R. Jones, Ed.). Richmond, IN: Friends United Press. (Original work published 1694)

Fox, M. (2000). *One river, many wells: Wisdom springing from global faiths.* New York: Jeremy P. Tarcher/Putman.

Francis, L., Kay, W., & Campbell, W., (Eds.). (1996). *Research in religious education.* Macon, GA: Smyth & Helwys.

Frankl, V. (1969/1988). *The will to meaning: Foundations and applications of logotherapy.* New York: Penguin. (Original work published 1969)

Freud, A. (1936/1966). *The ego and the mechanisms of defense.* In *The Writings of Anna Freud* (Rev. ed., Vol. 2). New York: International Universities Press. (Original work published 1936)

Freud, A. (1936/1966). Instinctual anxiety during puberty. In *The Writings of Anna Freud* (Rev. ed., Vol. 2, pp. 152–72). New York: International Universities Press.

Freud, A. (1946). The psychoanalytic study of infantile feeding disturbances. *Psychoanalytic Study Child, 2,* 119–32.

Freud, A. (1963). The concept of developmental lines. *Psychoanalytic Study Child, 18,* 245–65.

Freud, A. (1966–1980). *The writings of Anna Freud* (8 Vols.). New York: International Universities Press.

Freud, S. (1900/1953). The interpretation of dreams. In J. Strachey (Ed. and Trans.), *The standard edition of the complete psychological works of Sigmund Freud* (Vols. 4-5). London, UK: Hogarth Press. (Original work published 1900).

Freud, S. (1905d/1953). Three essays on the theory of sexuality. In J. Strachey (Ed. and Trans.), *The standard edition of the complete psychological works of Sigmund Freud* (Vol. 7, pp. 125–245). London: Hogarth Press. (Original work published 1905)

Freud, S. (1905e/1953). Fragment of an analysis of a case of hysteria. In J. Strachey (Ed. and Trans.), *The standard edition of the complete psychological works of Sigmund Freud* (Vol. 7, pp. 3–122). London: Hogarth Press. (Original work published 1905)

Freud, S. (1912x/1953). Totem and taboo: Resemblances between the psychic lives of savages and neurotics. In J. Strachey (Ed. and Trans.), *The standard edition of the complete psychological works of Sigmund Freud* (Vol. 13, pp. 1–162). London: Hogarth Press. (Original work published 1912)

Freud, S. (1917e/1957). Mourning and melancholia. In J. Strachey (Ed. and Trans.), *The standard edition of the complete psychological works of Sigmund Freud* (Vol. 14, pp. 239ff.). London: Hogarth Press. (Original work published 1917)

Freud, S. (1920g/1955) Beyond the pleasure principle. In J. Strachey (Ed. and Trans.), *The standard edition of the complete psychological works of Sigmund Freud* (Vol. 18, pp. 1–64). London: Hogarth Press. (Original work published 1920)

Freud, S. (1923b/1961). The ego and the id. In J. Strachey (Ed. and Trans.), *The standard edition of the complete psychological works of Sigmund Freud* (Vol. 19, pp. 3–66). London: Hogarth Press. (Original work published 1923)

Freud, S. (1927c/1953). The future of an illusion. In J. Strachey (Ed. and Trans.), *The standard edition of the complete psychological works of Sigmund Freud* (Vol. 21, pp. 1–56). London: Hogarth Press. (Original work published 1927)

Freud, S. (1953–1974). *Standard edition of the complete psychological works of Sigmund Freud.* (J. Strachey Ed. and Trans., 24 Vols.). London: Hogarth Press.

Freud, S., & Breuer, J. (1895d/1955). Studies on Hysteria: Chapter 2. Case histories: Fraulein Anna O. (Breuer). In J. Strachey (Ed. and Trans.), *The standard edition of the complete psychological works of Sigmund Freud* (Vol. 2). London: Hogarth Press. (Original work published 1895).

Freud, S., & Jung, C. G. (1974). *The Freud-Jung letters: The correspondence between Sigmund Freud and C. G. Jung* (W. McGuire, Ed., R. Manheim & R. F. C. Hull, Trans.). Princeton, NJ: Princeton University Press.

Friedman, E. H. (1985). *Generation to generation: Family process in church and synagogue.* New York: Guilford Press.

Friedman, L. J. (1999). *Identity's Architect: A Biography of Erik H. Erickson.* New York: Scribner.

Fulmer, E. M., Shenk, D., & Eastland, L. J. (1999). Negative identity: A feminist analysis of the social invisibility of older lesbians. In J. D. Garner (Ed.), *Fundamentals of feminist gerontology* (pp. 131–48). New York: Haworth.

Fulmer, R. (1999). Becoming an adult: Leaving home and staying connected. In B. Carter & M. McGoldrick (Eds.), *The expanded family life cycle: Individual, family and social perspectives* (3rd ed., pp. 215–30). Boston: Allyn & Bacon.

Galatzer-Levy, R. M., & Cohler, B. J. (1993). *The essential other: A developmental psychology of the self.* New York: Basic Books.

Gardner, H. (1983). *Frames of mind: The theory of multiple intelligences.* New York: Basic Books.

Garner, J. D. (Ed.). (1999). *Fundamentals of feminist gerontology.* New York: Haworth.

Gavin, L., & Furman, W. (2000). Work experience, mental health, and behavioral adjustment in adolescence. In G. Adams (Ed.), *Adolescent development: The essential readings.* Malden, MA: Blackwell.

Gay, P. (1998). *Freud: A life for our time.* New York: W. W. Norton.

Gee, H. (1991). The Oedipal complex in adolescence. *Journal of Analytical Psychology, 36,* 193–210.

Geertz, C. (1973). *The interpretation of cultures.* New York: Basic Books.

Geertz, C. (1973). Thick description: Toward an interpretative theory of culture. In C. Geertz, *The interpretation of cultures* (pp. 3–32). New York: Basic Books.

Gelman, S., & Taylor, M. (2000). Gender essentialism in cognitive development. In P. Miller & E. Scholnick (Eds.), *Toward a feminist developmental psychology* (pp. 169–90). New York: Routledge.

Gerkin, C. V. (1979). *Crisis experience in modern life.* Nashville, TN: Parthenon Press.

Gerkin, C. V. (1994). Projective identification and the image of God: Reflections on object relations theory and the psychology of religion. In B. Childs (Ed.), *The treasure of earthen vessels: Explorations in theological anthropology in honor of James N. Lapsley* (pp. 52–65). Louisville, KY: Westminster John Knox Press.

Gerston, K. (1993). *No man's land: Men's changing commitments to family and work.* New York: Basic Books.

Gibbs, J. (1977). Kohlberg's stages of moral judgment: A constructive critique. *Harvard Educational Review, 47*(1) 43–61.

Gibson, K., Lathrop, D., & Stern, M. E. (1991). *Carl Jung and soul psychology.* New York: Harrington Park Press.

Gilkey, L. (1988). A retrospective glance at my work. In D. W. Musser & J. L. Price (Eds.), *Whirlwind in culture: Frontiers in theology: In honor of Langdon Gilkey* (pp. 1–35). Bloomington, IN: Meyer-Stone Books.

Gilligan, C. (1982). *In a different voice: Psychological theory and women's development.* Cambridge, MA: Harvard University Press.

Ginsburg, H. P., & Opper, S. (1988). *Piaget's theory of intellectual development* (3rd ed.). Englewood Cliffs, NJ: Prentice Hall.

Glaser, C. (1996, September 16). Marriage as we see it. *Newsweek, 19, C1.*

Glaz, M., & Stevenson Moessner, J. (Eds.). (1991). *Women in travail and transition: A new pastoral care.* Minneapolis, MN: Fortress Press.

Goethe, J. (1808/1995). *Faust: Parts I & II* (H. Brenton, Ed., & C. Weisman, Trans.). London: N. Hern Books. (Original work published 1808)

Goin, M. K. (1990). Emotional survival and the aging body. In R. Nemiroff & C. Colarusso (Eds.), *New dimensions in adult development* (pp. 518–31). New York: Basic Books.

Goldman, D. (1993). *In search of the real: The origins and originality of D. W. Winnicott.* Northvale, NJ: Jason Aronson.

Goldwert, M. (1992). *The wounded healers: Creative illness in the pioneers of depth psychology.* Lanham, MD: University Press of America.

Goleman, D. P. (1997). *Emotional intelligence.* New York: Bantam.

Gooden, W. (1989). Development of black men in early adulthood. In R. Jones (Ed.), *Black adult development and aging* (pp. 63–90). Berkeley, CA: Cobb & Henry.

Goodman, L. (1981) *Death and creative life.* New York: Springer.

Graebner, W. (1980). *A history of retirement: The meaning and function of an American institution, 1885-1978.* New Haven, CT: Yale University Press.

Grant, B. (2001). *A theology for pastoral psychotherapy: God's play in sacred spaces.* New York: Haworth Pastoral Press.

Graves, R. (1980). *The Greek myths* (Vol. 2). New York: Penguin.

Green, R. J. (1998). Traditional norms of masculinity. In R. Almeida (Ed.), *Transformations of gender and race: Family and developmental perspectives* (pp. 81–83). New York: Harrington Park Press.

Greenspan, S. I. (1997). *The growth of the mind.* Reading, MA: Addison-Wesley.

Grof, S. (1986). *Beyond the brain: Birth, death, and transcendence in psychotherapy.* Albany, NY: State University of New York Press.

Grosskurth, P. (1995). *Melanie Klein: Her world and her work.* Northvale, NJ: Jason Aronson.

Grotstein, J. S. (1997). Internal objects or "chimerical monsters?" The demonic "third forms" of the internal world. *Journal of Analytical Psychology, 42,* 47–88.

Guntrip, H. (1961). *Schizoid phenomena, object-relations and the self.* New York: International Universities Press.

Guroian, V. (1996) *Life's living toward dying: A theological and medical-ethical study.* Grand Rapids, MI: Eerdmans.

Gutmann, D. (1987). *Reclaimed powers: Toward a new psychology of men and women in later life.* New York: Basic Books.

Gutmann, D. (1997). *The human elder in nature, culture, and society.* Boulder, CO: Westview Press.

Haley, J. (1991). *Problem solving therapy.* San Francisco: Jossey-Bass.

Haley, J., & Richeport-Haley, M. (2003). *The art of strategic therapy.* New York: Brunner-Routledge.

Hamburger, M. (Ed.). (1972/2002). Introduction. In *Poems of Paul Celan* (Rev. ed., M. Hamburger, Trans., pp. xix–xxxiv). New York: Persea Books. (Original work published 1972)

Hannah, B. (1976). *Jung: His life and work.* New York: Perigee Books.

Hansen, M., & Harway, M. (Eds.). (1993). *Battering and family therapy: A feminist perspective.* Newbury Park, CA: Sage.

Hargrave T. D., & Hanna, S. M. (Eds.). (1997). *The aging family: New visions in theory, practice, and reality.* New York: Brunner/Mazel.

Harris, J. (1997). *I kissed dating goodbye.* Sisters, OR: Multinomah books.

Harris, J. (1998). *The nurture assumption: Why children turn out the way they do.* New York: Free Press.

Harrison, A. O. (1989). Black working women: Introduction to a life span perspective. In R. Jones (Ed.), *Black adult development and aging* (pp. 91–116). Berkeley, CA: Cobb & Henry.

Hart, P. P. (1990). Bisexuality. In R. Hunter (Ed.), *The dictionary of pastoral care and counseling* (p. 91). Nashville, TN: Abingdon Press.

Hartmann, H. (1958). *Ego psychology and the problem of adaptation.* New York: International Universities Press. (Original work published 1939)

Hartmann, H. (1964). *Essays on ego psychology.* Princeton, NJ: Princeton University Press.

Hay, D., Nye, R., & Murphy, R. (1996). Thinking about childhood spirituality: Review of research and current directions. In L. Francis, W. Kay, & W. Campbell (Eds.), *Research in Religious Education* (pp. 47–71). Macon, GA: Smyth & Helwys.

Hayman, R. (1999). *A life of Jung.* New York: W. W. Norton.

Hekman, S. (1995). *Moral voices, moral selves: Carol Gilligan and feminist moral theory.* University Park, PA: Pennsylvania State University Press.

Hendrix, H. (1988). *Getting the love you want: A guide for couples.* New York: Harper & Row.

Hendrix, H. (1992). *Keeping the love you find: A guide for singles.* New York: Pocket Books.

Hersch, P. (1998). *A tribe apart: A journey into the heart of American adolescence.* New York: Fawcett Columbine.

Hick, J. (1966). *Faith and knowledge* (2nd ed.). Ithaca, NY: Cornell University Press.

Hick, J. (1976) *Death and eternal life.* San Francisco: Harper & Row.

Hightower, J. (Ed.). (1999). *Caring for people from birth to death.* New York: Haworth Pastoral Press.

Hillman, J. (1992). *Re-visioning psychology.* New York: Harper Perennial.

Hillman, J. (1996). *The soul's code: In search of character and calling.* New York: Warner Books.

Hillman, J. (1999). *The force of character: And the lasting life.* New York: Random House.

Hillman, J., & Kerenyi, K. (1991). *Oedipus variations: Studies in literature and psychoanalysis.* Dallas, TX: Spring.

Hine, T. (1999). *The rise and fall of the American teenager.* New York: Bard.

Hollander, J., & Lehman, D. (Eds.). (1998). *The best American poetry.* New York: Scribner.

Hollifield, E. B. (1983). *A history of pastoral care in America.* Nashville, TN: Abingdon Press.

Hopcke, R. (1989). *A guided tour of the collected works of C. G. Jung.* Boston: Shambhala.

Hunsinger, D. (1995). *Theology and pastoral counseling: A new interdisciplinary approach.* Grand Rapids, MI: Eerdmans.

Hunter, R., & Couture, P. (Eds.). (1994). Aging and the conflict of generations. In *Social conflict and pastoral care.* Nashville, TN: Abingdon Press.

Hunter, R., Malony, H. N., Mills, L., & Patton, J. (1990). *Dictionary of pastoral care and counseling.* Nashville, TN: Abindgon Press.

Imathiu, G. (2000, April 1). *Sermon.* Auburn, WA: Pacific Northwest Annual Conference Clergy Retreat, United Methodist Church.

Imber-Black, E., & Roberts, J. (1998). *Rituals for our times: Celebrating, healing, and changing our lives and our relationships.* New York: Jason Aronson.

Irigaray, L. (1974/1985). *Speculum of the other woman* (G. C. Gill, Trans.). Ithaca, NY: Cornell University Press. (Original work published 1974)

Ivy, S. (1982). [Review of the book *Stages of faith: The psychology of human development and the quest for meaning.*] *Journal of Pastoral Care, 36* (4), 265–74.

Jacobi, J. (1962). *The Psychology of C.G. Jung: An introduction with illustrations.* New Haven: Yale University Press.

Johnson, C. L. (1996). Cultural diversity in the late-life family. In R. Blieszner & V. H. Bedford (Eds.), *Aging and the family: Theory and research* (pp. 307–31). Westport, CT: Praeger.

Johnson, R. (1994). *Lying with the heavenly woman: Understanding and integrating the feminine archetype in men's lives.* San Francisco: Harper Collins.

Johnson, S. (1987). *After a child dies: Counseling bereaved families.* New York: Springer.

Jones, E. (1953–57). *The life and work of Sigmund Freud.* New York: Basic Books.

Jones, J. (1991) *Contemporary psychoanalysis and religion: Transference and transcendence.* New Haven, CT: Yale University Press.

Jones, R. (Ed.). (1989). *Black adult development and aging.* Berkeley, CA: Cobb & Henry.

Jones, S. (2000). *Feminist theory and Christian theology: Cartographies of grace.* Minneapolis, MN: Fortress Press.

Jonte-Pace, D. (2001). *Speaking the unspeakable: Religion, misogyny, and the uncanny mother in Freud's cultural texts.* Berkeley, CA: University of California Press.

Julian of Norwich (1670/1978). Showings (E. Colledge & J. Walsh, Trans.). In R. J. Payne (Ed.), *Classics of Western spirituality.* New York: Paulist Press. (Original work published 1670)

Jung, C. G. (1917/1966). On the psychology of the unconscious: A study of the transformations and symbolisms of the libido (B. M. Hinkle, Trans.). In H. E. Read, M. Fordham, & G. Adler (Eds.), *The collected works of C. G. Jung: Vol. 7. Two essays on analytical psychology* (2nd ed., R. F. C. Hull, Trans., pp. 3–119). Princeton, NJ: Princeton University Press. (Original work published 1917).

Jung, C. G. (1925/1954). Marriage as a psychological relationship. In H. E. Read, M. Fordham, & G. Adler (Eds.), *The collected works of C. G. Jung: Vol. 17. The development of personality* (2nd ed., R. F. C. Hull, Trans., pp. 189–201). Princeton, NJ: Princeton University Press. (Original work published 1925).

Jung, C. G. (1930/1969).The stages of life. In H. E. Read, M. Fordham, & G. Adler (Eds.), *The collected works of C. G. Jung: Vol. 8. The structure and dynamics of the psyche* (2nd ed., R. F. C. Hull, Trans., pp. 387–403). Princeton, NJ: Princeton University Press. (Original work published 1930).

Jung, C. G. (1932/1954). The development of personality. In H. E. Read, M. Fordham, & G. Adler (Eds.), *The collected works of C. G. Jung: Vol. 17. The development of personality* (2nd ed., R. F. C. Hull, Trans., pp. 167–86). Princeton, NJ: Princeton University Press. (Original work published 1932).

Jung, C. G. (1934/1951). The archetypes and the collective unconscious. In H. E. Read, M. Fordham, & G. Adler (Eds.), *The collected works of C. G. Jung: Vol. 9. The archetypes and the collective unconscious* (2nd ed., R. F. C. Hull, Trans., pp. 3–41). Princeton, NJ: Princeton University Press. (Original work published 1934).

Jung, C. G. (1934/1969). *The soul and death.* In H. E. Read, M. Fordham, & G. Adler (Eds.), *The collected works of C. G. Jung: Vol. 8. The structure and dynamics of the psyche* (2nd ed., R. F. C. Hull, Trans., pp. 404–15). Princeton, NJ: Princeton University Press. (Original work published 1934).

Jung, C. G. (1936/1969). Concerning the archetypes, with special reference to the anima concept. In H. E. Read, M. Fordham, & G. Adler (Eds.),

The collected works of C. G. Jung: Vol. 9, part 1. The archetypes and the collective unconscious (2nd ed., R. F. C. Hull, Trans., pp. 54–72). Princeton, NJ: Princeton University Press. (Original work published 1936).

Jung, C. G. (1946/1969). On the nature of the psyche. In H. E. Read, M. Fordham, & G. Adler (Eds.), *The collected works of C. G. Jung: Vol. 8. The structure and dynamics of the psyche* (2nd ed., pp. 159–234). Princeton, NJ: Princeton University Press. (Original work published 1946).

Jung, C. G. (1946/1966). The psychology of the transference. In H. E. Read, M. Fordham, & G. Adler (Eds.), *The collected works of C. G. Jung: Vol. 16, The practice of psychotherapy* (2nd ed., R. F. C. Hull, Trans., pp. 163–323). Princeton, NJ: Princeton University Press. (Original work published 1946).

Jung, C. G. (1948/1969). A psychological approach to the doctrine of the Trinity. In H. E. Read, M. Fordham, & G. Adler (Eds.), *The collected works of C. G. Jung: Vol. 11. Psychology and religion* (2nd ed., R. F. C. Hull, Trans., pp. 107–200). Princeton, NJ: Princeton University Press. (Original work published 1948).

Jung, C. G. (1951a/1959). Aion: The ego. (R. F. C. Hull, Trans.). In H. E. Read, M. Fordham, & G. Adler (Eds.), *The collected works of C. G. Jung: Vol. 9, part 2, Aion* (2nd ed., R. F. C. Hull, Trans., pp. 3–7). Princeton, NJ: Princeton University Press. (Original work published 1951).

Jung, C. G. (1952/1967). Symbols of transformation, part 2. In *The collected works of C. G. Jung: Vol. 5. Symbols of transformation* (2nd ed., R. F. C. Hull, Trans., pp. 121–444). Princeton, NJ: Princeton University Press. (Original work published 1952).

Jung, C. G. (1953–1961). *The collected works of C. G. Jung* (2nd ed., Vols. 1–20, H. E. Read, M. Fordham, & G. Adler, Eds., R. F. C. Hull, Trans.). Princeton, NJ: Princeton University Press.

Jung, C. G. (1954/1969). Transformation symbolism in the Mass. In H. E. Read, M. Fordham, & G. Adler (Eds.), *The collected works of C. G. Jung: Vol. 11. Psychology and religion* (2nd ed., R. F. C. Hull, Trans., pp. 201–96). Princeton, NJ: Princeton University Press. (Original work published 1954).

Jung, C. G. (1963). *Memories, dreams, and reflections.* (A. Jaffe, Ed., R. Winston & C. Winston, Trans.). New York: Pantheon Books.

Jung, C. G. (1970). *Jung, C. G.: Psychological reflections; A new anthology of his writings, 1905-1961* (J. Jacobi & R. F. C. Hull, Eds.). Princeton, NJ: Princeton University Press.

Jung, C. G. (1979). *C. G. Jung: Word and image* (A. Jaffe, Ed.). Princeton NJ: Princeton University Press.

Jung, E., & von Franz, M. L. (1970). *The Grail Legend* (A. Dykes, Trans.). New York: Putnam's Sons.

Kagan, J. (1981). *The second year: The emergence of self-awareness.* Cambridge, MA: Harvard University Press.

Kagan, J., & Lamb, S. (1987). *The emergence of morality in young children.* Chicago: University of Chicago Press.

Kalff, D. M. (1970). *Sandplay: A psychotherapeutic approach to the psyche.* Boston: Sigo Press.

Kalsched, D. (1996). *The inner world of trauma: Archetypal defenses of the personal spirit.* New York: Routledge.

Kant, I. (1788/1956). *The critique of practical reason.* (L. W. Beck, Trans.). New York: Liberal Arts Press. (Original work published 1788)

Kasl-Godley, J. E., Gatz, M., & Fiske, A. (1998). Depression and depressive symptoms in old age. In I. H. Nordus, G. R. VandenBos, S. Berg, & P. Fromholt (Eds.), *Clinical geropsychology* (pp. 211–18). Washington, DC: American Psychological Association Press.

Kedem, P., Mikulincer, M., Nathanson, Y. E., & Bartov, B. (1990). Psychological aspects of male infertility. *British Journal of Medical Psychology, 63,* 73–80.

Kegan, R. (1982). *The evolving self: Problem and process in human development.* Cambridge, MA: Harvard University Press.

Kegan, R. (1994). *In over our heads: The mental demands of modern life.* Cambridge, MA: Harvard University Press.

Kegan, R., & Lahey, L. (2000). *How the way we talk can change the way we work: Seven languages for transformation.* New York: Wiley & Sons.

Keirsey, D. (1998). *Please understand me II: Temperament, character, intelligence.* Del Mar, CA: Prometheus Nemesis.

Kelcourse, F. (1998). Discernment: The art of attention in religious experience and psychotherapy. *Dissertation Abstracts International, 59*(5-B), 2472.

Kelcourse, F. (2001). Discernment: The soul's-eye view. In J. B. Ratliff (Ed.), *Out of the silence: Quaker perspectives on pastoral care and counseling* (pp. 27–49). Wallingford, PA: Pendle Hill.

Kelsey, M. T. (1973). *Healing and Christianity.* San Francisco: Harper & Row.

Kerr, J. (1993). *A most dangerous method: The story of Jung, Freud and Sabina Spielrein.* New York: Knopf.

Kierkegaard, S. (1938). *Purity of heart is to will one thing* (D. Steere, Trans.). New York: Harper & Brothers.

Kill, A. S. (1986). Kohut's psychology of the self as model for theological dynamics. *Union Seminary Quarterly Review, 41,* 17–32.

Kim, C. W. M., St. Ville, S. M., & Simonaitis, S. M. (1993). *Transfigurations: Theology and the French feminists.* Minneapolis, MN: Fortress Press.

Kimble, M., & McFadden, S. (Eds.). (1995). *Aging, spirituality, and religion: A handbook.* Minneapolis, MN: Fortress Press.

Kimmel, M. (1996). *Manhood in America: A cultural history.* New York: Free Press.

Kindlon, D., & Thompson, M. (1999). *Raising Cain: Protecting the Emotional Life of Boys.* New York: Ballantine.

Kinnell, G. (1982). Little sleep's-head sprouting hair in the moonlight. In *Selected poems* (pp. 112–15). Boston: Houghton Mifflin.

Kirschner, S. (1996). *The religious and romantic origins of psychoanalysis: Individuation and integration in post-Freudian theory.* New York: Cambridge University Press.

Klein, M. (1932). *The psycho-analysis of children* (Rev. ed.). London: Hogarth Press.

Klein, M. (1957). *Envy and gratitude.* London: Tavistock.

Klein, M. (1975). *Love, Guilt, and Reparation and other works.* New York: Delacorte Press.

Knefelkamp, L. (1990). Seasons of academic life: Honoring our collective autobiography. *Liberal Education, 76*(3), 4–12.

Koester, H. (1982). *Introduction to the New Testament.* Philadelphia: Fortress Press.

Kohlberg, L. (1958a). *The development of modes of thinking and choice in the years 10-16.* Unpublished doctoral dissertation, University of Chicago.

Kohlberg, L. (1973). Continuities and discontinuities in childhood and adult moral development revisited. In *Collected papers on moral development and moral education* (pp. 1–62). Cambridge, MA: Moral Education Research Foundation, Harvard University.

Kohlberg, L. (1981). *The philosophy of moral development.* San Francisco: Harper & Row.

Kohlberg, L., & Kramer, R. (1969). Continuities and discontinuities in child and adult moral development. *Human Development, 12*, 93–120.

Kohlberg, L., & Kramer, R. (1972). Development as the aim of education. *Harvard Educational Review, 42*(4), 449–96.

Kohlberg, L., & Mayer, R. (1972). *Development as the aim of education.* Cambridge: Harvard Educational Review.

Kohut, H. (1971). *The analysis of the self: A systematic approach to the psychoanalytic treatment of narcissistic personality disorders.* New York: International Universities Press.

Kohut, H. (1977). *The restoration of the self.* New York: International Universities Press.

Kohut, H. (1978). *The search for the self: Selected writings of Heinz Kohut: 1950-1978* (2 Vols., P. H. Ornstein, Ed.). New York: International Universities Press.

Kohut, H. (1984). *How does analysis cure?* Chicago: University of Chicago Press.

Korin, E., McGoldrick, M., & Watson, M. (2002). Individual and family life cycle. In M. Mengel, W. Holleman, & S. Fields (Eds.), *Fundamentals of clinical practice* (2nd ed., pp. 21–47). New York: Plenum.

Kornfeld. M. (1998). *Cultivating wholeness: A guide to care and counseling in faith communities.* New York: Continuum.

Kramarow, E., Lentzner, H., Rooks, R., Weeks, J., & Saydah, S. (1999). Health and aging chartbook. *Health, United States, 17-97.* Hyattsville, MD: National Center for Health Statistics.

Kristeva, J. (1986). *The Kristeva reader* (T. Moi, Ed.). New York: Columbia University Press.

Krüll, M. (1979). *Freud and his father.* New York: W. W. Norton.

Kübler-Ross, E. (1981). *Living with death and dying.* New York: Macmillan.

Kuhn, T. S. (1970). *The structure of scientific revolutions* (2nd ed.). Chicago: University of Chicago Press.

Kurtz, G., Lucas, G., & McCallum, R. (Producers), & Lucas, G. (Director). (1977). *Stars Wars Trilogy* [Motion picture]. (Available from LucasFilms Ltd., Los Angeles).

Lacan, J. (1966/1977). *Ecrits: A selection* (A. Sheridan, Trans.). New York: W. W. Norton. (Original work published 1966)

Laird, J., & Green, R. J. (1996). *Lesbians and gays in couples and families.* San Francisco: Jossey-Bass.

LaMothe, R. (2001). *Revitalizing faith through pastoral counseling.* Nashville, TN: Abingdon Press.

Landreth, G. L. (1991). *Play therapy: The art of the relationship.* Muncie, IN: Accelerated Development.

Larkin, P. (1955). *The less deceived.* London: Marvell Press.

Lash, J. (1993). *Twins and the double.* London: Thames & Hudson.

Leaper, C. (2000). The social construction and socialization of gender during development. In P. Miller & E. Scholnick (Eds.), *Toward a feminist developmental psychology* (pp. 127–52). New York: Routledge.

Lear, J. (1990). *Love and its place in nature: A philosophical interpretation of Freudian psychoanalysis.* New York: Farrar, Straus & Giroux.

LeGuin, U. (1969). *The left hand of darkness.* New York: Walker.

Leland, J. (2000, May 8). Searching for a Holy Spirit. *Newsweek,* p. 61.

Lerner, M. (1996). *The politics of meaning: Restoring hope and possibility in an age of cynicism.* New York: Addison-Wesley.

Leslie, K. (2002). *When violence is no stranger: Pastoral counseling with survivors of acquaintance rape.* Philadelphia: Fortress Press.

LeVine, R. A. (1977). Child rearing as cultural adaptation. In P. H. Leiderman, S. R. Tulkin, & A. Rosenfeld (Eds.), *Culture and infancy: Variations in the human experience* (pp. 15–27). New York: Academic Press.

LeVine, R. A. (1990). Infant environments in psychoanalysis: A cross-cultural view. In J. W. Stigler, R. A. Shweder, & G. Herdt (Eds.), *Cultural psychology: Essays on comparative human development* (pp. 454–74). New York: Cambridge University Press.

Levinson, D. (1978). *The seasons of a man's life.* New York: Ballantine Books.

Lewis, C. S. (1976). *A grief observed.* New York: Bantam Books.

Lewis, H. B. (1981). Shame and guilt in human nature. In S. Tuttman, C. Kaye, & M. Zimmerman (Eds.), *Object and self: A developmental approach* (pp. 235–65). New York: International Universities Press.

Lewis, M. (Ed.). *The genesis of behavior: Vol. 4. Beyond the dyad.* New York: Plenum.

Lewis, M., Feiring, C., & Kotsonis, M. (1984). The social network of the young child. In M. Lewis (Ed.), *The genesis of behavior: Vol. 4. Beyond the dyad* (pp. 129–60). New York: Plenum.

Liebert, E. (2000). *Changing life patterns: Adult development in spiritual direction.* St. Louis, MO: Chalice Press.

Lifton, B. J. (1994). *Journey of the adopted self: A quest for wholeness.* New York: Basic Books.

Liu, E. (1998, May 17). Notes of Native Speaker. *The Washington Post Magazine,* 15–18.

Llewellyn, N. (1991). *The art of death.* London: Reaktion Books.

Lock, A. (Ed.). (1978). *Action, gesture, and symbol: The emergence of language.* New York: Academic Press.

Loder, J. E. (1998). *The logic of the spirit: Human development in theological perspective.* San Francisco: Jossey-Bass.

Long, J. (1997). Alzheimer's disease and the family: Working with new realities. In T. Hargrave & S. M. Hanna (Eds.), *The aging family: New visions in theory, practice, and reality* (pp. 209–34). New York: Brunner Mazel.

Lopata, H. Z. (1996). Feminist perspectives in social gerontology. In R. Blieszner & V. H. Bedford (Eds.), *Aging and the family: Theory and research* (pp. 114–31). Westport, CT: Praeger.

Lyon, K. B. (1985). *Toward a practical theology of aging.* Philadelphia: Fortress Press.

Lyon, K. B. (1988). Aging in theological perspective. *Educational Gerontology, 14,* 243–54.

Lyon, K. B. (1994). Aging and the conflict of generations. In R. Hunter & P. Couture (Eds.), *Social conflict and pastoral care* (pp. 86–98). Nashville, TN: Abingdon Press.

Lyon, K. B., & Smith, A., Jr. (Eds.). (1998). *Tending the flock: Congregations and family ministry.* Louisville, KY: Westminster John Knox Press.

Lyotard, J. F. (1979/1984). *The postmodern condition: A report on knowledge* (G. Bennington & V. Massumi, Trans.). Minneapolis, MN: University of Minnesota Press. (Original work published 1979)

Mahler, M. (1968). *On human symbiosis and the vicissitudes of individuation.* New York: International University Press.

Mahler, M., Pine, F., & Bergman, A. (1975). *The psychological birth of the human infant: Symbiosis and individuation.* New York: Basic Books.

Maidenbaum, A. (1989). Foreword. In R. Hopcke, *A guided tour of the collected works of C. G. Jung.* (pp. ix–x). Boston: Shambhala.

Mairs, N. (2001). *A troubled guest: Life and death stories.* BostonMA: Beacon.

Malia, M. E. (1978). Adulthood refracted: Russia and Leo Tolstoi. In E. H. Erikson (Ed.) *Adulthood* (pp. 173–87). New York: W. W. Norton.

Manheimer, R. (1999). *A map to the end of time.* New York: W. W. Norton.

Margolis, D. (1996). *Freud and his mother.* Northvale, NJ: Jason Aronson.

Markides, K. S., & Mindal, C. H. (1987). *Aging and ethnicity.* Newbury Park, CA: Sage.

Markus, H. R., & Kitayama, S. (1993). Culture and the self: Implications for cognition, emotion, and motivation. *Psychological Review, 98,* 224–53.

Marshall, J. (1997). *Counseling Lesbian Partners.* Louisville, KY: Westminster John Knox Press.

Maslow, A. (1963). The need to know and the fear of knowing. *The Journal of General Psychology, 68,* 111–25.

Maslow, A. (1998). *Toward a psychology of being* (3rd ed.). New York: J. Wiley & Sons.

McAdams, D., & de St. Aubin, E. (Eds.). (1998). *Generativity and adult development: Psychosocial perspective on caring and contributing to the next generation.* Washington, DC: American Psychological Association Press.

McCourt, F. (1996). *Angela's Ashes: A memoir.* New York: Scribner.

McFadden, S. H. (1996). Religion, spirituality, and aging. In J. E. Birren & K. W. Schaie (Eds.), *Handbook of the psychology of aging* (4th ed., pp. 162–77). San Diego, CA: Academic Press.

McFague, S. (1987). *Models of god: Theology for an ecological, nuclear age.* Philadelphia: Fortress Press.

McGill, A. (1987). *Death and life.* Philadelphia: Fortress Press.

McGoldrick, M. (1980). *The family life cycle: A framework for family therapy.* New York: Gardner Press.

McGoldrick, M. (1995). *You can go home again: Reconnecting with your family.* New York: W. W. Norton.

McGoldrick, M. (1999). Becoming a couple. In B. Carter & M. McGoldrick (Eds.), *The expanded family life cycle: Individual, family and social perspectives* (3rd ed., pp. 231–48). Boston: Allyn & Bacon.

McGoldrick, M., & Carter, B. (1999). Self in context: The individual life cycle in systemic perspective. In B. Carter & M. McGoldrick (Eds.), *The expanded family life cycle: Individual, family and social perspectives* (3rd ed., pp. 27–46). Boston: Allyn & Bacon.

McGoldrick, M., Gerson, R., & Shellenberger, S. (1999). *Genograms: Assessment and intervention* (2nd ed.). New York: W. W. Norton.

McKee, P. (1982). *Philosophical foundations of gerontology.* New York: Human Sciences Press.

McKelway, A. J. (1964). *The systematic theology of Paul Tillich.* New York: Dell.

McLynn, F. (1996). *Carl Gustav Jung.* New York: St. Martin's Press.

Meany, J. W. (Director), & Berger, M. (Ed.). (1990). *Jung on Film* [Video]. (Available from Video Finders, 4401 Sunset Blvd., Los Angeles, CA 90027, 800-343-4727)

Mehren, E. (1997). *After the darkest hour, the sun will shine again: A parent's guide to coping with the loss of a child.* New York: Simon & Schuster.

Meissner, W. (1984). *Psychoanalysis and religious experience.* New Haven, CT: Yale.

Meissner, W. (1987). *Life and faith: Psychological perspectives on religious experience.* Washington, DC: Georgetown University Press.

Meltzer, D. (Ed.). (1984). *Death: An anthology of ancient texts, songs, prayers, and stories.* San Francisco: North Point Press.

Menaker, E. (1982). *Otto Rank: A rediscovered legacy.* New York: Columbia University Press.

Menaker, E. (1995). *The freedom to inquire: Self psychological perspectives on women's issues, masochism, and the therapeutic relationship.* Northvale, NJ: Jason Aronson.

Mengel, M., & Holleman, W. L. (Eds.). (2000). *Principles of clinical practice: Vol. I. Patient, doctor and society* (2nd ed.). New York: Plenum Press.

Miles, S. H., & August, A. (1990). Courts, gender, and "the right to die." *Law, Medicine, and Health Care, 85*(92), 87–90.

Miller, A. (1981). *The drama of the gifted child: How narcissistic parents form and deform the emotional lives of their talented children.* New York: Basic Books.

Miller, D. L. (1981). *The new polytheism: Rebirth of the gods and goddesses.* Dallas, TX: Spring.

Miller, E. J. (2000). *Religion and families over the life course.* In S. J. Price, P. C. McHenry, & M. J. Murphy (Eds.), *Families across time: A life course perspective* (pp. 173–86). Los Angeles: Roxbury.

Miller, P. (1993). *Theories of developmental psychology* (3rd ed.). New York: W. H. Freeman.

Miller, P., & Scholnick, E. (Eds.). (2000). *Toward a feminist developmental psychology.* New York: Routledge.

Miller-McLemore, B., & Gill-Austern, B. (Eds.). (1999). *Feminist and womanist pastoral theology.* Nashville, TN: Abingdon Press.

Minuchin, S. (1974). *Families and family therapy.* Cambridge, MA: Harvard University Press.

Mitchell, K., & Anderson, H. (1983). *All our losses, all our griefs: Resources for pastoral care.* Philadelphia: Westminster Press.

Mitchell, R. R., & Friedman, H. S. (1994). *Sandplay: Past, present and future.* New York: Routledge.

Mitchell, S. A. (1988). *Relational concepts in psychoanalysis: An integration.* Cambridge, MA: Harvard University Press.

Modgil, S., & Modgil, C. (Eds.). (1986). *Lawrence Kohlberg: Consensus & controversy.* Philadelphia: Falmer Press.

Moe, T. (1997). *Pastoral care in pregnancy loss: A ministry long needed.* New York: Haworth Pastoral Press.

Moessner, J. S. (Ed.). (1996). *Through the eyes of women: Insights for pastoral care.* Minneapolis: Fortress Press.

Mogelonsky, M. (1996). The rocky road to adulthood. *American Demographics, 18*(5), 26–56.

Moi, T. (1985). *Sexual/textual politics: Feminist literary theory*. London: Routledge.

Morse, C. (1994). *Not every spirit: A dogmatics of Christian disbelief*. Valley Forge, PA: Trinity Press.

Morss, J. (1996). *Growing critical: Alternatives to developmental psychology*. New York: Routledge.

Munsey, B. (1980). *Moral development, moral education and Kohlberg*. Birmingham, AL: Religious Education Press.

Murphy, M. (1988). *New images of the last things: Karl Rahner on death and life after death*. New York: Paulist Press.

Musser, D. W., & Price, J. L. (Eds.). (1988). *Whirlwind in culture: Frontiers in theology: In honor of Langdon Gilkey*. Bloomington, IN: Meyer-Stone Books.

Nelson, H. (1987). *On the poetry of Galway Kinnell*. Ann Arbor, MI: University of Michigan Press.

Nerimoff, R., & Colarusso, C. (Eds.). (1990). *New dimensions in adult development*. New York: Basic Books.

Neusner, J. (2000). *Death and the afterlife*. Cleveland, OH: Pilgrim Press.

Newman, B. M., & Newman, P. R. (2003). *Development through life: A psychosocial approach* (8th ed.). Belmont, CA: Wadsworth/Thomson Learning.

Newmark, M., & Beels, C. (1994). The misuse and use of science in family therapy. *Family Process, 33*, 3–17.

Nichols, M., & Schwartz, R. (2001). *Family therapy: Concepts and methods*. With a foreword by Salvador Minuchin, (5th ed.). Boston: Allyn & Bacon.

Niebuhr, H. R. (1962). *The responsible self*. New York: Harper & Row.

Nordus, I. H., VandenBos, G. R., Berg, S., & Fromholt, P. (Eds.). (1998). *Clinical geropsychology*. Washington, DC: American Psychological Association Press.

Nussbaum, M., & Glover, J. (Eds.). (1995). *Women, culture, and development*. Oxford, UK: Clarendon.

Nydam, R. (1989). Teen suicide: The denial of grace. *The Journal of Pastoral Care, 53*(3), 210–20.

Nydam, R. (1999). *Adoptees come of age: Living within two families*. Louisville, KY: Westminster John Knox Press.

O'Bryant, S. L., & Hannson, R. O. (1996). Widowhood. In R. Blieszner & V. H. Bedford (Eds.), *Aging and the family: Theory and research* (pp. 440–58). Westport, CT: Praeger.

Obholzer, A., & Roberts, V. Z. (1994). *The unconscious at work*. London: Routledge.

O'Driscoll, P. (2000, July 17). Ted Turner builds the ultimate preserve. *USA Today*, A1.

Ogden, T. H. (1989). *The primitive edge of experience*. Northvale, NJ: Jason Aronson.

Orange, D. M. (1995). *Emotional understanding: Studies in psychoanalytic epistemology.* New York: Guilford Press.

Orange, D. M., Atwood, G. E., & Stolorow, R. D. (1994). *Working intersubjectively: Contextualism in psychoanalytic practice.* Hillsdale, NJ: Analytic Press.

Ornstein, P. (1978). Introduction. *The search for the self: Selected writings of Heinz Kohut: 1950-1978* (Vol. 2, pp. 1–106). New York: International Universities Press.

Ornstein, P. (Ed.). (1978). *The search for the self: Selected writings of Heinz Kohut: 1950-1978* (Vol. 2). New York: International Universities Press.

Osmer, R., & Schweitzer, F., (Eds.). (2002). *Developing a public faith: New directions in practical theology.* St. Louis, MO: Chalice Press.

Palmer, M. (1997). *Freud and Jung on religion.* New York: Routledge.

Parkes, C. M. (1996). *Bereavement: Studies of grief in adult life* (2nd ed.). Madison, CT: International Universities Press.

Parks, S. D. (1991). The North American critique of James Fowler's theory of faith development. In J. Fowler, K. Nipkow & F. Schweitzer (Eds.). *Stages of faith and religious development: Implications for church, education, and society.* New York: Crossroad.

Perry, B. D., Pollard, R. A., Blakley, T. L., Baker, W. L., & Vigilante, D. (1995). Childhood trauma, the neurobiology of adaptation and use-dependent development of the brain: How states become traits. *Infant Mental Health Journal, 16*(4), 271–91.

Piaget, J. (1926). *The language and thought of the child.* New York: Harcourt.

Piaget, J. (1929). *The child's conception of the world.* (J. & A. Tomlinson, Trans.). New York: Harcourt, Brace.

Piaget, J. (1932/1965). *The moral judgment of the child.* New York: Free Press. (Original work published 1932)

Piaget, J. (1937/1954). *The construction of reality in the child* (M. Cook, Trans.). New York: Basic Books. (Original work published 1937)

Piaget, J. (1953). *The origins of intelligence in the child.* New York: International Universities Press.

Piaget. J. (1955). *The language and thought of the child.* Cleveland: World.

Piaget, J. (1962). *Play, dreams and imitation in childhood.* New York: W. W. Norton.

Piaget, J. (1967). *Six psychological studies.* New York: Random House.

Pinkola-Estes, C. (1992). *Women who run with the wolves: Myths and stories of the wild woman archetype.* New York: Ballantine Books.

Pipher, M. (1994). *Reviving Ophelia: Saving the selves of adolescent girls.* New York: Ballantine Books.

Pollio, H., Henley, T., & Thompson, C. (1997). *The phenomenology of everyday life.* New York: Cambridge University Press.

Powell, S. (1993). Electra: The dark side of the moon. *Journal of Analytical Psychology, 38,* 155–74.

Pratt, C., & Garton, A. (Eds.). (1993). *Systems of representation in children.* New York: John Wiley & Sons.

Price, S. J., McHenry, P. C., & Murphy, M. J. (Eds.). (2000). *Families across time: A life course perspective.* Los Angeles: Roxbury.

Quadagno, J. (1988). *The transformation of old age security: Class and politics in the American welfare state.* Chicago: University of Chicago Press.

Rahner, K. (1961). *On the theology of death* (C. Henkey, Trans.). New York: Herder & Herder.

Randall, R. L. (1984). The legacy of Kohut for religion and psychology. *Journal of Religion and Health, 23,* 106–14.

Rank, O. (1932/1975). *Art and artist: Creative urge and personality development.* New York: Agathon Press. (Original work published 1932)

Rank, O. (1932/1971). *The double: A psychoanalytic study* (H. Tucker, Jr., Trans.). Chapel Hill, NC: University of North Carolina Press. (Original work published 1932)

Rank, O. (1932/1968). *Modern education* (M. E. Moxon, Trans.). New York: Agathon Press. (Original work published 1932)

Rank, O. (1932/1959). *The myth of the birth of the hero and other writings* (P. Freund, Trans.). New York: Vintage Books. (Original work published 1932)

Rank, O. (1936/1972) *Will therapy and truth and reality* (J. Taft, Trans.). New York: Knopf. (Original work published 1936)

Rank, O. (1958). *Beyond psychology.* New York: Dover Publications.

Rank, O. (1961). *Psychology and the soul.* New York: Barnes & Company.

Ratcliff, D. (1992). Baby faith: Infants, toddlers, and religion. *Religious Education, 87,* 117–26.

Ratliff, J. B. (Ed.). (2001). *Out of the silence: Quaker perspectives on pastoral care and counseling.* Wallingford, PA: Pendle Hill.

Rawls, J. (1971). *A theory of justice.* Cambridge, MA: Harvard University Press.

Reber, A. (1983/1995). *The penguin dictionary of psychology* (2nd ed.). New York: Penguin Books. (Original work published 1983)

Richardson, K. (2000). *Developmental psychology: How nature and nurture interact.* London: Macmillan.

Richardson, V. (1999). Women and retirement. In J. D. Garner (Ed.), *Fundamentals of feminist gerontology* (pp. 49–66). New York: Haworth Press.

Ricoeur, P. (1967). *The symbolism of evil.* Boston: Beacon Press.

Rizzuto, A. M. (1979). *The birth of the living God: A psychoanalytic study.* Chicago: University of Chicago Press.

Roazen, P. (1992). *Freud and his followers.* New York: DaCapo Press.

Roberts, J. (Ed.). (1994). *Escaping prison myths: Selected topics in the history of federal corrections.* Washington, DC: American University Press.

Robertson, J. F. (1996). Grandparenting in an era of rapid change. In R. Blieszner & V. H. Bedford (Eds.), *Aging and the family: Theory and research* (pp. 243–60). Westport, CT: Praeger.

Ross, L. W. (1997). The meaning of death in the context of life. In H. Pollio, T. Henley, & C. J. Thompson, *The phenomenology of everyday life* (pp. 298–333). Cambridge, UK: Cambridge University Press.

Roth, M. (Ed.). (1998). *Freud: Conflict and culture.* New York: Knopf.

Rubinstein, M. (1987). *The growing years: A guide to your child's emotional development from birth to adolescence.* New York: Atheneum.

Ruffin, J. (1989). Stages of adult development in black professional women. In R. Jones (Ed.), *Black adult development and aging* (pp. 31–62). Berkeley, CA: Cobb & Henry.

Russell, J. (1974). *The meaning of modern art.* New York: Harper & Row.

Ryder, R. (1965). The cohort as a concept in the study of social change. *American Sociological Review, 30,* 843–61.

Salovey, P., & Sluyter, D. J. (1997). *Emotional development and emotional intelligence: Educational implications.* New York: Basic Books.

Salthouse, T. A. (1998). Cognitive and information-processing perspectives on aging. In I. H. Nordus, G. R. VandenBos, S. Berg, & P. Fromholt, *Clinical Geropsychology* (pp. 49–60). Washington, DC: American Psychological Association Press.

Sanford, J. (1979). *Dreams and healing.* New York: Paulist Press.

Satir, V. (1964). *Conjoint family therapy, a guide to theory and technique.* Palo Alto, CA: Science and Behavior Books.

Satir, V. (1972). *Peoplemaking.* Palo Alto, CA: Science & Behavior Books.

Saussy, C. (1998). *The art of growing old.* Minneapolis, MN: Augsburg.

Schaefer, C., Briesmeister, J., & Fitton, M. (1984). *Family therapy techniques for problem behaviors of children and adolescents.* San Francisco: Jossey-Bass.

Schaie, K. W. (1996). Intellectual development in adulthood. In J. E. Birren & K. W. Schaie (Eds.), *Handbook of the psychology of aging* (4th ed., pp. 266–86). San Diego, CA: Academic Press.

Scharf, J., & Scharf, D. (2003). *A primer of object relations therapy* (2nd ed.). Northvale, NJ: Jason Aronson.

Schore, A. (1999). *Affect regulation and the origin of the self: The neurobiology of emotional development.* Hillsdale, NJ: Erlbaum.

Segal, H. (1957/1981). Notes on symbol formation. In H. Segal, *The work of Hanna Segal: A Kleinian approach to clinical practice* (pp. 49–65). Northvale, NJ: Jason Aronson. (Original work published 1957)

Segal, M. (1998). *Your child at play: Three to five years.* New York: Newmarket Press.

Seidman, S. N., & Reider, R. O. (1994). A review of sexual behavior in the United States. *American Journal of Psychiatry, 151*(3), 330–41.

Sells, S. P. (2001). *Parenting your out of control teenager: Seven steps to reestablish authority and reclaim love.* New York: St. Martin's Press.

Shakespeare, W. (1998). *William Shakespeare's Macbeth* (H. Bloom, Ed.). Philadelphia: Chelsea House.

Shapiro, C. H. (1988). *Infertility and pregnancy loss: A guide for helping professionals.* San Francisco: Jossey-Bass.

Shea, J. (2000). *Spirituality and health care: Reaching toward a holistic future.* Chicago: Park Ridge Center.

Sheehy, G. (1976). *Passages: Predictable crises of adult life.* New York: Bantam Books.

Sheehy, G. (1995). *New Passages: Mapping your life across time.* New York: Ballantine Books.

Shultz, M. M. (1999). Death does us part. *Journal of Gender-Specific Medicine, 1*(2), 72–76.

Siegel, D. J. (1999). *The developing mind: Toward a neurobiology of interpersonal experience.* New York: Guilford Press.

Simmons, R. (2002). *Odd girl out: The hidden culture of aggression in girls.* New York: Harcourt.

Singer, D., & Revenson, T. (1996). *A Piaget primer: How a child thinks.* New York: Penguin Books.

Singer, J. (1972). *Boundaries of the soul: The practice of Jung's psychology.* New York: Doubleday.

Singleton, D. (1989). *Language acquisition: The age factor.* Philadelphia: Multilingual Matters.

Slipp, S. (1991). *Object relations: A dynamic bridge between individual and family treatment.* New York: Jason Aronson.

Smart, N. (Ed.). (1964). *Philosophers and religious truth.* New York: Macmillan.

Smith, A. D. (1996). Memory. In J. E. Birren & K. W. Schaie (Eds.), *Handbook of the psychology of aging* (4th ed., pp. 266–86). San Diego, CA: Academic Press.

Soo-Young, Kwan (2001, November 17). Codependence and interdependence: Cross-cultural reappraisal of boundaries and relationality. Paper presented at the meeting of the Person, Culture and Religion group at the American Academy of Religion Annual Meeting, Denver, CO.

Spitz, R. (1945). Hospitalism: An inquiry into the genesis of psychiatric conditions in early childhood. *Psychoanalytic Study of the Child, 1,* 53–74.

Spitz, R. (1965). *The First Year of Life.* New York: International Universities Press.

Sroufe, L. A. (1995). *Emotional development: The organization of emotional life in the early years.* New York: Cambridge University Press.

Sroufe, L. A., Cooper, R. G., & DeHart, G. B. (1996). *Child development: Its nature and course* (3rd ed.). New York: McGraw Hill.

Stein, M. (Ed.). (1984). *Jungian analysis*. Boulder, CO: Shambhala.

Stein, R. (1973). *Incest and human love: The betrayal of the soul in psychotherapy*. New York: Third Press.

SteinhoffSmith, R. (1999). *The mutuality of care*. St. Louis, MO: Chalice Press.

Stern, D. N. (1985). *The interpersonal world of the infant: A view from psychoanalysis and developmental psychology*. New York: Basic Books.

Stevenson-Moessner, J. (2000). Incarnating theology: Restructuring developmental theory. In J. Stevenson-Moessner (Ed.), *In her own time: Women and developmental issues in pastoral care*. Minneapolis, MN: Fortress Press.

Stevenson-Moessner, J. (Ed.). (2000). *In her own time: Women and developmental issues in pastoral care*. Minneapolis, MN: Fortress Press.

Stigler, J. W., Shweder, R. A., & Herdt, G. S. (Eds.). (1990). *Cultural psychology: The Chicago symposia on human development*. New York: Cambridge University Press.

Stolorow, R. D., & Atwood, G. E. (1992). *Contexts of being: The intersubjective foundations of psychological life*. Hillsdale, NJ: Analytic Press.

Stolorow, R. D., Atwood, G. E., & Brandchaft, B. (1994). *The intersubjective perspective*. Northvale, NJ: Jason Aronson.

Storr, A. (1991). *Human destructiveness*. New York: Grove Press.

Stratton, P. (1988). Parents' conceptualization of children as the organizer of culturally structured environments. In J. Valsiner (Ed.), *Child development within culturally structured environments: Vol. 1. Parental cognition and adult-child interaction*. Norwood, NJ: Ablex.

Strozier, C. B., & Flynn, M. (1996). *Trauma and self*. Lanham, MD: Rowman & Littlefield.

Sue, D. W., & Sue D. (1990). *Counseling the culturally different: Theory and practice* (2nd ed.). New York: Wiley.

Sum, A., Fogg, N., & Taggert, R. (1996). The economics of despair. *American Prospect, 27*, 83–84. Cited in S. Coontz (1997), *The way we really are: Coming to terms with American's changing families* (p. 127). New York: Basic Books.

Tacey, D. (2001). *Jung and the New Age*. Philadelphia: Brunner-Routledge.

Tagliaferre, L., & Harbaugh, G. (2001). *Recovery from loss: A personalized guide to the grieving process*. Gainesville, FL: Center for Applications of Psychological Type.

Talbot, M. (2002, February 24). Girls just want to be mean. *New York, NY Times Magazine*, 24–65.

Taylor, C., & Finley, P. (1997). *Images of the divine in Dante's Divine Comedy*. New Haven, CT: Yale University Press.

Taylor, J. M., Gilligan, C., & Sullivan, A. (1996). *Between voice and silence: Women and girls, race and relationship*. Cambridge, MA: Belknap.

Taylor, R. J., & Chatters, L. M. (1989). Family, friend, and church support networks of African Americans. In R. Jones (Ed.), *Black adult development and aging* (pp. 245–71). Berkeley, CA: Cobb & Henry.

Taylor, S. E., Klein, L. C., Lewis, B. P., Gruenewald, T. L., Gurung, R. A. R., & Updegraff, J. A. (2000). Female responses to stress: Tend and befriend, not "fight or flight." *Psychological Review, 107*(3), 41–429.

Teilhard de Chardin, P. (1969). *The future of man.* New York: Harper & Row.

Tengbom, M. (2002). *When your spouse dies.* Minneapolis, MN: Augsburg.

Thomas, L. E., & Eisenhandler, S. A. (Eds.). (1999). *Religion, belief, and spirituality in late life.* New York: Springer.

Thorne, B. (Ed.). (1982). *Rethinking the family: Some feminist questions.* New York: Longman.

Tillich, P. (1952). *The courage to be.* New Haven, CT: Yale University Press.

Tillich, P. (1957). *The dynamics of faith.* New York: Harper & Row.

Tillich, P. (1951–1963). *Systematic theology: Vol. 1. Reason and revelation, being and God.* Chicago: University of Chicago Press.

Tillich, P. (1963). *The eternal now.* New York: Scribner.

Tomkins, S. S. (1962). *Affect, imagery, consciousness* (Vols. 1 & 2). New York: Springer.

Tornstam, L. (1999). Late-life transcendence: A new developmental perspective on aging. In L. E. Thomas & S. A. Eisenhandler (Eds.), *Religion, belief, and spirituality in late life* (pp. 178–202). New York: Springer.

Trevarthan, C., & Hubley, P. (1978). Secondary intersubjectivity: Confidence, confiders and acts of meaning in the first year. In A. Lock (Ed.), *Action, gesture and symbol.* New York: Academic Press.

Turner, V. W. (1995). *The ritual process: Structure and anti-structure.* New York: Aldine de Gruyter.

U.S. Census Bureau. (1995). *Global aging into the 21st century.* Washington, DC: Economics & Statistics Administration, U.S. Department of Commerce.

Ulanov, A. (1997). Jung and religion: The opposing self. In P. Eisendrath & T. Dawson (Eds.), *Cambridge companion to Jung* (pp. 296–313). New York: Cambridge University Press.

Ulanov, A. (2001). *Finding space: Winnicott, God and psychic reality.* Louisville, KY: Westminster John Knox Press.

Ulanov, A. (2001a). Memorial Address: Barry Ulanov 1918-2000. *Journal of Religion and Health, 40*(1), 11–14.

Ulanov, A., & Ulanov, B. (1975). *Religion and the unconscious.* Philadelphia: Westminster Press.

Ulanov, A., & Ulanov, B. (1982). *Primary speech: A psychology of prayer.* Atlanta, GA: Westminster John Knox Press.

Ulanov, A., & Ulanov, B. (1983). *Cinderella and her sisters: The envied and the envying.* Philadelphia: Westminster Press.

Ulanov, A., & Ulanov, B. (1987). *The witch and the clown: Two archetypes of human sexuality.* Wilmette, IL: Chiron.

Ulanov. A., & Ulanov, B. (1991). *The healing imagination.* New York: Integration Books.

Vaillant, G. (1993). *The wisdom of the ego* (Reprint ed.). Cambridge, MA: Harvard University Press.

Vaillant, G. (1995). *Adaptation to life* (Reprint ed.). Cambridge, MA: Harvard University Press.

Valsiner, J. (Ed.). (1988). *Child development within culturally structured environments: Vol. 1. Parental cognition and adult-child interaction.* Norwood, NJ: Ablex.

Van der Kolk, B. (1994). The body keeps the score: Memory and the evolving psychobiology of post traumatic stress. *Harvard Review of Psychiatry, 1,* 253–65.

Van der Ven, J. (1998). *Formation of the moral self.* Grand Rapids, MI: Eerdmans.

Vergote, A., & Tamayo, A. (1981). *The parental figures and the representation of God: A psychological and cross-cultural study.* New York: Mouton.

von Franz, M.-L. (1975). *C. G. Jung: His myth in our time.* New York: Putnam.

von Franz, M.-L. (1984/1986). *On dreams and death: A Jungian interpretation* (E. X. Kennedy & V. Books, Trans.). Boston: Shambhala.

von Franz, M.-L. (1999). *Archetypal dimensions of the psyche.* Boston: Shambhala.

Waelder, R. (1964). *Basic theory of psychoanalysis.* New York: International Universities Press.

Wagner, J. (1986). *The search for signs of intelligent life in the universe.* New York: Harper & Row.

Walker, A. (1982). *The color purple.* Boston: G. K. Hall.

Walsh, F. (Ed.). (1993). *Normal family processes* (2nd ed.). New York: Guilford Press.

Walsh, F. (Ed.). (1999). *Spiritual resources in family therapy.* New York: Guilford Press.

Walsh, N. (1996). Life in death. In C. B. Strozier & M. Flynn (Eds.), *Trauma and self* (pp. 245–54). Lanham, MD: Rowman & Littlefield.

Watts, F., Nye, R., & Savage, S. (2002). *Psychology for Christian ministry.* New York: Routledge.

Weil, S. (1951). *Waiting for God.* (Reprint ed., E. Craufurd, Trans.). New York: Harper & Row.

Welchman, K. (2000). *Erik Erikson: His life, work and significance.* Philadelphia: Open University Press.

Werner, H. (1948). *The comparative psychology of mental development.* New York: International Universities Press.

West, C. (1993). *Race matters.* New York: Vintage.

Whitaker, C., & Bumberry, W. (1988). *Dancing with the family: A symbolic-experiential approach.* Levittown, PA: Brunner-Routledge.

Whitbourne, S. (1998). Physical changes in the aging individual: Clinical implications. In I. H. Nordus, G. R. VandenBos, S. Berg, & P. Fromholt (Eds.), *Clinical geropsychology* (pp. 79–108). Washington, DC: American Psychological Association Press.

White, M., & Epston, D. (1990). *Narrative Means to Therapeutic Ends.* New York: Norton.

Whitehead, E. E., & Whitehead, J. D. (1982). *Christian Life Patterns.* Garden City, NY: Doubleday Image Books.

Wicks, R., Parsons, R., & Capps, D. (1985). *Clinical Handbook of Pastoral Counseling.* New York: Paulist Press.

Williams, K. (1995). *A parent's guide for suicidal and depressed teens: Help for recognizing if a child is in crisis and what to do about it.* Center City, MN: Hazelden.

Williams, M. (1975). *The velveteen rabbit.* New York: Avon Books.

Williamson, C. (1999). *Way of blessing, way of life: A Christian theology.* St. Louis, MO: Chalice Press.

Williamson, D. (1991). *The intimacy paradox: Personal authority in the family system.* New York: Guilford Press.

Willis, S. L. (1996). Everyday problem solving. In J. E. Birren & K. W. Schaie (Eds.), *Handbook of the psychology of aging* (4th ed., pp. 287–307). San Diego, CA: Academic Press.

Wimberly, E. (1976). A conceptual model of pastoral care for the Black church utilizing systems and crisis theories. *Dissertation Abstracts International, 36*(11), 7487. (University Microfilms No. AAT 7611642).

Wimberly, E. (1982). *Pastoral counseling and spiritual values: A black point of view.* Nashville, TN: Abingdon Press.

Wimberly, E. (1994). *Using scripture in pastoral counseling.* Nashville, TN: Abingdon Press.

Wimberly, E. (1997). *Counseling African American marriages and families.* Louisville, KY: Westminster John Knox Press.

Wimberly, E. (2000). *Relational refugee: Alienation and reincorporation in African American churches and communities.* Nashville, TN: Abingdon Press.

Wimberly, E., Wimberly, A., & Chingonzo, A. G. (1999). *Pastoral counseling, spirituality, and the recovery of village functions: African and African American correlates in the practice of pastoral care and counseling.* Paper presented at The Sixth International Congress on Pastoral Care and Counseling, Accra, Ghana.

Winnicott, C., Shepherd, R., & Davis, M. (Eds.). (1987). *Babies and their mothers.* Reading, MA: Addison Wesley.

Winnicott, D. W. (1953/1971). Transitional objects and transitional phenomena. In *Playing and reality* (pp. 1–25). New York: Routledge. (Original work published 1953)

Winnicott D. W. (1958/1965). The capacity to be alone. In *The maturational processes and the facilitating environment: Studies in the theory of emotional development.* (pp. 29–36). London: Hogarth Press. (Original work published 1958)

Winnicott, D. W. (1960/1965). The theory of the parent-infant relationship. In *The maturational processes and the facilitating environment: Studies in the theory of emotional development* (pp. 37–55). London: Hogarth Press. (Original work published 1960)

Winnicott, D. W. (1960a/1965). Ego distortions in terms of true and false self. In *The maturational Process and the Facilitating Environment: Studies in the theory of emotional development* (pp. 140–52). London: Hogarth Press. (Original work published 1960)

Winnicott, D.W. (1964). Book review of Jung's autobiography: Memories, dreams and reflections. *International Journal of Psychoanalysis, 45,* 450–55.

Winnicott, D. W. (1964/1987). Further thoughts on babies as persons. In *The child, the family, and the outside world* (pp. 85–92). Reading, MA: Addison-Wesley. (Original work published 1964)

Winnicott, D. W. (1965). *The maturational processes and the facilitating environment: Studies in the theory of emotional development.* London: Hogarth Press.

Winnicott, D. W. (1968/1971). Contemporary concepts of adolescent development and their implications for higher education. In *Playing and reality* (pp. 138–50). New York: Routledge. (Original work published 1968)

Winnicott, D. W. (1969/1971). The use of an object and relating through identifications. In *Playing and reality* (pp. 86–94). New York: Routledge. (Original work published 1969)

Winnicott, D. W. (1971). The place where we live. In *Playing and reality* (pp. 104–10). New York: Routledge.

Winnicott, D. W. (1971). Playing: A theoretical statement. In *Playing and reality* (pp. 38–52). New York: Routledge.

Winnicott, D. W. (1971). *Playing and reality.* New York: Routledge.

Winnicott, D. W. (1987). The ordinary devoted mother. In C. Winnicott, R. Shepherd, & M. Davis (Eds.), *Babies and their mothers* (pp. 3–14). Reading, MA: Addison Wesley.

Wirth, F. (2001). *Prenatal parenting: The complete psychological and spiritual guide to loving your unborn child.* New York: Regan Books.

Wittgenstein, L. (1922/1990). *Tractatus logico-philosophicus* (C. K. Ogden, Trans.). New York: Routledge. (Original work published 1922)

Wittgenstein, L. (1953). *Philosophical investigations* (G. E. M. Anscombe, Trans.). Oxford, UK: Blackwell.

Woodward, K. (1986). The mirror stage of old age. In K. Woodward & M. Schwartz (Eds.), *Memory and desire: Aging, literature, psychoanalysis* (pp. 97–113). Bloomington, IN: Indiana University Press.

Woodward, K. (1991). *Aging and its discontents.* Bloomington, IN: Indiana University Press.

Woodward, K., & Schwartz, M. (Eds.). (1986). *Memory and desire: Aging, literature, psychoanalysis.* Bloomington, IN: Indiana University Press.

Woollen, M. (Producer), & Wagner, S. (Director). (1990). *The world within: C. G. Jung in his own words and remembering Jung* [Video]. (Available from Video Finders, 4401 Sunset Blvd., Los Angeles, CA 90027, 800-343-4727)

Wordsworth, W. (1964). Ode: Intimations of immortality from recollections of early childhood. In A. K. Hieatt & W. Park (Eds.), *The college anthology of British and American verse.* Boston: Allyn & Bacon.

Wulff, D. M. (1997). *Psychology of religion: Classic and contemporary* (2nd ed.). New York: John Wiley & Sons.

Yates, J. (1999). *Jung on death and immortality.* Princeton, NJ: Princeton University Press.

Yerushalmi, Y. (1991). *Freud's Moses: Judaism terminable and interminable.* New Haven, CT: Yale University Press.

Zal, H. M. (1992). *The sandwich generation: Caught between growing children and aging parents.* New York: Insight Books.

Zimmerman, M. (2002). *Ovid's metamorphoses.* Adaptation of original work by Ovid (43 B.C.–ca. 17. A.D.), (D. R. Slavitt, Trans.). Evanston, IL: Northwestern University Press.

How are my views shaped by the fact
that I am in the dominant grouping—
white, male, middle-class, educated

?

LaVergne, TN USA
17 February 2011
216895LV00005B/67/A